Frankie Jones
1031 Broadmoor Ave.
Munster, IN 46321

LEGACY

LEGACY

PAYING THE PRICE FOR
THE CLINTON YEARS

RICH LOWRY

Since 1947
REGNERY
PUBLISHING, INC.
An Eagle Publishing Company • Washington, DC

Cataloging-in-Publication Data on file with the Library of Congress.

ISBN 0-89526-129-4

Published in the United States by
Regnery Publishing, Inc.
An Eagle Publishing Company
One Massachusetts Avenue, NW
Washington, DC 20001

Visit us at www.regnery.com

Distributed to the trade by
National Book Network
4720-A Boston Way
Lanham, MD 20706

Printed on acid-free paper

Manufactured in the United States of America

10 9 8 7 6 5 4 3 2 1

Books are available in quantity for promotional or premium use. Write to
Director of Special Sales, Regnery Publishing, Inc., One Massachusetts
Avenue, NW, Washington, DC 20001, for information on discounts and
terms, or call (202) 216-0600.

"In the opinion of all he was capable of rule—if he had not ruled."

—TACITUS

To Mom and Dad,
who surrounded me with books and love;

To Robert,
who laughs more than anyone I know

CONTENTS

Introduction

THIS BOOK WAS PROMPTED by the September 11, 2001, terrorist attack. From my New York City apartment, I heard the first plane scream down Fifth Avenue toward the North Tower of the World Trade Center, and for weeks afterwards we could smell the smoldering rubble from our offices at *National Review*. What had happened to leave us vulnerable to such a catastrophic attack?

The answer required a thorough examination of the assumptions of contemporary liberalism. It didn't take long, of course, to realize that most of the intellectual and temperamental flaws of liberalism were embodied in the Clinton administration. Thus, the mustard seed of this book.

It inevitably grew. The mistakes of the Clinton administration weren't limited to its policies toward terror and the Middle East. They infected its broader foreign policy. So, an account of its failure in the terror war entailed a wider-ranging analysis of its international performance. Then, the argument grew further from there.

Clinton's defenders might concede—although they usually concede very little—that he didn't do enough to fight terror or defend America abroad, but he would have done more if nasty, scandal-mongering Republicans hadn't distracted him. Or that any failings abroad were more than compensated for by his supposedly excellent stewardship at home. The Clinton legacy, then, is of a piece, and an account of part of it cannot really be undertaken without engaging across the board in all the controversies surrounding his presidency.

That is what I've done in this book. I have never considered myself a "Clinton hater," and have always regarded him with a kind of amused and not particularly passionate contempt. I have taken care to be fair-minded and factual in what follows. But it is stunning how little there was to the Clinton administration, less even than met the eye, and there wasn't much that did in the first place. Most Clinton "accomplishments" are just spin, and his failures are stark and—it seems to me—inarguable.

It doesn't take much time thinking, and talking to people about, Bill Clinton before you realize the absolute centrality of character. His character weaknesses affected everything he did. I always thought that the George H.W. Bush and Bob Dole campaigns against Clinton based on character were lame (and they largely were—a substitute for making arguments on the issues). But their essential point was correct: that Clinton's dishonesty and moral failings made it almost impossible for him to exercise responsible leadership.

The first chapter of the book is an overview of Clintonism in all its aspects. The rest is divided into three sections: domestic policy, in which I expose Clinton's "accomplishments" as having little or nothing to do with his policies; scandal and law, in which I argue that through his lawlessness Clinton brought his scandals on himself; and, finally, foreign policy, in which I examine Clinton's appalling international record.

This is not a book comparing and contrasting Clinton to George W. Bush, so I don't spend much time explaining differences or similarities between the two, although they occasionally come up. A note on style: I refer to comments made directly to me in interviews in the present tense and to comments culled from other sources in the past tense.

The argument over Clinton and his legacy has just begun. This book demonstrates that conservatives should have little trouble winning it.

"I may not have been the greatest president, but I've had the most fun eight years."[1]
—Bill Clinton

"If an actor can become a president, a president can be an actor."[2]
—Bill Clinton

THE CONTENT
OF HIS CHARACTER

B Y HIS SECOND TERM, BILL CLINTON'S presidency had achieved a kind of Seinfeldian self-referentiality. He was a president devoted to his presidential legacy, whatever that might be.

It might be economic growth, but that seemed prosaic, lacking the political grandeur of creating the Social Security system or winning a major war. Or it might be entitlement reform, if Clinton ever decided to support it. It might be his race commission, or his last-minute initiative to bring economic aid to poor areas. It might be a peace deal between the Israelis and the Palestinians, or failing that, another arms agreement with North Korea. It might be holding onto the presidency in the person of Al Gore, or taking back the House for the Democrats.

Who knew what it would be, but his presidency was going to be about something. Because, as the *New York Times* reported, Clinton was "a man who, friends say, values his legacy above all else."[3] "Legacy" became such a collective mania that White House aides had to be banned from using the word with the press.[4]

Clinton's preoccupation with how historians would regard him was, ironically, part of the self-obsession that kept him from attempting great acts. Political leadership requires taking risks and decisive actions, which, in turn, requires a commitment to convictions and principles that trump short-term considerations and make the risks seem worthwhile. Because Clinton's presidency was about him, he couldn't transcend the day-to-day, or put himself or his presidency on the line for any larger purpose. Because, in short, he was self-involved enough to talk constantly about his legacy, he was never capable of forging a positive one.

Clinton was the Navel-Gazer-in-Chief, the president as Narcissus, his truest political principle devotion to himself.

Clinton's very being was dependent on his political standing. When he lost the Arkansas governorship after one term in 1980, he was more than bereft. He went a little "crazy," roaming Little Rock like a boyish Ancient Mariner. He accosted everyone he could find, asking, "What did I do wrong?"[5] In losing the affection of the voters, in potentially losing his political career, Clinton faced a nearly existential threat.

That threat always loomed. Clinton told Al Gore, whenever he was making a major decision, "I'm risking my presidency on this."[6] To Clinton, everything felt like a risk, because he was so afraid of losing. This fear deterred him from large, truly risky acts—say, a major military operation against Osama bin Laden—while he took refuge in small, politically popular measures to keep his poll numbers up. They ensured public approval and reelection. That was legacy enough for Clinton, no matter what he might tell journalists during interviews or advisors during Oval Office bull sessions.

Clinton was a jumble of contradictions. He was dismissive of the lessons of history, yet entirely consumed by how history would judge him; personally audacious and reckless, he was politically timid and weak; his rhetoric was bold and visionary, but his policies miniature and often silly; he was self-pitying and victimized, but capable of acts of Nixonian callousness and spite. The common thread that gave it all a kind of coherence was his immediate self-interest.

Using a White House intern for oral sex was a gargantuan risk. But Clinton wouldn't take political risks with his Bosnian policy or to stop the slaughter in Rwanda. The risk with Monica Lewinsky seemed worth it because it satisfied his sexual appetite. His political caution, on the other hand, served another appetite: for popularity. Former Clinton strategist Dick Morris writes, "For Bill Clinton, positive poll results are not just tools—they are vindication, ratification, and approval—whereas negative poll results are a learning process in which the pain of the rebuff to his self-image forces deep introspection."[7]

Most of the Clinton contradictions can be resolved in this way. He loved bold rhetoric because it was a form of self-flattery, allowing him to speak the language of political greatness. He wouldn't take bold action, however, because it meant courting political peril and perhaps defeat.

He often descended into soggy self-pity because, through his solipsism, the world seemed uniquely aligned against him. On the other hand, he often treated his friends and aides with an unsentimental coldness because, through his solipsism, they seemed mere instruments to serve his convenience and interest.

If the unifying theme of it all was Clinton's self-interest, the means to Clinton's living and thriving among these contradictory impulses was his shamelessness. A political figure less immune to shame would have been forced to stop occasionally and try to make his political course cohere. Not Clinton. He lumbered right on. "As I wrote and rewrote," George Stephanopoulos comments in his memoir *All Too Human*, "I came to see how Clinton's shamelessness is a key to his political success, how his capacity for denial is tied to the optimism that is his greatest political strength."[8]

In the end, Clinton's ethic collapses into one simple word—win. Clinton's nominee to head the civil rights division of the Department of Justice, Lani Guinier, who was dumped in 1993 after her nomination became controversial, has best captured the animating spirit of Clinton's presidency. At the end of his second term, she said that Clinton "became more consumed with winning than leading," and was "such a good politician that he began to believe that in winning he was actually leading."[9]

A president operating from that logic will think a meaningless slogan like "building a bridge to the twenty-first century" is leadership, that promoting policy minutiae is leadership, that lying to survive a sex scandal is leadership (in fact, as we shall see, will think it is one of his proudest accomplishments), and that, above all, maintaining high poll numbers is leadership.

Those numbers generally stayed up. Times were good, after all. But a strong president would have led the country away from the folly inherent in the times, especially the sleepy belief that history had ended, buried with the end of the Cold War and the miracle of the Internet. Instead, Clinton happily swam in the froth of the 1990s, content to benefit from and feed its comforting conventional wisdom.

The sympathetic gloss on the Clinton presidency is that it was a substantive success despite Clinton's personal failings. It was really the opposite. The administration was a personal success, for both Bill and Hillary. Bill graduated into global celebrity-hood, giving him a perpetual forum to soak up adulation beyond his most fervent dreams. Elvis had been a demi-god in the Clinton household when Bill was growing up.[10] Both the Clinton boys aspired to be rock stars—Bill's half-brother, Roger, unsuccessfully, through the direct route of music; Bill himself, spectacularly, through the indirect route of politics. He left office having achieved P. Diddy stature and permanent entrée into the rarified precincts of the red-carpet world.

Hillary, meanwhile, graduated into the United States Senate. She finally gained a base of political power independent of her flawed and unreliable husband and a foothold for an assault on the presidency herself.

The most profound symbol of Clinton's personal shortcomings, his sex scandal, may have perversely helped advance both Bill and Hillary's personal ambitions. It won Clinton great sympathy among the sophisticated Hollywood, New York, and overseas social sets, and it gave Hillary's own political career an important boost with the wave of sympathy that came with being the wronged but brave wife.

It was substantively that Clinton failed, on his own terms and by any reasonable standard. On his own terms, because he won office with two heartfelt priorities, creating massive new government "investments" and a New Deal–style government health-care system, the first of which was largely abandoned—with the significant exception of expansions in the Earned Income Tax Credit for low-income workers—and the second of which went down in ignominious defeat. Thereafter, Clinton maneuvered his way to political survival and success, with small-bore, feel-good initiatives enshrined in his vacuous 1996 reelection campaign. The Clinton of 1992 would have scoffed at the exigencies of the Clinton of 1996, conducting a press-release presidency as he declared "the era of big government over."

Clinton's substantive failings were, in turn, connected to his personal failings. Clinton had important personal strengths. He was hyper-intelligent, empathetic, and had an amazing capacity for endurance, lasting through political setbacks and personal humiliations. "Clinton has the lowest center of gravity of anyone in American politics that I have ever met," says longtime friend and former administration official Mickey Kantor. "You cannot knock him over."[11] But his other personal traits crucially influenced his political character too: his indecision, his selfishness, his timidity, his inconstancy, and his self-pity.

Clinton was a weak person, and so ultimately a weak president. His weaknesses related to the kind of man he was. If Clinton's presidency was "post-greatness"—on a determinedly minor key—it also was "post-masculine." Clinton was the new, sensitive man elevated to high office: sentimental and easily moved to tears, undisciplined and self-indulgent, endlessly and thoughtlessly expressive, schooled in the language and attitudes of therapy, fundamentally out of sympathy with that center of another, different kind of masculinity, the military. He was a soft man for a soft age.

Ultimately, the ingredients of presidential leadership aren't complicated: It takes a clean set of governing principles and character. Clinton had neither.

"Bill's not going to apologize for being against the Vietnam War"

Who was Bill Clinton? The most elemental, and telling, Clinton controversy was over his Vietnam draft status. It captured so much: his opposition to the war in the first place, which stemmed from a liberal skepticism toward American power and the use of force that he would never entirely shake off; his unwillingness to put himself on the line, either as a soldier or conscientious objector, instead finding refuge in a deep straddle after excruciating indecision; his ready resort two decades later to evasions and outright lies to save himself politically, even when it implicated those around him in untruths.

When the draft issue began percolating in the national press in late 1991, press aide George Stephanopoulos urged Clinton in a meeting to provide better, cleaner answers. Stephanopoulos writes in his memoir, "You would have thought I had called Clinton a draft dodger. Hillary spoke first, and she was incensed. 'Bill's not going to apologize for being against the Vietnam War!' Ignited by her intensity, Clinton launched into a red-faced tirade against the war and said he'd rather lose the race than say it was right."[12]

That Bill and Hillary were still proud of their opposition to the war showed their attachment to their generation's own mythology, the belief that its protests against Vietnam were a sign of its unprecedented purity. The Vietnam War, whatever its flaws in execution, was a profoundly moral enterprise, a war to protect South Vietnam from a conventional invasion from the totalitarian North, to avoid a humanitarian disaster of nearly biblical proportions, and to protect America's position in the world against an expansionist Soviet Union. The attitudes behind Bill and Hillary's opposition to Vietnam—a readiness to believe the worst of America and extend sympathetic understanding to its enemies—lingered on in Clinton administration foreign policy.

Clinton's version of the draft story was that he never got a defer-ment because, although one was on offer if he enrolled in the ROTC program at the University of Arkansas Law School, he had decided to take his chances in the lottery instead. In fact, Clinton got a draft notice and had an induction date of July 28, 1969.[13] Clinton scram-bled like mad to get out of it, drawing on every resource and pulling every possible string. He eventually got a deferment by enrolling in the ROTC program at the University of Arkansas. But he didn't want to go to the University of Arkansas, or to join the ROTC, or, after school, to have to fulfill an obligation to go into the service for two years. He just wanted to avoid serving in Vietnam.

"My mind is every day more confused than it was before; and countless hours doing nothing save waiting for the phone to ring are driving me out of my head," he wrote to a friend, in a perfectly self-obsessed fit of pity as he was deciding his next move. "I know one of the worst side effects of this whole thing is the way it's ravaged my own image of myself, taken my mind off the higher things, restricted my ability to become involved in good causes or with other people— I honestly feel so screwed up tight that I am incapable, I think, of giv-ing myself, of really loving."[14]

Clinton didn't let his guilt stop him from putting on hold the ROTC program that had saved him from the draft, and going back for the second year of his Rhodes Scholar romp at Oxford instead.[15] As David Maraniss recounts in his Clinton biography, *First in His Class*, while Clinton was back at Oxford, President Nixon announced a series of changes that eased up on the draft. It was in these circum-stances, with the odds shifted significantly in his favor, that Clinton decided to forgo his deferment and take his chances in the new draft lottery. He drew a high number that would keep him from ever being drafted, and he was free to ditch the University of Arkansas altogether to go to Yale instead.[16]

Clinton had managed to maneuver his way to a nearly perfect result for himself, given the circumstances. It wasn't draft dodging so much as a draft pirouette. Maraniss writes, "He did not want to resist the draft, and thereby imperil his political dreams. He did not want to get drafted and fight in Vietnam. He did not want to spend three years in the safe haven of ROTC, and two years after that as a commissioned lieutenant, even if the war had ended long before then. He did not want to go to the University of Arkansas Law School, when so many of his Rhodes friends were heading to Yale. And he did not want to feel guilty about his deferment."[17]

Clinton had told *Washington Post* reporter Dan Balz in December 1991, "I've always been interested in and supportive of the military. That is something, you know, in some ways I wish I'd been a part of it. I wound up just going through the lottery and it was just a pure fluke that I wasn't called."[18]

This was self-justifying fiction, as became clear when Clinton's 1969 letter to Colonel Eugene Holmes, then–head of the Arkansas law school ROTC program, became public in February 1992.[19] Clinton wrote to Holmes after he knew that he was in the clear, despite dumping the ROTC slot that Holmes had helped him get when he had been desperate to find any safe harbor from the draft.

"Dear Colonel Holmes," Clinton's letter began, "I want to thank you, not just for saving me from the draft..."[20] He wrote of his time at the Senate Foreign Relations Committee one summer "working every day against a war I opposed and despised with a depth of feeling I had reserved solely for racism in America before Vietnam." And, in a famous passage, he explained why, after long wrestling, he decided not to become a draft resister: "I decided to accept the draft in spite of my beliefs for one reason: to maintain my political viability within the system." The letter was defined by a thoroughgoing self-involvement: "I didn't see, in the end, how my going in the army and maybe going to Vietnam would achieve anything except a feeling that I had punished myself and gotten what I deserved."[21]

A reporter gave Stephanopoulos a copy of the letter at the Manchester, New Hampshire, airport during the thick of the New Hampshire primary. The press aide, who had unknowingly been repeating Clinton's lies, huddled with Bill and Hillary and a few other aides for an emergency meeting in the airport men's room. "Bill, this is *you*! I can hear you saying this," Hillary blurted out.[22] Even at that moment of high personal tension and perhaps political disaster, she couldn't hide her pride in his opposition to serving in Vietnam. Clinton weathered the controversy with a combination of defensive bluster—complaining about being criticized "over a draft I never dodged"—and a cascading set of denials, each one abandoned after it was proved false, until the whole mess had become "old news."

The falsehoods still live on. In her thoroughly dishonest memoir, *Living History*, Hillary writes, "I knew that Bill respected military service, *that he would have served if he had been called* and that he would also have gladly enlisted in World War II, a war whose purpose was crystal clear" (emphasis mine).[23] This is a lie. The fact is that Clinton was called, and he wiggled his way out of it. If military service is to be considered optional in any war whose purpose is not "crystal clear," Clinton is fortunate that anyone was willing to follow his orders in Somalia, Haiti, Bosnia, or Kosovo. If it's nice to know that Clinton would have served in World War II, it is also a characteristically Clinton sentiment to feel cheated by history: If only he had been called to serve in that other war, he never would have had to go to the trouble of manipulating his way out of the service.

Contra Hillary, the path to military and political success in Vietnam may have been unclear, but not the purpose: to save South Vietnam from a Communist takeover. It's just that Bill Clinton didn't consider this purpose important enough to fight for. As the Cold War consensus fractured in the United States, Clinton was with the forces that were chipping away at it, doubting the necessity of America's contest with the Soviets and unwilling to fight against Communism in Vietnam.

This was the wrong position, but not necessarily a dishonorable one. Clinton invested it with dishonor, with his slippery maneuverings to serve his interests and career at the time, and with his evasions and lies to serve his interests and career when his draft status became a political issue later. Thus, Clinton achieved a kind of synthesis. He drew on the ideals of the baby-boom elite opposed to the Vietnam War, the careerism of the most super-ambitious members of that elite, and a personal unscrupulousness all of his own.

"The most promising graduates in U.S. academic history"

When Clinton won the White House, he brought with him talented baby boomers who had shared his feelings about Vietnam, whom he had collected at Georgetown, Oxford, Yale Law School, and Renaissance weekends, the annual high-achiever schmoozefest. These were McGovernites who had kept their opposition to the war within respectable bounds, but who likely never would have been trusted with power if the Cold War hadn't ended. They considered 1992 the beginning of their long overdue moment, a chance finally to shower the country with all their intelligence, passion, and idealism.

That Bill and Hillary had ascended into this elite is testament to the democratic dynamism of America. Both came from undistinguished backgrounds, Bill especially, of course, growing up in an alcoholic household in Hot Springs, Arkansas. Bill and Hillary joined the cream of the baby boomers on the basis of their smarts and their drive, at a time when a meritocracy defined by education was first coming into flower.

A tremendous investment of expectations was made in this generation. *Time* magazine put Robert Reich on its cover in 1968, as representative of what the magazine called "the most conscience-stricken, moralistic, and perhaps, the most promising graduates in U.S. academic history."[24] This elite's candidate for president, almost from the beginning, was Bill Clinton.

At least in the early going, his administration was run by and for Oxford and the Ivy League. Yale Law Graduates for Clinton raised $1.6 million for their fellow alumnus in the 1992 campaign. Eight Harvard professors initially joined the ranks of the administration. In a classic 1993 *New Republic* essay entitled "Clincest," Jacob Weisberg outlined all the academic and social ties of the Clinton team, making for "the increasingly cozy relationships among press, law, academia and government that now mark the Clinton era. In fact, there's rarely been a time when the governing elites in so many fields were made up of such a tight, hermetic and incestuous clique."[25]

An emblematic moment was the swearing in of Clinton's former Oxford roommate, Strobe Talbot, as a senior State Department official: "In Portland's Benson Hotel, Labor Secretary Robert Reich (Rhodes scholar, '68, University College) presided over the oath given by Bill Clinton (Rhodes scholar, '68, University College) to Mr. Talbott (Rhodes scholar '68, Magdalen College). 'It was a really beautiful moment,' commented George Stephanopoulos (Rhodes scholar, '82, Balliol College)."[26] This was an administration that looked like America—the portion of it that had happened to win Rhodes scholarships, go to Yale Law School, or be invited to Renaissance weekends.

This elite didn't just feel a call to run the country, it felt it deserved to run the country. "They think of themselves as entitled to power in a way their antecedents never did," Weisberg writes. "The Clinton circle has a pronounced class consciousness that tells them they're not just lucky to be here. They're running things because they're the best."[27] How could anyone reject the leadership of a group of people so intelligent and famously "conscience stricken?" In the Clintons, this sense of entitlement produced a deep anger at the fact that their ambitions encountered resistance.

Author Gail Sheehy wrote in a note to herself after first meeting Hillary in January 1992, "She is angry. Not all of the time. But most of the time."[28] In her memoir, Hillary writes of how independent counsel Kenneth Starr's probe "infuriated me."[29] To his cabinet, Clinton explained away his affair with Monica Lewinsky by referring to his own anger. Peter Baker writes in his impeachment book, *The Breach*: "He had woken up profoundly angry every day for the last four and a half years, he said, the same time frame that he had been under investigation by Starr and his predecessor. And that, he suggested, had created a behavior pattern that was not justified but could be explained because he was not at peace with himself."[30]

Here were two people, Bill and Hillary Clinton, given so much by their country and at the pinnacle of power—and they were mad at the world.

To this day, they express outrage that they had to battle a political opposition, and use it as an excuse for their failures. Hillary notes darkly that the protests that dogged her "Health Security Express" in 1994, when she toured to promote her health-care plan, were "[n]either random nor spontaneous."[31] *Organized* protests? Of a major piece of legislation—crafted by Hillary? What had the United States come to?

Similarly, Clinton's defenders save their most fervent indignation in the Lewinsky scandal for the fact that two conservative lawyers helped Paula Jones make her legal arguments, and two women worked to expose the fact that the president was using a twenty-two-year-old White House intern for oral sex. What could these people have been thinking? Didn't they know Clinton had been to Oxford, to Yale, and signed the Family and Medical Leave Act? If this didn't exempt him from the law and allow him to have his way with White House personnel with impunity, well, the nation didn't know what was good for it.

For the Clintons, their opponents were never just wrong or short-sighted, but bad, ill-intentioned people, seeking to harm "the children." Clinton's "axis of evil" was Bob Woodward,[32] Ken Starr,[33] and Bob Dole,[34] all of whom he considered "evil" for, respectively, writing an unflattering book about him, investigating him, and wanting to cut government programs more than he did. Opposing or even criticizing Clinton was an immoral act, because he had subsumed within himself, as the best politician of the best generation, truth, light, and progress. He was always willing to apologize for his country, but wringing an apology out of him for himself, say in the Lewinsky affair, was nearly impossible. He didn't apologize until he realized that it had to be part of his survival strategy—after which he, true to form, apologized promiscuously.

When Clinton took the presidency, it seemed there might issue a glorious new political epoch, led by all the well-credentialed former

McGovernites ready to make themselves the new establishment. It never quite happened.

First, there was the epic debacle of the health-care plan, a perfect concoction of baby-boomer elite arrogance (in thinking it could remake a seventh of the American economy) and condescension (toward Democratic lawmakers, who were ignored; toward insurance companies and drugmakers, who were labeled evil; and toward everyone else in the country, who were to be ministered to in great detail by government). The baby-boom elite had let the working class fight the Vietnam War, and now they were going to return the favor by telling the working class how to live. The plan's flop chastened the Clinton administration, forevermore.

Then there was the general unseemliness of the administration, topped off by the Lewinsky affair, which led to a souring of relations with the press, a major setback in the effort to forge a new establishment. This was devastating because it was impossible to create the Kennedy-like aura of glamour and goodness Clinton so craved without the fawning cooperation of the press.[35]

As conservative writer David Brooks pointed out at the time, press criticism of Clinton after the 1996 reelection fund-raising scandal and the exposure of his affair with Lewinsky was part of a changed inflection in the Clinton in-crowd during the course of his administration.[36] It began as good-government Kennedy School liberals and ended as the decadent Hollywood left. The entertainment world could implicitly understand and forgive Clinton's sexual use of a lower-level employee, since that is one of the privileges of Hollywood life.

But, for Clinton, sexual incontinence issued from considerably less glitzy roots.

"I was born at sixteen and I'll always feel I'm sixteen"

If growing up in a stable two-parent family is important to character formation, Bill Clinton started at a gross disadvantage. He grew up in the family equivalent of a log cabin, or perhaps a tar paper shack.

His mother, Virginia Kelley, married a ne'er-do-well traveling sales-man, Bill Blythe, who was a bigamist and died in a car accident six months before Clinton was born.[37] There is doubt whether he was actually Clinton's father. During the 1992 presidential campaign, Blythe's different marriages and his children by them began to turn up. Clinton aide and confidante Betsey Wright has said, "Virginia didn't know how many marriages [he had had], and every time a new child showed up, she would just tell the staff to have me return the call."[38]

The flirtatious Virginia eventually remarried, to a man named Roger Clinton, and they moved to the mob-infested gambling town of Hot Springs. There were three warning signs about Roger: he was a drinker, he was a gambler, and his nickname was "Dude."[39] He turned out to be a miserable bastard. Young Bill routinely heard the sounds of fierce, drunken late-night arguments between Virginia and a jeal-ous Roger, who beat and sometimes kicked her.[40]

All of this irresistibly lends itself to armchair psychoanalysis, about how Clinton utterly lacked a model of stable, affirming masculinity in his personal life, about the fast-and-loose ethos of Hot Springs where he grew up, about the promiscuity and sexual intrigue that surrounded Virginia.

The Clintons have talked about the impact of Bill's upbringing. Clinton has said that he had an irrational fear of death from the early loss of his father that drove him to seek political success, and seek it fast.[41] "He viewed his father's death as so irrational—so out of the blue—that it really did set a tone for his own sense of mortality," Hillary has explained. "Not just in his political career. It was reading everything he could read, talking to everybody he could talk to, stay-ing up all night, because life was passing him by."[42]

Clinton told Betsey Wright how he had come to understand that growing up in an alcoholic household had made him eager to please. Wright has said that Clinton experienced family therapy (after his brother Roger's drug arrest) as a kind of revelation: "He got a much better understanding of why he did things the way he did. It was in the context of learning about how that comes out of an alcoholic home. Most notable was why he was always trying to please people. He was fascinated by it, and it rang so true."[43]

Clinton has talked to various people about how everyone has an "addiction," which his listeners have taken as references to his own compulsive attachment to sex or to politics or both. He told a friend in the mid-1980s: "I think we're all addicted to something. Some people are addicted to drugs. Some to power. Some to food. Some to sex. We're all addicted to something."[44] When journalist Joe Klein asked him about the divergent paths between him and his brother Roger, a cocaine addict, Clinton said, "Well, there are different sorts of addictions."[45]

He has remarked on the pull of adolescence on him: "I always wondered if I'd want to be sixteen when I was forty, because I never felt like I got to complete my childhood."[46] When he entered family counseling after Roger's drug arrest, Clinton observed, "I was born at sixteen and I'll always feel I'm sixteen. And Hillary was born at age forty."[47]

Finally, the hostility in Clinton's early home life, by his own account, drove him inward. "The violence and dysfunction in our home," Clinton has said, "made me a loner, which is contrary to the way people view me, because I'm gregarious, happy, all of that. But I had to construct a whole life inside my own mind." Virginia would tell her children to put their troubles in "an airtight box," a strategy Clinton publicly referred to as president when he said he put Paula Jones's accusations "in a little box."[48]

According to his own lights, then, Clinton was a death-driven addictive personality with a strong streak of immaturity, an eagerness to please, and a tendency to live in his own private world.

Other presidents have faced hardship growing up, and others have had grave character flaws, but Clinton's emotional and psychological life must rank him among the all-time greats of presidential dysfunction. That he became president, rather than suffer some sad fate, is a testament to his intelligence, his determination, his marriage, and his character traits—the ambition, the compulsion to please, the ability to wall off bad news—that were adaptive to success in politics.

None of this is to absolve Clinton of moral responsibility for his actions. But he was a disaster waiting to happen. It is almost a marvel that his two terms featured—once the smaller flaps are put aside—"only" a reelection fund-raising scandal, a sex scandal, and a pardon scandal. Each of them highlighted a different character flaw—respectively, the desperation to win, his sexual obsession, and the need to seize every last vestige of power.

Dick Morris, the political consultant who knows him best, quite seriously refers to Clinton's "pathology,"[49] and the most important operative of his 1992 election and early presidency has said he never should have been elected. During the Lewinsky scandal, Diane Sawyer asked George Stephanopoulos, "Should a man capable of doing that ever have been elected president?" Stephanopoulos answered, "No, I don't think so. You know, the problem is that he hasn't been a bad president. He's achieved more than I ever could have imagined. But he is the head of state, where the person matters."[50] The equivalent would be former White House spokesman Ari Fleischer disavowing his support for George W. Bush. In his person, in his character—which is inevitably magnified by the office—Bill Clinton was always unfit to be president.

"Get with the goddamn program!"

Clinton seemed such a good fit for the 1990s because it was a time of plenty, a time of excess, a time of unseriousness, and, above all, a time of denuded masculinity and of regnant sentimentality.

Clinton, in a famous outburst, complained that he had become an Eisenhower Republican. Be that as it may, no one would ever accuse him of being an Eisenhower man. Clinton's generation had moved beyond the sterner model of manhood, emphasizing duty and sacrifice, that had characterized the generation that won World War II. They had been in therapy, were open to sharing their feelings, and were understanding and sensitive to a fault.

Joe Klein recalls his realization after an interview with Clinton's mother in which they talked about the family therapy the Clintons had undergone: "Bill Clinton was the first American president to admit that he had participated in a form of psychotherapy. One imagines him totally cooperative, wildly eloquent, emotionally accessible, flagrantly remorseful . . . and completely in control of the situation, three steps ahead of the therapist—the analysand from hell." Klein continues, "Certainly, I'd never met a politician like him before. I barely knew the man and we were talking, or seeming to talk, about the most ridiculously intimate things."[51]

Clinton's greatest talent was for feeling. His best moments on the 1992 campaign trail were acts of empathy, whether it was hugging a woman who said she had to choose between buying food or medicine,[52] or asking a female questioner during one of the presidential debates how the deficit affected *her*.[53] He stood perfectly at the crossroads of two distinct cultural trends that combined to put a premium on emotional display: the rise of confessional daytime television and Southern religiosity.

His ability to cry was prodigious. He read Ruth Bader Ginsburg's statement about her personal history prior to announcing her nomination to the Supreme Court, but still cried upon hearing her read it out loud.[54] He cried when he was cutting, after much calculation, Lani Guinier loose.[55] He would wipe tears from his eyes when he was laughing too hard at something not particularly funny Boris Yeltsin had said at a joint press conference.[56] He could cry and laugh uproariously at the same time.[57] The tears were always near the surface, available.

In his weepiness and his evocation of feeling, Clinton tapped into a philosophic wellspring that runs back to the philosopher Rousseau, who sought to create a public morality based on compassion. The political scientist Clifford Orwin has remarked, "The morality of compassion offers a relaxed alternative to moralities of self-restraint. Slackness in no way precludes compassion, and if the latter dictates being 'nonjudgmental,' then the slack have a head start on the rest of us." In an observation particularly apt to Clinton, Orwin identifies the problem with compassion as a public value: "Almost always too much or too little, too intense or too sporadic, liable alike to mindless excess and to calculated hypocrisy, compassion is anything but a reliable basis for public policy."[58]

Clinton was the daytime TV president, in his emotiveness, in his soap-operatic sex scandal—and in his electoral base. Clinton's typical voter was a single woman. According to pollster Mark Penn's analysis, Clinton did best among voters whose way of looking at the world was marked by intuition and feeling. "Clinton voters," Penn remarked in a memo, "are more likely to watch HBO, MTV, Oprah (and similar TV talk shows) and soap operas." Penn also noted that "Clinton voters are more likely to be afraid to walk alone at night, consider themselves overeaters, and visit department stores."[59]

Appropriately, Clinton's leadership featured a certain emotional fragility. One Clinton associate told author Elizabeth Drew: "It's amazing to me how many things turn on his mood. I've heard references to 'the knife edge of his confidence.' If he's thrown off his stride, he loses confidence. One of [appointments director] Nancy Hernreich's jobs is to assess his moods and adjust the pace according to his moods. I don't know how many former presidents were on such a sharp edge of emotion."[60] He needed constant pep talks. Both Robert Reich and pollster Stan Greenberg warned him against dissolving into self-pity when he was running third, behind Bush and Perot, in the early going in the 1992 campaign.[61] He may be the only president who had to be told by his vice president to "Get with the goddamn program!"[62] and "You've got to get your act together."[63]

This weakness helps account for the perception that Clinton lacked beliefs. Former Clinton national security advisor Tony Lake writes: "The charge that President Clinton is a cynic who believes in too little is flatly wrong. . . . Indeed, I think that [Clinton's] tendency has always been to believe too much, not too little. And, immensely talented, throughout his life he was able to have it all, to avoid making truly hard choices."[64]

With Clinton, it was always too much—too many beliefs, too many emotions, too many women. Such excess, joined with his indiscipline and weakness, accounts for his indecisiveness.

As Stephanopoulos told Bob Woodward, "The worst thing about [Clinton] is that he never makes a decision."[65] Making a crisp decision and sticking to it means implicitly telling someone "no." Clinton had little stomach for it. His default mode was agreement. Stephanopoulos writes, "Clinton's compassion was involuntary, fully felt yet entirely existential, an instinctive empathy so ingrained that he communicated commitment even when he thought he was creating space."[66]

Clinton specializes in portraits of indecision. In a 1985 incident as governor, Clinton agonized about whether to veto a bill ending the tax deductibility of donations to colleges. He decided so late that a state trooper had to slide a copy of the bill, stamped "Disapproved," under the door of the state clerk who had already left for the day. When Clinton told college presidents later that night of his veto, they talked him out of it, and a trooper had to fish the bill back out from under the door with a coat hanger so Clinton could scratch out the "Dis."[67]

As top Clinton diplomat Dick Holbrooke puts it, "Clinton is profoundly intuitive. His mind works like nothing I've ever seen. He's brilliant, and is able to see every side of each issue. This is usually an advantage, but not always."[68] Says Don Baer, a former Clinton communications director, "I think he never wanted to make snap judgments. He has a very, very active and engaged intelligence. I think he wanted to understand the various sides of issues before he came down hard on them, even though he started from a certain set of principles that he believed were right. It may be that the process of doing that, at the end of the day, required too much time and too much lack of discipline to really focus himself and his administration."[69]

Clinton's sensibility was more appropriate to a seminar room. Former Clinton congressional lobbyist Howard Paster recalls the question of the balanced budget amendment coming up early in the administration: "There wasn't a soul anywhere in the West Wing who was for it. So four of us went to see Clinton and said, 'Mr. President,

you're going to have to see Senator [Paul] Simon, he wants you to support a balanced budget constitutional amendment, and you've got to
tell him No, you can't support a constitutional amendment.' And one
of us said, 'This is a unanimous recommendation.' And Clinton said,
and this is a paraphrase, obviously, 'Have any of you taken constitutional law? I have, and let me tell you, it's not that simple.' And what
we saw was frustration because he was going to make a debate."[70]

Clinton's understanding and empathy and willingness to see all
sides were taken as an advance over the sterner virtues of an earlier,
more certain age. The latent danger of emotional expressiveness, however, is the relentless focus on the self that it encourages, unleashing a
solipsism unbounded by extrinsic restraints such as responsibility or
duty. Clinton was, in this sense, Woody Allen in the Oval Office: smart,
talented, hyper-articulate, but caught in a childish self-obsession.

"Peace and prosperity"

In his emotional style, as in much else, Clinton didn't define the
1990s, in the sense of fundamentally shaping the decade. Instead,
Zelig-like, he represented the decade—the obsession with the economy and the implicit belief that it would keep growing forever; the
apotheosis of globalization and the hope that it had fundamentally
altered international affairs; the unwillingness to grapple seriously
with the nation's enemies and the imperative to kill them; the willingness to kick problems down the road in the hopes that they would
disappear as if by magic. The business cycle wouldn't turn down, the
NASDAQ bubble wouldn't burst, the corporate lying and cheating
would never be exposed, the flimsy arms-control agreements and
peace deals would never come undone, the unwillingness to tolerate
combat casualties would never come home to roost, the terrorists
would never kill more than a dozen Americans here or there.

Upon taking office, Clinton inherited his share of international
crises. There was a dubious military deployment in Somalia, a war in
Bosnia, and a budding crisis with North Korea. But Clinton, funda-

mentally, was fortunate in his timing. He inherited a growing economy, and he would leave office before the economic bust and before the looming, grave threats to national security had become starkly clear. He could make "peace and prosperity" an endless mantra, when it was really illusory. Within a year of his leaving office, the depth of the illusion had become clear, in the exposure of the criminal acts of corporate leaders and in the smoldering ruins in downtown Manhattan.

None of this is to suggest that there wasn't real economic and social progress in the 1990s. But it bubbled up from below. The fantastic economy of the 1990s was not a Clinton creation. It stemmed from the strengths of corporate America and the dynamism of American society, not the minor deficit reduction Clinton managed early in his presidency. He wasn't central to "peace and prosperity," but was its accoutrement, the shiny red maraschino cherry plopped on top of rollicking good times.

The elimination of the federal budget deficit, in turn, was the result of galloping economic growth, not Clinton's anti-deficit program. He touts cutting the deficit as one of the crown jewels of his accomplishment, but it is really a case study in his dissonant governance. In 1992, he promised both to cut the deficit by half within five years and to create massive new spending programs. In his first year, he was saying deficit reduction was indispensable to economic growth, but his 1993 budget still forecast long-term deficits. In 1994, when Republicans took over Congress and proposed eliminating the deficit, Clinton suddenly proclaimed that deficit reduction was a threat to the nation's children and elderly.

After the 1996 campaign, when Clinton decided to cut a deal with Republicans to balance the budget, deficit reduction was once again indispensable to economic growth, and, in fact, one of President Clinton's great, principled acts for which future generations of Americans would remember him in reverence and awe.

Clinton, as these maneuverings suggest, was the ultimate situationalist. The comedian Jackie Mason says that if he is dropped anywhere in America, from midtown Manhattan to Utah, he will, within minutes, know what jokes work for that audience. Clinton had a similar ability. He could either defend or trash deficit reduction with equal passion, depending on whether it suited his interests at the time.

This didn't mean that he was infinitely malleable. Abortion rights and racial quotas were untouchable. He probably wouldn't ever himself propose a "tax cut for the rich," although he might sign one (and did in 1997). Getting him to accept the idea of block granting Medicaid to the states—as Republicans were proposing in 1995—would take more leverage than Republicans could bring to bear. But within a remarkably broad band of positions Clinton zigged and zagged as necessary.

If there is one cause for which Clinton consistently took career-endangering risks, for which he fought with unstinting vigor and toughness, and on which he was mostly vindicated, it was sex. In the Lewinsky scandal, Clinton fought for sex unbounded by moral strictures, sex that was a free-floating act of personal self-expression. He found a receptive enough audience in an American public that might not embrace this sexual ethic themselves, but was not willing to judge almost anything having to do with sex.

But his Lewinsky escapade still exacted a significant price in his other priorities. The scandal helped keep him, late in his administration, from pursuing entitlement reform, from pushing an aggressive free-trade agenda, from bombing al Qaeda targets, from confronting Saddam Hussein, and from getting Al Gore elected president. All this was sacrificed for a few sessions with Monica Lewinsky in the White House and over the phone.

Despite all his irenic rhetoric and his professions of wanting to unite the country, Clinton's personal failings and need to defend them polarized the country and made more stark what would become known after the 2000 election as the red-state/blue-state split.

The country divided over the importance of truthfulness, marital fidelity, and moral virtue. This was the kind of cultural split Clinton had sought to smooth over in 1992 (on the issues of welfare and crime), but it had returned by way of Clinton's own personal weakness.

In the end, the central conundrum about Bill Clinton is how a president who was so active—talking and doing constantly—could have done so little that is important. The answer is that Clinton's activism served as a substitute for performing government's most important tasks. The most fundamental function of the federal government is simply to defend the nation.

Dick Morris had a conversation with Clinton about his place in history that he recounts in his book *Behind the Oval Office*. Morris had three tiers of presidential greats, and thought Clinton could perhaps sneak into the third tier. Morris told Clinton that economic growth doesn't make for presidential greatness because it is cyclical, and neither does popularity while in office. He thought welfare and the elimination of the deficit were big accomplishments that boosted Clinton's case (although, as we shall see, Republicans more properly deserve credit for these). In Morris's mind, however, Clinton needed something else: "I think you have to break the international back of terrorism by economic and military action against the terrorist states."[71]

What Morris was recommending was a bold, far-reaching use of executive power toward an end central to the government's purpose. Clinton, for all his activism, wasn't up for it. As his administration wound down, Clinton and his aides became increasingly aware of the terror threat, but they were unwilling to take decisive action against it.

This was partly a function of Clinton personally. He was never entirely comfortable in his role as commander in chief, feeling awkward about his draft history and never culturally at ease with the military. Nor was he comfortable with that ultimate act of moral responsibility—sending men into combat, and giving orders to have people killed. Waging the kind of campaign Morris was talking about also cut against Clinton's intellectual grain.

The Clinton team believed that, in some sense, history had ended, at least as it had traditionally been known. The forces of the new economy were making borders irrelevant. Trade was the foremost factor in international affairs. Ancient hatreds were melting away. The world was inevitably slipping toward a liberal future on the American model. America would exercise its leadership in multilateral settings, shaping the world through arms control and peace negotiations. It sometimes would have to resort to force, but ideally on behalf of humanitarian causes one step removed from America's national interest. Defending that interest had about it an atavistic scent. The military engagements would be risk-free, and if not, abandoned (as in the case of Somalia), or not undertaken at all.

As Clinton was leaving office, the illusions of the 1990s began to give way. The NASDAQ bubble burst, the first step toward exposing how the miracles of the New Economy had been oversold, and that not everything that was new, young, and Internet-related would make a profit. The North Koreans had been cheating on their nuclear deal for years, and Arafat had returned to his terrorist roots, demonstrating how tyrants and terrorists wouldn't be restrained by soothing words and parchment bounds. Clinton talked incessantly of "peace and prosperity," but neither was quite as advertised.

Clinton had proudly shone with the fever flush of late 1990s America. He wasn't the only one, of course. Conservatives were complicit in the silliness over the economy. The political culture as a whole didn't take terrorism seriously enough. When the economy dipped and the terrorists struck, Clinton was—in a perfectly fitting end to the Clinton years—somewhere else, giving well-compensated speeches, attending glitzy parties, or explaining how he could have handled the whole ensuing mess better than his successor.

Clinton obviously would not have been the right man for this new, much harder moment, precisely because he had been the right man for the old, much easier moment. All his weaknesses had fit the spirit of the age.

Even as America had surged to unparalleled economic and military power in the 1990s, a haze of weakness hung over it. Our enemies concluded we were too weak to defend our borders, too weak to undertake serious domestic security, too weak to realize the terror alliance forming in the Middle East, too weak to give up the illusion of negotiations with unreformed enemies, too weak to take casualties in combat, too weak to hit back hard after terrorist attacks, too weak to lift our eyes from our gorgeous "peace and prosperity" to the murderous forces arising abroad.

On September 11, Clinton's most important legacy arrived in horrifying form, and settled in a pile of rubble seven stories high in downtown Manhattan.[72] History hadn't ended, after all. We had just ignored it.

Part One

POLITICS & POLICY

HIS PRESIDENCY:

Shrinking the Office

I N SEPTEMBER 1989, DEMOCRATIC theorists Bill Galston and Elaine
Kamarck wrote a monograph, "The Politics of Evasion," diagnosing
the party's presidential losing streak. "Too many Americans," they
wrote, "have come to see the party as inattentive to their economic
interests, indifferent if not hostile to their moral sentiments and ineffective in defense of their national security."[1]

A few years later, in May 1991, Galston and Kamarck were sitting
in a Cleveland hotel room with Bill Clinton before he delivered a
speech at the annual convention of the Democratic Leadership Council. "He had not only read our manifesto," says Galston. "He had
inhaled it. As we were sitting in his hotel room before the speech, he
played back to us—this is one of my strongest political memories—
what amounted to paragraphs from the monograph. He did it without
notes, and with total command of the material in a way that made it
clear to both of us that he had not only internalized the framework of
our argument but had decided how he was going to use it. It was a
total mind-meld."[2]

It was Clinton's understanding of the New Democrat critique of the Democratic Party—and his formidable ability to translate that understanding into practical politics as a candidate—that made it possible for the Democrats to win the presidency again. He seemed to exorcise the spirits of Mondale and Dukakis. This was a significant accomplishment, but it was quickly dissipated during the first two left-leaning years of his administration.

Thereafter, Clinton was just a survivor, allergic to taking risks and self-abasing in his taste for poll-tested minutiae.

The common thread to his time in office is smallness, of Clinton personally and of his politics. His malleability and his fear of risk kept him—after the crash of Hillary's health-care plan—from proposing or thinking anything grand. Napoleon talked of great leaders having "three-o'clock-in-the-morning courage."[3] Clinton had three-o'clock-in-the-morning jitters, whether he was up late deciding to bomb another country or formulating his latest impeachment defense or just feeling sorry for himself.

Clinton could have been a truly great campaign operative, helping some other, better man be president. But he was fundamentally miscast in an office that depended on his person, that couldn't be filled just with political strategy and campaign skills, and that required qualities his moral cowardice denied him. He trailed dishonesty like a plume of bad cologne, lying to protect himself, to reposition himself, and to make himself feel better. He created a private language of evasion memorialized in that haiku of Clintonism—"it depends on what the meaning of 'is' is."

Clinton shrank liberalism and the presidency. His 1992 campaign didn't lead to a liberal revival. Instead, liberalism atrophied, often able to check conservative reforms but not an independent creative force in its own right. It was a liberalism largely shorn of its idealism and of its ambition.

Clinton became comfortable in the presidency only as the job dwindled to an exalted governorship or school superintendency. He sought to help the public conduct better neighborhood watches, decide what kids should wear to school, improve its TV viewing habits, and cope with other annoyances of daily life. He kept busy by working on what didn't matter—it was safe and popular.

So Clinton managed to be an activist—speaking and proposing a lot—while never straying far from the status quo. It was hyperactivity almost for its own sake. Clinton rarely could do just one thing. He did crossword puzzles while getting briefings, he worked the phones while getting sexually serviced by an intern.

Clinton bucked his political base when it seemed imperative—e.g., signing welfare reform—and occasionally took measures that didn't necessarily poll well, such as bailing out Mexico during a financial crisis. Otherwise, he distinguished himself by his lack of distinction.

His presidency had four phases, as he adapted his coloration to the political moment.

- In 1993–1994, he governed to the left, reflecting as always the constellation of forces around him, in this case his liberal staff and the Democratic Congress.
- In 1995–1996, he confronted the new Republican Congress, blunting its charge by flip-flopping as necessary on important issues, by rediscovering his centrism, and by staying safely within the penumbra of popular micro-initiatives.
- In 1997–1998, he maintained the upper hand over Congress that he had won during the government shutdowns, but was distracted by scandal, first over his reelection fund-raising, then over his affair with Monica Lewinsky.
- In 1999–2000, finally, he backed off some of the centrism from the previous four years of his presidency, returning full-circle to his liberal phase. The Democrats soon enough would be in need of another Galston and Kamarck memo.

It makes for a dizzying panorama of political maneuver. It is all pudding and very little theme. Clinton represented the presidency in its post-heroic phase, and his successes were often selfish, not translating to his party at large. In the end, his political formula—a kind of deficit-hawk progressivism—was highly personalized, the key to popular governance in late 1990s America if you were a Democrat named William Jefferson Clinton.

It is an indication of the essential defensiveness of his administration that he told journalist Joe Klein as he was about to leave office that "two of the great achievements" of his presidency were fighting the Republicans during the government shutdowns and surviving his impeachment.[4] In other words, Newt Gingrich thrust, and he parried.

Several of his influences linger on. His speeches weren't memorable, but with slogans like "one hundred thousand new cops on the street" he affected the nature of sound bites. It was no longer enough to talk about the dollar amounts of a spending program. Instead, government programs had to be sold in faux-communitarian terms emphasizing their benefit to communities, families, or "the children." He blunted the edge of ideological politics for both Democrats and Republicans, which is a good thing if you consider "partisanship" an inherent evil, but not if you prefer politics to be a frank battle of ideas. He introduced a cloying sentimentality into American political life, which had a hand in creating the "compassionate conservatism" of George W. Bush. The props and style were largely the same.

In short, Bill Clinton introduced much that is small, fuzzy, or ridiculous in contemporary American politics. Despite his endless hankering after a new Camelot, there was little in his politics designed to edify or uplift. He represented the lowest common denominator of what you would get if you stopped people randomly at a shopping mall and asked them their opinions—which is no accident, because that is exactly what the Clinton team did.

After September 11, such methods seemed the artifact of another era, when America could float in a haze of good feeling, when school uniforms could be among the president's top concerns, when it seemed the country could thrive without strong leadership from the top. Clinton was the bridge from one epic era in American politics, defined by the Cold War, to another, defined by the war on terror. In between, there was mush, trivia, and wishful thinking.

Clinton's presidency ultimately was like a summer storm that produces teeth-rattling thunderclaps, but soon is gone without a trace—except for the fresher-smelling air when it's over.

"He's ad-libbing! He's ad-libbing the State of the Union!"

Clinton won a three-man race in 1992 with 43 percent of the vote, benefiting from President Bush's near abdication.[5] Even though there were ten million more voters than in the previous presidential election, Clinton collected only a million more votes than had Michael Dukakis when he went down to humiliating defeat in 1988.[6] Still, Clinton had reached the top of the heap, elected president at age forty-six, with the Democrats holding a 259 to 175 majority in the House and a 57 to 43 majority in the Senate. It was a moment pulsating with possibility—soon squandered.

The first two years of Clinton's presidency would track almost exactly his first disastrous term as Arkansas governor, after which he lost his bid for reelection in 1980. He surrounded himself with young aides who inspired little confidence in the public; he was disorganized and constantly late; he complained about how he was being run ragged, although it was of his own doing; lines of authority were tangled and vague; and he made mistakes that convinced voters—partly because of the callow sense of superiority given off by his administration—that he was too liberal and out of touch with their concerns.

These themes recurred because they reflected something enduring in Clinton's character. As David Maraniss writes of the Arkansas experience, "the staff's mistakes in large measure reflected Clinton's loose, free-ranging management style, his conflicted personality, and his urge to be all things to all people."[7] All of these qualities were still on display in 1993.

No one, including Clinton, seemed to realize he was president of the United States. Initially, his staff didn't stand when President Clinton entered the room. He could barely manage a salute, and National Security Advisor Tony Lake had to teach him how to do it.[8] His schedule was so chaotic he couldn't receive a regular morning CIA briefing.[9] Decisions were continually revisited.[10] His meetings were long and inconclusive, while—in a pattern that endured for years—his speeches were written in a process that required all-nighters, and in-the-car-on-the-way-to-the-event revisions.

The final version of his first address to Congress was so inadequate that he did impromptu riffs off of it. "On the House floor," speechwriter Michael Waldman writes, "standing on tiptoes, [economic aide Gene] Sperling and I were scanning our single-spaced copies of the speech. 'He's ad-libbing! He's ad-libbing the State of the Union!' we shouted, and gave each other a high five."[11] Like, cool![12]

Lower-level aides would try to make it into important meetings just for fun. "Senior staff meetings grew to thirty-five to forty-five people," says Howard Paster, Clinton's first congressional lobbyist. "Anybody could come. There wasn't any list circulated. They had chairs three deep in the Roosevelt room. You don't run a place like that."[13]

Then, the staff mouthed off to the press. "Most of the leaks were coming because people were trying to show to journalist friends of theirs that they were in the room and had a hand in big decisions," says a former senior official. "Many people who witnessed it would call it 'the Stephanopoulos problem.' There was just a lot of foul careerism on the part of some people around Clinton."[14]

The juvenile edge of the White House was slowly sanded away, but more than atmospherics and process were wrong. Clinton got off to a decidedly Old Democrat start. In 1992, Clinton ran an economically populist campaign, advocating new spending and tax hikes on the rich, but he still hugged the center and even managed to get to Bush's right. He endorsed free trade and middle-class tax cuts. He constantly invoked the middle class ("people who work hard and play by the rules"), and made bywords of "responsibility" and "opportunity."

He favored capital punishment. He famously called for "the end of welfare as we know it."

Once in office, the liberal staffing at the White House and the departments, the leftist orientation of the Democratic majority in Congress, and Clinton's ambivalence about some of his campaign centrism—he hated his tax cut proposal and opposed the idea of truly "ending" the welfare status quo—undid his moderation from the campaign trail. The leftward lurch pleased the Democratic faithful taking control of the White House for the first time since 1980.

"There was a euphoria once we won the election," says Bruce Reed, a centrist who was deputy campaign manager for policy, and who became a domestic policy advisor in the Clinton White House. "The hordes had been waiting at the gates for twelve years, and didn't really understand politics, that this wasn't a Kennedy School exercise."[15] It wasn't just the Democrats flowing back into the executive branch who yearned for a return to the Old Faith, but the Democrats who had long ago settled into the legislative branch. Clinton showed—most of the time—deference to congressional Democrats for whom it was still 1965, the heyday of "Great Society" liberalism.

The moderate Southern governor of yore went missing, as Clinton, always the reactive politician, reflected the forces around him. Howard Paster warns against assuming with Clinton "that there's ideology guiding decisions which are really made ad hoc." He says, "I don't think the decisions were consistently ideological, because there were different players in every decision. There's a risk to assume that there's any ideological shepherd in what he did."[16]

The first firestorm was over Clinton's pledge to allow gays to serve openly in the military. A week after his election, NBC reporter Andrea Mitchell asked Clinton whether he intended to keep it. His reply was a mild, "I want to." Clinton may have been trying to leave himself wiggle room,[17] but there was no backing out now. He had told a gay group during the campaign that overturning the executive order stipulating the ban would be one of his first acts, and that he would never compromise on such an important issue.[18] The military, which had not been consulted, was furious. Republicans and even some Democrats were unalterably opposed.

The resulting compromise—"Don't Ask, Don't Tell"—satisfied no one. The controversy permanently soured Clinton's relations with the military, and identified him with the sort of cultural liberalism his 1992 campaign had been designed to disavow. Typically, Clinton held himself blameless for the fiasco, and later complained that congressional Republicans had raised the issue in the first place by trying to write the ban on gays in the military into law. A Clinton aide who tried to sell this spin to the press later told Elizabeth Drew it had been "a lie."[19]

It got worse. Clinton jettisoned one of his significant feints to the right from the campaign, a 10 percent middle-class tax cut,[20] and proposed a $30 billion "stimulus bill" that represented old-fashioned public-works spending (it was defeated).[21] These moves gave an unmistakably liberal coloration to Clinton's economic program even as the rest of his budget plan shifted to the center, from an emphasis on public "investments" to deficit reduction. The irony was that, at the end of the day, the legislative centerpiece of Clinton's early administration, his economic plan, was almost exactly the same as that of George Bush in 1990.

After all the anti-Bush rhetoric, despite all the later self-serving claims of attempting an establishment-threatening "progressive presidency" (Clinton courtier Sidney Blumenthal writes, ridiculously, of "the challenge to the old order"),[22] Clinton in 1993 served up a huge helping of the status quo. Both the Bush plan from 1990 and the Clinton plan in 1993 featured modest increases in the top income tax rate, more Medicare payroll taxes on top earners, an expansion of the Earned Income Tax Credit for low-income workers, a gas tax increase, and an increase in the alternative minimum tax.[23] Clinton's other important economic initiative from this period, pushing to pass the North American Free Trade Agreement (NAFTA), had been conceived and negotiated by prior Republican administrations.

Meanwhile, Clinton's signature promise to change the status quo, on welfare policy, was nearly forgotten. Dropping welfare reform meant abandoning altogether the Bill Clinton of 1992. "I think that as a political matter, it's a demonstrable fact that we had welfare-reform TV spots running in the most contested battleground states in the ten days before the 1992 election," says Bill Galston, who became a Clinton domestic advisor. "From which I infer that the single most conspicuous domestic policy promise that candidate Clinton made was to end welfare as we know it."[24]

Welfare reform had been pushed aside by the health-care plan. The health plan was indeed a big and bold proposal, the last Clinton ever dared make. It enjoyed an initial burst of popularity, then gradually sank. Opposition to the plan energized a Right that was increasingly muscled up with think tanks, grass-roots groups, and the voice of Rush Limbaugh—making for a powerful, budding anti-Clinton coalition.

This coalition exercised its muscle in the fight against the Democratic crime bill in the summer of 1994, a harbinger of things to come. After the Black Caucus had failed to water down death penalty provisions in the bill, it was given a consolation prize of more spending for urban social programs, such as midnight basketball. This created an opening for conservatives to deride the bill as pork-barrel spending, and the traditional softhearted and softheaded liberal approach to crime. In the House, the GOP defeated "the rule" on the bill—a procedural vote that usually passes on party lines—with a stunning fifty-eight Democratic defections.[25]

The great Democratic unraveling was underway.

"I know who I am. I know what I believe!"

November 1994 was a body slam for Clinton. The Democrats lost eight Senate and fifty-two House seats. Republicans captured seven out of the eight largest governorships in the nation, with Democrat Lawton Chiles barely hanging on in Florida. A political party hadn't suffered such a midterm rebuke since the Republicans under Herbert Hoover, who had never been a Clinton role model.[26]

"1994 arose from fundamental, not incidental causes," writes Michael Barone. "It was the result of voters' rational responses to the parties' differences on major issues, not to some accidental events or irrational paroxysm of anger."[27] Or as Mark Penn and Douglas Schoen, who would become Clinton's key pollsters, put it in a memo at the time, "The 1994 midterm election was a complete rejection of what the Democratic Party has come to represent—bigger government, more taxes, higher spending, more bureaucracy. It was more than just a rejection of Bill Clinton's leadership. After all, Bill Clinton had a 50 percent approval rating on Election Day, and unemployment and inflation are at historically low levels."[28]

Newt Gingrich had prepared for the opportunity Clinton gave him in 1994 for over a decade,[29] building a cadre of House Republicans who were ideologically cohesive and unwilling to put up with minority status any longer. He had found a fresh, future-oriented way to talk about limited government and about reform—of everything from welfare to Congress to torts.[30] The agenda was enshrined in the Contract with America, and honed into a weapon to nationalize the midterm elections around the bedrock differences between the parties.

Gingrich's mistake was over-interpreting the election results. The GOP sweep was a historic readjustment of a Congress that was no longer representative of the country's politics, and a cultural reaction against the Clinton administration, especially in the South where "gays, guns, and God" motivated anti-Clinton voters. It was not an endorsement of all things Gingrich, nor did it make Gingrich the president of the country.

His lurch too far would prove to be the promise to balance the budget. In the Contract with America, Republicans had pledged only to vote on a balanced budget amendment to the Constitution. Gingrich made actually achieving a balanced budget the chief Republican policy goal. He decided on balancing the budget within seven years, partly out of a "mystical" sense that it was the right time frame.[31] "It was Newt's decision almost personally," says former Gingrich aide Tony Blankley.[32]

The decision was made during an impromptu vote at a small dinner meeting of Gingrich's key lieutenants.[33] "The guys who were voting didn't have a clue about balancing the budget in seven years," says John Kasich. "And neither did Newt, for that matter. It wasn't a decision that was driven by a bunch of people in the leadership. Newt just basically came up with something, and frankly, he didn't have a clue."[34]

The unpopular budget cuts inherent in the initiative provided Clinton's eventual strategic opening to turn back the Republican assault. In the meantime, the Republican victory shocked and disoriented the White House.[35] In almost any circumstance, Clinton is given to self-pity and juvenile outbursts.[36] The 1994 rebuke, then, prompted a thick miasma of blame-shifting, flip-flops, and temper tantrums. Stripped of his safety blanket of popularity, Clinton wailed against his fate.

He lashed out at his staff. An advisor who ventured after the election that Clinton hadn't taken enough strong stances got a presidential blast in reply: "Don't ever say that to me again! The problem isn't that I haven't taken strong stands. It's that I don't have any help around here."[37] Clinton blamed his political advisors for the loss. He told Dick Morris that they had forged ahead with a strategy of attacking the Contract with America while Clinton was in no position to stop that strategy because he was away on a Middle Eastern trip. "I agreed with you," Clinton told Morris, "that the Contract was initially pretty popular and that this wasn't the way to campaign. But they were there and I wasn't, and they kept attacking the Contract and it didn't work."[38]

Attacking the Contract as a return to the dark, Reaganite 1980s was indeed foolish, since both Reagan and the 1980s were fairly popular. But Clinton had eagerly participated in the assault. "It's the same old thing they did in the 1980s, and it poses a stark choice for the Americans in this election," Clinton told an interviewer as the Contract was unrolled, and he repeated the theme at almost every campaign stop.[39]

He made needy late-night calls to political confidantes, sitting alone, playing solitaire.[40] The bathos reached its nadir when Clinton pleaded with aides at a meeting in January, "You all have to *help* me.

I don't *want* to use their tactics. I don't want to be *mean*."[41] (He got over it.)

Clinton's first reaction to the defeat was to find his own inner "angry white male," the demographic group supposedly behind the 1994 results. He said of the electorate, "I think they were agreeing with me, but they don't think we produced [for] them. In other words—let me say it in another way. I'm saying that I agree with much of what the electorate said yesterday."[42]

After having abandoned his middle-class tax cut in what—we were told—was a deep act of political courage necessary to the economy's recovery, Clinton quickly re-adopted tax cuts in a speech to the nation on December 15, 1994.[43] In October 1995 he told a group of Texas contributors at a nighttime event that his 1993 tax hike, later spun as the foundation stone of all his accomplishments, had been a mistake. He said he understood they were "still mad" because they thought he had "raised your taxes too much" in 1993: "It might surprise you to know that I think I raised them too much too."[44] Clinton falsely suggested that he had wanted more spending cuts, but Congress had foisted the tax increases on him—when it had really been the other way around.[45]

Clinton's swings back and forth made it necessary for him to make a statement as extraordinary for a president as his famous avowal at a March 1995 press conference that he was still "relevant."[46] He had to assure *Newsweek* right after the elections that yes, he actually had beliefs: "I find it amazing that anybody could question whether I have core beliefs. This idea that there's some battle for my soul is the biggest bunch of hooey I ever saw. I know who I am. I know what I believe!"[47]

"The ultimate master of the Western world—the polls"

Well, he knew what he believed—provided he had the right advisor to win the battle for his soul. Dick Morris was crucial to imposing coherence on President Clinton's response to the 1994 debacle. Clinton's political consultants from the 1992 campaign had always been present in full force in the White House, and had had a say on every important policy question, whether the economic package or Somalia policy. Now, they had failed him. "They didn't see them coming," says Elaine Kamarck of the Democratic defeats. "That's what was really unforgivable: They didn't even see them coming."[48] Neither had Clinton, whose political antenna is supposed to be his best-developed attribute. In any case, the failure created the opening for Morris—and the occasion for a bizarre charade.

Clinton initially kept Morris secret, and when talking to his other aides, referred to him as "Charlie."[49] There was a series of episodes appropriate to a bedroom farce. In one, Stephanopoulos worked with Clinton on a speech in the White House residence, while Morris hid in the family quarters, secreted there to be available to knock down Stephanopoulos's advice.[50] "I don't fully understand," says Robert Reich, "why the president felt it necessary to sneak Dick Morris into the White House, and keep his operations secret from all the rest of us, even his closest advisors. That just doesn't make a great deal of sense, even if he was afraid of leaks. So what if it leaked out that Dick Morris was in the White House? I don't understand the purpose of that subterfuge."[51]

Famous for his indirection, Clinton partly wanted to avoid the pain of telling his advisors, Chief of Staff Leon Panetta and others, that they were being supplanted. He had trouble being tough and decisive even with his own staff.[52] Both Morris and the president also enjoyed the secrecy, with its whiff of betrayal and of their superior knowledge. As Clinton told Morris, "I like subterfuge. That's why I like you."[53]

Morris eventually came out of hiding, but his presence would be bitterly resisted by most of the rest of the staff even as he became a quasi–chief of staff.[54] The hatred of Morris by other Clinton aides was a combination of envy of his brilliance and influence, ideological differences (they were liberal, Morris wasn't), and genuine abhorrence at his methods. Stephanopoulos quotes Morris telling him at one point, "My team is like the politburo. We work together, everyone has a say, and when we disagree, we submit the decision to the ultimate master of the Western world—the polls."[55] Panetta says of Morris, "He was someone, who, I am convinced to this day, basically manipulated polls to kind of emphasize the positions he wanted to stress."[56]

Liberals would like to believe that Morris was a strange, incidental excrescence on the Clinton presidency. He wasn't. "Dick Morris made many mistakes in terms of handling people, and he obviously had a strange personal life," says Don Baer. "But he is one of the small handful of the smartest people about American politics I ever encountered. He did more to make the Clinton presidency a success than anyone else except for Bill and Hillary Clinton and Al Gore."[57]

His political brilliance, his insecurity, and his self-obsession made Morris a sort of Clinton soul mate. He first schooled Clinton in the dark art of the "permanent campaign," perpetual polling and political combat.[58] For all that Clinton admired and valued Morris's political skill, he had a tangled relationship with the consultant. He didn't want to admit to himself that he was just as cold-blooded as Morris. In Arkansas, he used Morris, then cast him off, then used him again, before having one argument so intense that Clinton knocked Morris to the floor in the course of trying to keep him from leaving the room.[59] It was a classic burst of Clinton anger and neediness. "I don't get shit from you anymore," he yelled at Morris. "You're screwing me! You're screwing me!"[60]

Morris's longtime intimacy with Clinton allowed him to talk to the president in brazenly frank terms. Morris recalls that at one meeting in the spring of 1995 he pointed his finger at Clinton and said, "You're the biggest problem. You've lost your nerve." When the meeting was over, Morris maintains that he grabbed Clinton by the arms and shook him violently, saying through clenched teeth, "Get your nerve back. Get your f— nerve back."[61]

Their strongest common bond was polls. According to the *Wall Street Journal*, Clinton spent nearly $2 million on polls in his first year in office, nearly ten times as much as the first President Bush spent in the first half of his administration.[62] By the end, more money would be spent on polling by the Clinton White House than in all other administrations in American history combined.[63] Polls were taken on everything from where he should spend his 1995 summer vacation (when polls said to go camping instead of to Martha's Vineyard, Clinton duly hit the great outdoors)[64] to whether he should tell the truth about Monica Lewinsky.

Morris pulled public-policy ideas out of obscurity and featured them prominently, based on polls. He decided which of Clinton's positions to emphasize and which not, based on polls. In other words, polls set the agenda. In fact, Clinton and Morris essentially ran the administration on polls.

Morris polled the language of speeches before Clinton gave them. He used a poll to figure out which tax cuts Clinton would endorse in December 1994. He had to take three polls about banning sales of handguns to those guilty of misdemeanor domestic violence before he could convince Clinton to endorse the idea. Before Clinton's 1995 State of the Union address, Morris conducted a huge national survey. "The core of the strategy that emerged from the poll results was to embrace parts of the Republican initiative and reject others." Morris polled the public on what the date should be for a balanced budget. Every possible scenario in the 1995–1996 budget fight was poll tested, so after any given event "we had only to push a button on the computer, and the mall test and the poll for exactly that situation would pop up."[65]

Robert Reich recounts Morris explaining how the policy process, in his mind, would work. "'You have a lot of good ideas,' [Morris] says. 'The president likes your ideas. I want them so I can test them.' 'Test them?' 'Put them into our opinion poll. I can know within a day or two whether they work. Anything under 40 percent doesn't work. Fifty percent is a possibility. Sixty or seventy, and the president may well use it.'"[66]

Clinton loved every minute of it. "In our Arkansas days together," Morris writes, "Clinton would spend hours reviewing each detail of a questionnaire before we gave it to the interviewers to field. Surely now that he was president, his review would be more cursory. That's what I thought when I took Clinton's call. But after two hours of reviewing each question, I realized that Bill Clinton's need for the micromanagement of polling had not lessened as his responsibilities had increased."[67] Clinton was a political consultant trapped in a president's body.

Morris's central insight was that the old liberalism, as represented by the Democratic Congress, was dead. Clinton needed to jettison it for a shrewder political mix, "triangulating" between the Republicans and Democrats in Congress. His great strategic insight was that Clinton had to be for balancing the budget before he could effectively attack Republicans. The deficit had become a values issue, it stood for governmental irresponsibility, and as long as Clinton opposed balancing the budget he was tainted with the out-of-touch values of big-spending liberalism.[68]

Morris also argued that many of the items in the Contract for America were similar to Clinton's campaign platform in 1992. Devastating midterm defeat meant Clinton had to embrace again the things he had campaigned on for president in the first place.

"The second most successful adolescent"

All through 1993, Clinton had declared that cutting the deficit was essential to American prosperity, and later, he would claim that reducing the deficit was one of his foremost substantive achievements. Even this core Clinton concern, notionally at the very heart of the American economy, was easily sidelined when it seemed to present risks.

The Clinton of 1995 was blissfully unconcerned with the deficit. "The president lost his nerve a bit on deficit reduction for a while," says Alice Rivlin, former deputy director of the Office of Management and Budget, "and that was a very discouraging period for those of us who thought it was really important."[69] When his budget was brought up in the Senate for a vote, it lost 99–0.[70]

What followed was a mind-bending series of flip-flops about whether he supported balancing the budget by a certain date, and if so, by which certain date.[71] At one point, deputy chief of staff Erskine Bowles had to ask Clinton, "Are you for a balanced budget or not?" Turned out that he was.[72]

Congressional Republicans were convinced they could make Clinton capitulate entirely and accept their plan to balance the budget. They planned to attach language mandating a version of their budget onto a so-called "continuing resolution" to keep the government operating in lieu of the passage of appropriations bills, which had been delayed.[73] If Clinton vetoed the bill, the government would shut down. Republicans thought the president would be too afraid to do that, and if he did, they were happy to wait him out.

The Republicans talked about their strategy out loud, early and often—ensuring they would get the blame for the shutdowns when they came. "The two people who I think were most harmful to us in that regard were Newt Gingrich and John Kasich," says former Republican House majority leader Dick Armey. "Because they started early talking about if the president doesn't come around to us, we'll shut down the government. It was easy to hang the rap on us, because we had two of our most important people talking about it."[74]

The boastful talk of the coming shutdown added to what was already an extreme Republican vulnerability on Medicare. To achieve the balanced budget in seven years, Republicans had to find $270 billion in Medicare savings. Trimming the program played perfectly into the image of Republicans as eager to slash benefits for the elderly. Dick Morris's polling showed that Medicare rivaled Social Security as an inviolate federal program. He ran into one White House meeting and declared: "Medicare's a winner!" If the Republicans passed their plans, Morris exclaimed, "old people will end up on the sidewalks where they'll curl up and die!"[75] Clinton's first Medicare ad, picking up on the theme, featured a hospital heart monitor flatlining.[76]

The Medicare charge in particular—Clinton made plenty of others—hit home because the Republicans' defensive spin on the program wasn't credible. They said they wanted to save the system from bankruptcy. Republicans really wanted to reform and trim Medicare primarily to meet their other priorities, especially balancing the budget.

Not that Medicare didn't deserve trimming. It was a budgetary monster that accounted for 3 percent of the federal budget in 1970, 11 percent in 1994, and was slated only to go higher.[77] Robert Reich complained that Clinton "demonstrates indignation only about Gin-grich's threat to slow the growth of Medicare spending. Yet this is the *least* offensive part of the Republican [budget] plan. Medicare *is* out of control, and too many of its beneficiaries are wealthy enough not to need it. The Republicans deserve credit for saying that something has to be done."[78]

The president once had thought so too. In 1993 and 1994, Clinton said that unless the cost of Medicare and other health-care programs was tamed, the federal budget would never be brought under control. Clinton said in his first address to Congress in February 1993 that, absent health-care spending restraint, "our families will never be secure, our businesses will never be strong, and our government will never again be fully solvent."[79]

Clinton returned to the theme in his health-care speech before Congress in September 1993, saying, "[W]e passed a budget which has ... Medicare increases of between 11 and 9 percent in an environment where we assume inflation will be at 4 percent or less. We cannot continue to do this. Our competitiveness, our whole economy, the integrity of the way the government works, and ultimately, our living standards depend on our ability to achieve savings without harming the quality of health care."[80]

So, even Clinton's "stand on principle" to defend Medicare, which many liberals call his finest moment, was a reversal based on a political calculus. The Clinton of 1995–1996 would have attacked the Clinton of 1993–1994 as a heartless extremist. Leave it to Clinton to flip-flop on whether to push the elderly onto "the sidewalks."

As a matter of cut-and-dried numbers, the GOP proposals were reasonable enough. If Republicans succeeded in trimming $270 billion from Medicare, the program would grow at a 7.2 percent rate, instead of a 9.9 percent rate.[81] But the politics were still awful for Republicans. They had undertaken one massive project for which they had no electoral mandate, Medicare reform and savings, in the service of another, even more massive project for which they had no electoral mandate, balancing the budget.

Gingrich compounded the political risk with his intemperate manner, bad tactical sense, and appallingly undisciplined comments.[82] The first Republican "continuing resolution" included a Medicare premium increase, for technical reasons having to do with a computer adjustment.[83] The premium increase provided convenient and popular grounds for Clinton to veto the resolution.

After the shutdown began, Gingrich said he had sent Clinton a tough resolution partly because the president wouldn't talk to him on Air Force One in transit to Israeli leader Yitzhak Rabin's funeral and made him exit from the rear ramp: "You just wonder, Where is their sense of manners? Where is their sense of courtesy?"[84]

Where was Gingrich's self-control? It was a sign of the times that the country had put Bill Clinton in charge of the executive branch and Newt Gingrich in charge of the legislative all at once. They shared the same immaturity and longing for father figures; the same starry-eyed faith in technology and taste for management-consultant psychobabble; the same emotional brittleness and self-involved obsession with their legacies. "I always said," recalls Dick Armey, "that Bill Clinton was the most successful adolescent I had ever seen in my life, and Newt Gingrich was the second most successful adolescent."[85]

After the initial shutdown skirmish in November,[86] Clinton went into the next shutdown fight in December confident that Republicans would be blamed.[87] Clinton could seem conciliatory in negotiations, while stringing things along, because he knew time was on his side.[88] After the government was shuttered for weeks, Republicans finally had to give up on making Clinton buckle. They had lost.[89]

The Republican "revolution" had been broken. "The House Republicans were the most courageous bunch of politicians you'll ever see," says Tony Blankley. "They stuck with the balanced budget because they thought it was right. After the shutdowns, when the January break came, they left an army and came back a rabble. It was every man for himself."[90]

Republicans had something to show for their perhaps foolhardy courage. Clinton had agreed in principle to a seven-year balanced budget, and a year or so later would cut a budget deal with Republicans. Even without a budget agreement, Republicans cut discretionary domestic spending in 1996.[91] And after two vetoes, Clinton relented and signed a GOP welfare-reform bill in August 1996.[92]

Clinton had found his role: taking the rough edges off a Republican Congress that—despite the hue and cry—he was essentially willing to accommodate. In his 1993 State of the Union address, Clinton said, "Tonight I want to talk to you about what government can do because I believe government must do more."[93] In his 1996 State of the Union address, Clinton proclaimed, "The era of big government is over."

"Turn off TV; see that homework is done"

Clinton was set to coast to victory in 1996. "I remember as we started going into '96," says former White House spokesman Mike McCurry, "Stephanopoulos and I, we'd just keep looking at each other and laugh."[94]

His reelection campaign was equal parts demagogy, corruption, and trivia. He fulsomely attacked GOP Medicare plans—plans addressing Medicare's out-of-control spending that he had said threatened the very future of the country a few years earlier. He ran a series of brutal negative ads against Bob Dole paid for by an unseemly and at times illegal fund-raising drive. And he positioned himself, shrewdly but inconsequentially, as a "conservative" on some "values" issues, like school uniforms. Thus, he won a mandate for nothing, except perhaps an investigation of his campaign's fund-raising.

Clinton's pollster Mark Penn conducted opinion surveys in shopping malls, and realized that among swing voters values determined how people voted.[95] Clinton's campaign would have to give up the Democratic myth, dating back to FDR, that lunch-bucket economics and redistributionist policies drove American politics.[96] It was out with class warfare, and in with values.

The word came up so often in strategy meetings that speechwriters occasionally would flash a "V" sign with their fingers for it. The Clinton campaign began to sell traditional Democratic positions not in terms of bread-and-butter economics, but in terms of "V." The first fusillade of the ad campaign against the Republican Medicare plan was entitled "Moral," and declared, "President Clinton: doing what's moral, good, and right by our elderly."[97] This thrust was followed up with a barrage of small-bore actions and positions meant to demonstrate Clinton's "V."

In 1992, Clinton had told his campaign advisors that he wouldn't get elected president advocating tougher child support enforcement.[98] In 1996, Clinton would, however, get *reelected* president advocating tougher child support enforcement.

The list of Clinton's rhetoric from the 1996 State of the Union that "tested well," according to Penn, included "pay child support, you deadbeat SOBs," as well as "school uniforms," and "turn off TV; see that homework is done; visit children's classrooms."[99] Clinton promoted the V-chip to screen out violent TV programming, endorsed teenage curfews, urged that schools be kept open as community centers during nights and weekends, advocated more efficient emergency telephone numbers, begged for three hours of educational TV programming per week, and declared that hospitals should allow women to stay longer than twenty-four hours after delivery.[100] Morris reportedly even wanted to endorse a rating system for violent children's toys, an idea that had to be discarded when no one could figure out how to rate squirt guns.[101]

The most important "V" Clinton was able to associate himself with was patriotism. Clinton used the April 1995 Oklahoma City bombing not just to bathe the nation in healing rhetoric, but—shamefully—to paint congressional Republicans as un-American. At an address at Michigan State University, Clinton said, "There is nothing patriotic about hating your country, or pretending that you can love your country but despise your government."[102]

Clinton wasn't, however, willing to challenge openly the congressional Republican vision of smaller government. "I traveled with Gore, and every time we met up with the president," says Elaine Kamarck, a former Gore advisor, "he said three things at the top of every speech: We've created more jobs (he gave the statistics on jobs); he said we've done 'x' in economic growth; and he said we've got the smallest government since Jack Kennedy was president. The three things he said basically gave the message of fiscal conservatism and economic growth. It was a very centrist message."[103] On top of this, in areas where he needed to, Clinton emphasized more than fiscal conservatism. "Clinton ran as almost a cultural conservative in southern Ohio, Kentucky, Tennessee," his pollster Doug Schoen has said.[104]

Only one piece was missing to make his reelection complete—a tired, uninspired opponent. Enter Bob Dole. "He was a terrible candidate," says a former Dole aide. "He had no business being the nominee. I can't remember a single substantive issue that we had. The case against Clinton was trust and style."[105]

Robert Reich recalls Penn briefing a cabinet meeting afterwards about how the election was won: "'We did this by co-opting the Republicans on all their issues—getting tough on welfare, tough on crime, balancing the budget, and cracking down on illegal immigration. . . . The suburban swing [voters] are busy at their jobs and worry about the values their kids are picking up. These aren't the sorts of things a president can do much about, of course. . . . But it was important to show the president was concerned. So we emphasized teen smoking, school uniforms, nighttime curfews, drug testing at school, and sex and violence on television. All these polled very well. . . . The third part of our strategy was to keep Dole down. Every time he approached 50 percent approval, we knocked him down ten or fifteen points with these ads.'"[106]

Even so, Clinton hardly rode a tidal wave to victory. Almost every economic and social indicator was improving in 1996, yet the public still didn't fully embrace him. According to the Pew Research Center, the average grade voters gave him a few weeks before the election was a C.[107] He had made himself a non-threatening mediocrity.

It was enough to get him elected, but not get him over the 50 percent mark he so coveted. His 49 percent showing significantly undershot the roughly 60 percent won by other presidents reelected in times of peace and prosperity.[108] He was, fundamentally, the under-50 percent president. He could have been presiding over Shangri-La, and still never won an absolute majority.

When a batch of stories about his shady foreign donors began to hit the press, stalling any momentum toward his prized percentage, Clinton lashed out in self-pity, asking his aides, "Where is the fairness in all this?"[109] Everyone on the Clinton team knew they were just holding on with flimsy explanations of the fund-raising until Election Day—and then what?

Clinton had made the mantra of his reelection campaign "Building a bridge to the twenty-first century." Where was the bridge going?[110]

It would be a second term in search of a purpose. As he thrashed about increasingly obsessed with his place in history, Clinton ended up chafing against his own vacuity. He was the King Lear of micro-initiatives. Alas—presidential greatness doesn't issue from shopping-mall polling results.

"I have been having a great time!"

Dick Morris and Robert Reich—right and left, operative and policy wonk—at least agree on the fecklessness of Clinton's second term. "I believe," says Morris, "that Bill Clinton totally and completely wasted his second term. Partially due to his laziness in 1997, in 1998 he was totally tanked up by Monica, and in 1999 and 2000 his entire presidency was devoted to the single goal of getting his wife elected to the Senate."[111] After the 1995–1996 budget battles and the Lewinsky scandal, according to Reich, "there wasn't very much political capital left in the second administration—the second term—for new initiatives."[112]

Clinton's major act was cutting a budget deal with congressional Republicans in August 1997. More than half the projected savings in the budget agreement were from Medicare, and it reduced Medicare spending much more than expected. It made the original GOP plan for Medicare savings, vociferously opposed by Clinton, look prodigal by comparison. In 1998 Medicare spending essentially held flat, and in 1999 it actually declined, something that had never happened before.[113]

In 1995–1996, Clinton would have pounced on such spending declines as certain to decimate the elderly. In the second term, he tucked away those savings, with their positive effect on the deficit picture, as part of his legacy.

Clinton's defenders point to the 1997 budget deal to make the case for his continued political vitality and policy creativity, because it did wring a few new spending programs out of Republicans. Clinton won $30 billion in tax credits for the first two years of higher education, which Joe Klein has puffed as "larger than the GI Bill of Rights."[114] Since community colleges and public universities were already heavily subsidized, the credits just took what was already a minimal private expense and made it close to zero. And some colleges simply increased their tuitions to absorb the full value of the credits.[115]

More important was a $24 billion program for children's health insurance, known as SCHIP (the State Children's Health Insurance Program).[116] The generous federal subsidy encouraged states to maximize their health benefits, essentially extending a federal entitlement to children living in families with incomes roughly 200 percent above the poverty line. Muting the program's effectiveness, many families simply dropped their private coverage to pick up the government insurance instead.[117] The program was basically defensive, intending to make up ground after Medicaid usage had declined with the passage of welfare reform. Coverage of children in low-income families was still lower in 1999 than it had been in 1995.[118]

If the locus of Clinton's legislative innovations isn't in the 1997 budget deal, it's hard to find it elsewhere. Early on, he signed the Family and Medical Leave Act, which mandated that businesses give up to twelve weeks of unpaid leave to workers with urgent family needs. Even its liberal advocates admit it is a minor achievement.[119] Public-employee unions, always jealous of anything that might intrude on their jobs, watered down Clinton's cherished AmeriCorps volunteer program.[120]

Besides defending the Medicare status quo, Clinton's main post-1994 themes were the environment and education.

The environment proved to be a winning political issue for Clinton, but there weren't any major departures in policy. The last big-bang piece of environmental legislation had been the reauthorization of the Clean Air Act in 1990. The air steadily got cleaner during the Clinton years and the fragmentary water quality data available suggest improvements in rivers, lakes, and coastal estuaries as well.[121] Of course, those developments were part of a long-running trend. The environment had been improving for decades for several reasons: increased industrial efficiency reduces pollution; the shift from an industrial to a service economy creates an inherently cleaner economy; and regulations already on the books tend to ratchet up restrictions automatically over time. Much of environmental policy is on autopilot.

Education was another Clinton political strength. Again, there was no policy departure. The first President Bush had tried to enshrine into law a set of national education goals, but the Democratic Congress turned him down. The Bush proposal, "America 2000," morphed into the Clinton proposal, "Goals 2000," that passed. The law had elaborate mechanisms to encourage states to set standards and meet goals. On paper, there were sanctions for failing to do so, but they were almost entirely ignored, in a flurry of waivers and general inertia. The result was the worst of both worlds, as the federal government intruded further into education policy, while little actually changed.[122] In terms of test scores, the national picture across the 1990s was basically flat.[123]

Politically, Clinton lurched from one scandal to the next. Having suffered a money scandal in 1997, Clinton moved on to the sex scandal in 1998.

Second-term presidents typically suffer big defeats in congressional elections in their sixth year in office. Clinton bucked the trend in 1998, benefiting from a backlash against his impending impeachment. Clinton likes to pretend that this was a great, historic benefit to his party. "[We] had a stunning election in 1998," Clinton told interviewers in 2000, "the dimensions of which still have never been fully appreciated by the political writers."[124] This is silly. Republicans lost just five House seats, and held even in the Senate. Republicans held the same very slight edge in the total congressional vote in 1998 as they had in 1996.[125] The fact is that Republicans had already had their big off-year win against Clinton in 1994.

Even as Clinton survived and even prospered, the Monica scandal washed away what had been important gains for the party. So much for "V," as the Democrats became associated again with personal irresponsibility.[126]

Clinton tacked right to survive Gingrich; he tacked left to survive Monica. Any chance of reforming Medicare and Social Security, which Clinton had repeatedly insisted was essential to the programs' futures, was shot. According to a former Clinton official, "The last two years made him even more beholden to the traditional interests of the Democratic party and the congressional Democrats. Because they're the ones who saved his butt in impeachment. He couldn't go against them on things like Social Security reforms and other challenges that he had wanted to tackle."[127]

His ability to create bipartisan coalitions faded. Clinton domestic policy advisor Bruce Reed says, "It made it harder in those closing years for Clinton to govern aggressively from the center. I worked with McCain at the time on the tobacco bill. There was pretty much no one else in the Republican caucus who would be seen in public with us."[128] Clinton moved left on trade, heretofore one of his trademark centrist causes. He temporarily blew up a free-trade deal with China in April 1999, and helped scuttle a World Trade Organization meeting in Seattle in December 1999. "There was a real cost to impeachment—in Seattle, in not confronting the left there," says a former foreign-policy aide. "There was only so much that Clinton could take on."[129]

"We need to demystify the job"

As entitlement reform faded, Clinton's other project to reach into the future also failed. Clinton had pledged to work "ceaselessly" for Al Gore's election. His own radioactivity helped queer the deal.

Gore felt compelled to distance himself from the personally disgraced incumbent, while running on his record. "Clinton sort of softened up the environment for Gore to be cast as someone who wasn't genuine," says Elaine Karmack. "Nobody ever thought that Gore had Clinton's exact problems; but they were willing to think that since Clinton was a sleazy guy, there was probably something sleazy with Gore, too."[130] Former Gore campaign chairman Bill Daley says, "I don't think there's any question that Clinton's personal failings complicated the election of 2000. But I'm not one who believes that Bill Clinton cost Al Gore the election by any stretch. You've got to deal with what you've got to deal with."[131]

The historical storyline that progressives tout is that after a period of conservative stasis and scandal, a progressive president arrives to clean up American politics. But in 2000, it was Clinton, the supposed progressive, whose scandals and proximity to moneyed interests prompted reform agitation. The punch line of every George W. Bush campaign appearance—a simple pledge to uphold the honor and dignity of the office—was aimed squarely at the incumbent, and was an implied promise of truth-telling and clean government. Clinton's loose ethics and promiscuous fund-raising drove the reform candidacies of Republican maverick John McCain, and—much more damaging to Gore—the Green Party candidate, Ralph Nader.

Clinton's success didn't translate to his vice president—or to the Democratic Party at large. There were fifty-eight Democratic senators and 259 House members when Clinton was elected in 1992. In 2000, Republicans had been in the majority in both bodies for six years and the party's hold on Congress was beginning to look like its post-McKinley congressional dominance.[132] The Democratic Party also suffered under Clinton at the state and local levels. By October 1995, forty-three state legislators and 137 Democratic officeholders overall had switched party affiliation to the Republicans.[133] Over the Clinton years, elected Democrats switched parties at a rate of almost one a week.[134]

What grand Clinton success compensates for these Democratic losses? His apologists say that he "restored trust in government." This is nonsense. The level of public trust in government fell precipitously in the 1970s, and has never truly recovered. When times are good—the mid-1980s and the late 1990s—the level of trust in government increases slightly, but it hasn't changed fundamentally.[135] It is true that the cause of government activism benefited from welfare reform and elimination of the deficit, both of which erased what had been powerful symbols of governmental failure. But if Clinton had been left to his own devices these reforms would not have occurred.

Clinton defenders also say the "Third Way"—the fancy phrase for his on-and-off moderation—was an important ideological departure. The Third Way amounts to macro-capitalism (a healthy respect for markets) and programmatic creeping socialism (federal programs for everything), packaged with occasional nods to conservative values. But even as a Third Way leader Clinton failed, at least compared to his fellow Third Way stalwart, British prime minister Tony Blair. Blair managed a much more thorough transformation of his party—Britain's Labour Party—along centrist lines than Clinton could accomplish. Blair was Clinton without the personal problems, making it possible for him to comfortably co-opt conservative cultural themes.

Clinton's personal scandals, in contrast, alienated and energized a conservative opposition that led to the deadlock of the 2000 election, and made Clinton beholden to the unreformed left-wing elements of his party. By the end, Clinton had forged a kind of amoral majority, consisting of Hollywood and the entertainment industry, pro-abortion feminists, urban secularists, and a swath of straying husbands and wives with a personal interest in a moral non-judgmentalism. This coalition's financial and cultural clout was considerable, and impeachment was a catalyzing event, signifying its growing influence. Even this was an accident, the product of the bizarre circumstances that brought together a sexual harassment suit and stained dress.

The reality is that Clinton, in keeping with his solipsism, operated in a sphere above his party, and above philosophy. He rode the tide of a rising America, making no real effort to try to fundamentally shape national events. Such big ambitions would almost violate Clinton's sense of the presidency. At the end of his administration, he told Joe Klein, "We need to demystify the job. It is a job."[136]

With the exception of Jimmy Carter, it's hard to imagine any president since FDR having, let alone expressing, an impulse to demystify his office—to make "leader of the free world" seem like any other job description, from alderman to House majority leader.

Then again, it was a different time. The Cold War, with its looming sense of national crisis, had passed, freeing the president to focus on increasing child support payments and urging parents to help their children with homework. These, as it happened, were Clinton's strengths.

"Bill Clinton is the president who, for better and worse, turned the White House into a governor's mansion," Jacob Weisberg wrote in a 1998 New York Times Magazine essay. "Clinton has downsized the office, both in the negative sense of stripping away some of its dignity and in the positive one of making adjustments demanded by the historical moment. Coming to the White House from the governor's mansion in Little Rock, Clinton has recast the presidency on the more modest model of his previous job. Unlike presidents, governors have few opportunities to be visionaries. Instead, they do what Clinton has done—a job of crisis management, political accommodation and governmental reform."[137] Clinton remade the presidency in his image and around his capabilities. Morris writes, "We really sought to redefine the job of president in such a way that he was uniquely qualified to fill it. Under Reagan, the presidency was redefined by ideology. In the second half of Clinton's first term, it was defined by compromise, reconciliation, values, and healing—skills at which this president was awfully good."[138]

This downsizing served another purpose. It made Clinton himself, and therefore his shortcomings, seem less important. In January 2000, a plurality of Americans—42 to 39 percent—said they were ashamed to have Clinton as president.[139] But—so what? Newsday captured the nonchalance during the impeachment fight: "He hasn't been much of a president and he's even less of a human being, but it's still not worth the strain of impeaching him."[140] In the new era, Weisberg argued, "leaders don't have to be ideal human beings, superior projections of ourselves. They merely need to understand our problems and help us grapple with them."[141]

Part of the key to Clinton's ability to endure in office, then, is that he didn't seem to matter much. He sought to bury his personal failings beneath his own inconsequence. Mission accomplished.

THE ECONOMY:
The 1980s, Part II

C LINTON'S POLITICAL IDENTITY IS INSEPARABLE from the economic boom
of the 1990s. When he was down and out after the 1994 elections, he repeatedly told his aides about the good economic
numbers and complained that he didn't get credit for them. When he
was on the campaign trail in 1996, he regaled crowds with indices of
the building boom. When he was impeached, when he was giving a
State of the Union, when he was arguing for Al Gore's election, when
he was savoring his legacy as a former president—he talked of how he
had "grown" the economy. It was all boom, all the time.

As with most Clinton boasts, this one is false. This is the record:
Clinton grossly exaggerated the severity of the 1990–1991 recession.
He inherited a growing economy, abandoned heartfelt campaign
pledges that would have been economically harmful, and presided
over good times that reflected deep strengths in the economy that had
nothing to do with him. On his way out of office, he bragged about
the boom, which was in fact ending, and handed George W. Bush an
economy sinking into recession.

Altogether, it was a characteristic Clinton performance, featuring dishonesty, double-mindedness, and good fortune. In no sense did he save, revive, transform, or "grow" the economy. All such claims are given credence only by the power of well-coordinated repetition.

Clinton's economic record has benefited from two big lies. The first is the dishonest picture Clinton painted of the American economy in 1992. At almost every campaign stop he talked of an economy that had already recovered from a brief recession as if it were Dresden in 1945— "it had to be rebuilt."[1] He called it "the worst economy in fifty years," a transparently false claim.[2] The 1990–1991 recession was relatively mild, especially compared to the downturn of the early 1980s. In that earlier recession, galloping inflation had to be wrung out of the system and the economy endured great dislocations, leading to the coining of the phrase "the rust belt."[3] The recession Clinton ran against ended in March 1991, seven months before he even announced his candidacy.[4]

The other lie is that his 1993 economic package transformed the federal budget, and hence the American economy. In fact, his plan was insignificant, a flea on the raging bull economy of the 1990s; and his plan failed in its three specific aims: it didn't cause interest rates to fall, it didn't significantly reduce the deficit, and it didn't cause the economy to grow.

The economy grew because of the vitality of corporate America, which during the 1980s and early 1990s had undergone the downsizing and retooling necessary to make it more efficient, more competitive, and more innovative. These strengths caused a surge of productivity that propelled the growth of the 1990s. Clinton thus presided over the second installment of an almost twenty-year-long boom that began in 1983. His contribution to it was mostly to let Federal Reserve Board chairman Alan Greenspan, operating in tandem with Clinton's more conservative economic advisors, emasculate his free-spending government "investment" program from the 1992 campaign. Then, a Republican Congress hamstrung him for his remaining six years in office, during which he had a quasi-Republican economic program.[5]

Of course, when it comes to his economic legacy, Clinton prefers to avoid talking up his near-Republicanism. This is why the stilted account of his supposedly world-changing 1993 economic plan is so crucial to him and his supporters.

"We are losing our soul"

Clinton's presidential campaign was predicated on opening the spigots for more government spending. The campaign plan called for $200 billion in new spending—"investments"—for education, job training, preschool, mass transit, a civilian Research and Development agency to convert "a defense-based economy to a peacetime one," a nationwide system of community development banks, and much else.[6]

According to Clinton's campaign book, *Putting People First*, it was to be the "the most dramatic economic growth program since the Second World War."[7] The federal government would spend the country back to economic health and vigor.

Clinton called these investments "the things I got elected for." He told aides, "If I do too little investment, then some other candidate won the election, not me."[8] His first budget, in this vein, maintained: "Deficit reduction at the expense of public investment has been and will continue to be self-defeating."[9]

The idea was that public investment was more important than private investment. All the private investment of the 1980s, according to liberals, hadn't "trickled down" to average Americans, and America's infrastructure was supposedly falling apart. "We're way behind Germany and Japan in modernizing infrastructure," Clinton said in March 1993.[10] This was a time when a presidential candidate, Democrat Paul Tsongas, could travel the country saying, without prompting derisive laughter, "The Cold War is over. Japan won."[11] Another purpose of the spending was Keynesian economic "pump-priming"—public spending to fuel economic demand and activity.

The plan was intellectually flawed in almost every respect. The 1980s were a boom rather than the economic backwater that Clinton's advisors made them out to be. Japan's economic system, with its cozy relations between government and business, was about to suffer an ongoing near-meltdown, while Germany's social-democratic economy would stagnate. The strength of the American economy in the 1990s was precisely that it wasn't like Japan's or Germany's. American companies were relatively unencumbered by regulation, free to fail and to innovate. As for Keynesian pump-priming, even many of of the people Clinton tapped to be his top economic advisors didn't believe that government spending was the key to economic health.[12]

The final flaw of Clinton's campaign program was that it was a classic instance of all-things-to-all-people Clinton incoherence. He promised to cut taxes, increase spending, and reduce the deficit. Not content to promise just a free lunch, he promised a free lunch *and* sharp deficit reduction. Reality set in after Election Day. His tax cuts were quickly jettisoned—Clinton was never enthusiastic about them—and at their first meeting in Little Rock, Alan Greenspan told Clinton that any package of spending to stimulate the economy would have no serious positive effect.[13] Then, there was the deficit. Clinton had promised in the campaign to cut the deficit in half by 1997 while spending massive amounts of new money.[14] Reconciling these priorities would have been difficult in any case, but became harder when the economic slowdown caused federal spending to increase, tax revenues to plummet, and deficit projections to worsen.[15]

The Clinton team decided to shoot for reducing the annual deficit by $140 billion in 1997, an arbitrary number that it thought would demonstrate to Congress and Wall Street that the administration had a credible commitment to deficit reduction. It meant, in effect, that the investments were fated to oblivion.[16] Clinton dumped them—but not without pouting about it.

When Clinton was first told how much the investments would be axed to abide by the spending caps set in the 1990 budget deal, he felt victimized. "Why didn't anyone *tell* me about the spending caps?" Clinton complained to his advisors. "We spent week after week going over every little budget item, and no one said a word about the caps! Why didn't they *tell* me?"[17]

He considered his new, investment-less budget a self-betrayal. "We have just gone too far," he said. "We are losing our soul."[18] Clinton called his new plan "a turkey," and was enthusiastic about a *New York Times* editorial that declared: "It won't be a budget that invests in the future and it won't be a victory for those who voted for an economic turnabout."[19]

Clinton's dismay was understandable. As we have seen, the final shape of his 1993 economic plan was almost exactly similar to President Bush's economic plan in 1990. It wasn't even "Bush Lite"—it was just "Bush."

The problem for the Clinton team was that it couldn't have the president critical of his own budget. So the White House made a crucial pivot in its communications strategy that has endured to this day: it decided to pretend to be enthusiastic about the new budget plan as a wonderful economic elixir.[20]

"Easy to state with conviction, impossible to prove"

The White House latched onto the argument that by lowering the deficit, it would lower interest rates, and thus stimulate the economy by reducing the cost of borrowing for consumers and businesses. But as Robert Reich, who served as Clinton's secretary of labor, noted, "This theory is easy to state with conviction, but it is impossible to prove. Look back several decades and you see no direct relationship between deficits and interest rates."[21] The reason for this is that inflation and the real return on investments,[22] not deficits, drive interest rates.[23] Indeed, in the first half of 2003, with America's budget deficit soaring toward record levels, interest rates fell to their lowest level in four decades.[24]

Alan Greenspan helped sell the Clinton team on the idea that deficit reduction would pay immediate economic benefits by reducing interest rates. "Greenspan believes that a major deficit reduction (above $130 billion) will lead to interest rate changes *more than off-setting"* any harm from reducing spending and increasing taxes, a Clinton aide wrote in a memo passed along to the president.[25] This suggests a quid pro quo, with Greenspan promising to cut rates if Clinton went along with the banker's fiscal priorities.

But the notoriously dry Greenspan must have his devious side, because, if this was the implicit bargain, he broke it. Republicans were always nervous of entering into negotiations with Clinton for fear that they would get snookered. In his dealings with Clinton, Greenspan apparently did the snookering.

Just months after the Clinton economic plan passed Congress, Greenspan raised the short-term rates over which he had direct influence. Long-term rates began to rise as well. So, Greenspan managed to get Clinton to abandon the most worrisome chunks of his economic agenda from the campaign,[26] while freely pursuing his own agenda, which was keeping inflation tightly under control (raising short-term rates is the Federal Reserve's chief anti-inflation tool).

Because the entire premise of the Clinton 1993 budget was lowering long-term interest rates, the fact that rates went up after its passage puts Clinton boosters in the odd position of arguing that its benefits came *before* it actually passed. They argue that interest rates fell in anticipation of the plan's becoming law, as the market prepared itself for the wonders to be wrought by the Clinton budget.

This is truly voodoo economics, attributing magical power to a budget before it became law, and before anyone could even know it would become law, since it scraped by Congress by the narrowest of margins.[27] Actually, the general trend in long-term interest rates had been downward for about a decade,[28] and had been dropping relatively steadily since March 1992.[29] Had the market been anticipating Clinton's 1993 plan since then?

The Clinton budget passed and was signed into law in August 1993. In February 1994, just six months later, Greenspan raised rates to address new inflation worries.[30] This was the first in a series of seven increases during the next year.[31] Clinton felt betrayed. After Greenspan began his program of rate increases, Clinton, in a huff, refused to meet with him during the second half of 1994, despite the urging of his aides.[32] By April 1994, long-term rates were 7.4 percent, higher than when Clinton took office,[33] and the ten-year rate peaked around the time Republicans captured Congress in November 1994.[34]

Many Clinton sympathizers simply omit the 1994 rate increases from their account of the 1990s economy. Joe Klein doesn't mention it in his moderately favorable Clinton book, *The Natural*.[35] The *Washington Monthly* didn't mention it in a December 2000 cover story lauding the Clinton legacy.[36] Sidney Blumenthal doesn't mention it in his 800-page apologia for all things Clinton.[37] Wonder why.

If Clinton's 1993 plan didn't lower interest rates, it didn't accomplish the other two things often attributed to it: significantly cutting the deficit and stoking economic growth.

The deficit reached its 1990s high of $290 billion in fiscal year 1992 and fell to $255 billion in fiscal year 1993, a roughly $40 billion reduction even before Clinton got started. (His tax plan was signed in August 1993, after the 1993 fiscal year, ending in September, was all but over.)[38]

Why was the deficit already declining? The deficit tends to rise during recessions, and fall during expansions. It climbed with the recession of 1990–1991, before declining again as the recovery took hold. So, just as Clinton was taking office, natural forces were already working to reduce the deficit.

The deficit further declined to $164 billion in 1995.[39] The Clinton spin is that the $126 billion reduction in the deficit between 1992 and 1995 must be attributable to him—he had a "deficit-reduction plan," after all. But the fall in the deficit had many causes, and the Clinton plan doesn't even top the list.

According to 1996 Congressional Budget Office numbers, $71 billion of the decline could be attributed to the upswing in the business cycle—naturally creating more tax revenue. This upswing was well underway when Clinton was campaigning against the "worst economy in fifty years." Another $21 billion was accounted for by reduced spending on deposit insurance as the worst of the federal cleanup of the savings and loan crisis had passed. Finally, the federal government gained one-time revenues of $8 billion by auctioning off exclusive licenses for the use of certain frequencies on the radio spectrum.[40]

That leaves $26 billion of deficit reduction between 1992 and 1995 that was the result of new policies. But without the restraint of Congress, it's not clear that Clinton's policies would have reduced the deficit at all. Congress killed his health plan, which purported to be deficit-neutral, although it wasn't. Congress killed his stimulus plan, originally proposed at $30 billion.[41] The spending caps from the 1990 budget deal, which Clinton railed against, provided some enforced restraint.

As a paper from the congressional Joint Economic Committee notes, even with Congress slowing spending, domestic expenditures increased enough to gobble up all the projected revenue increases from Clinton's tax hike. It was a $29 billion cut in defense spending from 1992 to 1995 that accounted for all of the deficit reduction from Clinton's policy changes. If defense spending had stayed at its $303 billion level of 1992, no deficit reduction at all would have resulted from Clinton policy changes.[42]

The bottom line about Clinton's 1993 economic plan is that it simply wasn't that important. Its tax increase prompted predictions of doom from congressional Republicans. "This will lead to a recession next year," said Newt Gingrich.[43] It was the sort of shrill and overstated rhetoric typically heard from any congressional minority, although some Democrats said the same thing. Democrats on the Joint Economic Committee in 1993 warned that the plan "will continue to exert downward pressure on economic activity through the next five years."[44]

The plan, including the increased bite of the Medicare payroll tax, effectively raised the top income tax rate from 31 percent to roughly 42 percent.[45] This top rate was still lower than the 50 percent rate after the first round of Reagan tax cuts in 1981, which conservatives had greeted at the time as tax-rate nirvana. Tax changes must be significant to have a large economic effect. Clinton's income tax increase wasn't big enough to stall a $6 trillion economy, although it might have dampened growth somewhat.

But the fact is that the economy was already growing before any Clinton policies took effect. In 1992, growth was 3 percent. From 1993 to 1995, it was 3.1 percent annually.[46] The plan's chief contribution to gross domestic product was an increased output of spin, as Clinton and his allies desperately sought to hype their budget as responsible for an economic miracle.

"Eisenhower Republicans, fighting the Reagan Republicans"

So, why did the economy grow so vigorously in the 1990s? The American economy had been shifted into a fundamentally different gear by Ronald Reagan in the early 1980s.[47] He drove a stake through the "stagflationary" economics—high unemployment and high inflation—of the 1970s. He cut the top tax rate from 70 percent to 50 percent in 1981 and then from 50 percent to 28 percent in 1986. Keynesians maintained that if you cut taxes, inflation would rise. Reagan economists saw the cuts as counter-inflationary. With more after-tax rewards, the workforce would be more productive, thus more goods would absorb more money.

The tax changes were coupled with a strong dollar, and inflation plummeted from roughly 15 percent in 1980 to roughly 4 percent in 1983.[48] As inflation declined, long-term interest rates dropped, easing borrowing. The economy and corporate profits grew, while the stock market exploded.[49] The seemingly perpetual economic doldrums of the 1970s had been replaced by economic renewal.

As *Wall Street Journal* editor emeritus Robert Bartley notes in his classic defense of the 1980s, *The Seven Fat Years,* from 1982 to 1990, the economy grew by a third, and created 18.4 million jobs. Despite the budget deficit, gross private investment increased 32 percent. And amid howls about the de-industrialization of America, manufacturing production grew 48 percent.[50]

Interest rate increases by the Fed, a mild oil shock with the price increases of the first Gulf War, and a credit crunch associated with the savings and loan mess contributed to a slowdown beginning in the middle of 1990.[51] Clinton jumped on the recession as the long overdue bill for the 1980s.

But the slowdown was only a blip before the economy produced another decade of growth. In a straight-on decade-to-decade comparison,[52] the 1980s and 1990s look very similar. Average economic growth in the 1980s was 3.02 percent. Average economic growth in the 1990s was 3.03 percent. The average stock market return in the 1980s was 18.58 percent. The average stock market return in the 1990s was 18.83 percent.[53] Upon taking office, Clinton was well positioned to take advantage of the 1980s, Part II.

Corporate America had slimmed down and toughened up through the restructuring of the 1980s and the downsizing of the early 1990s. As Alex Berenson writes in his book *The Number*, "U.S. manufacturers were finally competitive with their foreign counterparts. Consumer goods companies like Coke had strengthened their global dominance. American drug makers were on the verge of demolishing European competitors. And the United States had no peer in information technology."[54]

The strengths of the 1990s economy were apparent as Clinton settled into office. There was considerable life in the tech sector. The NASDAQ increased 57 percent in 1991, and another 16 and 15 percent in 1992 and 1993. Corporate earnings were taking off. Earnings for the S&P 500 increased 16 percent in 1993, on their way to a robust 40 percent rise in 1994.[55]

The Clinton team soon touted all of this as the product of Clinton's economic genius, but reality occasionally intruded. In July 1993, Laura Tyson demanded a change in a Paul Begala memo that promised Clinton's "plan will create JOBS—8 million of them." As Bob Woodward reports, "she insisted that the team agree to attribute the job growth of 8 million to the economy, not to Clinton's plan. Virtually all economists agreed that the 8 million jobs were going to be created, no matter what the impact of the plan."[56]

This is not to embrace a complete fatalism about the economy. Clinton got some things right. His presidency was bracketed by major free-trade successes.[57] Early on he pushed the North American Free Trade Agreement (NAFTA) through Congress, followed by the Uruguay round of the General Agreement on Tariffs and Trade (GATT), establishing the World Trade Organization (WTO) to settle international trade disputes and expanding world trade. Later, he got Congress to go along with an agreement guaranteeing China's ascension into the World Trade Organization.[58] American exports nearly doubled in real terms from 1991 to 2000, rising to more than $1.1 trillion from $613 billion (in 1996 dollars).[59]

While the American economy became more open to trade, Alan Greenspan throttled inflation (which was the purpose of his increase in short-term rates in 1994). In 1990, the consumer price index had been a relatively high 6 percent.[60] Over the course of the decade, the Federal Reserve squeezed inflation nearly out of existence.[61] Inflation after January 1992 stayed in a tight range of 1.34 to 3.32 percent for the rest of the decade.[62]

Low inflation was a tonic to the economy. It acted as a business tax cut, minimizing the bite of the capital-gains tax and increasing the value of depreciations.[63] Its effect on long-term interest rates, which stayed low as the economy boomed, was a major benefit to consumers and borrowers. Clinton's contribution was simply to get out of Greenspan's way.

He grumbled about the Greenspan rate increases in 1994, but didn't openly challenge him. His economic advisors had tried to condition him in such forbearance. Alan Blinder writes, "I vividly recall the day in Little Rock in January 1993 when I told President-elect Clinton that, where the economy was concerned, he had just been elected to the *second* most important position in the country."[64]

The last important piece of the economic puzzle in the 1990s was put in place with the Republican congressional sweep in 1994. The Republicans brought fiscal restraint to Washington, with a vengeance. Even after all the hoopla of Clinton's deficit reduction plan, the Congressional Budget Office in January 1995 projected annual deficits of more than $200 billion between 1997 and 2005.[65] Congressional Republicans forced Clinton into agreeing to achieve a balanced budget by 2002.

In the first months of his administration, Clinton had complained, "We're Eisenhower Republicans here, and we are fighting the Reagan Republicans. We stand for lower deficits and free trade and the bond market. Isn't that great?"[66] A couple of years later, he would be alternately fighting the Reagan Republicans and cutting deals with them. Clinton's 1997 budget pact with Congress cut into spending by significantly reducing Medicare payments and extending spending caps. Importantly, it cut the capital-gains tax rate from 28 to 20 percent.[67] It also provided estate tax relief, instituted a $500-per-child tax credit, and expanded Individual Retirement Accounts.[68] Robert Reich sourly called the deal "the largest federal tax cut on higher incomes since Ronald Reagan signed the tax reduction bill in 1981."[69]

Clinton joined Republicans in continuing a deregulatory trend that began in the Carter administration and carried through the Reagan years. He signed bills deregulating agriculture, telecommunications, banking, trucking, and financial services.[70] With the significant exception of its harassing antitrust suit against Microsoft, the administration had a hands-off attitude toward high tech. The first two principles of its policy on the Internet, crafted in 1997 by the former health-care guru Ira Magaziner, were, "the private sector should lead" and "government should avoid undue restrictions on electronic commerce."[71]

With Greenspan handling monetary policy, and a combination of the Eisenhower Republicans and Reagan Republicans managing fiscal and regulatory policy, the environment for the economy was nearly ideal.

Across all ten years, the 1990s were a good, but not unprecedented period of growth. They conformed with the pattern of the previous three decades—recession in the first couple of years, followed by growth.[72] It was the latter half of the decade that was extraordinary, largely because of astonishing new technology that invited widespread use of the Internet and cell phones. The stock market and

NASDAQ experienced stunning run-ups, and in the late 1990s, the economy achieved full employment for the first time since the 1960s. Inflation remained in check, while productivity growth soared to 2.5 percent a year from 1996 to 2000, up from 0.9 percent in the period 1993–1995.[73]

The private investment boom made a mockery of the early Clinton obsession with government "investment." Total research and development spending grew 6 percent annually between 1994 and 2000. By 1999, real private investment as a share of gross domestic product reached its highest postwar levels, led by information technology.[74]

Government investment didn't define the decade, individual investors did. They poured money into the stock market, as the rise of 401(k)s minted a new class of Main Street stock owners. Investment in mutual funds alone jumped from $240 billion to $4 trillion across the decade.[75] Some of this investment was wasted in the bubble economy, but the gains of the 1990s were real, in the higher productivity, increased living standards, and the deep integration of technological innovation and stock ownership into American life.

All of this created a massive, unanticipated surge of tax revenue—income, corporate, and capital gains—that balanced the budget.[76] Much of that revenue increase came from the stock market in the form of capital gains, taxed at the reduced rate of 20 percent, and the cashing-in of stock options taxed at ordinary income tax rates. This ephemeral revenue windfall made a stark irrelevance of Washington's tax and budgetary policy. From 1995 to 2000, individual income revenue as a percentage of GDP increased from 8.1 percent to 10.2 percent, even though there was no notable tax increase in those years, in fact the opposite.[77]

Clinton likes to take credit for the erasure of the deficit with his 1993 budget plan. Republicans like to take credit for it with their anti-spending charge of 1995–1996. Both were largely spectators as economic growth trampled the deficit, lending a retrospective air of credence to Reagan's old joke: "I'm not worried about the deficit—it's big enough to take care of itself."[78]

The budget went from a $200 billion projected deficit in 2002 to a projected surplus in about nine months.[79] As Robert Reich has noted, the deficit "began to vanish during the spring and summer of 1997, even before the White House and Congress reached agreement, with great fanfare, on how to make it do so officially."[80] The 1997 budget deal was even slated to increase the deficit slightly in its first year, by roughly $21 billion.[81] The revenue surge was wholly unexpected by the Office of Management and Budget or the Congressional Budget Office, and no Clinton administration document predicted it.

Partisan Clinton defenders boil this down to one simplistic argument: Clinton single-handedly "grew" the economy. Hillary writes of the "the giant economic strides Bill had made" in 1994—"the deficit was finally coming back under control, hundreds of thousands of jobs had been created and the economy was starting to grow."[82] This is an infantile view of economics—that "Bill" is responsible for everything that happens to the economy on his watch, and even before, if it's good news. Sidney Blumenthal is equally silly, calling the 1993 budget "the foundation stone of a new economy," as if a modest income tax increase created the Internet.[83]

Blumenthal and other former Clinton advisors love to pretend that Clinton was somehow manning the controls of the economy. "For five years," Blumenthal wrote in an August 1997 memo, "the administration has endured the harrowing ordeal of conducting the transition from the old to the new economy."[84] Clinton conducted nothing. And any "harrowing" transitions in the economy had come in the early 1980s, with the truly painful throttling of runaway inflation, and the early 1990s, with further corporate downsizing. All Clinton had to do was enjoy the results of broad, felicitous economic forces.

Less partisan former Clinton advisors admit as much. Mickey Kantor, a former Clinton secretary of commerce and trade representative, says, "No one should claim that what we did, what President Clinton did, created the eight most productive years in the history of the United States. No one should claim that."[85] Clinton didn't cause the growth, he just avoided sending unsettling—read: liberal—signals to the markets. "I think the action taken in the 1993 budget battle was as much a psychological statement as a political one," says Bill Daley, another former Clinton commerce secretary. "The budget fight, where they were willing to take on a tough one, and NAFTA, set a tone that this may not be your typical, liberal Democrat."[86]

As soon as Bill Clinton left office, the debate shifted ground from who should get the credit for the economy to who should get the blame.

"An end to the something-for-nothing ethic of the 1980s"

Depending on your point of view, the 1990s, and especially the latter part of the decade, should either shatter the Clinton critique of the 1980s, or damn him in exactly the same terms he used against Reagan. It is tempting to read the 1990s corporate scandals as a reflection of Clinton and his governance since they feature the same unchecked appetite, looseness with rules, and concern with appearances over reality. But this would be unfair.

A free market economy is an enormous, roiling affair subject to governmental control only at its margins. It will always offer opportunities for folly and novel forms of criminality, for which the only solution is to let the fools and scam artists go broke or go to jail or both. The system can then cleanse itself before lurching into the next period of progress, to be leavened with excesses all its own.

The Clinton team in the early 1990s didn't, however, have a sophisticated appreciation of the forces of "creative destruction" inherent in capitalism. They argued instead that all the economy's flaws emanated from the top—from Ronald Reagan—and that they would solve them once in office.

A 1992 campaign memo urged Clinton: "Look for an opportunity to pivot into a denunciation of the Decade of Greed. You know the riff—the worst legacy of the Reagan-Bush years is the greed, the get it while you can attitude; the to-hell-with-my-neighbor, quick buck mentality that created the S&L debacle, the looting of HUD, and the ransacking of our great companies."[87]

He didn't need much reminding. He often repeated the theme, including in his 1992 speech accepting the Democratic nomination: "I have news for the forces of greed and the defenders of the status quo: Your time has come and gone. It's time for a change in America."[88]

The Decade of Greed critique had several permutations. There had been an unseemly social celebration of wealth; "the 1980s were about acquiring—acquiring wealth, power, privilege," Hillary complained in 1993.[89] There had been an emphasis on easy money, fading into outright criminality; Clinton exhorted in 1992, "together, we must bring an end to the something-for-nothing ethic of the 1980s."[90] There had been a rise in income inequality; "We need to reject the greed and short-sightedness of the past," Begala wrote in a 1993 memo, "[reject] sitting idly by while an elite few profit as our economy erodes."[91] There had been rank business speculation and self-enrichment; Robert Reich wrote in a memo to Clinton after his election, "American business must NOT use the added resources to . . . (a) speculate as they did in the 1980s, (b) pad their executives' salaries."[92]

If the 1980s were allegedly focused too intensely on wealth, they were nothing compared to the 1990s. CEOs became celebrities and were showered with money and benefits. The supposed excess that stoked the Clintons' ire in the 1980s was that executive salaries had tripled over the decade, reaching an average of $1.9 million. According to some estimates, executive pay increased six-fold in the 1990s, and executives were by the end of the decade making roughly five hundred times more than the average worker.[93]

If the 1980s were supposedly a time of speculative waste in the stock market and real estate, they were merely a warm-up for the 1990s. In the frenzy over technology and Internet companies in the late 1990s, profit-making often didn't matter as their stocks were bid ever higher in the very apotheosis of an unsustainable "something-for-nothing" attitude.

If the 1980s, in the imagination of Democrats, featured "the ransacking of our great companies," the 1990s would bring their pillaging

and burning. During the decade, the pressure to fudge earnings statements steadily built, while stock analysts and accountants got too cozy
with the corporations doing the fudging—leading to the explosion of
corporate scandals.

If the 1980s "left the poor behind," so did the 1990s. Blaming
Reagan and his tax cuts for income inequality never had much plau-
sibility, since the trend began around 1970. (Nixon's fault?)[94] It was
the product of deep changes in the economy that put a premium on
education and skills. Public policy could not reverse this trend, unless
it could dramatically improve education, something it has signally
failed to achieve. "Most of the gains from the 1990s boom went to the
people at the top," says Robert Reich. "The rich have gotten substantially richer."[95]

Despite all the 1980s bashing, Bill Clinton became a kind of
covert adherent to "trickle-down economics." This mocking phrase for
Reaganism captured a very simple truth: if policies promote economic
growth, everyone will gain. Clinton later justified the abandonment of
his investment program by saying, "All the folks that I ran to help
would be more hurt by a slow economy than they would be helped by
a marginal extra investment program."[96] According to Robert Rubin,
Clinton told him, "I have a jobs program, and my jobs program is
deficit reduction"—because deficit reduction would supposedly cause
economic growth. [97]

In his general orientation toward growth, Clinton was onto something important. Pick your cliché: a rising tide lifts all boats, or wealth
trickles down. Lower-income earners gained later in the decade when
the boom tightened the labor market. As former Clinton economic
official Joseph Stiglitz writes, the decline in inequality at the end of
the decade "was due to ordinary market forces of supply and
demand."[98]

Given a choice between condemning themselves for presiding
over a second, more egregious "decade of greed," or taking a more realistic view of the difficult-to-control forces of capitalism, former Clinton officials, of course, choose the latter.

Says a former Clinton official who had a sterling leftist pedigree before joining the administration: "The '90s were both a time of well-structured economic expansion and a stock-market bubble. The Internet was real. The incredible change in the fiscal position was real. The rise of the United States in the global economy was real. The stock value of Amazon.com was not real. But the fact is that the excesses were inevitable during a long boom. But the boom was real. Jobs were real. Income growth was real. A lot of it was real, some of it wasn't. That's inevitable."[99]

Indeed, it is. Where does Ronald Reagan go to get his apology?

Where the Clinton administration can be faulted in the go-go 1990s is that it was excessively pro-business. Forging free-trade agreements, for instance, wasn't enough. Government had to work in active partnership with corporations to help them win business overseas, an operation centered in the Department of Commerce. It wasn't a new phenomenon for Commerce to be a tool of corporate interests, but the administration elevated corporate hackery into high political strategy.

"[Making overseas business deals could] help the administration politically, both through the jobs exports provided and by adding a new political constituency—American business—to the Democratic coalition," writes Steven Holmes in his biography of the late commerce secretary Ron Brown. "The Reagan and Bush administrations were presumably more business-friendly. But both were in the thrall of the conservative Republican ideology that shunned government intervention in the marketplace. As such, beyond negotiating contracts to open up foreign markets, they did little to help American companies."[100]

The administration often made business the business of the United States government. A host of corporations, including the soon-to-be notorious Enron, got extraordinary help from the federal government in winning overseas contracts.[101] This was corporate welfare on an enormous scale. So were the administration's repeated international financial bailouts. They saved American brokerage houses and investors from the consequences of their irresponsible gambles in overseas markets.[102]

The fact is that the administration was happy to enjoy the economic bubble. The loose 1990s should have been an opportunity for a self-styled "progressive" administration to tighten the rules that keep capitalism successful, and honest. Some of those rules had eroded with time and the unintended consequences of deregulation. But the Clinton administration was too identified with corporate interests and too occupied with cheerleading the boom to be the vehicle of such restraint.

It wasn't just free-marketer Phil Gramm, for instance, who opposed tightening up the accounting rules around stock options, a change that would not have made much difference but that Democrats touted as absolutely necessary to corporate honesty in the wake of the bust. Both the Clinton Commerce and Treasury departments wrote letters to the Financial Accounting Standards Board fighting a proposed change in the treatment of options.[103]

The administration simply did not want to hear, or utter, a discouraging word that would detract from its glorious economic narrative. It wanted to believe in the dream of a New World created by the New Economy, one in which the business cycle and other surly bonds of history were forever suspended. As Clinton expressed this chiliastic vision, "The blocks, the barriers, the borders that defined the world for our parents and grandparents are giving way, with the help of a new generation of extraordinary technology."[104]

The second part of the relentless Clinton catchphrase of "peace and prosperity" was significantly oversold (the first part, as we will see, was just false). Not only had the boom begun to stall in 2000—manufacturing output began to decline in August[105] and industrial production in October[106]—it had created a hangover of bad investment it would take years to work through. Clinton didn't have to deal with the consequences of this. On the contrary, he rode it for all it was worth. As Joseph Stiglitz writes, "Those who were supposedly guiding the country's economy benefited from the euphoria brought on by false accounting no less than did the CEOs."[107]

Crude Clinton partisans Paul Begala, James Carville, et al., would turn around and blame the downturn on George W. Bush, even though, as Stiglitz puts it, "the economy was slipping into recession even before Bush took office, and the corporate scandals that are rocking America began much earlier."[108]

There was something symbolically perfect about Clinton touting economic growth that was going bust, and leaving someone else with the consequences. Clinton's presidency had achieved a sort of symmetry. He took office overselling a slowdown, and left office overselling a boom. He couldn't help the timing. But he sure as hell benefited from it.

WELFARE & CRIME:

A Conservative Triumph

IN 1993, THE CLINTON ADMINISTRATION held a series of "listening sessions" on welfare reform. Experts were invited to talk briefly to a panel of Clinton officials about welfare policy. The Heritage Foundation's Robert Rector, a longtime advocate of reform, got an invitation to one of the forums, held at the Commerce Department. He soon realized that everyone else invited had created, and still supported, "welfare as we know it." "It's ironic," Rector told the panel, "that I'm the only one here who supports President Clinton on welfare reform—and I'm not a Democrat."[1]

Bill Clinton's pledge to "end welfare as we know it"—with a policy summarized as "two years and you're off"—was the phoniest of all his campaign promises. He had no intention of doing anything that would remotely resemble "ending welfare as we know it," or instituting a policy of "two years and you're off"—a departure so radical that even when Republicans took Congress in 1994 they didn't support such a drastic time limit.

Clinton wanted all the rhetoric of welfare reform, with very little of the reality. He hoped that saying it would make it *not* so—that his rhetoric would ease the political pressure for real change. It was temporizing posing as leadership, the status quo camouflaged as reform.

Clinton now considers the two foremost social advances of the 1990s, the drop in welfare caseloads and the reduction in crime, pillars of his presidential accomplishment. He's delusional. He deserves credit for neither. Meaningful welfare reform never would have happened if he hadn't been forced into it, as he vetoed GOP reform bills twice before finally signing Republican legislation in August 1996 under political duress. As for crime, Clinton took office when trends that had nothing to do with him sent crime rates tumbling.

Clinton's achievement was, in essence, coming aboard the USS *Missouri* and signing the Democratic Party's surrender papers. He admitted that conservatives were right: welfare traps its recipients into a culture of dependency, and locking up criminals reduces crime. He made these concessions rhetorically in the 1992 campaign. Acting on them—especially when it came to welfare reform—was another matter, involving the usual Clinton posturing and backtracking, before Republicans forced his hand.

"Clinton aides see problem with vow to limit welfare"

When Clinton ran for president in 1992, the last important piece of welfare legislation had been Senator Daniel Patrick Moynihan's Family Support Act in 1988. It was advertised as a way to "replace welfare with work," but was really a continuation of the status quo.[2] The bill fit a Democrat pattern—soon to be adopted by Clinton—of talking tough on reform to co-opt anti-welfare political sentiment, but passing legislation that changed nothing.

The Family Support Act had major new spending on education, job training, and medical and child care services.[3] The work requirements were so weak that by 1992 only 1 percent of parents on Aid to Families with Dependent Children (AFDC) were mandated to perform community service work, and only a slightly higher number had to enter into job training or search for work.[4] The welfare caseload continued its rise, increasing by some 30 percent.[5]

For its part, the Bush administration—not a hotbed of policy imagination—adopted a posture of passivity, content to try to let the Family Support Act work (or not). This created Clinton's opening. Widespread discontent with the system was out there, waiting to be exploited.[6]

"In 1991, he said people on welfare ought to work," recalls former Clinton domestic policy advisor Bruce Reed. "And when he said it, there were notable gasps from the audience because they'd never heard Democrats say that before. It was a radical notion."[7] Clinton repeated the phrase "end welfare as we know it" so often that campaign aides began to refer to it as EWAWKI.[8] With his supreme policy wonkery, Clinton could out-talk anyone on the issue. "Clinton wasn't the least bit scared of the Democratic backlash on welfare, because he felt he knew this issue better then the rest of the Democrats did," Reed says. "He had spent more time in welfare offices than most people in politics. He was from a poor state."[9]

Clinton's sound bites obscured the fact that he was a supporter of the sort of "soft" Family Support Act–style reform that never accomplished anything. When Clinton said "two years and off," people assumed that the phrase meant what it seemed to say—two years, then no more welfare. During the welfare reform debate in 1995–1996, some Republicans would even complain, remembering Clinton's words, that the five-year time limit in the GOP bill was too long. Hillary, in turn, says that this five-year limit—more than twice as long as the one Clinton implied that he supported in 1992—was the scariest aspect of the Republican bill.[10]

But Clinton's phrase never was what it seemed. In policy terms, it meant a recipient could be on welfare for two years, then might fall into a small category of people required to conduct some sort of job search. The emphasis was on giving welfare recipients more benefits, rather than forcing them to work. As the Clinton manifesto *Putting People First* characterized the plan, it would "[e]mpower people with the education, training, and child care they need for up to two years, so they can break the cycle of dependency."[11]

Once in office, Clinton's strategy of making himself sound like a reform radical while doing nothing was perfectly safe, and even smart, so long as Democrats controlled Congress. Liberal committee chairmen were never going to pressure him to act on his tough positioning.

So Clinton's words floated off into the ether, with no relation to his policy. In February 1993, he gave a speech to the National Governors Association extolling welfare reform, and complained that there wasn't enough money in the JOBS program, established by the Family Support Act to fund training and workfare programs. Then, he released his first budget, which had no additional money for JOBS. Instead, there were big increases for food stamps, public housing, the Women, Infants, and Children food program (WIC) and other traditional welfare-related spending.[12]

That pushed any promotion of work off until fiscal year 1995 at least. But the next budget didn't have any money for JOBS either. It would have taken a relatively small amount of money in Washington terms—$3 billion or less—to quadruple JOBS funding and make a down payment on reform. Instead, with 1994 and 1995 out, it would have to be 1996, Clinton's reelection year, before there would be any additional funding—if then.[13]

A couple of factors helped constrain the administration. One was the expense. Since the administration's reform wasn't predicated on reducing the rolls, it would cost lots of money. It was just adding new bells and whistles, job training and the like, on top of the current system. The administration wasn't adverse, of course, to spending money on its stimulus package, its health-care plan, and traditional welfare programs, but insisted it simply couldn't afford welfare reform (as a June 1993 *New York Times* headline put it, "Clinton Aides See Problem with Vow to Limit Welfare").[14]

Another problem was that the administration staffed itself with opponents of reform. Health and Human Services (HHS) secretary

Donna Shalala had served on the board of the Children's Defense Fund, which had opposed even the meek Family Support Act. This was like making a former Greenpeace official the secretary of energy. Shalala mentioned welfare reform in just one sentence during her confirmation testimony—and probably felt that she was overextending herself.[15]

Top policymakers at HHS would resign when Clinton eventually signed a reform bill, including assistant secretary for welfare Mary Jo Bane and two other HHS officials, Wendell Primus and Peter Edelman (husband of Children's Defense Fund honcho Marion Wright Edelman). They obviously never expected Clinton to do anything like "ending welfare as we know it," or they never would have signed up to work for the administration in the first place. Before the Republican takeover of Congress, their expectation was entirely reasonable.

The administration busied itself early on trying to squelch the one meaningful work requirement in the Family Support Act, on fathers in two-parent families on AFDC. The requirement was set to take effect in fiscal year 1994, which the administration sought to delay until fiscal year 1996 (New York Times headline: "Delay Sought in Law Meant to Trim Welfare Rolls"). When the Senate rebuffed the proposed change, HHS tried to weaken the requirement by regulation. It had to back off that, in turn, after a political firestorm (Wall Street Journal headline: "Clinton Backs Away from Plan to Weaken Welfare Work Rules").[16]

When the administration eventually got around to crafting its reform bill, it was a substantive disaster, a betrayal of most everything Clinton had seemed to be saying during his campaign. By Rector's calculation, once most of the caseload had been whittled away in an extensive series of waivers and exemptions, the bill's work requirement applied to roughly 7 percent of people on welfare. The biggest exemption, covering about 80 percent of the caseload, said that the work requirements wouldn't apply to parents born before 1972. Only fifteen hours a week of work would be required from those few recipients who happened not to be exempted.[17]

The balance of the bill tipped heavily toward providing further funding to welfare recipients rather than forcing them to work. As former Clinton officials Rebecca Blank and David Ellwood write, "[M]ore pages of that bill were devoted to child support enforcement changes than to classic welfare reform provisions."[18] The bill was the status quo, with more spending. It was unveiled in the spring of 1994 and immediately sank into oblivion. The Democratic majority in Congress soon followed it there.

"A moral blot on his presidency "

The administration's failure on welfare created the possibility for genuine reform.

Liberals held four deep-seated premises about welfare. First, they believed that there simply weren't enough jobs for single mothers, and even if positions were available, there were "structural obstacles" to work. So, single mothers in theory were eager and willing to work, but to make that happen massive public expenditures for day care, transportation, and training were necessary, along with programs that would create new jobs.

Second, they thought that it was somehow inappropriate—coercive and judgmental—to force welfare recipients to do anything against their will. Welfare law had developed so that recipients had a legal claim against the government for their welfare benefits, and liberals thought nothing should disturb this "right."[19] Left-wing advocates even called work requirements "slavefare."

Third, they believed poverty was at the root of social dysfunction, causing pathologies such as crime, illegitimacy, and a weak work ethic. If government could raise a family's income, middle-class behavior would break out all over.

Fourth, liberals worried that single mothers, at the end of the day, just couldn't hack it. "[L]iberals feared," writes Ron Haskins, a key Republican congressional staffer on welfare policy, "that many poor mothers would not be able to find jobs, would not be able to keep them even if they found them, and would receive low wages even if they managed to keep the jobs."[20]

This last assumption, of a frank inability to work, essentially conflicted with the first premise, of a frustrated willingness to work—but liberals held both at the same time. This is why they argued, on the one hand, that single mothers only needed more child care, etc. to send them jumping eagerly into the workforce, and, on the other, that if single mothers were forced to work they would utterly collapse and end up homeless on the street.

A band of conservative reformers blew through these premises, picking up where Charles Murray had left off in his classic 1984 indictment of the welfare system *Losing Ground*.

They rejected the argument that structural factors were preventing people from working, and instead focused on the perverse incentives of the welfare system itself. They thought it was imperative to force recipients into work—"coerce" them—since they believed it was what was best for them. They believed that it was social pathologies, especially single motherhood, that caused poverty, not the other way around. Finally, they assumed that, given the right structure of incentives, welfare mothers would act as responsible, moral agents, caring for themselves and their children.

This was fresh thinking that, before it had any chance to influence policy, still had to sweep the Republican Party. In 1994, a group of House members led by Tom DeLay forged a reform bill that made marginal changes within the existing system, on the assumption that that was all the political market would bear.[21] A former Clinton official says of the GOP bill: "That plan and what Clinton proposed were not that different."[22]

A small group of Republicans engaged in a political and intellectual takeover on welfare, demonstrating the power of ideas wedded to determination. With Robert Rector providing the policy inspiration, Republican congressmen Jim Talent of Missouri and Tim Hutchison of Arkansas, together with Republican senator Lauch Faircloth of North Carolina, lobbied internally for an entirely new approach, with different tactical, rhetorical, and policy emphases.

On tactics, the group embraced confrontation. "The idea was to polarize the heck out of this issue," says Rector. "Don't engage in split-the-difference with Clinton, because you'll never come out with the clothes on your back."[23]

On rhetoric, the reformers took the high ground. "We started talking about welfare reform not in terms of how to save money, or federalism, or welfare cheats," says Talent. "What we said was, 'No, the purpose of welfare reform is to replace a system that has destroyed families and punished work with a system that encourages marriages and requires work for everybody.'"[24]

On policy, they proposed a revolution. The group crafted a bill that required 50 percent of welfare recipients to find work in short order, attempted to discourage illegitimacy, and put sixty-five means-tested welfare programs into one block grant to the states. This last provision was an audacious move to export a large piece of the Great Society right out of Washington to the states, where the programs could be managed more sensibly.

The provisions largely went into the Contract with America, and with the Republican sweep in 1994, the "end of welfare as we know it" finally looked plausible. Clinton's rhetoric was about to get a shotgun wedding with reality. Republicans loved quoting Clinton. "It allowed us to present the issue and our proposals as comprehending a consensus that in reality maybe wasn't there," says Talent.[25] Such was the price of Clinton's saying things he didn't really mean.

The Clinton administration lurched into irrelevance. It didn't reintroduce its bill in 1995,[26] and didn't write a line of the eventual legislation. "I didn't even see David Ellwood once during the entire process," Rector says of one of the administration's top welfare officials. Everything shifted right. "Democrats unsuccessfully rallied around counterproposals," writes welfare expert Hugh Heclo, "that they would have rejected out of hand two years earlier."[27]

The Republican bill mandated roughly that states cut their case-loads in half, removed legal restrictions on work that had been in the Family Support Act, set a five-year time limit on benefits, and eliminated the perverse incentives of existing federal welfare spending that effectively penalized states for reducing their welfare rolls.[28]

A final priority of the conservative reformers was reducing illegitimacy, but moderate Republican senators refused to go along. "The illegitimacy provisions probably had too punitive a character to them, and I say that advisedly, since I wrote them," says Rector.[29]

Liberals were appalled by the new direction. Nothing so captured the way policy creativity had shifted to the right in the 1990s than the debate over welfare. Liberals jealously guarded the status quo against conservative reformers. Marion Wright Edelman warned that under the Republican welfare reform bill poor children would starve.[30] She said if Clinton signed the bill it would "leave a moral blot on his presidency and our nation,"[31] while Senator Daniel Patrick Moynihan said the law would be "the most brutal act of social policy since reconstruction."[32]

Yet another battle for Bill Clinton's soul was on.

"A welfare veto would cost him the election"

Elements of the administration joined in the liberal outrage, and worked to give the critics more ammunition. HHS official Wendell Primus produced numbers showing that Republican reform would allegedly drive a million children into poverty. The administration worked to quash the figures, knowing that Clinton could well sign the bill. "The administration disavowed that there was even a study," says a former administration official. "We put a lot of effort into that study. It was not something that was done overnight on the back of an envelope."[33] Eventually, the Urban Institute ran the same numbers, producing a widely quoted prediction that welfare reform would force 2.6 million people, including 1.1 million children, into poverty.[34]

Clinton wasn't in the same place as his Department of Health and Human Services. He had granted waivers—as had Reagan and Bush—

for state-level welfare reforms, a reflection of his gubernatorial pedigree.[35] Bruce Reed explains, "Clinton hated HHS as governor because he had to appeal for waivers and got jerked around."[36] Welfare reform at the state level, in turn, lent ammunition to conservative reformers in Washington. One of their heroes was Wisconsin governor Tommy Thompson. "The Wisconsin model made reform possible," says Talent. "It would not have happened without Tommy Thompson. Because what we were able to say at every step was that what we were proposing had already been tried."[37]

On the other hand, Clinton was fundamentally uncomfortable with the direction of the Republican reforms. "The real issues were illegitimacy and the seriousness of work requirements," says Rector. "Clinton opposed all these things." According to Congressman Talent, "What they tried to do, when they realized they couldn't stop a bill, was to twist the concepts so that in practice they wouldn't work. So, for example, they tried to define work to mean a whole lot of things that had nothing to do with work."[38]

Clinton first vetoed a version of the welfare bill attached to the Republican budget. Then, he vetoed it a second time, highlighting changes in the food stamps and the school lunch programs that he opposed.[39] After an internal debate over whether to give Clinton another chance at signing, or to save the welfare issue for the lackluster Dole campaign, Republicans decided to send him a welfare bill one more time in the summer of 1996.

Clinton now had a choice. His advisors split, but Dick Morris worked himself nearly into an apoplexy, begging him to sign.[40]

"I told him flatly that a welfare veto would cost him the election," Morris writes. "Mark Penn had designed a polling model that indicated that a welfare veto by itself would transform a fifteen-point win into a three-point loss. Of all the developments that could realistically happen to affect the race, a welfare veto and Powell as Dole's VP ranked the worst in their impact on the president's fortunes."[41]

If the Clintons were ready to bow to political reality, they weren't happy about it. Hillary told Morris, "I know the politics, I know the numbers, but it still bothers me deeply."[42] Clinton raged to him at one point, "You've just given me biased polling on this bill. Did you ever ask if they want me to sign or veto a bill that would let three-year-old children starve, go hungry in the street, because their mother was cut off? You didn't ask that, did you? You didn't want to know the answer, did you?"[43]

The welfare bill that Clinton signed was essentially the same as the second bill he had vetoed, although some Clinton defenders suggest there were important changes. Day care funding was increased. Food stamps wouldn't be block-granted to the states.[44] A contingency fund, set aside for a recession, was increased.[45] But this was marginalia. The substance of the bill didn't change. "I probably would have really raised Cain if it had," Talent says.[46] And Democrats who hated the bill thought the same. That the third bill didn't change much is "more right than wrong," says a former Clinton official.[47] "The latest Republican welfare bill," Robert Reich thought at the time, "is still a disgrace, almost as bad as the two [Clinton] already vetoed."[48]

The New York Times felt the same sense of ideological betrayal, noting in an editorial that Clinton had supported welfare reform based on more federal spending, not less:

> After the Republicans took control of Congress, however, the president did an about-face, agreeing early on to a Republican proposal to end Washington's sixty-year-old commitment to the poor. He temporarily backed off when he was embarrassed by estimates that showed the proposal would abandon millions of needy children. These estimates had been made by Mr. Primus, forwarded to the White House, where they were buried, then flushed out by the persistence of Senator Daniel Patrick Moynihan of New York. Unfortunately, the president's embarrassment was temporary. The bill he signed was little different from the one Mr. Primus had studied.[49]

Clinton's about-face created an enormous social experiment. Rarely is there such a direct test between two opposing theories—liberals maintaining that tightening the welfare system would be disastrous for helpless poor people; conservatives arguing that welfare recipients would respond to different incentives. The conservative vision has been starkly vindicated.

Welfare dependence has been cut by more than half.[50] The caseload dropped from 4.3 million families in August 1996 to two million families in September 2002.[51] Caseloads were all the way back to their 1968 levels, despite a growing population and more single mothers since then.[52] The poverty rate declined from 13.8 percent in 1995 to 11.7 percent in 2001.[53] The black child poverty rate fell by more than a quarter,[54] and the declines in the black child poverty rate in 1997 and 1999 were the biggest on record.[55]

The growing economy was useful background noise, but didn't account for the progress. From 1950 to 2000, no economic expansion caused a drop in the welfare caseload, and the caseload swung much higher during periods of growth in the late 1960s and early 1970s.[56]

Work requirements were the crucial change. Former Clinton advisor Rebecca Blank writes, "States with strict or moderate penalties for not working consistently show higher income gains among poor children throughout the income distribution than do states with lenient penalties. . . . [I]t is the more lenient states with softer penalties where children's income seems to have grown least."[57]

The effect of the legislation was amplified by its symbolism, by the message it sent to potential recipients and to welfare administrators that society would no longer tolerate dependence. "We basically had a system that said never get a job, never get married, and have children," says Talent. "No one ever has said that to their own daughter. We stopped saying it."[58] After rising roughly one percentage point every year for thirty years, the rate of out-of-wedlock births stopped growing in the mid-1990s.[59]

Clinton's most significant contribution to reform was working to increase the Earned Income Tax Credit (EITC).[60] The program is a refundable tax credit pegged to earnings. It is designed to boost the income of lower-income working people, including those leaving welfare. Reagan had been a supporter of the idea, calling it "the most important antipoverty policy in America."[61] It had been expanded in 1986 and 1990, and Clinton continued the trend, increasing spending on the EITC from $15 billion in 1993 to $30 billion in 2000.[62]

Other supports for former welfare recipients were more marginal. Clinton's defenders credit him with boosting childcare spending from $4.5 billion in 1993 to $12.6 billion in 2000.[63] But after 1996 most of the additional money came from unused funds in the welfare block grants, thanks to the reduction in the rolls,[64] and only a quarter of former welfare mothers used subsidized daycare.[65] Child-support enforcement, though a rhetorical winner for Clinton, yielded minute gains. In 1999 the average annual child support payment for poor female-headed families was only $112 more than it had been in 1993.[66]

It was, obviously, the welfare bill itself that made the biggest difference and, left to his own devices, Clinton never would have produced a bill as tough, and as effective.[67] Dick Morris's political pleading was clearly decisive in getting Clinton to sign the GOP bill.[68] Morris notes that Clinton told him at one point, "I want you to know I signed that bill because I trust you." Morris writes, "Trust me? I knew what he meant. He signed the bill because he believed that I could help him win by a sufficient margin to bring in a Democratic House and Senate to help him change the bad features of the bill."[69]

So it was that the foremost policy accomplishment of his administration, an effective reform of welfare, was foisted upon Clinton by the congressional Republicans.

"The greatest decline in crime"

As with welfare reform, liberals consider the falling crime rates of the 1990s as another bequest from the Great White Father. "Clinton's policies helped the nation to achieve," writes Sidney Blumenthal, "the greatest decline in crime in more than a generation."[70] As the Clinton team was fond of saying when Republicans took credit for the end of the Cold War, this is like the rooster taking credit for the sunrise.[71]

The few distinctive crime measures pushed by Clinton—new gun-control laws and his one hundred thousand cops initiative—had little or nothing to do with the sharp drop in crime. They represented political positioning, and—unusually for Clinton—not all of it was even that shrewd.

It was the get-tough measures the country had been gradually embracing since the 1970s that brought down crime rates. Behind these measures was a rejection of the liberal argument that criminal acts weren't really the criminals' fault. Most Americans were always hardheaded in their approach to crime, which had given Republican politicians since Nixon a significant advantage on the issue.

In the 1990s, Clinton saw the political upside of joining the bandwagon. As Henry Ruth and Kevin R. Reitz write in their history of recent American crime policy, *The Challenge of Crime*, "The basic elements of the conservative program coalesced in the 1970s, achieved growing political popularity, and were embraced by both political parties by the century's end."[72]

Three factors clearly contributed to the drop in crime in the 1990s: prisons, cops, and pot.

Since the 1960s, a rising rate of violent crime had seemed to become an inexorable part of American life. The rate was 160.9 per 100,000 citizens in 1960, 363.5 in 1970, 596.6 in 1980, and 731.8 in 1990.[73] The spike was initially greeted with softer, rather than tougher measures, as the prison population, and average time served, fell in the 1960s. The next three decades saw sentences and prison populations swing up.[74]

The number of prisoners increased roughly 6 percent every year over the next quarter century,[75] and tripled from 1980 to the mid-1990s.[76] In 1974, there were roughly 218,000 prisoners in state and federal prisons. By 1995 there were more than a million.[77] In the 1990s, longer sentences began to fuel the rise. A murderer served on average less than five years in the 1980s, but was serving more than eleven years by 1996.[78] This increased imprisonment eventually overtook the increased crime, as crime rates in the 1990s dropped back to the levels of the 1960s.[79]

As political scientist William Spelman puts it, "About as many police officers per capita are employed today as were employed twenty-five years ago; only a tiny fraction of probationers and parolees are assigned to intensive supervision programs; the courts behave about the same as they did in the early 1970s. But four times as many people are in prison. Even if imprisonment were an incredibly inefficient means of reducing crime—and there are strong arguments that it is exactly that—it could hardly have helped but have a substantial effect on the crime rate, given the enormous scale of the difference."[80]

Clinton took office as this wave of imprisonment had already been building for decades. "You saw a carry-over effect from the Reagan-Bush years," says former Clinton deputy attorney general Eric Holder, "with really substantial increases in imprisonments, taking hold in the late 1980s and early 1990s."[81]

Also driving the crime drop was more aggressive policing, in New York City and other urban areas. The improvement in New York was the doing of Mayor Rudy Giuliani and his police commissioners William Bratton and Howard Safir. For his trouble, Giuliani was smeared for most of the decade by the Left for allegedly sending a racist, brutal occupying force into the city's poor neighborhoods.[82]

Perhaps the most important change wrought by Giuliani was to reject such criticisms root and branch. He let the New York City Police Department know that it was okay to be a cop again.[83] A reinvigorated NYPD instituted intense crackdowns in high-crime "hot spots." It adopted a strategic approach, working, for instance, to get illegal guns out of the hands of kids in and around high-crime areas. Gun apprehensions began to fall after 1994 as people began to think it too risky to carry guns on the streets.[84]

New York led the way in the national drop in crime.[85] The crime rate dipped 1.1 percent across the nation in 1994, but fell 12 percent in New York. The number of homicides dropped almost 20 percent in the city in 1994, while the national drop was only 5 percent.[86] There are chinks in the NYPD's success story, however. Declines in crime had begun in every major city in the country except Philadelphia by 1994.[87] And the number of murders had peaked in 1990 (2,245), before Giuliani took office.[88]

It's hard to argue, though, with the success of New York's experience and that of Boston, which adopted intensive crackdowns on gang members.[89] Even sociologist Andrew Karmen, a liberal Giuliani skeptic, writes, "Only New York and Boston enjoyed a consistent drop in murders year after year throughout the entire 1990–1998 period." By 1998 New York had 633 murders, lower than Chicago, a city less than half its size.[90]

There was one final trend important to the crime picture. Around 1991 the crack-cocaine boom began to burn out, and this sent the levels of juvenile violence plummeting. This trend intertwined with— and to some extent was caused by—tougher imprisonment policies and policing practices. But it is hard for any politician to take credit for the turnaround on crack, since no one was touring the nation's cities urging kids to eschew the drug for "blunts" instead, the hollowed-out cigars filled with marijuana that became the inner city's drug of choice.

Crack made its debut around 1984, prompting gun-bristling, murderous turf wars between dealers.[91] When the drug went out of style, juvenile murder fell almost exactly back to where it had been before the epidemic. There were roughly five hundred non-gun-related juvenile murders a year from 1980 until the late 1990s. That number held stubbornly constant. It was the number of gun murders that had skyrocketed, and the ensuing decline in juvenile murder was all in these gun cases.[92]

Crack lost out to marijuana in popularity, and a new, less aggressive culture grew up around pot. Because profit margins from selling marijuana were relatively small, there was less incentive for armed-to-the-teeth turf battles. This change was another sign of the thirst for order in the cities after the chaos and murder of the late 1980s and early 1990s—and not just among Giuliani voters. The kids who switched to marijuana wanted to escape the fate of their older siblings, whom they had seen shot, or arrested and sent to prison in the crack craze.[93]

Bill Clinton glommed onto, and made the Democrats part of, this broad new consensus for order, which served to ratify and strengthen it politically. But he was following, not leading.

"A symbolic gesture"

One of Clinton's first instincts in attacking crime was to institute new gun control measures, a page straight from the hymnal of liberal orthodoxy.

Gun control as a crime-fighting strategy suffers from at least two fundamental flaws. First, there is nothing to suggest any connection between the level of gun ownership and violent crime. To cite just one datum: More guns were manufactured in 1997 than 1986, but the homicide rate in 1986 was 25 percent higher.[94]

Second, with some 240 million guns[95] in circulation, criminals simply won't have a problem getting access to guns unless all guns are banned *and* confiscated—and maybe not even then. Ruth and Reitz write, "No study has shown that criminals have ever had difficulty in acquiring firearms in the past forty years, no matter what the level of gun production, gun regulation, or the type of gun currently in favor among manufacturers and users." Criminals will often, not surprisingly, steal their guns.[96]

Making any dent in crime with gun control measures, therefore, is extremely unlikely, even if it makes liberals feel like they're "doing something" about crime.

Clinton signed the Brady Bill in November 1993, mandating a five-day waiting period and a background check for the purchase of handguns from federally licensed dealers. About half of the states already had waiting periods, so the Brady Bill served merely to extend them to others, most of them more rural and without intense crime problems.[97] (The waiting period gave way to a system of instant background checks, beginning in 1998.)[98]

Hillary writes that the law has stopped "600,000 fugitives, stalkers, and felons" from buying guns.[99] This figure is inherently an exaggeration since the number is for total denials. It therefore includes denials for administrative reasons, fouled-up records, and so on.[100] There's no telling, of course, how many "fugitives, stalkers, and felons" went on to acquire their guns by some different means.

There is no evidence that the Brady Bill reduced violent crime,[101] which makes sense given that its two component parts have, apparently, no effect on crime. There is no evidence that waiting periods have any effect on violence,[102] and while the research on background checks is murkier, they probably are as ineffectual. A study comparing states that adopted background checks in 1994 to states that had the checks before then found no effect on the homicide rate.[103]

Clinton's other gun control measure was the assault weapon ban, passed as part of the 1994 crime bill.[104] It makes the Brady Bill look substantive and effective by comparison.

"Assault weapon" is a manufactured term, and doesn't refer to easily defined characteristics of a gun, although it's usually taken to mean a semi-automatic that accepts a large-capacity magazine and—this is the crucial part—has a "military-style" appearance. The weapons are a bogeyman, and not the accessory of hardened criminals everywhere as portrayed. One study showed that less than 2 percent of all guns used in crimes were assault weapons.[105]

If one were to ban all semi-automatics that accept large-capacity magazines it would be a sweeping measure banning millions of guns. So, with the assault weapons ban, Congress arbitrarily picked out nineteen models. Criminologist Gary Kleck writes, "It is hard to imagine how the federal AW ban could even hypothetically prevent a death or injury by banning further sales and manufacture of just nineteen models of semiautomatic guns that accounted for less than 1.4 percent of guns used by criminals and that possessed no violence-relevant attributes to distinguish them from over 380 semiautomatic models not banned."[106]

Nonetheless, when the figures for crime in 1995 were released, Clinton absurdly declared: "Today we learned that the first full year of our Crime Bill produced the largest drop in violent crime in twenty-two years."[107]

The only demonstrable effect from the Brady Bill and assault weapons ban was to help defeat a slew of Democratic congressmen from conservative districts where guns are important to the local culture. Clinton himself said: "We lost probably a dozen members of Congress that the NRA took out."[108] For the Democrats, this represented wanton political destruction, real political sacrifice on behalf of empty symbolic policies. (The White House was misled by its own polling on the issue. Says Howard Paster, who was Clinton's first congressional lobbyist, "I think the polling data was not done in a sophisticated manner. The polling data showed overwhelming support for Clinton's views on guns. But that doesn't save Jack Brooks or Tom Foley," Democratic old bulls defeated in pro-gun districts.)[109]

The crown jewel of Clinton's law enforcement agenda was his call for one hundred thousand new cops. The initiative deserves a special, sainted spot in sound bite heaven right alongside "ending welfare as we know it." Clinton's COPS program to provide federal funding for one hundred thousand new police officers was hugely popular, won over an important interest group (police unions eager for new members),[110] and was oversold and meaningless.

Since America's crime is primarily in politically inconvenient places—i.e., large urban areas—the funding couldn't be focused on crime hotspots, but instead had to be sprinkled throughout the country to allow every congressman to brag about the federally funded police he was bringing home. "Half of the new cops," journalist Ted Gest writes, "were reserved for jurisdictions with populations under 150,000." Herman Goldstein, an academic who pioneered the idea of problem-solving police patrolling, dismissed COPS as "a symbolic gesture with relatively little practical use."[111]

Probably something on the order of fifty thousand cops ended up in departments, rather than one hundred thousand, although the number is controversial. Much of the rest of the money was spent on equipment—computers, fax machines, and the like. COPS was supposed to promote community policing, although departments tended to get money for pretty much anything they asked.[112] In any case, "community policing" was a trendy catchphrase that no one could precisely define and had no proven effect on crime.[113]

Fortunately, the social progress of the 1990s didn't depend on Bill Clinton. It bubbled up from below, a deep yearning for an end to social indulgence and a return to order. America, Michael Barone wrote in 1998, "has opted clearly, on both crime and welfare, for more discipline and less therapy. These were not the decisions of Washington elites or academic experts, who almost uniformly favor therapy; they were forced by the people on their national leaders, or were the product of local officials and citizens acting in disregard of elite opinion."[114]

An indication of the power of this public opinion was that Bill Clinton felt compelled to try to co-opt and appease it—and then pretend that he was leading the way.

"THE CHILDREN":

Nanny-in-Chief

I N JUNE 1995, WHILE SHE and the president were in Canada for an economic summit, Hillary Clinton was honored by a women's university for her attempt to reform American health care. A few weeks
earlier, an official in Ukraine had asked her to sign a copy of her
Health Security Act, long since dead and forgotten in the United
States. "You know," Hillary complained, "this is getting really embarrassing. I travel around the world, and this has happened to me dozens
of times now, somebody from another country tells me that they've
read and analyzed it. More people have read it in the Ukraine
probably than read it in the United States."[1]

She might have been right. The bureaucratically sprawling and
intricate plan was more naturally pitched to Ukrainian than American
political culture.

If Hillary could—notwithstanding her reputation for greater ideological purity—be as pragmatic and cold-blooded as Bill, she embodied a distinct strand in his liberalism: the suffocating succor of the
nanny-state, with its constraining net of rules and regulations and its

touchy-feely sensibility. Bill, with his ready tears and warm hugs, best represented the emotional style of this liberalism. Hillary best represented its substance—its emphasis on health and safety, feminism, and above all, "the children."

Hillary had always considered children the thin edge of the wedge for her politics. In her writings in the 1970s, she portrayed children as the oppressed subjects of the American family, awaiting their liberation by a cadre of lawyers, advocates, and bureaucrats.

In the 1990s, the harsh edges of her prior advocacy had been shorn away. In her book *It Takes a Village*, the 1970s activist has grown up and joined the PTA. She praises traditional childrearing, and avoids blatant association with the cultural left. But the key themes are still there.

If Hillary doesn't call for the liberation of children, she still holds them up as beacons of enlightenment bearing lessons for the rest of us. She maintains, ridiculously, "Some of the best theologians I have ever met were five-year-olds" (move over, Reinhold Niebuhr).[2] If she doesn't engage in harsh anti-corporate rhetoric, she still maintains that children are beset with business-generated threats—everything from tobacco to inappropriate television programming.[3] If she doesn't express the full measure of the progressive movement's traditional distrust of ordinary parents, she still relates a study on how working-class parents raise their children poorly compared to better-educated parents.[4] If she doesn't call for child ombudsmen to supplement the inadequacies of traditional families, she still emphasizes the need for children's advocates and for a panoply of governmental interventions for any ill that potentially could face any child.

Children are the perfect left-wing constituency. They don't have a political voice of their own, so they don't have the annoying habit of objecting to an agenda undertaken in their name. They are politically popular, with an implicit place right alongside "motherhood, baseball, and apple pie." Those opposing legislation for "the children" therefore seem by definition nasty people, exactly what the Left naturally wants to call its opponents. Finally, a "children's" agenda will be inherently meddlesome, since its assumption is that families can't manage their kids on their own.

One of Hillary's favorite quotes was from John Wesley: "Do all the good you can, by all the means you can, in all the ways you can, at all the times you can, to all the people you can, as long as you can."[5] Note the preposition—good is done "to" people. On that little word turns a whole attitude toward public policy.

Alexis de Tocqueville gave a classic description of nanny-state government when he wrote that it could be compared to "parental authority if, fatherlike, it tried to prepare its charges for a man's life, but on the contrary, it only tries to keep them in perpetual childhood. . . . [I]t daily makes the exercise of free choice less useful and rarer, restricts the activity of free will within a narrower compass, and little by little robs each citizen of the proper use of his own faculties. . . . [G]overnment then extends its embrace to include the whole of society. It covers the whole of social life with a network of petty, complicated rules that are both minute and uniform, through which even men of the greatest originality and the most vigorous temperament cannot force their heads above the crowd. It does not break men's will, but softens, bends, and guides it. . . . [I]t does not destroy anything, but prevents much being born; it is not at all tyrannical, but it hinders, restrains, enervates, stifles, and stultifies so much that in the end each nation is reduced to nothing better than a flock of timid and hard-working animals with the government as its shepherd."[6]

This tendency was at a political high tide in the 1990s, when the "soccer mom" was made an icon and her presumed desires for government intervention and regulation to better ensure health, safety, and comfort dominated public discourse. The nanny-state impulse was starkly evident in two 1990s initiatives: the Clintons' socialistic health-care plan, and the feminist fight against the molten core of white-male backwardness, the warrior culture of the military.

The first project was an unmitigated disaster, while the second had some success through cultural mau-mauing and Clinton administration regulations. Hillary was directly involved only in the health-care debate, but the same spirit animated both fights, the same impulse to "soften, bend, and guide."

The background to both was a broad cultural struggle. Liberals sought to smooth away America's ruggedness, reducing its freedom via regulation (in the health-care initiative especially) and its penchant for risk-taking and aggression (in the fight over the military and in the related struggle over gun control). It's no accident that Western European social democracies with a wide array of government-provided benefits are essentially demilitarized societies. The waning of self-reliance and liberty is related to a declining tolerance for conflict and risk—something vital is bleached away from society's spirit.

Culturally, the 1990s battles over the nanny state were fought by the social and political elite, urban dwellers, and those parts of "soccer mom" suburbia that lived up to the stereotype against the rest of the country, especially the South and the West and rural areas. These areas were The Other America. The continued existence of this Other America—gun-toting, Bible-believing, un-Ivy League—was a continual cause of chagrin for the left.

It is a reason why Hillary never entirely lost her tinge of contempt—expressed in her writings from the 1970s—for America as it actually exists. Hillary said the reverence for her failed health plan abroad was embarrassing. For her? Or for her country, which had spurned her good works? In *It Takes a Village*, she recounts asking politicians in France how all of them came to agree on public spending for children. "One after another of them," she writes, "looked at me in astonishment. 'How can you not invest in children and expect to have a healthy country?'"[7] Hillary, no doubt, shared some of that Gallic disbelief at America's atavistic ways.

Hillary and her allies were arrayed against The Other America as they attempted to enmesh it in regulations and feminize its sensibilities, hoping to make it ever more well disposed to the ministrations of its Nanny-in-Chief.

"A president who was tiptoeing around the person in charge"

After the 1992 election, the Clinton team considered making Hillary the domestic policy advisor.[8] That was rejected as too formal a role. She got responsibility for remaking American health care instead.

Politically, it is impossible to overstate the importance of the health-care plan. Creating a system of government-guaranteed universal health coverage was considered by the Left the last missing piece of the New Deal. It would potentially create a new Democratic majority, hooking the middle class on governmental benefits and, thus, by extension on the political party of governmental benefits.[9]

When it all collapsed, it was a characteristic Clinton failure. The rush for a sweeping plan stemmed from the Clintons' romantic self-conception as the new Roosevelts. The process that created the plan reflected their Ivy League/Oxford-knows-best attitude at full flower. The flaws in their marriage impeded their internal deliberations. Their righteousness prompted them to reject compromise and demonize their opponents in the business community. Finally, the mandates, controls, and other strictures reflected their core belief that good is something you do *to* other people.

In the health-care fight, the First Lady was Hillary Unleashed. Clinton aides were afraid to contradict her, and she existed in an isolation tank born of others' adulation and fear. David Gergen writes, "When she was 'collecting facts' at public forums around the country, speakers were often chosen who would say what she wanted to hear. When she expressed views, few wanted to contradict her. When she went to Capitol Hill, senators and congressmen were deferential and reluctant to speak candidly. She was like an extremely wealthy person with many suitors who can never be quite sure who is telling the truth."[10]

Among those wary of challenging the First Lady was the president himself. He couldn't undercut her the way he could any other advisor when it suited his interests, and he couldn't ask her to resign. He may not even have felt himself to be in a position to talk frankly with her.

In late 1993, the story of how Arkansas state troopers had procured women for him broke, and Clinton appeared to adopt a supine position toward Hillary. "We were heading into the most important months of the health-care fight," according to Gergen, "with a president who was tiptoeing around the person in charge. I cannot recall him publicly confronting her on any health-care issue after that."[11]

Hillary's health-care soul mate was Ira Magaziner, a one-man distillation of everything wrong with early Clintonism. Asked why health-care reform failed, Clinton domestic policy advisor Bruce Reed says, "I hate to lay the blame entirely on Ira, but..."[12] Under Magaziner's guidance, the moral and intellectual superiority of the Oxford/Ivy League set was joined with a complex, all-encompassing bureaucratic liberalism. He was New Deal bureaucracy-builder Harry Hopkins on speed.

Magaziner got to know Clinton at Oxford, where he organized protests against the Vietnam War.[13] He had a history, from his student days to his career as a multimillionaire business consultant, of leading large-scale, totalist reforms that failed.[14] His rationality was prodigious. It was only a feel for reality that Magaziner lacked.

This is the man the Clintons entrusted with scrapping and rebuilding from scratch the American health-care system. Bill and Hillary were taken by his description of his (failed) efforts to reform health care in Rhode Island at—where else?—a Renaissance weekend in January 1992.[15]

After the 1992 election, Magaziner presided over a health-care task force of more than five hundred people, in a secret, byzantine policy process involving, by Magaziner's count, some 840 major decisions.[16] Meetings were of a punishing, Maoist length. One lasted twenty-two hours.[17] Magaziner himself pulled "double all-nighters," and when Clinton gave his health-care address to Congress in September 1993, Magaziner had gone without sleep for sixty-five hours.[18]

Out of this frantic, enormously complex process was born a plan of...enormous complexity. The health-care plan was truly epic, lunatic even, and if passed, could have changed the character of the country, making it more a Western European-style social democracy. The health-care system would have been drastically different today. There would be far fewer medical specialists, fewer new drugs, less innovation both in treatment and ways of delivering it, less research by academic medical centers, and drastically diminished private capital available for investment in health care.

The plan would have made for an ever-growing line in the federal budget, and would have been a serious drag on the economy, as it disrupted a huge 15 percent sector of it. It would have endangered the economic boom of the 1990s, and made it much harder to balance the budget, putting in doubt two of Clinton's favorite bragging points. Thus, one of the most important and beneficial policy legacies of the Clinton administration is simply that its health-care plan was crushed, never to be seen again.

"I can't save every undercapitalized business in America"

In an August 1993 memo to the First Lady, Magaziner wrote, "The U.S. has probably never done anything as big or comprehensive as what we are proposing." It wasn't idle boasting. The bill was 1,342 pages long.[19]

The plan micromanaged everything, stipulating how many specialists and primary-care doctors (and of what race and ethnicity) would be trained by teaching hospitals. It created obstacles to individuals spending their own money on traditional fee-for-service care. It set up committees to decide what new technologies and drugs could be approved. It essentially exported the restrictions on doctors and medical technologies from Medicare to the health-care system at large, and when that wasn't possible, imposed new Canadian-style regulations instead.

Two provisions in particular roiled the business community. The first was the "employer mandate," requiring businesses to provide coverage to their employees. It was bitterly opposed by small businesses as a hidden tax increase. The second was a cap on insurance premiums that was an ill-disguised form of price controls, guaranteeing the opposition of most insurance companies.

Most important, the plan set a global budget on what Americans could spend on health care, to be imposed by regional health-care alliances (originally called health insurance purchasing cooperatives, a name dropped because of its socialist connotations).[20] This was a massive rationing scheme that would have relentlessly squeezed medical providers.

The planned spending restraint—limiting spending growth to inflation—was tighter than that achieved in outright socialist systems that were explicitly rationing care.[21] In other words, the limit was wholly unrealistic without a reduction in how much health care Americans consumed. Either providers like hospitals would have gone out of business, or they would have had to petition for relief, which would have meant new federal spending, and either increases in the deficit or higher taxes or both.

The Congressional Budget Office, in an estimate excessively kind to the administration, projected the plan would add $74 billion to the deficit over six years.[22] Democratic congressman Dan Rostenkowski of Illinois, in an unwelcome burst of candor, said in an April 1994 speech that the plan would require "a broad tax increase that has some impact on virtually every American."[23]

"It was a breathtakingly huge expansion of government and became even more complicated because of its attempt to masquerade that fact," says a former administration official. "The bill sank of its own incomprehensibility."[24] In a telling contrast, Democratic congressman Jim McDermott of Washington introduced a "single-payer" government health-care plan—to the left of the Clinton plan—that was much simpler. It was frank in its reliance on tax increases and re-distribution from taxpayers to the uninsured.[25] It took the Clinton plan nearly 1,400 pages to try to hide the same redistribution and tax increases.[26]

The administration advanced two rationales for its plan: reducing health-care costs and reaching universal coverage. Actually, the first goal was already being addressed by the marketplace—and to some extent by the administration's jaw-boning about increased costs—even as Magaziner was suffering through his long, sleepless nights. From 1991 to 1994, big firms saw the annual increase in their insurance premiums fall from 14 percent to 6 percent.[27] Managed-care plans were at the time engaged in an intense war for market share, so they were willing to eat costs.[28]

The Clinton focus on health-care costs was wrongheaded in any case. There are inefficiencies in the health-care system,[29] but as a general proposition, increased medical costs are a product of people using more health care—a good thing—not price inflation or "price gouging."[30]

The second Clinton rationale was to provide coverage for everyone. At the time, thirty-seven million Americans had no insurance.[31] All these people were not, however, the dispossessed of the earth. At any given time, a segment of the uninsured are people without coverage only because they are changing jobs, are temporarily unemployed, or are young people in their early to mid-twenties whose health-care costs are typically very low and who choose not to bother with coverage.[32]

That said, there are indeed working-class Americans who can't afford insurance and who either don't sign up for, or are ineligible for, Medicaid. A package of limited subsidies would address this genuine problem. For that, you don't need a 1,342-page bill or Ira Magaziner's endless meetings. The Clintons instead proposed a monster, and tried to sell it in increasingly confrontational and left-wing terms.

Going back to their Arkansas days, the Clintons had sold their policy agenda by finding opponents to demonize. In the health-care fight, it would be, as a former campaign advisor put it, "greedy hospitals, greedy doctors, greedy insurance companies."[33] To the Clintons, health-care companies weren't well-meaning firms caught up in a bad system. They were positively rotten, enjoying their depredations. A memo from a Clinton advisor early in the administration called for an attack on "the evil pharmaceutical companies."[34]

Hillary grooved to this theme. In November 1993, she denounced the insurance companies, saying they "*like* being able to exclude people from coverage because the more they can exclude, the more money they can make" (emphasis mine). She returned to the theme in a February 1994 speech, denouncing both the insurance and drug industry as "rife with fraud, waste, and abuse." "We are basically taking the billions and billions of dollars we spend on financing health care," she said, "and dropping it in a black hole as far as I'm concerned."[35]

Hers was a most unusual charm offensive, based on telling anyone worried about the effects of her plan, effectively, to drop dead. In testimony before the House Small Business Committee, when asked about the burden of her plan on small businesses, she famously said, "I can't be expected to go out and save every undercapitalized business in America."[36] She told a health insurance agent worried about losing her job, "I'm assuming anyone as obviously brilliant as you could find something else to market."[37]

Polls showed 70 or 80 percent approval for the Clinton plan as it was emerging,[38] prompting A.M. Rosenthal of the *New York Times* to write that Clinton could already consider universal coverage one of his accomplishments.[39] The Clintons played this potentially winning hand awfully. By cutting Congress out of the process of developing the plan, they alienated even liberal congressmen. They might have been able to cut an early deal for a compromise (inflexibility wasn't usually Bill's problem), before their position became unrecoverable. Pollsters began to find that merely calling the health-care plan "the Clinton plan" was enough to drop support for it by thirty to forty points.[40] The phrase itself became a term of derision.

Republican and business opposition had not been—to use the terms of the health-care debate—universal or guaranteed. Republican Senate minority leader Bob Dole, above all a legislative weathervane, serially co-sponsored compromise plans that became steadily less regulatory over time. He backed off each one in turn as the political climate kept turning right.[41]

The American Medical Association,[42] the Health Insurance Association of America (HIAA),[43] the Chamber of Commerce,[44] and the Business Roundtable[45] all initially endorsed aspects of the Clinton plan, reversing themselves as the full scope of the plan became clear and the White House's position deteriorated. The *Washington Post* reported how the Business Roundtable's change of heart had been prompted by the administration's earlier dishonesty: "Big business had backed the administration in its budget fight with Congress on the strength of White House promises of additional cuts in domestic spending. But the cuts never came. Many now believed the health plan would become an open-ended entitlement that would raise taxes and the federal deficit."[46]

The Clintons obsessed over ads run by the HIAA featuring a husband and wife, "Harry and Louise," discussing worries about the Clinton plan. "The format was being for reform, because Harry and Louise were always for reform, but questioning the details," says former HIAA official Chip Kahn. "The initial motivation of Harry and Louise was not to beat health care reform. We didn't think we could. We didn't think we were important enough in the big picture, and that wasn't the objective of our members. They were trying to play along. Just find a role."[47]

The Clintons made the ads more important by attacking them. Hillary was offended that the industry would dare express itself on an issue determining its very future. "They have the gall," Hillary said in November 1993, "to run TV ads that there is a better way, the very industry that has brought us to the brink of bankruptcy because of the way they have financed health care."[48]

The focus on the ads accorded with the Clintons' view that they were undone by a vast profit-making conspiracy of special interests. There was indeed plenty of business spending against the plan. HIAA alone dropped $50 million.[49] But conservative groups like Citizens for a Sound Economy and the National Federation of Independent Businesses, both of which opposed the plan on principle from the beginning, launched a genuine grassroots opposition. It was the sort of intense political engagement the Clintons claimed to welcome—provided it wasn't opposed to them. "It was not the campaign contributions," writes David Gergen, "but the field operations of the opponents that were devastating."[50]

The ferment at the grassroots level made a last-ditch Hillary bus tour, meant to gin up support for the plan, an embarrassing fiasco. The anti-Clinton crowds were better organized and more boisterous than the supporters.[51] It was one of the most stirring political moments of the 1990s, as the public resisted an effort led by a political party with considerable power—controlling both the presidency and Congress, and with a generally sympathetic media—to reduce individual freedom and change the nation's economy and political culture.

For Hillary, naturally, the people involved in this grassroots revolt were creatures emerged from some black lagoon. "I had not seen faces like that since the segregation battles of the '60s," she said of the demonstrators.[52] In *Living History*, she characterizes the opposing crowds as "militia supporters, tax protesters, clinic blockaders."[53] Actually, they were Hillary protesters. They detected her sense of superiority and utter disdain for them. They opposed her unwieldy plan for a radical makeover of a sector of the economy that touched on everyone in the country. And they had the audacity to express their views in a boisterous and mocking way (a broken-down bus, covered in red tape, was placed on the side of a highway as Hillary's caravan got underway).[54] Hillary will never forgive them.

In the end, the political meltdown was so complete that neither house of Congress held a floor vote on any health-care reform plan.[55] The plan was its own undoing. Senator Daniel Patrick Moynihan was asked after health-care reform ended in ashes, "Who misunderstood Clinton's program? The American people or Mr. Clinton?" He responded: "Possibly the president. The American people got it clear enough. . . . And we didn't do any harm. *Primum non nocere*. That's the Hippocratic oath."[56]

Say this for the Clinton plan: at least it was ambitious. Nothing of remotely similar ambition would be advanced through the rest of the administration. Hillary's status was considerably diminished, and wouldn't rise again until her cuckolding in office—not quite the route to stardom she had imagined. At a downbeat New Year's Eve party in

1999, Bill and Hillary took questions. Asked what would be her legacy, Hillary bitterly referred to her recent pose on the cover of a fashion magazine: "Oh, I don't need a legacy—I was on the cover of *Vogue*. Nothing could equal that legacy. Health care is but a distant memory. So the epitaph should read, 'She was on the cover of *Vogue*.'"[57]

"A very narrow, all-white coterie of exclusively men"

After the rebuke of the 1994 election, the Clintons sought comfort and advice from self-help gurus. Two of them proved especially important to Hillary: Jean Houston, a co-director of the Foundation for Mind Research and a believer in the efficacy of trances and hypnosis, and Mary Catherine Bateson, an anthropology professor at George Mason University whose *Manual for the Peacekeeper: An Iroquois Legend to Heal Self and Society* both Bill and Hillary read and enjoyed.[58]

During their sessions together, Houston shared an insight with Hillary: that five thousand years of women's oppression were on her shoulders.[59] It was supposedly because Hillary represented a decisive break from this long history of victimization that she was so hated.

Hillary herself related a version of this theory to Gail Sheehy, explaining how she threatened men who were made vulnerable by their loss of dominance. "I know I'm the projection for many of those wounded men. I'm the boss they never wanted to have. I'm the wife who went back to school and got an extra degree and a job as good as theirs. I'm the daughter who they never wanted to turn out to be so independent. It's not me, personally, they hate—it's the changes I represent."[60]

This is nonsensical on its face. The men who so opposed Hillary loved, for instance, Margaret Thatcher, the very embodiment of a strong woman.

The "wounded" men of whom Hillary spoke are the white males who represent, in her view, the core of opposition to herself and her political project. "White male" is a way of thinking and of being, the ethnic and gender markers for backwardness. This is why the superficially white and male Bill Clinton could manage to be "the first black presi-dent," as an admiring Toni Morrison put it.[61]

Hillary condemned the first President Bush by remarking, "Bush is advised by a coterie of men who are, frankly, all of one mind—a very narrow, all-white coterie of exclusively men."[62] After Clinton's election in 1992, when the question of what to do about the Southern white male vote came up, her reaction was sharp and instant: "Screw them. Let's move on."[63] She remarks in her memoir, in what she surely takes to be a devastating criticism, "Each of Ken Starr's eight male deputies looked just like him."[64]

In her writings on children, Hillary had called for liberating children from the "empire of the father."[65] White males represent that empire: the patriarchy, the emotionally repressed, politically retrograde, and unfairly entrenched establishment that Hillary had been battling from the beginning. During the Clinton administration, the fight against white males was carried out through the administration's personnel policies, through its defense and extension of racial quotas, and, above all, through its battle against the traditional culture of the most power-ful and respected "white male" institution in the country—the military.

In the early Clinton administration, the push to avoid seeming overly white and overly male reached a kind of mania. Warren Christopher, of all people, the most stereotypically buttoned-up of all white males, boasts of Clinton's cabinet: "a twentieth-century record low of seven were white males."[66] Sidney Blumenthal notes with a similarly admiring tone, "If there was any ethnic deficit in the Clin-ton White House it was of white Anglo-Saxon Protestant males, espe-cially wealthy ones."[67]

Hillary strongly backed Clinton's pledge to have a government that "looks like America," a pledge that was painstakingly enforced. "No for-mal presentation of nominees could have on display only males, and this led to scrambles to get the right combination before the cameras," writes Elizabeth Drew. "Sometimes a whole slate would be returned to a Cabinet officer because it wasn't diverse enough. Sometimes Clinton would question a single potential appointee's credentials, and the whole group of nominations would be returned so that it could come back in correct balance."[68]

The tokenism extended into the administration's internal meetings. Sidney Blumenthal recounts, "Once, a small group of about six senior advisors met to brief the president in the Oval Office. We presented the policy options and the political implications. We thought we had covered all the bases. Clinton waited patiently for us to finish. Then he said, 'You are the dumbest bunch of white boys I have ever seen.' He reprimanded us for coming into the Oval Office as an all-white, all-male group. He mentioned the names of several minority women whom he expected to have included the next time. 'Don't let it happen again,' said the president. It didn't."[69]

This impulse is formalized, of course, in racial quotas. The issue of race preferences created one of the administration's most famous, and dishonest, catchphrases: "Mend it, don't end it." It purported to describe the administration's policy in response to the Supreme Court's 1995 *Adarand* decision holding that federal affirmative action programs have to meet the "strict scrutiny" test to be constitutional.[70] That means, roughly, that they should redress some specific, past act of discrimination. George Stephanopolous describes Clinton as "[o]paque with both political anxiety and honest intellectual uncertainty" as the administration undertook its review of affirmative action.[71]

He landed firmly on the side of the status quo, thus eroding the very principles of equal opportunity under the law that he had so admirably backed during the civil rights revolution. The administration pushed ahead with a program that aggressively extended, but didn't mend, the quota regime. Why disturb quotas when white males are the ones who lose out?

"I don't talk to the military"

The biggest institutional target in the crusade against white males was the military. In no meaningful sense is the military a "white male" institution. It just features qualities that are associated in the liberal mind with unreformed attitudes: strict discipline, unstinting standards, tradition, an absence of individual self-expression, hierarchy, patriotism, and, of course, bellicosity. In other words, it is backwardness personified, and riding in a Bradley Fighting Vehicle.

In its major combat arms, the demographic of the military tends to be Southern, white, male, and lower-middle-class—think NASCAR. However, anyone of any race, obviously, can join, and thrive in, the military, given the requisite mix of virtues and abilities. Women can as well, within limits. It is that qualifier—"limits"—that eats at feminists and the left.

In the military, cold reality is ever present in the possibility of combat and death. So, attention must be paid to natural limits. This is taken as great prejudice, and in the 1990s two values trumped the military's innate conservatism: the belief that women can, as a general matter, do whatever men do, and that personal choice and individual career advancement should be held uppermost in nearly every circumstance. Both beliefs are illusory, but both were in keeping with the spirit of the times, when limits were thought to be on their way toward obsolescence.

In the 1991 Gulf War, thirteen women were killed while serving in a combat zone, but none were in direct combat, and two became enemy POWs.[72] It was a four-day ground war that was a rout, so few men experienced actual combat either. But that these female casualties were suffered without significant political or military fallout was considered evidence enough to wipe away the accumulated wisdom of most of human history about putting women in combat.

An even more important blow in the feminist's favor came after the 1991 Tailhook convention of naval aviators. It was, as usual, a raucous drinkfest. Some of the misbehavior at Tailhook was appalling, but no more so than what would be happening in the Oval Office a few years later. Fatefully, however, there were sexual assaults, probably three that might be deemed criminal. From the kernel of this misconduct, a massive years-long witch hunt ensued that would keep defenders of the traditional military rocked perpetually back on their heels. The Navy—and the Bush administration—groveled before their feminist critics. Pat Schroeder welcomed the fact that, after Tailhook, "one could hear the sound of a culture cracking."[73]

The culture in question was the traditional warrior culture—i.e., the "white male" culture—of the military. Admiral Frank B. Kelso II, chief of Naval Operations, explained to a congressional hearing in 1992 that "until Tailhook, we dealt too often with sexual harassment at the local level, one case at a time, rather than understanding it as a cultural issue" (read: a white male problem). In 1992, Barbara Spyridion Pope, assistant secretary of the Navy for Manpower and Reserve Affairs, said of boot camp, "We are in the process of weeding out the white male as a norm. We're about changing the culture."[74]

The most direct way to "change the culture" was opening combat opportunities to women. The military had become increasingly dependent on women with the creation of the All Volunteer Force in the 1970s. But women had been kept from combat positions and certain dangerous support positions.[75] Feminists sought to remove all such barriers to women in combat.

Hillary had little direct involvement in this struggle. Her closest engagement with the military was pressuring it in 1996 to devote $20 million of its funds to breast cancer research.[76] In its hostility to white males and its roots in feminism, however, the anti-warrior campaign bore the marks of Hillary's style of liberalism. The military had to be wrenched, in this vision, from its traditionalist moorings and made a force for progressive social change. Clinton Navy secretary John Dalton said, looking back at his tenure, that he had wanted to have the Navy "lead society as a model for gender relations."[77]

The military might be doubly discomfiting to a Clintonite because it was an institution associated with old-line WASP patriots (e.g., the "out-of-touch" George Herbert Walker Bush) and Southern jingoists (i.e., "angry white males"). Clinton's generation had displaced the old-line WASP patriots at the top of the social heap in America. And the Southern "angry white males" were the despised leading edge of political anti-Clintonism in the country. So it's no surprise that the military was the one government program Clinton was most eager to cut, steadily reducing its funding and level of personnel.

There was also the lingering post-Vietnam "loathing"—as Clinton put it in his letter about the draft so many years ago—of the military.[78] A female White House staffer, capturing something of the administration's ethos, told a military official in the administration's early days, "I don't talk to the military." The story has the ring of an urban legend about it, but Elizabeth Drew vouches for its accuracy.[79]

The military would become much more tolerable to such critics if it were emasculated—literally. Duke University law professor Madeleine Morris, who became a paid consultant to Clinton's secretary of the Army, Togo West, in 1997, expressed this sentiment in its purest form, writing of the need to change the "military culture from a masculinist vision of unalloyed aggressivity to an ungendered vision."[80]

In April 1993, Les Aspin—a kinder and gentler defense secretary—began throwing open the doors to women in combat.

He ordered the Navy to seek congressional repeal of the exclusion law against women on combat ships. He approved of women in combat aviation.[81] He junked the "risk rule" that had kept women out of a host of support positions because there was a risk they might experience combat. He announced new, laxer rules on ground combat. The "substantial risk of capture" clause would no longer bar women from service in any given unit.[82] "The new policy," a Defense Department press release said, "means that women will no longer be excluded from military specialties simply because the jobs are dangerous."[83]

From here, the march steadily continued. Another important push in 1994 was for sex-integrated basic training. The Army buckled, but the Marines fought back and successfully resisted. For this, Sara Lister, assistant secretary of the Army for Manpower and Reserve Affairs, later called the Marines "extremist" (she was forced out within about forty-eight hours of her comment being publicized).[84]

The Marines argued that the normal stresses and temptations when men and women interact were incompatible with the values they inculcate in basic training. "We were very vocal and very

adamant that we were not going to gender-integrate our recruit training," says General Charles C. Krulak, the then–commandant of the
Marine Corps. "I got flak from the Department of Defense, some of
it probably generated from the White House, and some from the Senate and the House. But we got a great deal of support from the American people."[85]

The facts were on his side too. Many female Marines cannot
heave a hand grenade beyond its blast radius.[86] Moreover, chiefly
because of pregnancy, women are non-deployable at three times the
rate of men—an important factor for often-deployed Marine fighting
units.[87] In her book *The Kinder, Gentler Military*, Stephanie Gutmann
describes the ineluctable physical facts of life this way: "The average
woman is about five inches shorter than the average man, she has 55
to 60 percent less upper body strength, a lower center of gravity, a
higher fat-to-muscle ratio, lighter bones that are more subject to frac-
ture, a heart that can't move oxygen to the muscles as fast as a man's
(20 percent less aerobic capacity), and a rather more complicated
lower abdomen full of reproductive equipment."[88]

The conundrum faced by the services that moved to sex-integrated
training is that women will drop out and get hurt if training is attuned
to the capabilities of men. On the other hand, if the training is pitched
to a level that can be handled by women, the men aren't challenged.[89]
Basic training was duly watered down, and physical standards lowered. A commission headed by former Kansas Republican senator
Nancy Kassebaum Baker and appointed by Clinton defense secretary
William Cohen concluded in 1997 that gender-integrated training
resulted in "less discipline, less unit cohesion, and more distraction
from training programs."[90]

The political push to demonstrate a fervent belief that women are
exactly as capable as men in all areas created a climate of fear and dishonesty in the military. Reality had to be denied. As Marine critic Sara
Lister noted, the Army avoided discussing pregnancy and strength
issues because "those subjects quickly become fodder for conservatives seeking to limit women's role in the Army."[91]

On top of all this, the military had to accommodate itself to the fact that its soldiers were, given the dictates of nature and contemporary sexual culture, going to behave as if they were on the set of *Friends*. Roughly three-quarters of members of the Army and Marines said in a survey that there had been sexual activity in their units during the first Persian Gulf deployment.[92] Fifty-five percent of those reporting sexual activity said it adversely affected morale.[93] In 1991, 10 percent of the female crew of the destroyer tender USS *Acadia* left mid-cruise because they were pregnant.[94] In the initial stages of the Bosnian peacekeeping mission, a servicewoman had to be evacuated on average every three days for pregnancy.[95]

The military made its peace with its mini–sexual upheaval. First, secretary of the Navy John H. Dalton insisted in 1995 that "pregnancy and parenthood are compatible with a naval career" and being with child shouldn't create a "presumption of medical incapacity."[96] And the military more fully embraced single moms. It simply had to— roughly 40 percent of pregnant sailors were single.[97] The military became an arm of the welfare state. Feminist Linda Bird Francke, author of *Ground Zero: Gender Wars in the Military*, calls the services "a particular mecca for single parents."[98]

The military's policy of providing a generous package of supports that encourage single mothers to stay in the service, together with the feminist push to expose women to more dangerous duties interact to raise the question: What kind of country sends its young mothers into harm's way?

Well, feminists might ask, What if they choose it? The vast majority of women in the military aren't choosing to be exposed to danger, although the Aspin regulations make it more likely that they will be. There is a tiny number of women who want to be in combat and are capable of it. Canada has opened combat positions to women. In 1997, there were sixty-six women in combat positions and 10,450 men.[99] Distorting the military—reducing its standards, and blunting its warrior culture—to accommodate and encourage a tiny number of women who might choose to take up arms makes no sense. This is the more fundamental point: Choice should have nothing to do with it. Anyone in the military should be combat-ready and able.

By the late 1990s, the military as "empire of the father" had been dealt a serious blow: It had seen its leadership forced to pay obeisance to feminism, watering down its physical training and opening more and more combat positions to women, while pretending to enjoy every minute of it and refusing to acknowledge any negative consequence to the changes.

The military began to reflect its commander in chief, in its politicization, in its defense of preferential treatment for a special group, in its creeping softness, and in its dishonesty. The crucial difference was that the commander in chief felt entitled to obstruct a sexual harassment suit, whereas most military officers, cowed by the career-threatening consequences of such behavior, would never have dared such a thing.

The erosion of the traditional warrior culture in the politicization and feminization of the military helped account for a near-crisis in recruitment and retention as the decade closed.[100] Almost 80 percent of Air Force pilots decided not to extend their service in 1998.[101] Some of the adventure, challenge, and honor had been bleached out of the service. As historian S.L.A. Marshall has remarked of the man in combat, there is "one thing that he is likely to value more highly than life—his reputation as a man among other men."[102] In the 1990s, that impulse was treated as somehow disreputable.[103]

This could not last. The country doesn't just need something it can call a military, it needs warriors who can fight and win wars on the ground. There is a reason that the feminization of the military made such strides during a decade when America's wars were mostly fought from fifteen thousand feet. The war on terror brought an abrupt reality check, making it clear that violence couldn't be held at a safe, sterile distance.

On September 11, it was men who trudged up into the burning twin towers. There were no female casualties among the 343 firefighters who died that day.[104] It was men in Special Forces—where women need not apply—who were the sharpest edge of the American military in Afghanistan and Iraq. Even the most hardened feminist, indeed even Hillary Clinton, had to cheer these firefighters and front-line warriors. They were doing what women couldn't, acting on masculine virtues that, if not timeless, had at least, as Jean Houston might estimate, been in evidence for the last five thousand years. They had always been admirable and always been indispensable. In the 1990s, the era of the soccer mom, we just forgot.

Part Two

SCANDAL & LAW

INVESTIGATION:
Watergate's Revenge

L OOKING BACK AT THE SCANDAL WARS during his presidency, Clinton would complain that Democrats weren't tough enough to assassinate the character of their political enemies: "*We* don't have the stomach for it. *We* argue the issues."[1]

Actually, the contemporary tactic of using scandal allegations to destroy opponents was virtually invented by Democrats. Reagan labor secretary Raymond Donovan was one of the first victims. "Donovan was labeled a mobbed-up contractor," recalls former Clinton scandal lawyer Lanny Davis.[2] "Investigations followed, all ending with the wonderful phrase, 'There is no substantial evidence to find Mr. Donovan guilty.' What does that mean? But each time Democrats kept up the drumbeat and each time they would support a new independent counsel investigation. That was us. I was on the sidelines cheering. We used the scandal machinery. We abused it. And we set the precedent."[3]

The political and legal conflagrations that led to Clinton's impeachment were almost entirely the result of the world built by post-Vietnam, post-Watergate liberals. They created the independent counsel statute; they celebrated a powerful, adversarial press; they wrote exacting campaign finance rules; they instituted a strict anti–sexual harassment regime in the workplace—and then they supported an attempt to defy all of it when it became inconvenient.

The scandal wars of the Clinton administration represented the revenge of 1970s liberalism on 1990s liberalism. The first iteration of liberalism was bent on changing the world through the force of its own righteousness, the second bent on clinging to presidential power in the person of a corrupt Lothario.

The independent counsel statute carried in its DNA the attitudes and priorities of the 1970s, a time of retrenchment of the "imperial presidency" at home and of American power abroad. The statute was a mechanism for the American government to feast on itself in ever-repeating ethical crises. The Iran-Contra affair represented the ideal efflorescence of the statute from the standpoint of 1970s-style liberalism, since it damaged two Republican presidents, facilitated an attack on the executive's foreign-policy powers, and made more difficult the cause of aiding anti-Communist rebels in a Cold War flashpoint.

As Justice Antonin Scalia wrote in his dissent from a decision upholding the independent counsel statute in 1988: "The context of the statute is acrid with the smell of threatened impeachment."[4] Democrats wouldn't recoil from it until a Democratic president got a good strong whiff.

In politics, the hypocrisy of one side is usually met with a corresponding hypocrisy on the other. So it was in the 1990s, when many Republicans and conservatives learned to love the apparatuses of post-Watergate liberalism. They attempted to hype mini-flaps into bigger scandals, and sometimes used scandal as an excuse not to engage in frank political and ideological argument. But all the tools had already been put in place for them to harass a Democratic president—by the Democrats. It almost would have transgressed human nature for them not to use them. The laws were on the books, and all Republicans had to ask was for them to be enforced.

The line of Clinton loyalists is that most of the scandals proved to be "pseudoscandals," fakeries foisted on Clinton by his enemies. The scandals actually fall into three categories. Some of them were indeed minor controversies hyped into something bigger. Filegate, in which White House officials were found with the FBI files of former Bush officials, turned out to be a "bureaucratic snafu," exactly as Clinton said. And the Travel Office firings were ultimately a trivial matter involving the bumbling of the early Clinton staff, together with its peculiar mix of self-righteousness (they thought they were cleaning up a corrupt operation) and of cronyism (they thought their friends were just the people to clean up a corrupt operation).[5]

More serious were scandals that fell in an intermediate category, involving grave allegations that were never proved or alleged misconduct from Clinton's days as Arkansas governor, or both. The investigation into the Whitewater land deal resulted in substantial convictions. The allegations were that the Clintons participated with their Whitewater partner, S&L criminal Jim McDougal, in various fraudulent schemes. The charges were never proved, and may well have been false, although there was enough heat around them that Clinton was forced to ask for a special counsel in the case. Another early controversy, Troopergate, precisely foreshadowed the Monica affair, suggesting the level of Clinton's sexual irresponsibility and his willingness to dangle jobs and other inducements to cover it up.

Finally, there were the Big Three scandals, all very real, all involving official misconduct by Clinton while president. The 1996 reelection fund-raising scandal represented a massive and deliberate effort to subvert campaign fund-raising laws. At the end of his presidency, Clinton pardoned an international fugitive whose estranged wife happened to be a major contributor. And in the most consequential scandal of all, the Lewinsky affair, he lied under oath in two separate sessions, urged Monica to lie under oath, coached a potential witness in his employ in an attempt to get her to repeat falsehoods, asserted bogus executive privileges, and lied to everyone in the White House and the nation.

By the time Clinton was finished, he had taken a wrecking ball to post-Watergate political reform. He had eviscerated the campaign-financing regime that had been one of contemporary liberalism's proudest creations and killed off the independent counsel statute that liberalism had considered essential to ethical government. On top of this, he managed to separate feminists from their passion for sexual harassment law. His survival was more important to him than any of these supposed sociopolitical advances, and he survived—but not without a price, a price exacted in the tarnished idealism of his allies.

"You'll have to speak to Hillary"

The independent counsel statute (the "Ethics in Government Act") was the crown jewel of post-Watergate liberals' reform agenda, but it was a rotten idea from the beginning. The statute compelled the executive branch to investigate itself on the slightest instigation. This represented not only a bad practice, but a constitutional deformation.

Under the Constitution, the executive branch was meant to investigate and prosecute crimes—period, full-stop, end of discussion. But with the independent counsel statute, Congress lifted that power out of the executive branch, and let it roam free, unhinged from any serious constraint or from any political accountability.[6] Almost every aspect of the act was a trespass on the executive branch: Congress *required* the attorney general to ask for the appointment of an independent counsel in certain circumstances; gave to a panel of *judges* the power to make the appointment; and vested in the independent counsel, once selected, prosecutorial powers with almost *no check* from the rest of the executive branch. This kind of unbounded authority is just what the Constitution is designed to avoid. The Supreme Court upheld the statute anyway in *Morrison v. Olson* in 1988.[7]

In a dissent in the Olson case so prescient that it provides a kind of guide to the 1990s scandal wars, Scalia forecast the problems that the statute would create in practice: "What would normally be regarded as a technical violation (there are no rules defining such things), may in [an independent counsel's] small world assume the proportions of an indictable offense. What would normally be regarded as an investigation that has reached the level of pursuing such picayune matters that it should be concluded, may to him or her be an investigation that ought to go on for another year. How frightening it must be to have your own independent counsel and staff appointed, with nothing else to do but to investigate you until investigation is no longer worthwhile."[8]

In the new Clinton administration, White House counsel Bernie Nussbaum understood the nature of the statute. "It is an institution that is designed to get the president," he says of the independent counsel. He notes how independent counsel Lawrence Walsh issued indictments of former Reagan officials on the eve of the 1992 election, creating a last-minute controversy that hurt George Bush. "Lawrence Walsh," he says, "was probably responsible for Clinton's election when he totally sandbagged the Bush administration."[9] Bush attorney general Bill Barr, in a conversation on his way out the door, advised Nussbaum not to revive the statute, which had lapsed in December 1992: "As a Republican, I'd love to see you live under it, but as an American, I can tell you it would bad news if you get that thing going again."[10]

There might have been a small window to bury the reauthorization. "In the fall of 1993," recalls Nussbaum. "I got a call from [Senate Democratic majority leader] George Mitchell or his office. They said we can put reauthorizing the statute on the back burner. I told them I thought that was a very good idea. But I couldn't do it on my own, so I took it to the president. I went to the Oval Office. I told him that 'The majority leader had said we could try to avoid doing it, under the radar screen. Nobody's calling for it.' He said, 'We can't do that, Bernie. We made a promise during the campaign.' I told him 'You made a lot of promises. You are not going to keep them all. It's not a big issue. Let's just go slow, since it's not necessary.'" Clinton stood firm. "It was crazy," says Nussbaum.[11]

Clinton was doing the shortsighted, politically expedient thing. As Scalia wrote in his dissent: "It is difficult to vote not to enact, and even more difficult to vote to repeal, a statute called, appropriately enough, the Ethics in Government Act."[12]

Clinton's willingness to renew the law was also a telling statement about his self-image. Once out of office he would joke about how much money was spent proving that he was a "sinner." But in 1993 he didn't give off a casual, realistic sense of his own capacity for sin. Used to invoking Watergate, the Reagan "sleaze factor," and Reagan-Bush Iran-Contra problems, the Clinton team could almost be forgiven for thinking that corruption is something liberal Democrats, especially if they've been to Oxford, simply don't "do." This exalted sense of self-righteousness led to Clinton's impossible boast that he would conduct the "most ethical administration ever."

When he signed the new Independent Counsel Act, Clinton called it "a foundation stone for the trust between the government and our citizens. It ensures that no matter what party controls the Congress or the executive branch, an independent nonpartisan process will be in place to guarantee the integrity of public officials and ensure that no one is above the law."[13] Soon enough Clinton took a sledge-hammer to this "foundation stone," and attempted to destroy the agent of this "independent nonpartisan process."

While Nussbaum was losing the fight over the reauthorization of the counsel statute, he was outgunned in a related argument over a Whitewater special prosecutor. The question was, while the statute was still lapsed, whether to have Reno appoint a special prosecutor who would morph into a full-fledged independent counsel once the law kicked in again. "I told them," Nussbaum says, "the prosecutor would be investigating things years from now, investigating things we never dreamed of—Monica then was a junior in college."[14] Other aides rolled their eyes at Nussbaum's dire warnings, while a shaky Clinton ("I don't know how much longer I can take this")[15] was too cowed by criticism from the press to hold his ground against asking for a counsel.

"The problem was Clinton's weakness in response to all that criticism," says Nussbaum. "His mother, in her autobiography, talks of how, if there's a room of one hundred people, and ninety-nine of them like him, he'll spend all his time with that one person, trying to win him over. It's a dangerous prescription for leadership. But trying to get everyone to like him is an essential part of his personality. He thought if he did this, maybe the *Washington Post* and the *New York Times* would love him. He would gain peace—by giving in."[16]

As an institution, the independent counsel was essentially allied with an adversarial press that was liberal (especially on social issues), but mostly sought, as a matter of professional obligation, to bring low whoever was in high office. Like the independent counsel, the contemporary news media arose out of the post-Vietnam, post-Watergate era, which shifted power from discredited government officials to the press. The media took on a quasi-governmental role, and—prior to Clinton's ascendance—was almost universally praised by liberals for advancing the cause of truth and social justice.

The rise in the 1990s of new alternative media institutions—Rush Limbaugh, cable news, and the Drudge Report and other news websites—eroded the authority of the establishment media. It made the media more interesting, more diverse, and more informative. Even as Matt Drudge broke several important Monica-related stories, scandal coverage of the Clintons did not emanate mainly from these new outlets. *Newsweek* was working the Monica story before anyone else, and the White House's big, tone-setting fallout with the media came in a dispute with the *Washington Post*.

In December 1993, the *Washington Post* asked the White House to hand over documents related to Whitewater, a request with an implicit threat of sustained, negative coverage if it were rebuffed. David Gergen tried to convince his colleagues at the White House to cough them up, as a way of placating the editors at the *Post* who, in his words, "already sensed that the Clinton team had misled them several times in the past." Clinton told Gergen, "I agree with you. I think we should turn over all of the documents." Then, he delegated to Gergen talking to his wife about it: "*You'll* have to speak to Hillary and get her agreement. If she agrees, we'll do it."[17]

Hillary's implausible version is that Clinton was too "[c]onsumed with the demands of the presidency" to make this crucial decision himself.[18] Gergen writes that Clinton said he couldn't decide alone because Hillary was a party to Whitewater, and speculates that she was worried about her cattle trades being exposed. In any case, Hillary wouldn't agree to hand over the documents.[19] The *Post* would subsequently run sixty-two articles on Whitewater in three months, leading the way for other news organizations.[20]

Clinton loyalists portray this as an unprecedented assault against the new president, although it was actually a typical "feeding frenzy" of the sort that had been common in Washington over the previous fifteen years. What the White House lost in the excessive early Whitewater coverage, it made up in the media's relative reluctance to cover Troopergate or the Paula Jones suit—and in its brutal coverage of Newt Gingrich.[21] The Clintons would have been well advised to whine less about the press and cooperate with it more. "With the wisdom of hindsight," says Lanny Davis, "I would have advised Mrs. Clinton to be fully transparent with all the reporters, understanding that she had a right to be concerned about people who might criticize her for client representation while she was the wife of the governor. The basis of that management-crisis advice is that she did absolutely nothing wrong, by anything she did. But by not being fully transparent you leave the impression that there's something to worry about."[22]

The Clintons' tactical judgment about the press was clouded not just by short-term worries over making new revelations, but by their own sense of virtue and victimhood: How could anyone question the practices or motives of this utterly public-spirited couple, the finest fruit of the best generation in American history?

When Jeff Gerth broke, in an inchoate form, the Whitewater story in the *New York Times* on March 8, 1992, Hillary saw a threatened establishment at work: "What's really terrible is finding out that things your father told you are true. He used to tell me, 'Hillary, don't ever forget two things about the establishment: it hates change, and it will always protect its prerogatives.'"[23] Why the *New York Times* would be threatened by a candidate it endorsed heartily is a mystery.

Joining the two long-established power centers of scandal in the 1990s—the independent counsel statute and the press—were Republicans and conservatives in a position to turn ethics allegations against a Democratic White House. They too were bowing to a political phenomenon identified by Scalia: "Nothing is so politically effective as the ability to charge that one's opponent and his associates are not merely wrongheaded, naïve, ineffective, but, in all probability, 'crooks.'"[24]

Conservatives were heeding the lesson of their own Watergate-style victory, the takedown of House Speaker Jim Wright on ethics charges in 1989 that proved the effectiveness of scandal politics. The anti-Wright campaign was a Newt Gingrich project, and Democrats never forgave him. Indeed, when taking out Gingrich personally seemed the best way to blunt the Republican revolution after 1994, they made more than seventy ethics charges against him in the House—this even as the White House was expressing outraged disbelief that anyone might make exaggerated corruption charges in the cause of partisan advantage.[25]

On the fringes of the right, anti-Clintonism became a poisonous paranoia about murder in high places. But much of the Republicans' scandal-obsession was old-fashioned partisan opportunism, unedifying, but not unusual or nefarious. They were given plenty of targets by a White House and a president that, at best, couldn't do anything cleanly, and at worst were willing to break the law when it suited their purposes.

"So I need to roll over one more time"

Janet Reno first requested an independent investigation of President Clinton in the Whitewater controversy. She soon added probes of Vince Foster's suicide, Travelgate, and Filegate. She asked for counsels to investigate agriculture secretary Mike Espy, commerce secretary Ron

Brown, HUD secretary Henry Cisneros, former chief executive officer of the Corporation for National Service Eli Segal, interior secretary Bruce Babbitt, and White House aide Alexis Herman (later the
labor secretary).[26] It got to the point where no Clinton cabinet officer
seemed complete without an independent counsel. Robert "Bear"
Bryant, former deputy director of the FBI, recalls, "I jokingly said to
Reno, 'You are the only one left.' She didn't laugh."[27] In a sign of the
times, Linda Tripp testified in five different independent counsel
investigations.[28]

Congressional hearings would have been sufficient for most of the
early Clinton scandals. Indeed, Bernie Nussbaum's advice to the Clintons on Whitewater was to hand over all the documents to a congressional committee for hearings, which might obviate the need for
a special counsel and put the issue behind them.[29] In the first two
years of the administration especially, the hearings would have been
tame affairs, because Democrats controlled all the committees.

Later, the White House experienced much more aggressive Whitewater hearings held by New York Republican senator Al D'Amato. His
hearings were a model of how the normal political process should handle scandals. The hearings aired the Whitewater charges, extracted a
political price from the White House, and produced a few criminal
referrals.[30] But the Clinton counterattack was so effective that D'Amato has said privately that he lost his reelection bid in 1998 partly
because voters reacted against his work on Whitewater.[31]

Instead of embracing this rough-and-tumble process, Clinton
endorsed politically insulated independent counsels working mostly
in secret. Clinton's enemies did not refer the scandals to independent
counsels; his own attorney general did, as part of a lawful process
endorsed by the president and a Democratic-controlled Congress.
When the statute he supported proved to be a mistake, when his own
attorney general inconveniently acted in accord with the law, when
the complicated Whitewater case dragged on after he had asked for a
counsel to investigate it, Clinton's team responded by waging war on
Ken Starr.

The original Whitewater counsel was Robert Fiske, appointed by Reno while the independent counsel statute was still lapsed. Once the statute was reauthorized in June 1994, she asked the three-judge panel that appoints counsels under the statute to retain Fiske, but instead it replaced him with Ken Starr. For Clinton's defenders, this is the foundational act of the "right-wing conspiracy," insinuating its hit man Starr into the center of the Clinton investigations.

The three-judge panel argued—not unreasonably—that it had to replace Fiske because he had originally been appointed by Reno and the entire point of the independent counsel statute was to achieve an exquisite independence from the Department of Justice. Was this argument simply a ruse to sic a right-wing cheap-shot artist on Clinton? If it was, Ken Starr would seem an odd choice. Starr was a conservative, yes, but he was moderate in temperament, and responsible in practice. Journalist Stuart Taylor wrote of Starr in 1993 that he was "liked and respected, with an extraordinary degree of unanimity, by lawyers and judges of all political stripes all across the country—among them, most (and perhaps all) of the justices of the Supreme Court."[32]

There is a fundamental weakness with the Clinton storyline that the Whitewater investigation was not a problem under the "confident, careful, and experienced" (in the words of Sidney Blumenthal) Fiske, but ratcheted out of control under the wild-eyed Starr. By the time he was replaced, Fiske had already embarked on a wide-ranging investigation.[33] "In Little Rock," says Starr, "we found that there were underway investigations into a variety of matters hitherto unknown to me."[34] There were 120 investigators and lawyers already there. Fiske had struck three plea bargains, was about to charge Webster Hubbell for bilking the Rose law firm, and was probing a host of other far-flung matters.[35]

Starr scored a major victory in 1996 when he successfully prosecuted Arkansas governor Jim Guy Tucker and the Clintons' partners in the Whitewater land development, Jim and Susan McDougal. Convicting a bank president and a sitting governor who are friends of the president in their home state is a considerable feat. The *Washington Post* editorial writer Benjamin Wittes, a moderate Starr critic, has called the 1996 convictions "a significant prosecutorial accomplishment that was entirely justified and has, in retrospect, been significantly underappreciated."[36]

A political impresario and S&L owner, Jim McDougal had a taste for get-rich-quick deals that he liked to share with politicians. Whitewater was meant to be such a sweetheart deal, but went sour from the beginning. It was part of McDougal's imagined financial empire that became dependent on various Ponzi schemes and frauds to stay afloat, including one that involved fraudulently obtaining Small Business Administration funds through an Arkansas operator named David Hale. Starr prosecuted the McDougals and Tucker for that loan deal.[37] After nailing them, the next step was to see whether they would turn on the Clintons.

The investigation of the Clintons, in essence, sought to learn whether they were party to any of Jim McDougal's frauds, or lied about their knowledge of them. Starr's chief witnesses against the Clintons were David Hale, who had pled guilty while Fiske was still in charge of the investigation, and Jim McDougal, who flipped against the Clintons and changed his story after his prosecution. Both were felons with credibility problems, and Starr couldn't make a case on the basis of their testimony alone.

So, Starr ended up in a death-match with recalcitrant witnesses. Susan McDougal refused to testify, going to jail on civil contempt charges for eighteen months instead. One of the questions she found too outrageous to answer, even with an offer of immunity, was "To your knowledge, did William Jefferson Clinton testify truthfully during the course of your trial?"[38] She made the odd choice of preferring to go to jail. "It's certainly unusual; it isn't unheard of," former Starr prosecutor Sol Wisenberg says of Susan's behavior. "It traditionally happens in mob cases or gang cases where the person just isn't going to go against, either for fear, or loyalty, or both, just isn't going to go against the crooked organization."[39]

Clinton's defenders worked to make Susan McDougal a martyr and symbol of Starr's excess. Clinton claimed her treatment proved "we had totally innocent people prosecuted because they wouldn't lie."[40] Susan was a convicted felon, not "totally innocent." And no one asked her to lie. It was Judge Susan Webber Wright who had Susan McDougal jailed for contempt, of which she was flagrantly—proudly—guilty.[41] Her famous perp-walk in chains had nothing to do with Starr, but was standard U.S. marshals' practice.[42]

Starr's contribution was to prosecute her in 1999 on two charges of criminal contempt and one of obstruction of justice. An Arkansas jury acquitted on the obstruction charge and hung on the contempt charges. Since the evidence against Susan McDougal was well established—she was eagerly trumpeting her non-cooperation with Starr's grand jury—the outcome of the trial was widely interpreted as a sign, not that she was innocent, but the jury thought she had been punished enough.[43]

The other uncooperative witness was Webb Hubbell. Between the time he resigned under the cloud of an imminent indictment as associate attorney general in April 1994 and pled guilty to cheating the Rose law firm in December 1994, he collected several hundred thousand dollars' worth of no-work retainers. They came from various Clinton allies—not old Arkansas friends of Hubbell's, but typical DNC corporate donors—after he resigned from Justice on the verge of his indictment. Once in prison, Hubbell was recorded in ambivalent, but suggestive phone calls with his wife discussing protecting Hillary, during which he uttered the famous line: "So I need to roll over one more time."[44] If he had been paid for his silence, it was impossible to prove. Starr went after him again twice on other charges, losing a tax case and winning a guilty plea in a conflict-of-interest case stemming from Hubbell's work at Rose.[45]

The charge the White House would make against Starr to demonstrate his out-of-bounds zealousness was that he spent years investigating Clinton. Indeed, he did. There were numerous reasons for the slow pace. Upon his appointment a raft of Fiske's lawyers left, forcing a wait as he re-hired staff. Starr tended to be painstakingly methodical.[46] And, through no fault of his own, Janet Reno kept piling new cases on top of his Whitewater work.

Starr was also slowed by the White House's efforts to delay him. The common expression used to characterize the White House's scandal strategy from the beginning was the f-word. Back in the 1992 campaign, the attempt to keep Whitewater information away from the *New York Times* was known as the "F— you, Jeff Gerth" strategy.[47] The Clinton team adopted toward Starr what Harold Ickes called a "foot-dragging, f— you" attitude.[48] Emblematic was the production of Hillary's Rose law firm billing records two years after they had been subpoenaed.[49]

"The Whitewater thing was bogus from day one," Clinton said in June 2000.[50]

As a general matter, this was simply untrue. There was ample criminality around the Whitewater scandal. Aside from the McDougals, the counsel's office won guilty pleas from or convictions of twelve other people.[51] If the Clintons were squeaky-clean on Whitewater, it would have been logical to follow the Nussbaum strategy: release everything to Congress and don't ask for a special counsel. They didn't want to do that because they, at the very least, had things to be embarrassed about.

In 1992, Democrats were still beating up Republicans over the savings and loan fiasco. Ron Brown called it "one of the biggest scandals in the history of our country."[52] Anything that would have filled in details of the Clintons' involvement with a crooked S&L operator was a potential political problem. As journalist Joseph Lelyveld has pointed out, releasing the Clinton 1978–1979 tax returns when they were first requested by Jeff Gerth also would have exposed Hillary's cattle trades, foisting yet another controversy on Clinton's rocky primary campaign.[53]

Besides any potential criminality, the nub of what the Clintons had to hide was that they had availed themselves, through McDougal and through Hillary's trades, of the sort of opportunities to make easy money made available only to politicians and the otherwise well connected.[54] This offended against their self-image of public-interested purity and contradicted their campaign rhetoric. They had done their bit to partake in the "decade of greed."

The imperatives of damage control did not change from 1992 onward, meaning the White House had inevitably to obstruct and attack Starr. It would have eventually done the same thing to Robert Fiske, if he hadn't been removed from the crosshairs. By what theory, for instance, are we supposed to believe that the "careful and experienced" Fiske would have been less suspicious of the payments to Hubbell than was Ken Starr?

The fact is that independent counsels, by their nature, grind on relentlessly and prosecute every crime within their purview. In the end, the worst that can be said about Ken Starr is that he was an independent counsel. The White House's real problem was not with Starr, whom it attacked so ferociously, but with the independent counsel statute, which it had supported so reverently. It would eventually turn against the statute, and so would Attorney General Reno.

"I can't do anything but go to fund-raisers"

In 1974, locked in a tight congressional race, his first, word had come down to candidate Clinton that dairy interests were willing to provide money to buy votes. Some of his aides were in favor of it, Clinton seemed ambivalent, but Hillary was adamantly opposed.[55] The campaign eschewed the money, and Clinton lost.

He wouldn't make the same mistake in the run-up to 1996. According to George Stephanopoulos, the White House was committed to "pulling out all the stops," and did: The party raised three times as much in 1996 as it had in 1992.[56] If one believes Dick Morris, Mark Penn, and Clinton himself when they say that his early campaign advertising was crucial to his 1996 victory, then it was a tainted win, bought partly on fund-raising excess and illegality.

The ad campaign was always on the verge—just days away—of running out of money, and entailed a massive fund-raising push.[57] It ran Clinton ragged. He told Morris at one point, "I can't think. I can't act. I can't do anything but go to fund-raisers and shake hands."[58] Clinton's fund-raising depended on three unseemly or illicit methods:

selling access, laundering campaign contributions through the DNC, and tapping foreign money.

President Clinton and Vice President Gore made fund-raising calls from the White House, with Gore raising roughly $800,000.[59] The campaign auctioned off meetings and photo opportunities with the two.[60] It systematically rewarded large donors with overnights in the Lincoln Bedroom, and it instituted a program of fund-raising coffees at the White House. There were as many as fourteen coffee klatches a month, with attendees expected to contribute $50,000 each.[61]

The schedule was so intense that deputy chief of staff Evelyn Lieberman wrote a memo to White House staff explaining that the time pressures meant that presidential briefings "may be considerably truncated or eliminated."[62] The coffees reaped in total, according to one estimate, $26 million, with the contributions averaging out to— funny how that works—a little over $50,000 per attendee.[63] The White House would expend considerable energy later insisting that the coffees weren't fund-raisers, an effort, Lanny Davis admitted, "to deny the obvious."[64]

The greatest fund-raising bonanza came with the Clinton campaign's inspiration that it could subvert the post-Watergate campaign finance regime through the DNC. In exchange for public financing, a presidential campaign must abide by limits on its spending and raise money only in $1,000 increments. Clinton had raised so much money so early in 1995, to stave off a primary challenge, that he was already bumping up against the limits.[65] The Clinton campaign considered turning down public financing and blowing by the spending limits altogether, but decided instead to take the public financing—and still blow by the spending limits to the tune of $44 million.[66]

There are no limits on DNC "soft money" fund-raising, but the funds are not to be used to support a political campaign directly. Taking a distinction that had eroded over the years and destroying it utterly, the Clinton campaign made the DNC its wholly owned subsidiary. When the fund-raising controversy grew after the election, Clinton blamed it all on the DNC, dishonestly saying "That was the other campaign that had problems, not mine."[67] Actually, Harold Ickes spelled out in an April 1996 memo how every budgetary decision at the DNC was "subject to *prior* approval of the White House."[68] Clinton reviewed every DNC ad script so, in the words of Morris, they were "not the slick creations of ad men but the work of the president himself."[69]

The Clinton team knew, in effect, that they could outrun the law, with regard both to the campaign's direct control of the DNC advertisements and to all the foreign fund-raising. Justice Department investigator Charles La Bella summarized notes taken from a White House meeting during the 1996 campaign. "The notes reflected comments by a White House staffer who, amid reports of foreign money finding its way into the reelection effort, opined that any [Federal Election Campaign Act] violations would not be addressed by the FEC until *after* the election. What was not said—but what was clearly understood—was that any election abuse addressed *after* the election will likely be forgotten long before the next election and chalked up to the cost of doing business."[70]

The campaign adopted a studied negligence to shady funds. Former Little Rock restaurant owner Charlie Trie gave the president's legal expense trust a bag—literally, a bag—with $460,000 worth of checks and money orders in March 1996. The executive director of the trust, Michael Cardozo, felt uneasy, and an investigation determined that the money should be returned. The matter was discussed at a large White House briefing including Harold Ickes. The money was sent back, but the reporting requirements of the trust were quickly changed, so the return of the money wouldn't have to be publicly disclosed.[71] And nothing was done to keep Trie from continuing his other fund-raising activities.

Three days after the White House meeting at which his shady contributions were discussed, Trie gave $10,000 to the DNC, and the day after that he coughed up another $5,000 to sit at the president's table during an event. "Trie continued to attend dinners with the president, enter the White House, and function as a major solicitor and fund-raiser through Election Day," LaBella writes. "In August of 1996—not two months after [the trust] returned the Trie donations— the DNC accepted $110,000 solicited by Trie in connection with the Presidential Birthday Gala. We have confirmed that $100,000 of these solicited funds were [illegal] conduit contributions."[72]

The epicenter of the foreign fund-raising was James Riady and his Lippo Group, an enormous Indonesian business with ties to the Chinese government. Riady had gotten a head start on the 1996 fund-raising scandal in 1992 by donating $750,000 in illegal contributions to the DNC. Riady confidante John Huang raised $1.6 million in illegal money in 1996.[73] There was, needless to say, not much restraint from White House officials on Huang's illicit activity. At a coffee in the White House Map Room in June 1996, Clinton himself watched John Huang directly ask two Thai businessmen for funds.[74] At one Huang-organized event, Clinton thanked "those who come from other countries to be with us tonight."[75]

The DNC eventually returned $2.8 million in illegal money all told, 80 percent of it donated or raised by Charlie Trie (thirty-one White House visits in 1994 and 1995) or John Huang (sixty-seven White House visits in an eighteen-month period).[76] Clinton personally expressed an interest in having Huang move from the Commerce Department to the DNC, where he could work full-throttle on his fund-raising. And he issued an executive order to make a spot for Trie on the Commission on U.S. Pacific Trade and Investment Policy.[77]

Tennessee Republican senator Fred Thompson led hearings examining the scandal. His committee concluded that there was "strong circumstantial evidence that the government of the People's Republic of China (PRC) was involved in funding, directing, or encouraging some of these foreign contributions."[78] The Chinese government connections of Clinton fund-raisers and donors in 1996 are stunning.

The Thompson committee said intelligence information concluded that James Riady and his father perhaps had a "long-term relationship with a Chinese intelligence agency," while Huang "may possibly have had a direct financial relationship with the PRC government."[79]

Maria Hsia, according to the Thompson report, "has been an agent of the Chinese government."[80] She was the organizer of Al Gore's famous fund-raiser at the Hsi Lai Temple, and funneled approximately $150,000 in illegal funds to the Democrats in the 1996 election cycle.[81]

Ted Sioeng, according to the FBI, was a "cultural agent" of the Chinese government. The Thompson committee said he "has worked, and perhaps still works, on behalf of the Chinese government."[82] Sioeng's English was extremely limited, but he sat next to Gore at the Hsi Lai Temple, and sat next to Clinton at another fund-raiser. His family and his business contributed $400,000 to the DNC.[83]

The head of Chinese military intelligence, General Ji Shende, told Johnny Chung, according to Chung's own account: "We like your president very much. We would like to see him reelected. I will give you 300,000 U.S. dollars. You can give it to the president and the Democrat Party."[84] Chung would funnel $100,000 of this stash into the DNC.[85]

Np Lap Seng, "a hotel tycoon in Macao with reputed links to organized crime who advises the Chinese government," according to the committee, transferred $1.4 million to Charlie Trie to fund his contributions.[86]

Wang Jun—as the committee puts it, "a Chinese arms dealer and adviser to the Chinese government"—attended a February 1996 White House coffee.[87]

So, it is an indisputable fact that the president's fund-raising operation was infiltrated by Chinese agents, many of whom were warmly welcomed as valued contributors and given intimate audiences with the president and other senior administration officials. For Clinton, this was all just the price of victory. He said, "You know, I'm not ashamed of the fact that I did the best I could within the present system. I knew we would be outspent badly in 1996, but we weren't outspent as badly as we would have been if I had laid around and done nothing."[88]

This statement betrays the kernel of lawlessness in Clinton's attitude. Its hidden premise is that any excess or illegality was justified by the self-evident goodness of his own reelection. Campaign finance

rules never could have been intended to prevent such a just and progressive result. So, Clinton could push unashamedly for new, tighter
campaign finance rules without logical contradiction. Rules were
meant for other campaigns, less golden and well intentioned.

The fund-raising scandal fizzled politically because most of the
major witnesses cut and ran. As many as 120 individuals took the
Fifth or fled the country to escape the various investigations.[89] On top
of this, the White House was able to defuse the Thompson committee's work with a shrewd combination of preemptive leaks and foot-
dragging to wait out the committee's nine-month deadline.[90]

There were several levels of wrongdoing. Some of it was just gross—
for instance, the sleepovers in the Lincoln Bedroom. Some of it was
borderline illegal. The majority view on the Federal Election Commission is that the sort of control exercised by the Clinton campaign over
the DNC fund-raising and advertising was illegal, although the law is
tangled and vague. Gore's fund-raising calls from his office without
question violated a prohibition on fund-raising from federal property,
although such a case had never been prosecuted (thus Gore's famous
phrase, "no controlling legal authority"). Finally, the foreign money and
contributions made through "straw donors" were brazenly illegal.

The administration won the political battle over the Thompson
committee's investigation. For good or ill, one of the purposes of the
independent counsel statute was precisely not to leave potential
wrongdoing to the vagaries of the political process in this way. And the
statute was still on the books. At least it appeared to be.

Attorney General Janet Reno had entered office mouthing all the
usual pieties about the statute. She told Congress in 1993, "It is
absolutely essential for the public to have confidence in the system
and you cannot do that when there is a conflict *or an appearance of
conflict* in the person who is, in effect, the chief prosecutor."[91] Her
worries about conflicts got considerably less exacting over time.

Upon his reelection, as the fund-raising allegations were swirling,
Clinton conspicuously declined to say that he would keep Reno. The
Associated Press reported that White House aides "have privately said

they wish Reno would leave in part because of her readiness to send allegations of official misconduct to independent counsels."[92] Former deputy attorney general Eric Holder says of White House officials, "They were aghast at the number of ICs she appointed."[93]

Around this time, Reno conveniently changed her interpretation of the statute. Originally, she maintained that it had to be invoked when she had an appearance of a conflict of interest. That is why she asked for independent counsel investigations in Clinton's first term of all sorts of people she didn't have any direct conflict with, friends of the president and former White House officials. By 1997, she had flipped. She decided that she had to have a potential for an actual conflict, and that she did not have one with the president or the vice president of the United States.[94]

The independent counsel statute became, perversely, a way to shield the White House from further investigation. Reno accepted a novel interpretation of the statute from career lawyers in her department, who hated the statute because it took investigative work out of their hands. They read the law as creating a high threshold for investigating senior officials, when its intent had been the opposite: to create a hair trigger to prevent the attorney general from investigating and exercising discretion in cases where she might have a conflict.[95]

She exercised such discretion, for instance, in the case of Al Gore's illegal fund-raising calls from the White House. She found interpretations of the law and facts to give him a pass, and when those were exploded, fell back essentially on the argument that Gore could not have had criminal intent.[96] This is exactly what the independent counsel statute was intended to keep her from doing in such cases. As a 1998 Congressional Research Service study pointed out, "Congress believes that the attorney general should rarely close a matter under the independent counsel law based upon finding a lack of criminal intent, due to the subjective judgments required and the limited role accorded the attorney general in the independent counsel process."[97]

Both FBI director Louis Freeh and the head of a special task force investigating the fund-raising, Charles La Bella, strenuously dissented from Reno's interpretations. La Bella argued in 1997 that "if these allegations involved anyone other than the president, vice president, senior White House, or DNC and Clinton/Gore '96 officials, an appropriate investigation would have commenced months ago without hesitation." FBI officials argued that leaving the case to the Federal Election Commission, as Justice wanted, would mean a resolution of the case long after anyone cared about it anymore.[98] Indeed, it wasn't until September 2002 that the FEC issued more than $700,000 in fines against the DNC, the Clinton/Gore campaign, and various other entities in the scandal.[99]

High officials at the Justice Department had simply grown tired of the independent counsel statute. "I always thought that the independent counsel statute made sense, just for appearance's sake," says Eric Holder. "Over time my attitude changed." So did Reno's. According to Holder, "She was pretty much like me, spoke a lot like me, but I'm not sure what the turning point was for her."[100]

By 1998, Justice officials had no stomach for subjecting more targets to independent counsel investigations nor for bypassing the career investigators at Justice: "We were looking at it from the perspective, 'Oh God, we've got to do another one of these things.' It's hard to ignore the human dimension, the real world impact on someone like [interior secretary] Bruce Babbitt's life, how it will affect that person. You also had the career guys in the department, walking around with hang-dog looks." Then there was added pressure on top of all that: "She [Reno] knew all along that she had the fate of the president—or the next president—in her hands."[101]

So, the liberal ethical apparatus had suffered a double blow. The Watergate-era campaign finance rules had been vacated, and the Watergate-era independent counsel statute had been rendered inoperative. Somewhere, Nixon must have been smiling—all of this work of his enemies undone by the very "pointy-headed liberals" who had hounded him from office. And there was more yet to come.

SEX:

Grope First, Smear Later

T HE STANDARD LINE OF CLINTON DEFENDERS after the Lewinsky scandal burst on Washington would be that Clinton's falsehoods "were just lies about sex." To say that they were "just" lies about sex, however, is to minimize what was a key aspect of Clinton's public life. Lies about sex were important to Clinton. They were deeply intertwined with his career, so much so that almost every aspect of the Lewinsky scandal had been forecast by some earlier scandal or controversy, giving the eventual conflagration an aspect of inevitability.

Clinton told Monica that he had had hundreds of affairs in Arkansas.[1] Even if he was exaggerating, he had had enough Arkansas flings that when his sex with Monica was about to be exposed, and then was made public, a variety of deceptive machinations were ready at hand: the advice to Monica to file a false affidavit, the coaching of his secretary, Betty Currie, the lying to his intimates and the public. None of these tactics was novel to Clinton, nor did he evince the least hesitation in resorting to them. They were second nature, part of the grease that had fueled his political rise.

One school of Clinton defenders long maintained that Clinton was victimized by an unfair reputation as a womanizer. By this way of thinking, the stories about Clinton's Arkansas sexual exploits were always exaggerated, the product of the fevered imaginations both of his political enemies and of flaky women trying to cash in with the tabloids.[2] This line of defense was destroyed by the Lewinsky affair. Are we really to believe that Clinton led an upright existence, piously fighting off the schemes of greedy, lying women, right up until the moment that he decided—out of the blue, in the midst of fighting a sexual harassment suit and waging high-stakes political warfare—to receive oral sex from a White House intern he had barely exchanged pleasantries with?[3]

Make no mistake: sex, and arguments about it, consumed a large part of Clinton's presidency out of his own volition. No one in the 1990s thought a president could have sex with an intern in the White House and not create an enormously distracting firestorm.

Would the nation have been better off if the bygone JFK-era journalistic ethic of covering for politicians' peccadilloes still applied? Perhaps. Clinton certainly thought so. Asked what question he would ask of JFK if given the chance, he said, "I'd want to ask him, you know, how did you do it? How'd you get away with it?"[4] But even Clinton knew those days were long gone, that he lived in a political culture of suspicion and exposure. In an appearance before Ken Starr's grand jury, he self-pityingly described how he had no curtains in the Oval Office to avoid whispering campaigns about what he might be doing there.[5]

On December 6, 1997, his lawyer in the Paula Jones case, Bob Bennett, brought Clinton a witness list with Lewinsky's name on it to talk about the case. In the course of running through all the names, Bennett asked Clinton if he had been carrying on with her. Clinton seemed offended: "Bob, do you think I'm f— crazy? Hey, look, let's move on. I know the press is watching me every minute. The right has been dying for this kind of thing from day one. No, it didn't happen." (Clinton had talked to Lewinsky on the phone and in person for a total of nearly two hours immediately prior to issuing this stark denial to Bennett.)[6]

He would, indeed, have to be "crazy." The dire consequences of such a thing were screamingly obvious. As Bennett thought to himself, "If you're caught f— around in the White House, I'm not good enough to help you."[7] Clinton did it anyway, knowing the risk, knowing it could destroy his presidency or at the very least keep him from devoting energy to much more important things.

Or seemingly much more important things. Through his actions, Clinton demonstrated the hierarchy of importance that he lived by as a politician, and sex was near the top. It was never his critics who were "obsessed with sex," but Clinton himself. Overcautious in all his other endeavors, he took enormous risks for sex. Often soft and non-confrontational, he played hardball in defense of sex. Cautious as a politician, the one area in which he was bold was in the pursuit of adultery.

The most inarguable part of Clinton's legacy is not in foreign or domestic policy. Both his critics and defenders can agree that what people will remember about Bill Clinton is that he forged a greater public tolerance for infidelity and aberrant sexual behavior. This was a project for which he was ideally suited.

"A pudgy little guy who wasn't a football star"

Of few people is it truer to say that he had "a weakness" for women than Bill Clinton. His weakness—of self-image and character—drove his affairs. When Clinton became governor of Arkansas, he was delighted by the increased availability of women. "This is fun," he told Susan McDougal. "Women are throwing themselves at me. All the while I was growing up, I was the fat boy in the Big Boy jeans."[8] Political power was a way to make up for what had been his deficient adolescent sex appeal, while the embrace of women seemed to provide him the same kind of existential affirmation he derived from political success.

This is roughly the consensus view of even Clinton loyalists. Betsey Wright, the Clinton operative who coined the phrase "bimbo eruptions" and whose job it was to deny that Clinton ever strayed, explained Clinton's character this way: "I do think his being a pudgy little guy who wasn't a football star at the time the hormones raged . . . is where a lot of his needing to be loved and absorbing the flattery comes from."[9] Blumenthal writes of Clinton's fling with Lewinsky, "It was part of the same personality that got him to the White House, with his need for affirmation, attention, and affection."[10]

When he was governor of Arkansas, Clinton's need for political and for sexual affirmation could exist mostly in harmony. As president, things got more complicated. The Lewinsky scandal featured a collision of two relative innovations in American life, both of them, as it happens, supported by feminists.

The first was the rise of oral sex. The sexual emancipation of the 1970s drove the popularity of the practice. Fellatio was a bit of a rallying cry for feminists seeking freedom from the tyranny that linked sex to the burdens of procreation.[11] Clinton apparently was a student of the trend. The Arkansas state troopers who had accompanied Governor Clinton in Little Rock said that Clinton had "researched the subject in the Bible," and with Talmudic precision, concluded that oral sex didn't count as sex.[12] Soon enough, David Kendall and a host of other Clinton lawyers would embrace this hitherto laughable distinction.

Journalist Jeffrey Toobin recounts a bizarre incident during Clinton's 1992 campaign. Clinton heard that a young woman on staff had had an erotic dream about George Stephanopoulos. This prompted Clinton to conduct a kind of on-and-off seminar with his aides about sexual fantasies. "When it was Clinton's turn to talk," Toobin writes, "he often returned to the same scenario: that he was standing in a doorway as a woman kneeled before him and performed oral sex."[13]

The other, countervailing innovation was sexual harassment law. A creation of feminists led by Catherine MacKinnon, it had its roots in the notion that all sex was, to some extent, coercive, a product of the inherent power of the patriarchy. As sexual harassment law developed, it eroded the distinction between harassment and consensual sex. "Indeed, evidence that a defendant had engaged in consensual sex in the workplace came to be seen as evidence that he also engaged in sexual harassment," writes Jeffrey Toobin.[14]

The Clintons, of course, expressed their deep support for sexual harassment law. In 1992, Hillary Clinton lionized the feminists' sexual harassment icon, Anita Hill: she had "transformed consciousness and changed history with her courageous testimony."[15] In 1994, liberal Republican congresswoman Susan Molinari proposed amending the Federal Rules of Evidence to open the past conduct of those accused of sexual harassment to more scrutiny. Clinton supported her, and was "shocked" at the possibility that her amendment might be excluded from the 1994 crime bill.[16]

So, when it came time to consider the Paula Jones sexual harassment suit, Judge Susan Webber Wright felt compelled to allow the Jones lawyers to ask Clinton about allegations regarding women five years before and five years after the incident with Jones.[17] As Judge Wright said to the Jones lawyers at one point, "I'm also aware that in sexual assault cases, the Rules of Evidence promulgated by the Violence Against Women Act [i.e., Molinari's amendment] has certainly opened it up. So I can't say that you can't call any of the witnesses."[18] Even Bob Bennett thought this was a reasonable reading of the law.[19]

It was the mix of sexual harassment law with Clinton's sexual practices and ingrained habits of hiding them that would create the combustion of the Monica scandal. The essential pattern of Clinton's conduct in the case had been set long before, as Michael Isikoff argues in his book *Uncovering Clinton*, a work of sustained reportorial brilliance. Isikoff almost from the beginning had the central insight into Clinton's corruption, which is that sex and its interaction with his official duties and the law would be his foremost vulnerability.

Isikoff chronicles what was a multi-layered "affidavit strategy" to deal with Clinton's woman problems: Clinton would deny the allegation of sexual contact with a given woman; if possible, the woman would deny it, ideally in a signed affidavit; a job might be offered to induce her cooperation if she were reluctant; if that failed to produce an affidavit of denial, Clinton's aides or friends would provide alibis for him, again ideally signed in affidavits; investigations would be undertaken into the woman's life; and accounts would be given to the press questioning her truthfulness and sexual past.

Now, sexual allegations are inherently murky and problematic, especially if they stem from incidents years past. Some charges against Clinton were genuinely outlandish and sleazy—that, for instance, he fathered a son by a prostitute.[20] But it was his continual, successful discrediting of truthful allegations that deeply corrupted Clinton's political character. His dirty-tricks operations against women and his epistemological solipsism—*if you deny it, it's not true*—reached absurd heights in the impeachment fight.

The affidavit strategy would break down in the case of Monica. For the first time, Clinton was faced with the grinding machinery of the law and with incontrovertible evidence in the form of Monica's stained dress, which made it impossible to reduce the case to a he said/she said and to attack her character.[21] The loss of the affidavit strategy was disorienting, because it had until that point stood him in such good stead. "The guy," White House chief of staff John Podesta assured congressional Democratic aides early in the Lewinsky scandal, "can f— Miss America and nobody gives a damn."[22]

"We have to destroy her story"

Clinton's 1992 campaign was a long exercise in the affidavit strategy, handled by longtime loyalist Betsey Wright. According to Isikoff, the campaign spent $100,000—with various subterfuges meant to keep the payments out of FEC reports—on private detective work related to women. Women linked to Clinton could either sign affidavits denying any relationship, or be threatened with a campaign of character assassination.[23]

The affidavit strategy had its earliest national test in the fall of 1991. *Penthouse* published an article based on the diaries of a notorious rock groupie named Connie Hamzy. In a 1984 entry, she recounted being approached by an Arkansas state trooper on behalf of Governor

Clinton at a Little Rock hotel pool. According to her account, she and Clinton looked for a place where they could have some privacy for an assignation, but couldn't find one.[24]

George Stephanopoulos strategized with Clinton about the case: "As he quickly recounted the story over the phone, I imagined his eyes getting wider and detected a little laugh in his voice. They had run into each other in the lobby of the North Little Rock Hilton. The governor was leaving a speech with a few associates when Hamzy, who had been sunbathing by the hotel pool, ran up to him, flipped down her bikini top, and asked, 'What do you think of these?' Clinton seemed to take great pleasure in picturing the scene again." Hillary, a hard-core supporter of the affidavit strategy, wasn't so amused. "We have to destroy her story," she said.[25]

Stephanopoulos gathered affidavits from three Clinton staffers confirming his innocent account that she had flashed him, and Hamzy's story died. Next was a January 1992 report in the *Star* tabloid that Clinton had affairs with five Arkansas women, among them Gennifer Flowers. "I read the just-received *Star* story to Clinton," Stephanopoulos writes. "Although he said it was false, his manner was less breezy than with Hamzy, more agitated and insistent."[26]

The allegations about these five women had first surfaced in 1990, when they had all sworn affidavits denying that they had had affairs with Clinton. That gave the campaign a good hook with which to attack the *Star* story. Stephanopoulos explains how it worked: "Since Clinton had admitted to 'problems' in his marriage, we knew there had to be at least one woman out there whose charges he couldn't deny. More likely, many more. So we tried to avoid the trap by attacking the tabloid messenger. . . . A single demonstrably wrong accusation could call an entire story into question, allowing us to focus attention on the accusers rather than the accused. Beating back the first *Star* story was relatively easy—the sworn affidavits did the real work."[27]

Then, Gennifer Flowers flipped from denying an affair to alleging an affair after the initial *Star* story appeared. The cabaret singer said she had a twelve-year romance with Clinton and had captured some

of her conversations with him on tape. The Clinton campaign immediately got the upper hand, thanks to her decision to sell her story to
a tabloid.

Flowers was typical of how Clinton had an inherent advantage—
even when he was caught on tape, as he was in conversations with
her—in rebutting womanizing allegations. For most women, coming
forward publicly would always be difficult and embarrassing; they
often needed some countervailing incentive (money, publicity,
revenge), which made their motives ripe for attack. The Clinton coun-
terattacks applied a kind of catch-22. If they had long stayed silent or
initially denied an allegation out of embarrassment or shame, changing their story opened them to accusations of lying opportunism. If
they came forward with little or no hesitation, they were dismissed as
Clinton-haters or blackmailers. In any case, since they came from a
poor state and had had an affair with a married man, they were almost
by definition dismissible as "white trash" or "floozies." Stephanopoulos was delighted by Flowers's appearance: "Gennifer's red suit and
dark-rooted hair sent exactly the right message."[28]

In many ways, the Flowers episode forecast the Lewinsky affair.

It was immediately clear that there was something to the Flowers
allegations, but those around Clinton believed a higher purpose meant
ignoring it. Stephanopoulos writes, "When Clinton wasn't listening,
James [Carville] and I speculated on exactly what that something
might have been: A blow job in a car ten years ago? A one-night stand
or two? But I couldn't bear the thought that an old dalliance dredged
up by a tabloid would curtail the professional experience of my life,
or the promise I saw in Clinton."[29]

It presaged Clinton's carefully evasive testimony in the Lewinsky
affair. During Clinton's crucial *60 Minutes* appearance with Hillary,
Steve Kroft asked, "She's alleging...a twelve-year affair with you."
Clinton replied, "That allegation is false," meaning, we now know, that
the affair must have run eleven years or less.[30] In his Paula Jones
deposition, Clinton admitted to having sex, in the sense of inter-
course, with Flowers only once, in 1977.[31]

In both cases, Clinton relied on Hillary's active and willing support. Hillary was a full participant in the debate among Clinton's top strategists over whether the Clintons should use the word "adultery" during the 60 *Minutes* semi-confession. They decided (wisely) to keep it vague, referring to "problems" in their marriage.[32]

As in the Lewinsky affair, Clinton believed that lying was the best—and unbeatable—policy. On the tapes, Clinton tells Flowers to "hang tough.... all you got to do is deny it."[33] He elaborated, "They don't have pictures. If no one says anything, then they don't have anything."[34] He suggested she sign an affidavit.[35]

And, as with Lewinsky, there were the perks of office, with Clinton attempting to keep Flowers happy by getting her a state job. Clinton took an active interest in her job search, having her call one of his staffers who helped her fill out the application for the slot. The job requirements were bent to accommodate her hiring.[36]

"I never offered anyone a job"

Allegations about women from Clinton's Arkansas past followed him into office, where they were eventually replaced by allegations about women from his White House present.

The affidavit strategy was applied with a vengeance in the case of the Arkansas state troopers. The *American Spectator* and the *Los Angeles Times* reported in December 1993 that the troopers said Clinton had used them to procure women. The troopers were credible. Bill Rempel of the *Los Angeles Times* confirmed some of the details of their tales, and reported that Clinton as president had dangled the prospect of a job when he got word that they were cooperating with the press.[37]

Stephanopoulos had a familiar feeling: "When I asked Clinton about the rumors a few days before the stories broke, his abrupt shift to fast-talking, lawyerly, hyper-explanation mode convinced me something was up. 'I never offered anyone a job,' he insisted. But he didn't deny calling the troopers (and as I soon learned, he had discussed the subject with at least one of them), which gave me a sickening sense of déjà vu. I was back in Little Rock, hearing Clinton's voice on the Gennifer tapes."[38]

He shouldn't have worried. The usual tactics would kill off the trooper story, a shrewd combination of personal pressure, a cleverly worded non-denial denial affidavit, and character attacks. There were four troopers who forged a pact to tell their story to the press and to hang together. Two of them, Roger Perry and Larry Patterson, stuck to their decision to go public until the bitter end, while the other two, Danny Ferguson and Ronnie Anderson, pulled up short, although they initially spoke to the reporters.[39]

Given the troopers' intimacy with Clinton during his governorship, which implied a certain amount of guilty knowledge, preemptive pressure had been applied on them beginning in the 1992 campaign not to talk. According to James Stewart's book *Blood Sport*, a Clinton loyalist named Buddy Young, who headed the security detail, told Larry Patterson repeatedly during the campaign to keep quiet. "If you know what's good for you, you'll keep your mouth shut."[40]

After the 1992 election, Clinton made Buddy Young the regional head of FEMA in Denton, Texas. When the troopers talked to reporters, Young, at Clinton's request, warned them about the consequences. "I represent the president of the United States," Young told Roger Perry. "If you and whoever do that, your reputations will be destroyed, and you will be destroyed." Young called the wavering Danny Ferguson and Ronnie Anderson and delivered similar messages, while dangling the possibility of a White House job for Ferguson's wife. Governor Jim Guy Tucker reinforced the point with Trooper Perry: "Roger, you will not survive this." Clinton called Danny Ferguson three times, offering him and Roger Perry federal jobs like Buddy Young's, which paid $92,300 a year. Ferguson recalled the president saying, "Dan, would you like to have a job? Would you like to come to D.C.?"[41]

The strategy was to pit Ferguson against Perry and Patterson. Once the *Los Angeles Times* and *The American Spectator* stories broke, Betsey Wright started to work the case. She tried to get Ferguson to sign an affidavit contradicting the other troopers, although she had told David Gergen that she believed the troopers solicited women for Clinton.[42] She told *Washington Post* reporter David Maraniss the same thing.[43]

Wright managed to get Ferguson's lawyer to issue a statement: "President Clinton never offered or indicated a willingness to offer any trooper a job in exchange for silence or help in shaping their stories." It was a typical semi-denial. It was technically true since, of course, the job offers hadn't been made explicitly on the condition of the troopers' silence, although everyone involved knew their purpose.[44]

If the statement from Ferguson's lawyer took the air out of the story, revelations that Perry and Patterson had lied about a car accident in 1990 to get an insurance payoff killed it. It was a classic instance of attacking the messengers, and it worked. When efforts to discredit him had reached a high pitch, Roger Perry said at a press conference, "I'm scared to death. Larry [Patterson] is scared to death. I've never felt so alone in all my life."[45] He couldn't say he hadn't been warned.

The trooper story led directly to the Paula Jones suit. In his trooper report, David Brock, with the kind of commitment to accuracy that prompted him eventually to denounce his own work as a pack of lies, described a visit by a "Paula" to a Little Rock hotel room where Clinton had beckoned her. According to Brock's fallacious account, Paula left the room after a "consummated and satisfying sexual experience with Bill Clinton."[46] After the story was published, Jones denied it, describing instead a gross come-on by Clinton that she had rebuffed. She launched a sexual harassment suit against Clinton that was legally dubious from the beginning.

When her suit was first filed in May 1994, Jones contended that Clinton's conduct had served "to impose a hostile work environment" on her.[47] This claim was hard to credit given that Jones had no contact with Clinton on a routine basis at her job at the Arkansas Industrial Development Commission. After the incident, she alleged she was "treated in a hostile and rude manner" by her superiors, and denied merit pay increases.[48] That was false. She got merit pay increases, and was bumped up in grade a few months after the incident.[49] One of her legal advisers now calls this "the weakest aspect of her case."[50]

All that said, flimsier sexual harassment suits surely have gone to trial. Clinton defenders would make much of the fact that Jones wanted money from the suit.[51] But if women claiming to be sexually harassed weren't allowed to ask for money, the sexual harassment plaintiff's bar would go out of business. And under the sexual harassment regime created by feminists, it's not unusual for women to seek monetary compensation by bringing suit for a gross incident that doesn't actually constitute harassment under the law, which is murky anyway.

According to the Supreme Court, to incur liability harassment has to be "sufficiently severe or pervasive to . . . create an abusive working environment."[52] Although it's rare, some courts have held that one "severe" incident (for instance, slapping a woman's backside) can be enough.[53] Suffice it to say that in this legal environment, a governor soliciting oral sex from a state employee, with the help of one of his troopers, certainly risked legal fallout.

As for the incident itself, what Jones alleged, or something close to it, almost certainly happened in the hotel room that day. Initially, the White House said the hotel encounter with Jones "never occurred," and that the president had never even met her.[54] The insistence on this point got dropped quickly. Early in his negotiations with the Jones lawyers, Bob Bennett was willing to have Clinton concede, "I do not challenge her claim that we met there."[55] Jones had a detailed memory of the unusual furniture arrangement of the room that would have been impossible without her having been in it.[56] In addition, the prelude to the hotel room encounter isn't really in dispute.

Clinton and Jones were at a "total quality management" conference at a Little Rock hotel. Ferguson got Clinton a room, per his usual procedure in such circumstances, by telling the hotel the governor briefly needed one to take a call from the White House.[57] Jones and Ferguson agree that the trooper chatted her up as she worked at a registration table. According to Jones, Ferguson told her that Clinton said she "made his knees knock."[58] At the time, Jones was twenty-four years old, two years older than Monica during her fling with Clinton.[59] Then, Ferguson took her to Clinton's room.[60] Presumably, she was not invited up to discuss the finer points of total quality management or the New Democratic synthesis that Clinton had rolled out for the national press in a speech two days earlier.[61] After Jones enters the room, the story inevitably dissolves into a he said/she said.

Jones says that Clinton laid on the charm, telling her, "I love the way your hair came down your back, the middle of your back, and your curves." Clinton got steadily more aggressive with her, his face growing "beet red." He dropped his pants and asked her—in a "horny ass way," according to Jones—to perform oral sex on him.[62] Offended, she left. Clinton never gave his version of events aside from fuzzy denials through his lawyers.[63]

Clinton's defenders made much of the fact that Jones's older sister Charlotte and her husband eventually denounced Paula and called her story "a stupid lie."[64] There was plenty of corroboration for Paula's story, however, including from Charlotte herself. She originally told Isikoff that Paula had told her the night of the incident that Clinton asked for sex in the hotel room. Paula's other sister, Lydia Cathay, also told Isikoff that Paula had told her about the incident that night, and cried about it, worried about losing her job. Pam Blackard, who worked with Jones at the conference that day, says that a shaking Jones told her all about it as soon as she returned from the room. Another woman, Deborah Ballantine, said Jones also told her about the incident at the time.[65]

The discrediting machinery inevitably began, hitting the usual themes. James Carville dismissed Jones's complaint as what happens when you "drag a hundred dollars through a trailer park."[66] As soon as he was hired as Clinton's counsel on the case, Washington super-lawyer Bob Bennett began telling reporters that there were nude pictures of

Jones.[67] Bennett had a lawyer for Danny Ferguson (sued for defamation by Jones) subpoena men who supposedly could speak to Jones's promiscuity.[68]

Conservative lawyers from Dallas—paid for by the conservative Rutherford Institute—took over the Jones case in September 1997 from two Virginia lawyers who had a falling out with her over a proposed settlement.[69] The Dallas lawyers broadened the suit to include the charge that Clinton rewarded women who had sex with him.[70] This opened the way to rummaging more widely, if not in Clinton's bedroom, at least in his hotel rooms and hideaway offices. Given Clinton's vulnerabilities, it made obvious sense for him to settle (even Monica thought so[71]), but Hillary was against it. In her memoir, she implausibly writes that she opposed a settlement for the sake of the presidency: "[I]t would set a terrible precedent for a president to pay money to rid himself of a nuisance suit."[72] Did she help discredit Gennifer Flowers for the sake of the institution of the presidency too?

Disentangling the various strands that make the knot of the Clinton marriage is work appropriate for an army of marriage counselors, psychotherapists, and novelists. But one thing is clear: Hillary was an adamant supporter of the affidavit strategy. In the Jones case, she interviewed Bob Bennett for the job and drove the hard-line posture in the case. Clinton was in no position to contradict her. He told Bennett that he didn't want to disappoint Hillary by settling.[73] Her determination and toughness in such circumstances reflected the fact that the career she was ultimately saving was her own. But in this fight, the affidavit strategy had met its match.

"I may have even kissed her on the forehead"

Jones's charge was initially disbelieved as mere scandal mongering. Surely no one as smart and as sensitive as Clinton could do something so stupid and crude. But the evidence of Clinton's sexual recklessness began to mount.

Kathleen Willey, a Richmond socialite and former White House volunteer, emerged to tell her story of a visit with Clinton in the Oval Office. She went to see him about a job in November 1993 because her husband was in grave financial trouble (she apparently had more access than the director of Central Intelligence, the director of the FBI, and most of the cabinet). Clinton allegedly took her to his hide-away office, groped her, and put her hand on his erect penis. Willey says Clinton's face was, in a detail that echoed Jones, beet red. Bennett originally told Isikoff that Clinton had "no specific recollection" of meeting Willey that day. But by the time Clinton made his deposition in the Jones case, he was willing to concede that he had met Willey that day, but had done nothing sexual, although he tried to comfort her: "I embraced her, I put my arms around her, I may have even kissed her on the forehead."[74]

Willey had corroborating evidence from the time. She told Linda Tripp, who noticed her lipstick was smeared off, about the incident immediately afterwards. A friend of Willey's, Julie Hyatt Steele, initially confirmed Willey's story to Isikoff, but later said that Willey told her to lie. Prompted by Clinton's lawyers, Steele signed what was almost certainly a false affidavit denying any knowledge whatsoever of the incident. The case eventually got very confusing, but it remains likely that Kathleen Willey was telling the truth about her encounter with Clinton. When Julie Hyatt Steele was prosecuted by Starr for false statements in the controversy, two new witnesses said Willey had told them about Clinton's come-on at the time, giving Willey's version additional credibility.[75]

Nevertheless, the affidavit strategy still worked in discrediting her. There was the false Steele affidavit, and attempts to influence Willey. Big-shot Democratic fund-raiser Nathan Landow flew Willey from Richmond to his Maryland home and suggested she not tell her story in the Jones case.[76] After Willey appeared on *60 Minutes* to describe her encounter, the White House released fond letters she had written to Clinton after he had allegedly groped her.[77] The fact was that her

husband had committed suicide, and Willey, who had been a political supporter of the president, needed job help.

Clinton's fling with Lewinsky—about which there is no doubt—
sheds light on both the Jones and Willey allegations. It wouldn't even
occur to someone to receive oral sex from a near-stranger[78] unless
such quick assignations were a practice. And there were others. Isikoff
got an anonymous call in the summer of 1997 from a woman who said
she had an experience similar to Willey's. She included one detail that
would seem fantastic until the Starr report was released. When she
had rebuffed Clinton, she told Isikoff, the president turned his back
on her. "I think," she said, "he finished the job himself."[79]

Such rushed sex and attempted sex would be impossible without
brazen come-ons perhaps slipping into physical aggression. During the
1992 primaries, when rumors linked Clinton with former Miss America Elizabeth Gracen, Harry Thomason helped Gracen get a part in a
TV miniseries that was filming—conveniently—in Croatia. Gracen
issued a statement denying that she had ever had sex with Clinton.
But she later admitted that she had had a one-night stand with Clinton, when she was twenty-one years old and serving her term as Miss
America. Her testimony included one crucial, chilling detail—Clinton bit her lip that night. Juanita Broaddrick said Clinton had bitten
her lip in her allegation that Clinton had raped her in 1978.[80]

It was from a vulnerable position amidst the stew of his satyriasis
that Clinton would be deposed in the Jones case. Going forward with
the deposition was an act of near-insanity, but was driven by the same
damage-control logic that applied in Whitewater: it was never a convenient time to deal with the embarrassment that would attend coming clean—in this instance, settling the case. Bob Bennett's job was
to try to get the Supreme Court to declare the president immune from
civil suits, and failing that, at least push the case beyond the 1996
election. He succeeded in the latter, but failed in the former when the
court ruled 9–0 in May 1997 that the case could go forward.[81]

Bob Bennett worried about Clinton lying in his deposition—in
particular lying about Marilyn Jo Jenkins, an executive with the

Arkansas Power and Light Company. Trooper Danny Ferguson said that he had brought her to the basement of the Arkansas governor's mansion four times for forty-five-minute visits after the November 1992 election, usually before 6 a.m. Bennett urged Clinton not to lie about his relationship with her, telling him if he committed perjury, "You are dead. You are dead!" Clinton was noncommittal. "I hear you," he said.[82]

It was, of course, another woman on the witness list who presented Clinton with an unavoidable problem.

"Very soul-searching, very wanting, very needing"

Lewinsky started flirting with Clinton at the beginning of her internship in July 1995. Lewinsky described their first meeting thus: "When it came time to shake my hand, the smile disappeared, the rest of the crowd disappeared and we shared an intense but brief sexual exchange." Clinton told Monica later, according to her account, that upon first seeing her, "I knew that one day I would kiss you."[83]

During the government shutdown, when the White House staff was reduced from 430 to about ninety, Monica had her opportunity for closer contact. Briefly alone with the president the afternoon of November 15, 1995, she flashed her thong. Clinton got the message. Later in the evening, he kissed her. His eyes were, according to Lewinsky, "very soul-searching, very wanting, very needing, and very loving."[84] Later that night, they arranged to meet again. She took off her underwear prior to this encounter.[85] He put his hands down her pants and she performed oral sex on him, while he talked to a congressman on the phone.[86]

Immediately, Clinton realized that being sexually serviced by an intern could be a political problem. He pulled on her intern pass, and told her so. Even when Clinton testified before Ken Starr's grand jury, he wouldn't admit to having had sex with an intern, insisting that the sex didn't begin until early 1996, when Lewinsky had been made a low-level full-time employee.[87] Clinton included a version of this lie in his "confession" to the grand jury: "I regret that what began as a friendship came to include this conduct."[88] Clinton blandly described to the grand jury his encounter with Lewinsky during the government shutdown this way: "One night she brought me some pizza. We had some remarks."[89]

Clinton and Lewinsky settled into an on-again, off-again relationship that would continue until May 1997.[90] It was usually tawdry, sometimes farcical. It wasn't until their third session that Clinton wasn't on the phone while she performed.[91] They usually repaired to a windowless hallway off Clinton's private office. He didn't allow her to bring him to completion until their two last encounters, fatefully staining her dress. He often stood up to ease his sore back by leaning against a doorway—an almost exact enactment of the fantasy he told his aides about in 1992.[92] So, at least one of his presidential ambitions had been accomplished by 1995.

There was always a bit of a dance with the Secret Service agents, and, in one incident, Clinton had to zip up quickly because someone walked into the Oval Office and he had to go out to investigate. "I just remember laughing," Lewinsky said, "because he had walked out there and he was visibly aroused, and I just thought it was funny."[93] In yet another incident, when Lewinsky tried to sneak out of the hideaway office, she was blocked by a locked door and had to find an alternative exit. She came across Clinton masturbating in the office of the deputy assistant to the president.[94]

Lewinsky wasn't just an easy partner for Clinton; she understood, and enthusiastically embraced, the ethic of the affidavit strategy. This is why Sidney Blumenthal, who pours scorn on nearly all women alleging to have had sexual encounters with Clinton, showers Lewinsky with warm understanding.[95] It was almost unnecessary for Clinton to suggest that she sign a false affidavit in the Jones case. "You know the truth, Linda?" Lewinsky asked Linda Tripp, who was secretly taping their conversations. "What's the truth? The truth is you're either an FOB [Friend of Bill's] or not." She understood implicitly the subjective idea of truth that animated the affidavit strategy. "This is gonna sound really stupid," she told Tripp, "but other than how you feel yourself, like inside, what is the advantage of telling the truth? What advantage do you see for yourself? Where will that put you? What does that do for you?"[96]

The desirability of the convenient lie was, nonetheless, hammered into her constantly. Lewinsky said that the president told her, "If the two people who are involved say it didn't happen—it didn't happen."[97] She asked Vernon Jordan, who did his share of lying to Starr's grand jury,[98] "What if someone's been tapping my phone?" He answered, "Well, as long as you say it didn't happen, it didn't happen."[99] Lewinsky shared the theory with Betty Currie: "As long as no one saw us— and no one did—then nothing happened." Currie replied, "Don't want to hear it. Don't say any more"—presumably because if she didn't hear it, it didn't happen.[100]

In her "points to make in an affidavit" memo to Tripp, Lewinsky had the lines down almost exactly. Early sinister speculation was that this memo had been written by someone other than Monica, but this underestimated both her intelligence and how thoroughly she had absorbed the Clinton ethic. With regard to Kathleen Willey, Lewinsky recommended that Tripp swear: "You now do not believe that what [Willey] claimed happened really happened. You now find it completely plausible that she herself smeared her lipstick, untucked her blouse, etc. You never saw her go into the Oval Office, or come out of the Oval Office. You have never observed the president behaving inappropriately with anybody." Lewinsky even suggested in the memo how to denounce herself: she was "this huge liar," and "I found out she left the WH because she was stalking the P[resident] or something like that."[101]

Through all the deception, Clinton maintained a remarkable posture of self-righteousness. The Clintons initially insisted that in the Lewinsky scandal Clinton was suffering for his sheer, reckless, dogged generosity. Hillary told Sid Blumenthal that Bill had "ministered" to Monica: "He ministers to troubled people all the time. He's done it dozens if not hundreds of times. He does it out of religious conviction and personal temperament." When Blumenthal in turn told the president that he had to be more careful about his tendency to help others, Clinton explained: "It's very difficult for me to do that, given how I am. I want to help people."[102]

Help people . . . do what?

"Everybody around here is crying and helpless"

There were two overriding factors that would ultimately save Clinton in the Lewinsky affair: his wife and a broad cultural shift in the American public that predisposed it to go easy on him (the impeachment fight will be examined in the next chapter).

Hillary's support was never in much doubt. All she was being asked to do was what she had always done, in a more spectacular setting: cover for her husband and stick with the affidavit strategy. Hillary writes that at the end of August 1998 she "hadn't decided whether to fight for my husband and my marriage, but I was resolved to fight for my president."[103] This is a self-serving and highfalutin way of saying: 1) she was making a political decision; 2) yes, she was going to stay with Clinton because a breach would have doomed his presidency, and her own political future.

As always, she was Clinton's fiercest fighter. When the Lewinsky story broke, she called Harry Thomason. "Harry, you've got to get to Washington right away—everybody around here is crying and helpless."[104] When in her famous *Today* show appearance, she said twice that the charges against her husband would not be "proven true," she was speaking the language of the affidavit strategy.[105] Upon returning from the appearance, she told Thomason, "I guess that will teach them to f— with us."[106] Clinton's famous line after a Dick Morris poll showed that he couldn't confess and survive politically was, "Well, we just have to win, then."[107] According to Blumenthal, Clinton used the same phrase with Hillary: "Well, we'll just have to win."[108]

They did win, at least in a sense that they survived, and it would have been impossible without Hillary. In retrospect, she would depend on a couple of key dishonesties to explain her support. The spectacle of a wife complicit in her husband's infidelities and in his efforts to attack those telling the truth about them would be too creepy for comfort. So Hillary wrote in her memoir that—after eight months of defending her husband in utter good faith—she was shocked when Clinton told her on August 15 that he had been lying and had actually carried on with Lewinsky.[109] If she was surprised, she was one of few people in the country. Even Sidney Blumenthal, whose loyalty was absolute, had "nagging doubts."[110]

Two days after Hillary supposedly first learned of this betrayal, and was crushed and infuriated by it, Clinton delivered a confession speech to the nation that was partly a blistering attack on Ken Starr. After the speech, Blumenthal writes, "I could hear the president and Hillary bantering in the background. Whatever they would have to do between themselves to get over this episode, in the challenge to their marriage and the presidency they were still working as a team. Without that, nothing was possible."[111] Exactly.

Hillary also dishonestly suggests that Judge Susan Webber Wright absolved Clinton of having made the come-on that launched the Jones suit. She writes that in April 1998, "Wright had decided to throw out the Paula Jones lawsuit, finding that it lacked factual or legal merit."[112] Wright, however, did not find that the incident had never happened—how could she, given the weight of evidence?—only that it didn't constitute sexual harassment. Jones appealed the decision, but before her appeal could be heard Clinton settled the case for $850,000.[113]

Besides Hillary, Clinton also had a few powerful cultural currents on his side. He represented a new masculine ideal that came to prominence in the 1990s—the perpetual adolescent. It was an ideal borne of an age of divorce and feminist assertion, of absent fathers and the erosion of adult authority generally, of self-expression and psychobabble. It could be seen in the Internet billionaires with their teenage affectations, and the studied immaturity of superstar actors like Sean Penn and Brad Pitt. As the protagonist of the novel *Fight Club*—a book that grapples with the discontents of contemporary masculinity—says, "I'm a thirty-year-old boy. I knew my dad for about six years, but I don't remember anything.... What you see at fight club is a generation of men raised by women." Clinton—in 1998, a fifty-two-year-old boy—would understand.[114]

There was much that was gross and exploitative in Clinton's behavior—not knowing Monica's name when they first had sex, the gesture of contempt of talking on the phone while she was performing. But there was something prissy and weak at the same time—the strict rules Clinton imposed on how far she was allowed to go with him, his whiny defensiveness in arguments with her (he pathetically told her at one point, "It is illegal to threaten the president").[115] All of this is what one would expect from a libidinous, insecure seventeen-year-old boy. Lewinsky was the aggressor with Clinton, creating in their relationship, as Richard Posner puts it, "virtually a reversal of the traditional sex roles."[116]

One of the disturbing aspects of the relationship is that, even though it was sex first, conversation later, eventually there was a fair amount of conversation. The president and the twenty-two-year-old had a connection. They talked approximately fifty times over the phone (roughly a dozen of the conversations included phone sex). They spoke the same language, the same apotheosis of feelings and pop psychology, with a strong a dash of egotism on top. As Clinton put it, according to Lewinsky, they were both "emotive and full of fire."[117]

There was a connection between Clinton's promiscuous expression of his feelings and his sexual promiscuity, between his lack of emotional control and his lack of self-control in general. The sterner, traditional masculine virtues of loyalty (including to one's spouse), responsibility, courage, honor, duty, and chivalry were all alien to him. Clinton's masculine ideal, in contrast, was all about selfishness. He even talked of his exposure in the Lewinsky affair as an excellent adventure in self-discovery.

"You know, some people say to me, 'I feel so terrible for you. It's been so awful what has been publicized to the whole country; the whole world,'" he said in September 1998. "Believe it or not, and I know it's hard for people to believe, that has not bothered me very much because of the opportunity I've had to seek spiritual counseling and advice and to think through this and to try to focus much more on how I can properly atone, how I can be forgiven, and then how I can go back to healing with my family."[118]

It was Clinton's good fortune that one of the aspects of heedless maleness he was most drawn to—sexual gratification—happened to have become a core value of contemporary liberalism. Clinton's liberal defenders professed outrage at the invasion of his privacy. This was an imprecise expression of their true concern.

Journalist Ramesh Ponnuru has written of the liberal solicitousness of privacy in 1998 this way: "They would not go to the ramparts for freedom of association in private clubs, or defend taxpayers' financial privacy from the IRS. The danger that child welfare agencies might intrude on private matters of family discipline does not stir them. It is the allegedly privacy-trampling religious right that is most exercised about schools' probing of the emotional and family life of children. In the Lewinsky scandal, privacy simply meant sex. Nothing else would be protected by the shield of privacy."[119]

Sex would be protected to buffer it from any moral judgment that might endanger the gains from the sexual liberation of the 1970s. On the issues of crime, welfare, and race, the public was repudiating cultural liberalism, and Clinton tried to restrain liberalism in these areas. But when it came to sex, cultural liberalism had swept the field, except for the isolated "religious right." Clinton exploited this. His Lewinsky defense advanced a radical claim: that it's "just sex." It is not adultery. It is not the exploitation of a young woman. No moral judgments need apply.

If people didn't necessarily embrace this sexual amoralism in their own lives—the 1990s experienced a slight retreat from sexual irresponsibility—they weren't willing to judge anyone who did. As Francis Fukuyama notes of this non-judgmentalism, "It is as if Emile Durkheim's prediction that in a modern society, the only values uniting people would be the value of individualism itself had come true:

people reserve their greatest moral indignation for moralism on the part of other people."[120]

Despite having this significant factor in his favor, Clinton inevitably lost moral authority through his sex with Lewinsky and lies about it. A piqued Hillary, of all people, captured it best. During a strategy session before his August 17 confession speech, she remarked to her husband, "You're the president of the United States—I guess."[121]

IMPEACHMENT:

An Indelible Stain

B Y THE END OF 1997, THE ERA of the independent counsel seemed set to end in a whimper. "We were essentially through with the Whitewater case," Starr says, "and would have moved on to a report-writing phase."[1] Then came Monica.

"It was in January 1998, relatively early," Starr recalls, "when I was at an ABA meeting with the board of editors of the *ABA Journal*, on which I was serving at the time. And I was calling into the office several times a day on various matters and that's when I learned that some important information might be coming to our attention." The information was shocking—at least to anyone who hadn't been grappling with the Clinton White House for years. "I was not shocked," says Starr. "I guess chagrined and disappointed."[2]

Once the essentials of the Lewinsky story became clear—sex with an intern, attempts to get her to lie and win her silence, false statements in sworn testimony—Starr's path was obvious and nearly inevitable: an investigation leading to an impeachment referral to Congress.

Defending Clinton in the Lewinsky affair depends largely on attacking his critics: they hated Clinton, they talked to one another ("the vast right-wing conspiracy"), they funded efforts to investigate him (often through the infamous anti-Clinton billionaire Richard Mellon Scaife), they didn't really care about sexual harassment, they were frustrated at his political success, they were fascinated ("obsessed") by his sexual transgressions.

All of this, to some extent, is true. It's called having a boisterous opposition. That is not something new in American life, nor, obviously, should it be unwelcome. It is political competition that, despite its simplifications and passions, achieves a rough sort of justice by ensuring that the vulnerabilities of each side are exposed rather than safely hidden away.

Even if Clinton's opposition was wrong about certain particulars or countenanced excesses along the way, its essential critique of him proved dead-on. Clinton vindicated it both by his selfish and reckless behavior and by lying about it under oath and to the American public. "We didn't do anything to him," says George Conway, one of the conservative lawyers who secretly aided Paula Jones. "He did it all to himself."[3] Mickey Kantor, former Clinton secretary of commerce and trade representative, makes exactly the same point: "It's his own fault. No one did this to him. He did it to himself. No one brought this on him except himself."[4]

Clinton was justly impeached by the House, and should have been removed from office by the Senate. He escaped that fate, but impeachment turned out to be a condign punishment anyway: an indelible stain on his legacy that he and his defenders will spend all time railing against and futilely attempting to erase.

"I never touched her, right?"

When Linda Tripp called Starr's office with her tale of Clinton's efforts to keep the former intern quiet, she was offering evidence of a possible ongoing crime. Her allegations had a thematic connection to the rest of Starr's work, since they involved attempts to ensure someone's non-cooperation with a court proceeding by offering job help. Vernon Jordan was the human bridge from Whitewater to Monica. Of Webster Hubbell's post-Justice Department, pre-indictment retainers, $62,775 had come from Revlon, thanks to the good offices of Vernon Jordan, who was on the company's board.[5] And here was Jordan again, aiding in the job search of a young woman whom it was very important to keep happy.

When Starr's deputy Jackie Bennett called deputy attorney general Eric Holder to apprise him of the situation, Holder's reaction was, "Wha-wha-what?" There was really no option but expanding Starr's authority to deal with the case. With *Newsweek* close to publishing an article on the affair, Holder says, "It was pretty clear to us—there wouldn't be time to get somebody else in there," and if the opportunity had been missed to move against Clinton and Jordan before they were aware of the investigation, "we would've been criticized, justifiably."[6]

It is fantastical to suggest that Ken Starr or any other independent counsel should have—or even could have—winked at a president's lying under oath and encouraging someone else to do the same. As journalist Byron York has pointed out, these were exactly the sort of crimes the independent counsel statute was written to address. "The law's authors were particularly concerned about perjury and obstruction of justice because they believed those were the crimes that future Nixons might engage in to keep secrets from the American people. In fact, Section 593(b)3 of the law, which laid out the scope of the independent counsel's jurisdiction, gave him the authority to prosecute any crimes that he might discover in the course of his investigation, 'including perjury, obstruction of justice, destruction of evidence, and intimidation of witnesses.' These were the only crimes specifically mentioned in the statute—and they all involved concealment of the truth."[7]

There's no escaping the fact that President Clinton committed crimes in the Lewinsky affair. First and foremost, he perjured himself repeatedly—though his defenders would perform legalistic dances to try to keep the "p-word" from applying to his false statements.

Their chief argument was that his lies about Lewinsky in the Jones deposition were immaterial to the case, and therefore not technically perjury. Judge Wright did ultimately exclude evidence related to Lewinsky from the Jones case, but that was not because it was immaterial. She stipulated at the time that Clinton's Lewinsky testimony "might be relevant."[8] Later, she elaborated. "Contrary to numerous assertions, this court did not rule that evidence of the Lewinsky matter was irrelevant or immaterial to the issues in plaintiff's case."[9] She was making a prudential judgment that once the Lewinsky matter had come under investigation by Starr—who would want to tightly control anything touching on his work—keeping it in the Jones case would only make for needless complications. In any event, as Richard A. Posner writes in *An Affair of State*, "materiality is assessed as of the time the lie was uttered, and not with the wisdom of hindsight."[10]

Besides materiality, there are two other elements to perjury: falsehood and the intent to deceive. Clinton's defenders say his testimony was literally truthful by the definition Clinton assigned his words. But witnesses cannot create their own private languages. Their words must be understood by their common meaning, by which standard Clinton's testimony was clearly false.[11] As for intent, Clinton was open about his desire to deceive. "I misled people . . ." he said in his August 17, 1998, confession speech to the nation. "I can only tell you I was motivated by many factors. First, by a desire to protect myself from the embarrassment of my own conduct."[12]

Clinton's lies in the Monica affair descended in a thick fog. When he testified in his Jones deposition on January 17, 1998, he lied, most fundamentally, when he denied having sex with Lewinsky. The Jones lawyers offered a definition of sex drawn from the Violence Against Women Act, and Wright pared it down to: "contact with the genitalia, anus, groin, breast, inner thigh, or buttocks of any person with an attempt to arouse or gratify the sexual desire of any person."[13] Even by Clinton's solipsistic and implausible interpretation of this definition—i.e., that it was possible for Lewinsky to have sex with him while he wasn't having sex with her—Clinton lied, since it is obvious that he touched Lewinsky in places that qualified as sex under the definition.

When at the end of the deposition Clinton's attorney Bob Bennett brandished a copy of Lewinsky's affidavit denying that she had had sex with the president, Clinton maintained that her affidavit was "absolutely true."[14] Yet, even accepting Clinton's interpretation of the definition of sex, and even accepting his version of their encounters in which he never touched her inappropriately, Lewinsky's statement was absolutely false. Bennett wouldn't have helped lock his client into this categorical denial unless he thought Clinton was denying sex entirely—which by any reasonable understanding he was.

From his denial of sex with Lewinsky, Clinton's lies rolled steadily on. He lied when he said he had no memory of being alone with Lewinsky. He lied when he said he didn't recall giving any gifts to Lewinsky (three weeks earlier, he'd given her a Rockettes blanket, a New York City skyline pin, sunglasses, cherry chocolates, a stuffed animal, and other trinkets). He lied when he said that he talked to Lewinsky about the possibility of her being subpoenaed in the Jones case only once, and that in passing and jokingly. He lied when he said that he didn't know about Lewinsky's subpoena in the Jones case when he talked to her for the last time. He lied when he denied that Vernon Jordan kept him updated about Lewinsky's status in the Jones case.[15]

After the impeachment fight had burned out in April 1999, Wright—the same judge Hillary hails for allegedly totally vindicating Clinton in the Jones suit—sanctioned Clinton for contempt of court. She wrote that there is "simply no escaping the fact" that Clinton gave "intentionally false" answers to questions from the Jones lawyers in a way "designed to obstruct the judicial process."[16] Even Abbe Lowell, chief investigator for the Democrats on the House Judiciary Committee, had told his fellow Democrats upon first evaluating the evidence, "Perjury in the deposition. No question that he lied."[17]

Clinton's testimony before Ken Starr's grand jury in August, after he had finally decided to admit to the affair, was an encore performance of his civil deposition lies. He lied when he denied having sex with Lewinsky, and lied when he said their "inappropriate" relationship didn't begin until 1996.[18] He lied when he said his civil deposition in the Jones case had been truthful. He lied when he denied being alone with Lewinsky. He lied when he said that, when he coached Betty Currie with a series of rhetorical questions based on falsehoods, he was merely trying to jog his own memory. He lied when he said he hadn't told Currie to get back the gifts he had lied about not remembering giving to Lewinsky. And he lied in denying that he had lied to his aides in the wake of the Lewinsky revelations.[19]

With Clinton, the lies double back on themselves until he's telling lies about his lies, in a perfect storm of dishonesty and obfuscation.

The lies to his confidantes alone are extraordinary. There's nothing criminal, of course, about lying to your friends and advisors, but it is a damning statement about how you view them, and your obligations to them, as people and colleagues. Clinton told his chief of staff, Erskine Bowles, as soon as the Lewinsky story broke in the *Washington Post*, "Erskine, I want you to know that this story is not true." Clinton denied the story to presidential aide Sidney Blumenthal, telling him that Lewinsky had demanded sex and "threatened him." Blumenthal told the grand jury, "It was a very heartfelt story, he was pouring out his heart, and I believed him." Clinton went further with deputy chief of staff John Podesta, maintaining that he hadn't had sex with Lewinsky "in any way whatsoever... including oral sex."[20]

In addition to his perjury, Clinton was guilty of obstruction of justice. By suggesting to Lewinsky that she give an affidavit to the Jones lawyers, Clinton couldn't have been suggesting anything other than that she lie, and deny the relationship, in order to avoid being deposed.[21] That is the only possible interpretation, unless we believe that Clinton was urging Lewinsky to expose the relationship preemptively and launch the near-destruction of his presidency.

It seems almost certain that—although both he and Currie deny it—Clinton sent Betty Currie to pick up from Lewinsky the gifts he had given her, in order to keep this evidence safe from a subpoena.[22]

As a general matter, Currie went out of her way to protect Clinton in her testimony, which was understandable. As Clinton speechwriter Michael Waldman writes in his memoir, "Betty was one of us; an experienced political operative who had worked in the War Room for Carville and then as Warren Christopher's secretary."[23]

Clinton's defenders say his astonishing coaching of Betty Currie was only meant to prepare her for the coming media storm, i.e., to get her to lie to colleagues and to the press, not necessarily in a court proceeding.[24] In his Jones deposition, however, Clinton repeatedly invoked Currie, and told the Jones lawyers, "Those are questions you'd have to ask her."[25] He knew, then, that she was a potential witness. The next day he repeated a series of lies to Currie in the form of questions: "Monica came on to me, and I never touched her, right?"[26] And Clinton's second session with Currie came after he knew that she had been subpoenaed by Starr's grand jury—so there is no doubt that he knew he was tampering with a witness.[27]

Clinton's supporters make much of the fact that Clinton never starkly told anyone to lie. That kind of explicitness, however, is not necessary to commit obstruction. Nor should it be. Clinton apparently never explicitly asked Monica Lewinsky for oral sex either—he just made gestures or unzipped.[28]

"Within inches of losing the presidency"

Clinton's offenses created a one-way road to an impeachment referral. The independent counsel statute essentially demanded it as a matter of law: an independent counsel, said the statute, "shall advise the House of Representatives of any substantial and credible information . . . that may constitute grounds for an impeachment."[29] Creating this automatic pilot toward impeachment was one of the purposes of the misbegotten statute in the first place. It relieved Congress of the political risk of initiating impeachment proceedings itself.[30]

After the opinion polls held up for Clinton and the Democrats stood firm behind him, the defense of Clinton's conduct would be that it was unreasonable to conclude that it constituted grounds for impeachment. Few had this reaction at first blush.[31] Even Hillary allowed during her famous *Today* show appearance that if the charges against Clinton were proven true, it "would be a very serious offense."[32] It was only later that Clinton sympathizers downgraded perjury and obstruction of justice as crimes, indeed almost read them out of the criminal code.

Later, when the controversy neared its end, it seemed outlandish to think Clinton could have been forced from office over it. But that was only an illusion created after the fact. It could have been different—for instance, in August when Democratic senator Joe Lieberman of Connecticut condemned Clinton from the Senate floor, along with fellow Democratic senators Bob Kerrey of Nebraska and Daniel Patrick Moynihan of New York. "I'm pretty convinced," says Lanny Davis, who had left the White House, but was assisting in its defense, "that Clinton was within inches of losing the presidency then. Because that could have sent a wave of Democratic senators away from him under the cover of Joe Lieberman and Bob Kerrey. And then he would have been very, very hard pressed to stay in office."

Davis continues, "I was actually one of the point men on the Lieberman side. But I had a belief that turned out to be right: That if Joe Lieberman made a moral statement on the floor of the Senate but did not call for Clinton's resignation, he would save the Clinton presidency. He would serve as an outlet for the pivot that I thought the American people were prepared for: He would condemn the conduct, pivot, 'but it's not worth driving him out of office.' So all I did was call Joe and ask him what his intentions were. He told me, and I thought it was exactly the right pivot, and I told the White House, 'I wouldn't touch Lieberman.'"[33]

The pivot, of course, worked. So did Clinton's grand strategy from the beginning. Clinton took the path of a calculated and deliberate lie to the public ("I did not have sexual relations with that woman, Ms. Lewinsky") to hold him over during the period of initial peril when a dip in the polls might have sent Democrats fleeing. Time was on his side. The shock of the allegations wore off and patience with the investigation wore thin. Clinton worked to string the scandal along with delaying tactics that required personalizing the office of the presidency and leveraging it to the protection of his crimes.

Clinton tried to make the presidency a kind of sultanate. White House counsel Lloyd Cutler had issued an opinion in 1994 saying that the administration would never invoke executive privilege in a case involving an official's personal wrongdoing. Four years later, Clinton's personal lawyer was filing briefs maintaining: "In a very real and significant way, the objectives of William J. Clinton, the person, and his administration (Clinton White House) are one and the same."[34] The personal hadn't just become the political—it had enveloped the presidency in a fleshy embrace.[35]

The White House and its allies took advantage of delays caused by its unwarranted claims of executive privilege and other stonewalling to dirty up Starr.

They accused Starr of resorting to "Gestapo" tactics in the course of trying to create a "police state"—for undertaking an investigation authorized by Clinton's own attorney general.[36] They accused him of being "obsessed with sex"—although Starr couldn't help it that Clinton had happened to perjure himself over his sexual conduct during a deposition in a sexual harassment case. It was a little like attacking a bank examiner for being "obsessed with fraud."

They complained about the harsh treatment of Monica Lewinsky when she was confronted in a room of the Ritz-Carlton Hotel at the Pentagon City Mall by the FBI and Starr's prosecutors, who tried to flip her against the president. This is nonsense. As even Starr critic Jeffrey Toobin writes, "Lewinsky's treatment in the hotel room was entirely appropriate for an important witness in an unfolding criminal investigation."[37]

Much is made of the fact that Starr's team tried to dissuade her from calling her lawyer, Frank Carter. That was because Starr's prosecutors feared that he was a party to the effort to have Lewinsky lie in the Jones suit, and that Carter was in league with Vernon Jordan.[38]

Clinton's defenders placed such emphasis on Lewinsky's not calling Carter because if she had, they argue, Carter could have given Clinton's lawyer Bob Bennett a heads-up that the president's assignations with Lewinsky had been exposed.[39] In that circumstance, Clinton may have found an excuse—although it would have been difficult given the firestorm of speculation it would have ignited—to put off his fateful Jones deposition the next day to play for more time and devise a new strategy. But if the deposition had gone forward anyway, it is hard to believe that Clinton would have told the truth even with a heads-up.

He knew the political consequences of admitting an affair with an intern. If Clinton thought that Lewinsky was not cooperating with Starr, he certainly would have lied, because his operating theory in all such cases was that if both parties denied the affair there was no way it could be proven. After all, it was only Clinton's stain on Monica's dress—and the knowledge Clinton gained that Starr's office was on to it when it asked him for a blood test—that later forced him into admitting to the affair.

As it was, Clinton already had plenty of warning not to lie. Feeling Bill's pain *and* his self-pity, Hillary writes, "Bill had been blindsided, and the unfairness of it all made me more determined to stand with him to combat the charges."[40] But, even without the benefit of a tip-off from Carter, Bennett warned Clinton prior to the deposition, "The only thing you have to worry about is if you lie in there. The crazies will come after you. They will try to impeach you if you lie. That's the only thing to worry about."[41] What more did Clinton need to keep him from lying—a muzzle?

There were many other anti-Starr attacks. Clinton's defenders accused Starr of being so zealous that he wanted to wire Monica Lewinsky and send her into incriminating encounters with the president and Vernon Jordan. "That was never a viable option," says Starr deputy Jackie Bennett.[42] Clinton was distrustful of Lewinsky already. The thought was, if everything broke the right way, to have Lewinsky talk to Betty Currie in recorded conversations, and perhaps flip Currie.

But even that was unlikely, given that Michael Isikoff was preparing to break the story in *Newsweek*.

Clinton's defenders excoriated Starr for setting a "perjury trap" for the president, by allowing him to testify in the Jones case without telling him that his affair with Lewinsky had been exposed. A true "perjury trap," however, involves manipulating someone predisposed to tell the truth into lying. Clinton was perfectly prepared to lie, and the moral responsibility for his lies is all his own.

They charged that Starr leaked grand jury material to the press in violation of federal statutes, a bogus accusation. The D.C. Circuit Court of Appeals upheld Starr's understanding of grand jury secrecy rules, and a special investigator cleared Starr's office of any illegal grand jury leaks.[43]

Above all, Clinton's allies screamed about Hillary's "vast right-wing conspiracy," of which Starr was allegedly a member in good standing.

"Bingo, you've got to tape her"

In the Jones case, this conspiracy consisted mostly of three conservative lawyers in private practice, subsequently dubbed "the elves," who surreptitiously provided legal help to the Jones lawyers. Paula Jones's official representation—initially, two Virginia-based lawyers—was not top-notch,[44] especially considering that they were matched up against the best lawyering the president of United States could buy, in the form of Bob Bennett, one of the heaviest hitters at the enormous firm of Skadden, Arps.

A conservative Chicago lawyer named Richard Porter hooked the Paula Jones camp up with a bright, conservative litigator in Philadelphia named Jerome Marcus, who was eventually joined by George Conway, a partner at the high-flying New York firm of Wachtell, Lipton, Rosen & Katz.[45] These three were "the elves." It was Marcus and Conway who did almost all of the elves' legal work, slipping the Jones lawyers high-octane briefs making the argument that the Jones case should go forward while Clinton was president and that Clinton should be subject to routine discovery—efforts to find similar sexual incidents in his personal history—in the case.

Marcus and Conway were Davids to the president's Goliath. "I was not out there leading a jihad," says Marcus. "I was sitting in the back with my little laptop, and George was sitting in the back with his, doing what we did. And it's an amazing country that is sufficiently governed by the rule of law that you can have two guys with laptops and they could do this."[46]

If circumstances had been different, if they had been two lawyers secretly working to keep a conservative Republican president from dodging a sexual harassment suit, they would have been celebrated in verse and song. A movie would already have been made, a sort of legal sequel to *All the President's Men,* hailing their against-the-odds work to expose arrogance and corruption in high office. Instead, of course, they are attacked as part of an out-of-bounds, secret cabal the very existence of which excuses Clinton's misconduct.

There's no doubt that the elves' work was extremely important. "They probably couldn't have done it without us," Conway says of the official Jones lawyers.[47] The question is whether the elves did anything wrong, and the answer is "no."

Pro bono work is obviously perfectly legitimate, even secret pro bono work. Marcus and Conway didn't want to go public with their legal help because they worked in largely Democratic firms. "The chairman of my firm," says Marcus, "is a very, very committed supporter of President Clinton's. It would have embarrassed him, and I didn't want to do that."[48]

The two lawyers wanted to see the Jones case proceed out of a mix of motives, with exposing Clinton and making him live by the laws he himself had supported high on the list. "The guy struck me viscerally," Marcus says, "as a fraud. The way he talked, the way he acts, the things he says. He seemed like a fraud, top to bottom. And it struck me that this was a mechanism that could—if everything went as well as it possibly could—be a way to unmask him."[49] Conway explains, "If these laws and rules are on the books—on sexual harassment, broad rules of discovery, the independent counsel—the liberals who support them should live by them. All we did was to put the shoe on the other foot."[50]

So of course there was a political subtext to the elves' work, but Clinton and his defenders were looking at the Jones case from a political framework as well. Everything Bob Bennett did early on was predicated on delaying the case past the 1996 elections.[51] Conway wanted the opposite to happen. "I wouldn't have minded seeing the whole thing blow up in 1996 before the election. Did I have a political motive? Sure. Just like they had a political motive to put it off beyond the 1996 election, or put it off entirely."[52]

Political motives also explain why all the people and organizations who usually support sexual harassment suits wanted nothing to do with Paula Jones, who as far as they were concerned might as well have been a member of the patriarchy. "Had a Republican president been accused of sexual harassment," Conway argues, "big law firms and liberal organizations—a whole raft of them—would have fallen all over themselves to provide direct assistance and amicus briefs. In comparison, what little we could do in our spare time was a pittance."[53]

The way the case worked out was beyond the elves' imagining. Conway maintains, "I never thought that any of this would happen. I thought the case would settle. It was just insane for Clinton to go through with the deposition, even without the Monica business. I didn't think he was stupid enough to lie his ass off instead of settling."[54]

The elves got wind of Clinton's efforts to tamper with Monica Lewinsky's testimony through their contacts with another leg of the "vast right-wing conspiracy," Tripp and her friend and advisor Lucianne Goldberg,[55] a New York-based literary agent (the initial connection was between Goldberg and Richard Porter, but things got very tangled).[56]

"I remember trying to figure out," says Marcus, "when we first became aware that this was going on [with Clinton and Lewinsky], who I could go to. Starr's office were the only people we could go to. We couldn't go to Janet Reno. We had no reason to think that she'd do the right thing. I thought about the U.S. attorney for the District of Columbia. Same problem. They're appointees of Bill Clinton's."[57]

Marcus was good friends with a lawyer in Starr's office named Paul Rosenzweig, and arranged for Rosenzweig to have dinner with the elves in Philadelphia in early January 1998. Before the dinner, Marcus told Rosenzweig about Lewinsky, the tapes of her conversations with Tripp, and the efforts to get her to lie in the Jones case.

Conway says that right before the dinner, "Marcus pulled me aside, and said, 'I told him.' I thought to myself, 'Holy s—.'" Rosenzweig took the information back to Starr's office, which expressed an interest in the matter, although it stipulated that Linda Tripp had to bring her allegations to the office directly. "I figured that Starr's office in the end wouldn't do it," says Conway, "that they would never jump on this, because all hell would break loose." He recalls telling fellow elf Richard Porter, "Starr's going to get killed. It's going to be a bloodbath for both sides."[58]

The Rosenzweig connection to the elves would later prove embarrassing. When Starr's office was getting the authority to investigate the Lewinsky matter from the Justice Department, Jackie Bennett assured the department that the office had had no contacts with the Jones lawyers, not realizing that Rosenzweig's friends had been writing briefs for Jones.[59] "That's what I believed at the time," Jackie Bennett says of his assurance. Some prosecutors in Starr's office were angered when the full story came out. "We were very disappointed to learn that there had been that contact," says Jackie Bennett. "If we had known Paul's friends had been writing briefs obviously we would not have made an explicit point of denying that there were any Jones contacts when we went to the Justice Department."[60]

It probably wouldn't have affected Starr's decision to pursue the case, or Reno's decision to expand his authority. As Bennett puts it, "These were well-informed private citizens privy to ongoing criminality on the part of the president of United States. I don't know why they should be disqualified from being tipsters. The government has a right to receive evidence of wrongdoing from any source."[61] Deputy attorney general Eric Holder, who would engage in a low-key battle with Starr's office throughout 1998, has a more sour, if not exactly dissimilar take. "If we'd known, we'd probably have gritted our teeth, rolled our eyes, and done it anyway—probably. I think, in some ways, we were had."[62]

While the elves were secretly helping Jones, Lucianne Goldberg and Linda Tripp had been engaged in secret work of their own. Goldberg was always straightforward about her motivations. She was appalled by Clinton, and wanted to reveal him as a fraud and have a good time riding the story of the decade in the process. "In my mind, I wanted the world to know what a scum-bucket this guy was," says Goldberg. Once that is your goal, she says, "everything's fair."[63]

Linda Tripp was a more complicated case. She was the one who had a friendship with Lewinsky, and betrayed it. She secretly and illegally taped conversations with her, and lied in the course of doing it. She lied repeatedly to Lewinsky, and to everyone else. "I did not volunteer to become a witness in the Paula Jones lawsuit," she insisted, at one point.[64] That's exactly what she did. She would go to Starr partly to get immunity for her illegal taping, which had been Goldberg's idea.

Goldberg says, "When Linda told me about this girl, I told her she had to have some way to prove it. I asked her what her contacts were. She said they talked on the phone. I said, 'Bingo, you've got to tape her.'" She didn't even think of its legality. "It did not even occur to me that taping the conversations in Maryland was illegal," she says. "And you see how peripherally illegal it was—federally, it was legal. In New York state, it's totally legal and people do it all the time. If I had actually known it was illegal, I would have told Linda, 'Drive over the District line and call her.'"[65]

There are a couple of misconceptions about the Goldberg-Tripp intrigue, according to Goldberg. One is that Tripp was trying to sell a book. "The second time Linda came to me, she didn't have a book," says Goldberg. "She wanted help getting this story out. When the story broke it was not about a book. The first time, a year before, when she came to me, she did have an outline."[66]

Another misconception, retailed by Sidney Blumenthal, is that Goldberg was employed by the *New York Post* to provide it with tips.[67] She had been paid by the *Post* for years to acquire book excerpts for it, not to find news. She did, however, go to the *Post* when the story broke. "Every single wood they had for eight days," she says, using the insider's term for a cover story, "was stories I had given them. Because I like the *Post*. And this was their story—if I had ever, ever seen a story purely made for the *New York Post*, this was it. And I trusted them. I didn't trust the *Times*. I didn't trust the *Daily News*."[68]

By the time the Lewinsky matter had been brought to Starr's attention, things were increasingly byzantine and bizarre. Tripp, for instance, decided to dump her lawyer, Kirby Behre, because she feared he was too close to the Clinton camp. Her new lawyer would be James Moody, who was legally blind.

Goldberg recalls, "Linda gave me the laundry list on what she needed for a lawyer. She had to have him in twenty-four hours. He had to be in Washington. He had to be willing to work pro bono. He couldn't have any Clinton connections whatsoever. There were like nine different things this lawyer had to have, for her to leave Kirby and take her tapes. And so he came to meet Linda at Kirby's office, and Moody had typed up an agreement between them. She signed it and handed it back to him. He held it right up to his nose. She called me from home that night and she said, 'I know I said the lawyer had to have this and that, but I went through my checklist. I never said he had to be blind.'"[69]

Elements of the "vast conspiracy" weren't even aware of each other's existence. Goldberg, for instance, didn't know George Conway's name until she read it in the newspaper, and Starr's office was unaware of almost all of the plotting. More important, by the end, the major players were at cross-purposes. Goldberg had been working a long time to get Isikoff to break the story, but Isikoff's editors held it. "I was just furious," says Goldberg, "that it almost got out in a reputable magazine where it would be irrefutable, and when I heard that they weren't going to do it, I was just steamed." She continues, "And

I tell you, the next person who would have called me, I don't care if it had been *Parade* magazine, I would have given them the story. The fact that Matt [Drudge] called me was everybody's dumb luck."[70]

From the perspective of Starr's office, the airing of the story was a disaster. Starr's prosecutors were convinced that Clinton had engaged in criminality in the past, but this was finally a chance to be ahead of the curve, to investigate an inchoate crime. "It sure would have been better if they'd kept their mouths shut," says Jackie Bennett. "Prosecutors like to get evidence before their targets are aware of the investigation. We wanted to bring pressure to bear on other witnesses in a traditional prosecutorial fashion. We wanted to try to flip someone else in the White House. All of that ended as of the time the Drudge Report came out. The story breaking helped Clinton."[71]

Investigators in Starr's office would be made uncomfortable by elements of the Goldberg-Tripp plotting as they became public. For instance, Tripp had encouraged Lewinsky to messenger her letters to the president with a service to which Goldberg had a connection so Goldberg could get copies of the delivery tickets.[72] "It was very unseemly," says former Starr prosecutor Sol Wisenberg. "When that came out, I was very depressed. It was a tough time. You had to wonder whether we had done the right thing."[73]

But Clinton's conduct and his lies were always the ultimate issue. "Any sympathy for Clinton always passes very quickly," says Wisenberg. "What you ended up with is: He had a choice, he didn't have to lie."[74]

"I do not recall the precise wording of the oath"

So, let's concede that sexual harassment law is too broad and that the Jones suit was quite weak, that ideally there shouldn't have been an independent counsel waiting to pounce on Clinton's crimes, that a pair of conservative lawyers gave legal advice to the Jones team with the ulterior purpose of harming the president, and that Linda Tripp wasn't very nice to Monica Lewinsky or very honest—that still leaves the fact that Bill Clinton, the president of the United States, had sex with an intern, perjured himself about it, suborned the perjury of someone else, and obstructed justice.

What were House Republicans supposed to do with these alleged high crimes and misdemeanors of the president? Ignore them? Nearly everyone agreed on the need for the House to undertake an impeachment inquiry. Thirty-one Democrats voted for the Republican inquiry plan, and the rest voted for an alternative Democratic plan.[75]

There was a consensus in the country in favor of punishing Clinton. In December 1998, Clinton himself asked to be censured.[76] As one of the Democratic censure resolutions said, Clinton had "egregiously failed" his constitutional oath, "violated the trust of the American people," and "dishonored the office which they have entrusted to him."[77] This language echoed Lieberman's August floor statement, when he said Clinton's behavior was "disgraceful" and "immoral," and had "profound public consequences"—prompting Clinton to respond, "Basically, I agree with what he said."[78]

If all those things in the censure resolution and Lieberman's statement were true, then why shouldn't Clinton be impeached? He had committed crimes far more serious than the speeding ticket his defenders were wont to compare them to. People go to prison for perjury, and a prominent person or celebrity is usually likelier to get the attention of a prosecutor than a run-of-the-mill defendant.[79]

Alexander Hamilton wrote that the subjects of impeachment "are those offenses which proceed from the misconduct of public men, or, in other words, from the abuse or violation of some public trust."[80] Clinton had undoubtedly violated the "public trust." Judges had been impeached and convicted for perjury—although it's open to debate whether a president should be held to higher or lower standards than a judge. Whether Clinton's violation was grave enough to constitute "high crimes and misdemeanors" and warrant his removal from office was an inherently political question, which is why the Founders had impeachment proceedings begin in the raucously political House of Representatives.

The Republican House in 1998 was not necessarily a lost cause for Clinton. He could perhaps have peeled Republican moderates away from impeachment by making a full confession.[81] The problem was that such was the nature of his crimes, that he couldn't fully admit to them without making a damning case against himself, i.e., "He's a confessed perjurer." So he had to stick with the word games. Ridiculous word parsing had gotten him into this mess, and he hoped ridiculous word parsing could get him out.

Asked in one of eighty-one written questions by Henry Hyde if he had sworn to tell the truth, the whole truth, and nothing but the truth in his Jones deposition, Clinton responded, "I do not recall the precise wording of the oath." His unresponsiveness and his repetition of his lies in response to the questions—he talked to Currie only "to get as much information as quickly as I could"—helped seal his fate in the House.[82]

It impeached him by 228–206 on an article charging him with perjury before Starr's grand jury and by 221–212 on an article charging him with obstruction of justice.[83] It foolishly rejected the article charging perjury in the Jones deposition, which was rock-solid and was the basis of Clinton's perjury before the grand jury. Three factors would save Clinton's presidency. They can be summed up in the catchphrases: "old news," "it's all about sex," and "partisanship."

First, there was the length of time it took Starr to nail down his case. Starr could have speeded things up if he had accepted an initial "proffer"—a written promise of certain testimony in exchange for immunity—from Lewinsky in February 1998 instead of waiting until July.[84] But the office had been burned once before by a witness, Webb Hubbell, making unreliable promises of assistance. "I don't think Monica was trustworthy and we felt that it was important that the person with whom we would be dealing would in fact be cooperative with us," Starr says of the decision to forego the first proffer. "She was quite intelligent, manipulative, and calculating."[85] Indeed, it turned out that Lewinsky sent backchannel information to the White House right up until the time she reached the July agreement, when Starr's office was

more confident that it had at least secured a greater level of cooperation from her.[86]

Starr also could have speeded up his case by compelling the president's testimony before his grand jury much sooner, possibly locking
him into much more damning lies before he had decided to admit
"inappropriate" conduct. Starr issued six invitations to Clinton to testify voluntarily,[87] before pursuing a subpoena—a case, perhaps, of
excessive deference to the office of the president. "I think an argument can be made that I should have," Starr says of getting Clinton's
testimony sooner. "I felt very strongly, however, as a matter of separation of powers that the president and the presidency had to be assiduously respected and so we had to both in reality exhaust, and be seen
by a fair-minded judge as having exhausted, every possible avenue of
securing the president's voluntary, not compulsory, testimony."[88]

Second, there was the graphic detail in Starr's report, and its
release to the public, which badly weakened the Republicans' case by
making it seem "all about sex." "I had not contemplated," says Starr,
"that Congress would simply send the report out sight unseen."[89]
Republicans had a bitter argument about releasing the report, with
Gingrich prevailing over an adamantly opposed Henry Hyde. "I'm not
going to be the Larry Flynt of the House of Representatives," Hyde
proclaimed, to no avail.[90]

Lastly, there was the partisan strategy of the Democrats, which
was to decry the partisanship of the process from the beginning to
make impeachment seem a political vendetta. This strategy was a winner, although it doesn't tell us much about the merits of impeachment. Rather than a "political impeachment," it may well have been
a "political acquittal." Indeed, if the polls had been different, the
Democrats likely would have had a different attitude about the whole
controversy, whereas the Republicans resolutely defied the polls, convinced they were pursuing a just cause.

In any case, the public considered the issue and didn't want Clinton removed from office. The argument over impeachment might best
be framed by two concessions made by advocates on the different

sides. On one hand, there was Clinton's lawyer Charles Ruff. Before the House Judiciary Committee, Ruff explained how Clinton had tried to walk a narrow line. "Reasonable people—and you maybe have reached this conclusion—could determine that he crossed over that line and that what for him was truthful but misleading or non-responsive and misleading or evasive was, in fact, false."[91] Although Ruff would not interpret his concession this way, he was essentially saying that in the course of attempting to deceive the court, Clinton told lies—i.e., he committed perjury.

On the other hand, there was House impeachment manager Congressman Lindsey Graham of South Carolina. When asked during the Senate trial if reasonable people could conclude that Clinton shouldn't be removed from office even if he was guilty of the crimes of which he was accused, Graham said "absolutely."[92]

The Senate obviously wasn't going to convict—it took a two-thirds vote—so even impeachment leader Henry Hyde was briefly considering alternatives. A censure resolution floated by Dianne Feinstein was enticing, with its statement that Clinton's conduct "is unacceptable for a president of the United States, does demean the office of the president as well as the president himself, and creates disrespect for laws of the land."[93] "At one time," says Hyde, "I was looking for a way to resolve this. We couldn't walk away from pursuing the president, but it was clear that we would not get the two-thirds vote in the Senate. I had hoped to get the majority anyway, and had a couple of our distinguished, courageous senators remained distinguished and courageous, we would have. I thought, having seen the text of Feinstein's resolution of condemnation—which was stronger than our bill of impeachment, it was excoriating—I would not have been unhappy if that had been adopted by the Senate."

Hyde continues, "But as the chief manager, I was not going to take that position. I honestly believe that it was unconstitutional, there's no provision for it in the Constitution, and the notion of Congress writing a report card on the president seemed to me to violate the principle of separation of powers. Technically I didn't like it, but practically, we weren't going to get the sixty-seven votes we needed to remove him from office, so one condemnatory statement is as good as another, but I just could not take the lead on it."[94] The Senate voted 55–45 to acquit on the perjury count, and 50–50 to acquit on the obstruction count.[95]

The American political system tends to get big questions right, and in the Lewinsky controversy, it reached a reasonable, if not perfect, result—an impeachment that ended up serving as a sort of monster censure.[96]

The public's acquiescence to having Clinton continue in office sent some conservatives into paroxysms of outrage. Had the public lost all sense of virtue? Its non-judgmentalism in matters of sexual morality and its aversion to frank political argument were indeed distressing. But the public's discomfort about impeachment reflected understandable, and even healthy, tendencies as well.

There was a limit to how much people wanted to hear about sex, and by the end, Republicans more than Clinton were blamed for making it a national topic. There was an innate conservatism in the public—times were good, so why remove the president? People already knew that Clinton was a womanizer and a liar, so that the force of the Lewinsky revelations was blunted. Finally, there was a sense that the nation's political leadership had better things to be doing. The administration shrewdly played to this sentiment by creating a false image of a president doggedly focused on substantive work.[97]

Clinton won acquittal, but was still a loser. His allies will perpetually be involved in the fundamentally defensive action of trying to explain away impeachment. A desperation clings to their argumentation. Both Bill and Hillary have said that impeachment was an offense against the Constitution.[98] But impeachment is a process set out in the Constitution. Republicans assiduously followed that process—at least up until the time the Senate short-circuited the impeachment trial.

Sidney Blumenthal thunderously claims of Clinton's prospective removal, "the devastation to democracy would [have been] irreparable."[99] The fact is that if Clinton had left or been removed at any point, his duly elected vice president, Al Gore, would have taken over. There would have been a nearly seamless continuity in the American government, and the Democrats probably would have had a better chance to hold the White House in 2000.

In the end, Clinton bracketed an era with Nixon, with an almost perfect symmetry. Nixon's corruption brought to power a cadre of aggressive liberals. Clinton's corruption exposed liberals' thirst to defend what power they still had. Nixon's corruption attracted critics whose idealism was forged in their fight against his misconduct. Clinton's corruption attracted defenders whose idealism was blunted in their fight to defend his misconduct. Nixon's corruption led to the creation of a new edifice of ethics legislation in Washington. Clinton's corruption led to its dismantling or irrelevancy.

Clinton forced liberals, a couple of decades after the advent of the independent counsel statute, after the rise of sexual harassment law, after the creation of new campaign financing rules, to say, "Uh, never mind—those rules were intended for the *other* party."

DOMESTIC SECURITY:

Queen of the Bunny Planet

"**W**OULD IT BE BETTER if she had some federal experience?"
That's the sheepish question President Clinton asked
Florida senator Bob Graham, a Janet Reno booster, when
Clinton was mulling whether to make the Dade County prosecutor the
attorney general of the United States. "Probably," Graham said.[1]

Probably, indeed. Janet Reno entered the attorney general's office
a local prosecuting attorney and left, more or less, still a local prosecuting attorney. She was innocent of how Washington works; devoted
to school-marmish causes more appropriate not just to the head of the
Department of Health and Human Services, but to the head of a state
or local department of health and human services; and tone deaf to
national security matters. She survived in office partly because the
White House disliked her so much that firing her would have seemed
embarrassingly self-serving.

Yet, Janet Reno sat atop the country's domestic security apparatus
for eight years. It would be difficult to find a person who could more
fully anthropomorphize the administration's lack of seriousness—and

193

that of the political culture at large—about matters of high state. Her department contained the FBI and the Immigration and Naturalization Service and what she cared about most was delivering social services for "the children" and chasing deadbeat dads.

During the Clinton years, the United States systematically tied its own hands in dealing with national security threats, left its borders unprotected, and allowed politically correct concerns to trump commonsense security measures. Republicans were complicit in much of this, but the tone was set at the top, and exemplified by Janet Reno.

"We wanted a woman"

What Reno lacked in federal experience, she made up in chromosomal desirability. Hillary had insisted that Justice be headed by a woman.[2] Clinton's first two choices as women nominees were deep-sixed because of "nanny problems," a failure to pay Social Security taxes on household help. The search went on.[3]

Unfortunately, there weren't many women with top-level Justice Department experience. And now the administration wanted to find a childless woman who wouldn't have any nanny problems. So, Reno suddenly looked very qualified—she was a spinster.

She had managed to get elected district attorney several times in rough-and-tumble Miami. And she hit it off with Hubbell and Vince Foster in her interviews. Hubbell's assessment: "She was human." The Clinton vetting committee, less impressed by Reno's humanness, declined to recommend her nomination because of her lack of federal experience.[4]

"We wanted a woman," explains former Clinton White House counsel Bernie Nussbaum, who was involved in the choice. "She had run for office. She was thick-skinned, tough. She was not necessarily brilliant. In the end she was one of the most successful people in the administration. She was right in saving Clinton/Gore from an independent counsel in the fund-raising scandal. Was she a legal genius? No. Was she a legal scholar? No."[5]

In Florida, her passions were fighting domestic violence, improving child welfare, and tracking down deadbeat dads.[6] Among her first acts as state attorney was to spend a day at a conference of county librarians, because reading would help prevent crime.[7]

In Washington, she became, in essence, the Children's Defense Fund's attorney general. "We've got to figure out," she said, "how to take the federal bureaucracy and weave it together as a whole, so that we can reweave the fabric of society around our children."[8] She campaigned relentlessly for "investments in children."[9] In 1994, in a typical Reno itinerary, she traveled to day care centers, elementary schools, and rehabilitation clinics in thirty-seven states, talking about the importance of early childhood education and the role of her mother in her own life.[10]

She is the only attorney general in the history of the United States ever to be asked by a *New York Times* reporter—and please God, may she be the last—"Is it true that you are Janet, Queen of the Bunny Planet?"

The question referred to a children's book series that Reno enjoyed called "Voyage to the Bunny Planet." In the story, Queen Janet gives succor to a sad little boy and a sad girl bunny. Reno's aides noted her identification with Queen Janet. "It's not a joke," former Reno deputy Jamie Gorelick told the *Times* reporter. "It's not just the similarity of the names. The Bunny Queen tries to make the world a better place for kids. It's really her vision of a better world for children."[11]

When it came to law enforcement issues, Reno was an old-style liberal, who attacked "demagogic promises to build more jails and put all the criminals away."[12] As her deputy Eric Holder puts it, in the kindest possible formulation, "She had an ability to reach out to different constituencies that didn't necessarily think of law enforcement as allies."[13] This ability was a natural product of her unsuitability to be the nation's top law enforcement official.

Reno's liberalism on criminal justice issues put her into conflict with the administration's New Democratic posture of being tough on crime. "The biggest problem we encountered in getting tough criminal justice measures approved," writes Dick Morris, "was the attorney general, Janet Reno."[14]

The solution should have been simple: fire her. But even before Clinton's scandals made that politically problematic, she had achieved a kind of invincibility after the Branch Davidian disaster in Waco, Texas. On February 28, 1993, the Branch Davidian cult killed four Bureau of Alcohol, Tobacco and Firearms (ATF) agents during a raid that may have been unnecessary if the ATF had opted for the less confrontational approach of trying to arrest Branch Davidian leader David Koresh when he was outside the compound.[15] A fifty-one-day standoff ensued, before Reno approved a nonsensical FBI plan to encourage negotiations by gassing the Davidian compound.[16] The Davidians torched the place, and themselves, during the FBI action. More than eighty people died.[17]

Afterwards, it was clear that Reno didn't know why she had approved the FBI plan. She maintained, "We had information that babies were being beaten. I specifically asked, 'You really mean babies?' 'Yes, he's slapping babies around.' These are the concerns that we had." She was insistent on the point, recalling "the clear impression that, at some point since the FBI had assumed command and control for the situation, they had learned that the Branch Davidians were beating the babies." There was no evidence of anything of the kind.[18]

Despite her cluelessness, Reno rode a counterintuitive post-Waco wave of popularity, based on her willingness to *say* that she took responsibility for the raid. She wouldn't actually do anything to demonstrate her responsibility—e.g., resign—but her faux accountability was still a refreshing contrast to Clinton's weasely statement of non-support support for Reno after the disaster: "I told the attorney general to do what she thought was right, and I stand by that decision."[19]

His slippery calculation cast her well-meaning incompetence in a better light. And so it would go for the next eight years.

"Fire him, you're the president"

The White House's relationship with FBI director Louis Freeh made its relations with Reno look warm by comparison. Freeh was appointed in September 1993. A former federal judge who was upstanding to a fault, he was not well suited to thrive in Washington, especially in Bill Clinton's Washington.

"If there is a problem with Louie Freeh," says a former FBI official, "it is that he is too ethical. In Washington, you don't have to play the game entirely. But there is some point at which you have to compromise to get the maximum leverage to achieve your goals. Louie wouldn't compromise. He wouldn't even go to the White House. You can imagine what that did to our budgets and to our standing."[20] Freeh didn't even have a White House pass—he was the choirboy at the bacchanal.[21]

The White House provided plenty of reasons for Freeh to keep his distance. There was a flap about the misuse of the FBI from the very beginning of the administration during the Travel Office controversy, eventually compounded by the FBI files, fund-raising, and Lewinsky scandals. "He strongly believed that the FBI needed some political insulation," says former FBI executive assistant director Dale Watson. "If you're up there socializing, sooner or later someone is going to get in trouble about something, and you're going to have to get involved in an investigation."[22]

For its part, the White House treated Freeh with outright hostility. He proved far less prone to domestication than Janet Reno, who switched her views on the independent counsel statute to accord with those of the White House. With his determination to pursue the 1996 reelection fund-raising scandal, Freeh had made himself into what the White House hated most—a political inconvenience.

Clinton regarded the FBI director with sputtering, impotent hatred. "Louis Freeh is a g— f— a—!" Clinton said in the summer of

1998, enraged by Freeh's support for an independent counsel in the fund-raising controversy.[23] According to Sidney Blumenthal, it was a joke around the White House that Vince Foster must have had a premonition of what would happen after Freeh's appointment. Immediately after Bernie Nussbaum told him of it, he committed suicide (ha-ha).[24] "The White House was offended by our investigations," says former deputy FBI director Robert "Bear" Bryant. "That caused a lot of problems in government. They cut off the FBI—that was wrong."[25]

If there is a dysfunctional relationship between the president and the FBI director, it is the president's responsibility to fix it. Bernie Nussbaum remembers, after he had left the White House, talking to Clinton when he was particularly enraged at Freeh. "I told him, 'Fire him, you're the president.'"[26]

That Clinton was unwilling to exercise his most basic presidential power again demonstrated how his character affected his governance. His scandals made it politically risky to fire the director of the FBI, and his innate caution meant it was impossible. Says a former FBI official, "He didn't have the guts to do it."[27]

While he waved his arms and complained about FBI investigations into his own scandals, Clinton did nothing about the true weaknesses of the FBI—and there were plenty of those.

The 1990s was a bad decade for the FBI. There were the fatal shootings at Ruby Ridge, the mistreatment of the falsely accused Richard Jewell after the 1996 Olympic Park bombing, and the bungling at the FBI crime labs. And there were two cases—the FBI's failure to catch Russian spy Robert Hanssen before he did his damage, and the utterly incompetent investigation of Los Alamos scientist and suspected spy Wen Ho Lee—that highlighted the FBI's gravest weakness: its lumbering nature.

The FBI was experienced at solving domestic crimes after the fact. But it was ill suited to the sort of imagination and predictive analysis necessary to stay ahead of the emerging terror threat. "The FBI is like an oil tanker," says Bryant. "To change its direction takes five years. It was very frustrating at the time. The criminal culture at the FBI is very reactive. The FBI is the best in the world after a crime has been committed, in finding the facts. But we had to be more predictive to deal with the terrorist threat, otherwise you're still in law enforcement world."[28]

The starkest example of the FBI's failure to keep up to date was its antiquated computer system, a disaster to this day. At the time of an information revolution, the FBI had barely moved beyond the abacus. "The automation was terrible, it was backwards, it was slow," Bryant says. "I had a saying, 'we don't know what we know.' We wanted more resources for automation. We had numerous requests, but Congress pencil-whipped us to death. I told them, 'You can pay us now, or pay us later.'"[29]

The FBI didn't exist in isolation, and it absorbed—oftentimes as a matter of law—the priorities of the political culture around it. With the end of the Cold War, it was assumed that the old intelligence and counterintelligence capabilities necessary to protect against foreign threats were dated. They were "so 1980s." "The program was basically languishing," Bryant says of the FBI national security division he took over in late 1993, before later becoming deputy director of the FBI. "It all went away in a year or so. It was part of the 'peace dividend.' There was supposedly no war left to fight."[30] The FBI turned its attention instead to fighting global organized crime.[31]

The FBI also had to deal with the steady accumulation of additional, often frivolous, federal criminal jurisdiction. There are probably more than three thousand federal criminal statutes on the books. Almost all of these statutes overlap with state and local laws.[32] This meant federal agencies like the FBI were devoting resources to law enforcement work that could be handled by state and local police, mostly so politicians in Washington could pose as tough on crime.

The federal statutes continued to accumulate in the 1990s. "Some of the political structure was more interested in guns and drugs and civil rights," says Bryant, "than what are these cowardly outlaws going to do to us. They had their agendas and terrorism wasn't one of them."[33]

Someone had to act on Clinton's emphasis on chasing down dead-beat dads, since it polled so well in shopping centers. It was the FBI. Reno called cracking down on fathers who owed child support to children living in another state "one of the most critical responsibilities of state government in partnership with the federal government."[34] Says Bryant: "We didn't want anything to do with it."[35]

An FBI forced to try to do everything wouldn't do anything particularly well, and the nation was beginning to face threats much graver than deadbeat dads.

"We were making it more difficult"

In the wake of the Oklahoma City bombing in 1995, Clinton proposed new federal police powers to combat terrorism.[36] A cadre of House Republicans delayed and stripped down the legislation, in tandem with left-wing civil libertarians.

The left didn't trust the FBI because of 1970s revelations about its wiretapping of civil rights groups, and thought nearly anything to increase its powers would lead to such abuses again. But the right had doubts about the FBI too. In part, this was a healthy preference for state and local law enforcement over federal. But an element of the right overreacted to the debacle at Waco and the FBI shootings at Ruby Ridge, lurching into paranoia about federal power and becoming "black helicopter" civil libertarians. Henry Hyde complained that one House Republican told him during the debate over the terrorism bill, "I trust Hamas more than I trust my own government."[37]

The bill was delayed a year before it finally passed. It made a few small steps in the right direction. It banned fund-raising for groups that supported terrorism, a tool that would prove useful after September 11, 2001, when the government actually began to use it aggressively.[38] But, crucially, the right joined forces with the ACLU to deny the government the ability to acquire so-called "roving wiretaps" in terrorism cases. Such a tap allows the government to monitor every phone used by a suspect, rather than having to get new authority to tap each and every phone. The FBI already used "roving wiretaps" in organized crime cases, so denying it this authority when surveilling suspected terrorists was perverse.[39]

When it came to FBI powers, Reno shared important attitudes with the right-left civil libertarian coalition, as became clear in her handling of the Foreign Intelligence Surveillance Act (FISA).

Much of the FBI's anti-terrorist work is done under the rubric of the 1978 act. The law created a special court to which the FBI would bring wiretap requests in terrorism and counterintelligence cases. The standard for a FISA warrant isn't as high as that for an ordinary criminal wiretap warrant, but does require a finding of "probable cause" to believe that the target is an agent of a "foreign power," or a "group engaged in international terrorism or activities in preparation thereof."[40]

Properly understood, FISA strikes an appropriate balance between liberty and national security concerns. But almost from the beginning its language was misconstrued as limiting FBI surveillance more tightly than Congress had intended. Reno's Justice Department took this mistake and magnified it until the power was nearly unworkable. Foreign intelligence surveillance, apparently, wasn't nearly as imperative as "investments for children."

Reno ratcheted up the standard for applying for counterintelligence warrants, making it not so much "probable cause" as "near certainty," and created firewalls between the FBI's counterintelligence agents and the Justice Department's criminal division, so they would no longer be able to talk and share information. Reno's theory was that FISA was for counterintelligence, not criminal matters, and too much contact between FBI agents and Justice Department prosecutors could impermissibly blend the two purposes. But there had always been loose cooperation between counterintelligence agents and the criminal division, since monitoring of foreign agents (a counterintelligence matter) could easily turn up evidence for espionage cases (a criminal matter).[41] Indeed, applications for FISA and investigations under it had been a smoothly running process—until Reno's team changed all that.

The Justice Department's Office of Intelligence Policy and Review (OIPR) is responsible for vetting the FBI's FISA requests and deciding if they will be passed along to the court for approval.[42] Reno's head of OIPR, Richard Scruggs, zealously enforced the tighter rules.[43] He and OIPR created a climate of fear around FISA, thus making one of the government's most important surveillance tools radioactive.

It was as if the ACLU had been given stewardship of Justice Department surveillance policy. Ronald Kessler writes in his book *The Bureau*, "Scruggs pursued his separation doctrine with religious fervor, and FBI agents and Justice Department prosecutors considered crossing the line he imposed to be a 'career stopper.' It was exactly the opposite of what was needed to pursue successful investigations and prosecutions."[44]

Thus the government's handling of counterintelligence and terrorism cases was made dysfunctional for no good reason. No court had suppressed evidence on grounds that it had been improperly gathered under FISA, and the special FISA court had at this point never even rejected an application.[45] The Patriot Act in 2001 explicitly tore down the wall between the FBI and Justice Department lawyers,[46] and a subsequent decision by the FISA appeals court concluded that the Reno-Scruggs interpretation of FISA had been wrong and unjustified by the law all along.[47]

"Year after year after year it became more difficult to share information, not less difficult," says Jim Kallstrom, assistant director in charge of the New York office of the FBI from 1995–1997, and chief of its special operations division before that. "So while all those terrorist events were happening, we were making it more difficult, at the FBI. When you look at the Chinese wall and the naïve way that we restricted the sharing of information, if you take the word of the appellate court, that wall wasn't necessary even in the first place. When you read the FISA law, it wasn't even necessary. So not only did we create an obstacle that wasn't necessary, we made it bigger."[48]

So during the very years that Osama bin Laden declared and waged terrorist war on the United States, the FBI was unnecessarily hamstrung. The culmination of the terrorists' campaign came on

September 11, 2001, nine months after Clinton left office. Nine months wasn't enough time for the system to undo eight years of folly. Perhaps the two best chances for the FBI to unravel the plot were when "twentieth hijacker" Zacharias Moussaoui was detained in August in Minneapolis and when an agent in Phoenix wrote a memo suggesting canvassing flight schools where Arab men might be training for terrorist flights.[49] The administration's unduly restrictive interpretation of FISA, its opposition to "racial profiling," and a more general culture of timidity lingered on, and discouraged the FBI from acting on these potential leads.[50]

FBI whistleblower Coleen Rowley, an agent in the Minneapolis field office who wanted to search Moussaoui's computer prior to September 11, captured the atmosphere in her famous May 2002 memo. She wrote, "Our best real guess is that, in most cases, avoidance of all 'unnecessary' actions/decisions by FBIHQ managers (and maybe to some extent field managers as well) has, in recent years, been seen as the safest FBI career course."[51]

This chilling effect played into the decision that, understandably, so enraged Rowley: the conclusion of FBI headquarters that there wasn't "probable cause" to request a FISA warrant on Moussaoui prior to September 11 to search his computer. For years, it had been drummed into the FBI that it must err on the side of not asking for FISA warrants if it was a close call. The Justice Department's criminal division might have had advice for the FBI about how to develop the information necessary on Moussaoui to get a FISA warrant in the case—but the FBI had been taught not to talk to the criminal division.[52] And so Moussaoui's right to privacy was strictly respected.

The other tantalizing lead prior to September 11 was a July 2001 memo written by FBI agent Kenneth Williams recommending an investigation at flight schools.[53] This would have been a massive undertaking, and almost impossible given the legal and political environment at the time, especially the sensitivity around racial profiling.

Mike Rolince, then the head of the FBI's international terrorism division, now the special agent in charge of the Washington field office of the FBI, imagines how it might have gone: "Now we're knocking on every university's door: 'Hi, we're the FBI, we're going to go through your files.' 'Looking for what?' 'Information on Middle Eastern males between the ages of twenty and forty.' 'Do you have subpoenas?' 'No.' 'Court order?' 'No.' 'Do you have a pending case on these people?' 'No.' How long do you think it would have taken for us to be dragged up to Capitol Hill and charges from the ACLU to come out? The FBI is not going to target Middle Eastern males who don't even have cases open on them."[54]

And it wasn't easy for the FBI to open cases. The political culture had deliberately made it that way since the 1970s. The so-called "attorney general's guidelines" kept FBI agents from going inside houses of worship, attending public meetings, surfing the Internet, or using commercial data services—all activities anyone else in the country could engage in—unless they had opened a formal investigation. That, in turn, required a showing of probable cause, or information that persons to be surveilled were engaged in criminal activity.[55]

Such was the state of the regulations that an internal debate dragged on for months over whether to open an investigation of Sheik Omar Abdel Rahman prior to the first World Trade Center bombing, because he was a religious figure—even though he was known to have terrorist connections.[56] These strictures had no grounding in the Constitution, and were imposed merely because handcuffing the FBI seemed like a good idea at the time.[57]

The FBI had no confidence that the White House or Congress or anyone else would defend it if it got into a fight with ethnic or civil liberties groups, over, say, the surveillance of mosques.

"What was the feeling of the U.S. public and what was the policy at the time about what you want the FBI to do?" asks Dale Watson, former FBI executive assistant director for counterterrorism and counterintelligence. "Don't criticize us for not penetrating the mosques if by regulation we can't do it. Do we think we should do it? Well, that probably would have been helpful. Would we have liked to have amended the FISA order and made it easier to make it for something other than an intelligence purpose? Yes, we would have. Did we have any support to do that? No—no one wanted to do it."[58]

The tone was set at the top, by Clinton's attorney general. The FBI had known, for instance, since the early 1990s that a supposed charity, the Holy Land Foundation, was an American fund-raising front for the Palestinian terror group Hamas. Nothing was done as the evidence steadily accumulated against the foundation—even after Clinton officially designated Hamas a terrorist organization in 1995. The treasury department and the FBI recommended a freeze on the foundation's assets in 1997. Reno blocked it. According to a report in the *Wall Street Journal*, "Whenever FBI agents discussed moving against the foundation, more senior officials at the Justice Department would ask them, 'How can you prove to us this money isn't saving children's lives?'"[59]

And so it went. Jim Kallstrom summarizes the policy on terrorism cases: "The AG guidelines ended up at, and this is not much of an exaggeration, that we had to show three things to start an investigation: That somebody was associated with a known terrorist organization; that someone had the mentality to actually carry out a terrorist act; that they had the wherewithal to obtain the materials to carry out an act of terrorism. So basically, you had to wait until they blew something up."[60]

Collectively, that's exactly what the country did.

"Out of one, many"

One reason that the FBI and others had to fear the reaction of ethnic groups to any given policy was that these groups had become increasingly potent politically as their numbers grew in the 1990s. A massive wave of immigration that had begun in the late 1960s continued to wash over the country during the decade.[61] By 2001, annual legal immigration had hit one million a year, and the illegal population was estimated to be growing by an additional 500,000 a year.[62] This doesn't count the more than one million people allowed into the country on a long-term temporary basis each year, such as guest workers and foreign students, many of whom are functionally equivalent to immigrants.[63] The record level of immigration in the 1990s eclipsed the previous record set in the first decade of the 1900s.[64]

This demographic-rattling wave of immigration helped transform the idea of "multiculturalism" from a marginal academic theory into a mainstream movement.[65] Large-scale immigration makes dissolving America's common culture seem only a common sense reaction to demographic reality. President Clinton occasionally gave voice to multiculturalism's assumptions, as when he worried that the idea of "tolerance" unacceptably suggested "that there's a dominant culture putting up with a subordinate one." And Al Gore inadvertently expressed one of its core aspirations when he mistranslated *"E Pluribus Unum"* as "Out of one, many."[66]

On the ground, high levels of immigration create large, seemingly permanent ethnic enclaves in which assimilation is made unnecessary, and make it much harder to curtail immigration, because immigrants, voting as a self-conscious bloc, wield greater political power. Record-level immigration, in other words, begets a constituency for record-level immigration. This wasn't the only reason that American immigration policy wasn't reformed in the 1990s, but it was a significant one.

In 1996, a congressional commission led by the respected black former congresswoman Barbara Jordan recommended cutting legal immigration by a third. The commission also recommended establishing a computerized identification system that would make it easier to catch and punish businesses that hire illegals. A right-left coalition of business and ethnic groups killed both the legal immigrant reductions and the computer registry.[67] Clinton initially endorsed the Jordan commission's work—Barbara Jordan was a powerful liberal voice—but he flipped after she died in January 1996.[68]

Reform should have been a desperate priority since it was clear to anyone paying attention in the 1990s that the INS simply had no idea who was coming in and out of the country. If anyone had a doubt, the

INS's inspector general spelled it out in a harsh September 1997 report.[69] What should have been a national scandal was ignored, or worse, deliberately preserved. Even efforts to secure the country's borders in specific ways that didn't involve large reductions in the number of immigrants were resisted and torn apart by the business-ethnic alliance.

One provision of the immigration law that eventually passed in 1996 called for the creation of a comprehensive system to track foreign visitors to the United States, so they could be identified if they overstayed their visas. The system was supposed to be operational by 1998, but the business-ethnic lobby got Congress to delay implementation of the system until 2001. Then, it successfully pushed a new law mandating a watered-down version of the system to be phased in by 2005. Several of the September 11 hijackers overstayed their visas—unbeknownst to anyone, because that's the way the business-ethnic coalition liked it.[70]

Foreign student visas were identified as a particular problem in the early 1990s. The driver of the truck in the 1993 World Trade Center bombing came to the United States on a student visa in 1989, quickly dropping out of school and working illegally. A Department of Justice task force formed to examine the case issued a stinging report in December 1995 about the state of the foreign student visa program. Adopting the recommendations of the task force, Congress voted as part of the 1996 immigration law to overhaul the system: significantly broadening the information collected about students, computerizing the student records so they could be cross-referenced with law enforcement databases, issuing foreign students "smart" ID cards with a "biometric identifier" (e.g., a fingerprint), and providing for the constant, automatic updating of students' status.[71]

As Nicholas Confessore has reported in the *Washington Monthly*, a group representing the advisors of foreign students worked together with internal opponents of immigration restriction in the INS to gut the new program, delaying it then watering it down so it wouldn't be any better than the status quo.[72] Hani Hanjour, thought to be the pilot of the September 11 plane that crashed into the Pentagon, never showed up at a California language school after entering the United States on a student visa in December 2000.[73] The proposed new system might have picked up his violation.[74]

Dick Morris proposed a creative idea to make traffic stops part of the nation's immigration enforcement. Morris writes, "Since our most frequent police contact is on the highway, I believed this would be an easy way to identify illegals: if people found to be driving without a license were citizens or legal immigrants, they would be ticketed; if they were here illegally, they could be sent to the Immigration and Naturalization Service—the INS—for deportation. But the INS killed this idea by saying that it didn't want to know of any more illegals since it couldn't deport those it already knew about—an odd response."[75]

Odd, but entirely in keeping with the times, and the administration's priorities. Other Clinton aides were appalled by Morris's suggestion. Stephanopoulos writes that the program would have targeted people who were "suspiciously brown-skinned" and that he worried about the "political harm to our Hispanic base."[76] Such a system might have caused problems for terrorist ringleader Mohamed Atta when he was stopped for driving without a license months before the September 11 attacks.[77]

The fact is that in the 1990s, immigration laws simply didn't matter. It was vaguely thought that everyone had a right to be in America, for whatever purpose, and that enforcing laws against people who were from minority groups—Hispanics, Asians, Arabs—was somehow out of bounds. In any case, in an increasingly "borderless world," only retrograde fetishists could care about America's borders.[78]

Tighter rules were not implemented, and the ones on the books were ignored, in essentially a massive act of officially sanctioned civil disobedience. Amazingly, aliens in deportation proceedings or with asylum claims usually weren't even detained by the INS, but simply released.[79]

For law enforcement agents on the ground, it made for a dismaying picture. "Every day," says former FBI official Jim Kallstrom, "you'd

see people coming into Kennedy airport, undocumented, phony doc-
umentation, and INS would just let them go because there was no
way that they could track them. Agents watched and looked at this
thing, and the talk over beer every night was, 'Doesn't anybody give a
s—? We have these people coming in here by the thousands, and we
don't have a clue about who any of them are. Not a clue.'"[80]

"People who fit the stereotype of a terrorist"

Once the FBI had been hamstrung, once the borders had been kept
dangerously porous, then it was only left to make a terrorist hijacker's
job easier at the airports, and the Clinton administration duly obliged.
The same political correctness, ethnic lobbying, and lack of tough-
mindedness that characterized the administration's treatment of the
FBI and immigration policy were in play at the airports.[81]

Profiling of a sort had been an official practice of the nation's airlines for years. In 1994, Northwest began to develop a computer-
assisted passenger pre-screening system (CAPPS) to single out
high-threat passengers. After the TWA Flight 800 disaster in July
1996, the Clinton administration convened a commission led by Al
Gore to study aviation security. It was quickly reined in by ethnic and
civil liberties groups.

Journalist Heather Mac Donald writes, "When word leaked out that
the commission was considering a profiling system that would take into
account a passenger's national origin and ethnicity, among other factors, in assessing the security risk he posed, the anti–law enforcement
advocates, along with the Arab lobby, went ballistic. The counsel for
the ACLU fired off an op-ed to the *Washington Post* complaining that
'profiles select people who fit the stereotype of a terrorist. They frequently discriminate on the basis of race, religion, or national origin.'"[82]

The Gore commission recommended that the Northwest system
be adopted by the airline industry generally, but was scared of anything
that could be called racial profiling. Under pressure from Arab-American and civil liberties groups, the commission insisted that profiling

not rely "on material of a constitutionally suspect nature—e.g., race, religion, or national origin of U.S. citizens." The profiles instead would use factors such as whether someone had bought a one-way ticket or paid cash for it.

Even this prompted howls of outrage. After the commission issued its final recommendations in 1997, a dozen Arab-American and civil liberties groups sent a letter to Gore warning that "the risks to privacy are enormous" and reminding him that "passengers check their luggage, not their constitutional rights." The Gore commission had gone out of its way to address such concerns. It had convened a group of civil liberties experts to worry officially about the dangers of profiling. The group's contribution was an appendix to the report. "Efforts should be made," the group advised, "to avoid using characteristics that impose a disproportionate burden of inconvenience, embarrassment, or invasion of privacy on members of minority racial, religious, or ethnic groups."

Because it had been so watered down, the CAPPS airline security program eventually won some Arab-American support. The Justice Department examined CAPPS in 1997 for evidence of racism, and found none, although it recommended that the Federal Aviation Administration (FAA) require airlines to take steps to keep profiling from becoming discriminatory or insensitive. The FAA obliged, focusing on preventing personal searches that might make passengers feel uncomfortable. "Manual screening has been criticized by persons who perceived it as discriminating against citizens on the basis of race, color, national or ethnic origin, and gender," warned the FAA.

No one flagged by CAPPS, therefore, would be searched or even know they had been profiled. Instead, their checked luggage might be screened for bombs, and security might check that they actually boarded the plane. (The pre–September 11 assumption was that no terrorist would get on the same plane as a bomb.) The Clinton administration had hit on a perfect policy: sensitive, hands-free profiling!

This politically correct system had its intended politically correct result. According to the Council on American-Islamic Relations, profiling complaints dropped from twenty-seven when CAPPS first came online in 1997 to two in 1999, and finally none in 2000.

CAPPS, then, had served its political function. Its security function was another matter, as it was painfully easy to circumvent. If terrorists bought round-trip tickets and used credit cards, they slipped by two of the CAPPS criteria. According to the *Wall Street Journal*, CAPPS managed to flag two of the September 11 hijackers, Nawaf Alhazmi and Khalid Al-Midhar, who commandeered Flight 77, the Pentagon plane. They had reserved their tickets by credit card, but paid in cash. While their checked bags were supposedly more carefully checked, neither of them was searched or questioned at the airport—lest, presumably, they complain to the Council on American-Islamic Relations.

On their way they went. If ethnicity and national origin were among the CAPPS criteria, all of the September 11 hijackers probably would have been flagged. And if personal searches and questioning had been routine, a bizarre pattern might have become clear—Why so many Arabs in first class? Why so many box cutters?—and the plot come undone.[83] But that would have required a system that offended people's racial and ethnic sensitivities, something from which the Clinton administration recoiled.[84]

It's not as though Attorney General Janet Reno and the administration were incapable of ever being tough. When she thought a Texas cult was involved in child abuse, she approved drastic measures. When right-wing Cuban émigrés wanted to keep Elián González from being shipped back to Cuba's totalitarianism, she approved a raid to rip him from their arms. It's when get-tough measures would offend minority groups allied with the Democrats or clash with a tenet of liberal faith (e.g., the FBI is a threat to the nation's liberties) that laxity ruled.

So life rolled merrily along on the Bunny Planet, the dreams of little bunnies undisturbed by FBI surveillance, border control, racial profiling, or any other nasty things that might make them sad—or protect Americans from mass murder.

Part Three

FOREIGN POLICY

THE WORLD:

McGovern Without the Conscience

I N EARLY 1996, WARREN CHRISTOPHER sent a memo to the rest of the State Department addressing what he thought had been a historic weakness in the department's work, endangering America's security. It was entitled, "Integrating Environmental Issues into the Department's Core Foreign Policy Goals."

Christopher maintained that "America's national interests are inextricably linked with the quality of the Earth's environment." He mandated that all his overseas trips include an environmental event, and that embassies make environmental issues part of their "Mission Program Plan." In a speech at Stanford in April 1996 he elaborated on the theme, exhorting the nation to "contend with the vast new dangers posed to our national interests by damage to the environment and resulting global and regional instability. As the flagship institution of American foreign policy, the State Department must spearhead a government-wide effort to meet these environmental challenges."[1]

Thus, in the view of the Clinton team, the challenges to America with the end of the Cold War would no longer be characterized by power politics and war, but by problems that dovetailed with traditional liberal domestic priorities. The Environmental Protection Agency was going global.

The Clinton administration affected nostalgia for the days of competition with the Soviet Union. Clinton would often say, "Gosh, I miss the Cold War."[2] Secretary of State Warren Christopher remarked, "It was easy when we could simply point to the Soviet Union and say that what we had to do was to contain Soviet expansion."[3] Actually, facing down a totalitarian empire bent on world conquest was not "easy." Even if it had been, few Clinton advisors had pointed to the Soviet Union as an expansionist threat to be contained.

The formative experience of many Clinton foreign policy aides was in the anti–Vietnam War movement. They were veterans of the George McGovern presidential campaign in 1972, which had as its motto, "Come Home, America," and wanted the country to quit the twilight struggle with the Soviets. Then, many of them went on to serve in the Carter administration, led by a president who had warned his fellow Americans against having an "an inordinate fear of Communism." A defeatist, apologetic attitude toward American power was instinctual for much of the Clinton team.

On the lips of Clinton officials, then, "the end of the Cold War" was a dangerous phrase. It meant the end of what most of the Clinton team had never supported: traditional geopolitics in which the United States defends its interests, with the vigorous application of its power. The fall of the Berlin Wall meant kissing good-bye to all that.

Madeleine Albright—initially the U.S. ambassador to the UN, then Christopher's successor as secretary of state—maintained that there was no reason to read books of scholarship written before 1989: "They are about as useful now as archaeology; they are ancient history."[4] In place of old-style power politics, the Clinton administration offered a blindingly sunny vision of global interconnectedness and cooperation. The new globalizing world would make traditional instruments of state power less important, as the world converged in a benign network of commerce.

American policy reflected, and encouraged, a bleaching away of the nation. The United States intervened in Somalia, Haiti, Bosnia, and Kosovo in response to what were—with the semi-exception of Bosnia—internal matters within the borders of sovereign states. American sovereignty itself would be constrained by a commitment to multilateralism and—if the administration got its way—such far-reaching trans-national institutions as the International Criminal Court. Interventions strictly in defense of the national interest were considered atavistic.

Bill Clinton so often apologized for America because, in this new world, America as a sovereign nation was a kind of embarrassment. He apologized for slavery and American neglect of Africa,[5] denounced U.S. Cold War policies in Latin America,[6] and made apologetic sounds to Iran.[7] His posture toward the rest of the world was a proudly defensive cringe—proud of his own enlightenment and virtue, cringing at his nation's failings.

Apologizing was a Clinton strong suit, because it was so easy. His modus operandi was to make grand rhetorical sounds about problems, whether it was weapons proliferation or terrorism, then recoil from the tough measures necessary to deal with them, whether cracking down on American exporters or killing extremists. The qualities that defined 1990s America domestically—the obsession with business, an increasingly feminized politics, and a general silliness—were broadcast by the Clinton administration onto the international stage, and augmented by Clinton's own personal temporizing and "Can't we all get along?" bonhomie.

It made for a foreign policy of McGovernism, but without the conscience. The Clinton administration had McGovernism's guilt about American power and reluctance to deploy it in the national interest. But it combined them with a blind focus on the bottom line and a cynical disregard for its own idealistic rhetoric.

The administration left the world a more dangerous place. It winked at weapons proliferation around the globe, got diplomatically outdueled by Saddam Hussein, ignored a growing threat from Islamic extremism, coddled the lunatic regime in North Korea, and generally projected an image of American weakness at what should have been a moment of unparalleled strength.

Of course, there is much continuity in any American administration's foreign policy, with a general leaning toward promoting democracy and open markets. Differences are often in shading and degree. And the Clinton administration did get a few big questions right, most importantly expanding NATO and maintaining trade relations with China. But three distinctive themes of Clinton foreign policy jump out, joined by a connective tissue of dishonesty: frivolity, cash, and wishful thinking.

They can be seen in the administration's focus on international social work and the elevation of it to high strategic status; in a commercialism that was considered more important than confronting weapons proliferation and much else; in a devotion to the pieties of arms control, even as they were proving utterly inadequate to a new, more dangerous world; and in a commitment to peace deals that meant ignoring the nature of, and even empowering, nasty interlocutors, from African warlords to totalitarian North Korea.

"We are all one family"

When Warren Christopher issued his 1996 memo on the environment, it demonstrated that the administration considered the world serenely safe enough to concentrate on marginalia. Madeleine Albright told a reporter she rejected the idea that the environment and other "global issues"—e.g., migration, public health, and women's rights—are "soft issues that you do when you don't have anything better to do."[8] That is exactly what they were. If they seemed trivial at the time, they looked positively laughable after the September 11, 2001, terrorist attacks provided a crushing reminder that the world was still a dangerous place.

The administration's foreign policy idealism went well beyond the traditional American impulse to promote self-determination, democracy, and free markets abroad.[9] In Madeleine Albright's original conception of "assertive multilateralism," Clinton would bury American power in the United Nations and other multilateral institutions, where it could be used to remake broken societies in strategically marginal parts of the world. "I think Mother Teresa and Ronald Reagan were both trying to do the same thing, one helping the helpless, one fighting the Evil Empire," said national security advisor Tony Lake, in a fundamental confusion of religious charity with international politics.[10]

The Clinton administration had the gooiest foreign policy in American history. It took social services-oriented domestic issues and hoisted them high onto its international agenda, as a way to craft an aggressive foreign policy for people who didn't otherwise believe in an aggressive foreign policy.[11] "This is what people care about," Albright said of the warm-and-fuzzy issues. "This is the reason to care about foreign policy."[12]

No, it was the reason *she* cared about foreign policy. Albright was the embodiment of the administration's soft focus. She was the foreign policy equivalent of Janet Reno. Like Reno, she was chosen largely because she was a woman, and had ties to Hillary's feminist network.[13] She relished events with "the children."[14] And she was given to sounding themes one wouldn't naturally associate with her office—and shouldn't associate with her office.

Her foreign policy thought moved to the beat of the syrupy 1980s rock ballad, "We Are the World." In 1997, she visited an isolated camp in northwestern Guatemala for former Communist guerrillas, and addressed the villagers. "As I look at all the young children here," she said, "you need to know that the peace is for you. Some of you may wonder why in heaven's name the secretary of state is here. Why would she and the United States care about what is happening here? The reason is that we are all one family, and when one part of our family is not happy or suffers, we all suffer."[15]

In a 1998 commencement address she declared, "We are about to enter a century when there will be far more of us around the world, living closer together, consuming more, demanding more, using more, and throwing more away. Isn't it only common sense that we take reasonable steps to restrain population growth and safeguard the health of our air and the cleanliness of our rivers, lakes, and coasts? For if we fail to do that, we will deny our children and our children's children the legacy of abundance we ourselves inherited. That would be a felony against the future. And it is not acceptable—to you, or to me."[16]

These were not idle musings, but central to the administration's strategic thrust. The Clinton team's emphasis on "global," transnational issues occasionally proved useful—it provided insight into the rising danger of terrorism—but it inevitably spun off into the insignificant.

In its 1994 national security strategy, the administration listed its top priorities, a dog's breakfast of the worthy and the strategically marginal: NATO expansion, American trade competitiveness, implementing NAFTA, market-opening measures under the General Agreement on Trade and Tariffs, reducing greenhouse gases and ozone-depleting emissions, implementation of the Biodiversity Treaty, global family planning, reform in Russia, support for post-apartheid democracy in South Africa, the promotion of democracy in Guatemala and Haiti, and forging a new policy for peacekeeping.[17]

The administration declared in its 1998 "National Security Strategy for a New Century": "[P]roblems that once seemed quite distant—such as resource depletion, rapid population growth, environmental damage, new infectious diseases, and uncontrolled refugee migration—have important implications for American security. Our workers and businesses will suffer if foreign markets collapse or lock us out, and the highest domestic environmental standards will not protect us if we cannot get others to achieve similar standards. In short, our citizens have a direct stake in the prosperity and stability of other nations, in their support for international norms and human rights, in their ability to combat international crime, in their open markets, and in their efforts to protect the environment."[18]

The cost of such a broad focus was detracting attention from the essential. As Osama bin Laden built his worldwide terror network, for instance, the CIA was instructed to undertake duties related to law enforcement and environmental protection.[19]

The soft issues also sent the administration into the arms of Non-Governmental Organizations (NGOs), a network of international groups that shared the administration's leftish politics and vision of a world beyond traditional national sovereignty. When the administration was doing the work of NGOs, it assumed it was fighting for truth and justice.

It joined forces with the NGOs to give unprecedented attention to a dizzying array of international agreements that had been kicking around for years: the UN Conference on Straddling Fish Stocks and Highly Migratory Straddling Stocks;[20] the Basel Convention on the Control of Trans-boundary Movements of Hazardous Wastes and Their Disposal;[21] the Montreal Protocol on Substances That Deplete the Ozone Layer;[22] an international campaign to require fishermen in the Third World to use turtle-excluder devices to protect endangered sea turtles;[23] the UN Convention to Combat Desertification;[24] the Inter-American Convention for the Protection and Conservation of Sea Turtles (not just sea turtles—but Spanish-speaking sea turtles!);[25] the Convention on Biological Diversity;[26] the Convention on International Trade in Endangered Species of Wild Fauna and Flora;[27] the International Coral Reef Initiative;[28] and a Global Treaty on Persistent Organic Pollutants.[29] In the 1990s, this was your nation's foreign policy apparatus at work.

Many NGOs have an explicitly anti-American bias, because as the world's foremost military power, the United States is a standing rebuke to their animating world vision. In working with them, then, the administration inevitably tilted toward policies against America's national interests.

The Clinton administration signed the Kyoto Treaty that would drastically reduce American carbon emissions, while giving the developing world a free pass. It signed on to the International Criminal Court, which would subject American soldiers and officials to international war crime trials and supersede American courts. Neither

Kyoto nor the International Criminal Court had any chance of winning Senate ratification, but Clinton signed them anyway as political theater. He was demonstrating that, though hampered by the provincials back home, his instincts were truly that of a Citizen of the World.

In the 1990s, NGOs constantly sought to constrain the United States in the course of trying to ban or discourage nasty activity that had nothing to do with America.

For example, because Third World armies use landmines irresponsibly, the NGOs demanded that America be banned from using landmines. "Our policy on landmines turned out to be a compromise," says a former Clinton Pentagon official. "There was this incredible drive to get rid of them altogether, yet valid military reasons for us to keep them. It was the first time that we got full-bore the whole NGO-driven, resent-the-United States campaign against us. There's no question that we were really surprised. It was like, 'What is this?' And this was coming from our allies."[30]

When the administration advanced the causes of the NGOs and its other favorite multilateral bodies, the UN and the European Union (EU), it was bolstering institutions with agendas hostile to American power. The EU had the most resources of the three, seeking to make itself the first trans-national state and international counterweight to the American "hyperpower." This project should have been deeply anathema to the United States, but Clinton shared important attitudes with the continental Europeans pushing the EU. They saw the bureaucratic centralism of France and Germany as a superior model to Anglo-American free-market liberalism, and Clinton couldn't say they were necessarily wrong.

Sidney Blumenthal proudly writes that Clinton "was the most sophisticated, knowledgeable, innovative—and European—American president" that the Europeans had ever experienced.[31] Clinton's Third Way was largely about blending the differences of continental European and American politics into a multilateral center-left stew.[32] This U.S.-EU concord inevitably broke down when an American president,

George W. Bush, again pursued a national interest–based foreign policy, putting the underlying anti-Americanism of the French and Germans in stark relief.

When he wasn't joining hands with European social democrats as part of his soft-touch international agenda, Clinton offered as a sign of his progressive attitudes an interest in Africa and Latin America that was innocent of any untoward attachment to pursuing America's strategic interests.[33] Notably, however, Clinton brought the same fecklessness he exhibited in important foreign policy projects to the unimportant ones as well.

What Clinton had to offer was essentially V-chips for Africa. With the significant exception of an African trade bill, he proposed microinitiatives that carried no political risk. He never offered anything of the sweep of George W. Bush's Global AIDS Initiative. When confronted with an opportunity to stop a slaughter somewhere in Africa, he always backed off, too fearful of the political and military risks.

Talk was always the administration's best game. In 1999 Albright fretted that democracy itself was at risk in Colombia.[34] Clinton went so far as to warn in his 2000 State of the Union that Colombia's success in the war on drugs was "important for the long-term stability of *our* country" (emphasis added).[35] Colombia's civil war was a genuinely serious issue, yet the administration's policy was explicitly not to aid the government in its fight against vicious leftist guerrillas threatening the government, because fighting such a Third World insurgency was reminiscent of Vietnam.[36]

The administration offered only anti-drug aid. "The primary focus of the Colombia initiative," said an administration document in August 2000, "is to provide support for Colombia's intensifying counterdrug effort. As a matter of administration policy, we will not support Colombian counterinsurgency efforts." Despite Colombian democracy and the stability of America supposedly being at risk, the administration supported accommodation with the Communist guerrillas. "The administration remains convinced that the ultimate solution to Colombia's longstanding civil conflict is through a successful peace process, not a decisive military victory, and believes that counterdrug progress will contribute to progress toward peace."[37]

At least the administration was consistent, evenly distributing its weakness across the globe.

"We are now drawn together by shared economic interests"

All the administration's foreign policy idealism was significantly leavened with a solicitousness about the corporate bottom line.

Warren Christopher traveled to China in March 1994, pushing President Clinton's policy of linking trade with China's human rights record. Clinton had bludgeoned Bush in the 1992 campaign for trading with the "butchers of Beijing" and said that continuing to extend "most favored nation" trading status to China was "unconscionable." The Chinese greeted Christopher with the arrest of dissidents and diplomatic insolence.[38]

When the secretary of state returned, he told the rest of Clinton's cabinet at a meeting that the trip wasn't quite the debacle it seemed, and that they should at least support the president's policy to the extent of not leaking criticisms of it to the press. "When I finished," Christopher writes, "there was only silence. No one spoke in defense of continued linkage of China's trade status to its human rights progress. It was as if our policy had died in my absence or, as some at the meeting would have it, had never existed. All that remained was to arrange a decent burial."[39]

Christopher should have been used to it. In explaining other early administration reversals of policy in Bosnia and Haiti, Christopher had to plead on *Meet the Press*, "I don't suppose you'd want anybody to keep a campaign promise if it was a very unsound policy."[40] In the case of China, Christopher was encountering the power of the dollar, the almighty icon of business executives and campaign fund-raisers. During the Clinton years, American security policy would often be subordinated to it.

As soon as Clinton announced in May 1994 that not only did he support "most favored nation" status for China, but that Beijing's human rights record would no longer be a factor in its consideration, Commerce Secretary Ron Brown jetted to China. Christopher had petitioned for human rights advances, Brown would scrounge for business deals. He cemented $5 billion worth.[41]

"China's long history is deserving of respect and even deference that she has not always received," he told the Chinese. According to Brown, "Once divided by ideology, we are now drawn together by shared economic interests."[42] Chinese officials loved the fact that Brown said "the United States has some of the worst human rights problems." "You're the first American who has come here," Jiang Zemin gushed (if a Chinese official can do such a thing), "and admitted that your situation is nothing to brag about."[43]

The odiousness of Ron Brown's money-grubbing aside, the decision to keep open trade with China was the right one. There is a sound case for the benign political effects over the long term of economic development, spurred by trade.[44]

Where the Clinton approach was flawed was in its soft-headedness. The hard-nosed business advocacy and focus on the bottom line dovetailed with a naïve view of the world and the strategic environment. Little else was thought to matter besides business.[45] In 1993, just prior to joining Ron Brown's Commerce department, Jeffrey Garten described the administration as having placed trade "at the center of foreign policy, becoming at least as important as political and security questions."[46]

For Clinton, an economic focus served to give foreign policy a domestic political salience—it too was about the economy, stupid. "He conceived of foreign policy," says Dick Morris, "much as he conceived of economic policy and believed that the purpose of foreign policy was to create jobs."[47] According to Tony Lake, "The theme of globalism was in Clinton's mind from being governor of Arkansas and from being a smart guy. And so while we were talking to him about some of the arcane details of past foreign policy negotiations, he was talking to us about the nature of the economy. He was ahead of the foreign policy folks, and I expect ahead of Bob Rubin and some of the others on this issue."[48]

The administration could afford to give economics such a high priority because the world was thought to be getting better and better all the time, minimizing the need for America to shape geopolitics. Jeffrey Garten wrote after his tenure at Commerce ended, "The administration does not spend a lot of time worrying about holding the free world together, as the momentum everywhere is toward democracy and capitalism."[49] So, for instance, the administration squeezed Japan in 1994 to make trade concessions to the United States, rather than concentrating on getting its help to force North Korea to abandon its nuclear program.[50]

Trade trumped all even when the tiniest of markets were involved, and even when it meant trampling human rights in extreme cases, including those involving terror states. The administration exempted dirt-poor Sudan from the 1996 anti-terrorism act to open the way for an oil deal for Occidental Petroleum, even though the terrorist-connected Sudanese government was waging a genocidal campaign against the country's Christians and animists. The administration also exempted Syria and Lebanon, the former an active sponsor of terrorism, the latter a host state for terrorists. As the head of the Export-Import Bank said of Lebanon in 1996, "They always pay their bills. . . . Our purpose is to create American jobs, not promote peace."[51]

Not since the 1920s had an administration made the Commerce Department such a crucial part of its foreign policy.[52] This created obvious ethical problems. Ron Brown wanted not just to win contracts for American business, but to win corporate political support and contributions. He also wanted the support and contributions of ethnic groups with ties to other countries.

In this borderless, dollar-driven world, things like "ethics" and "national security" seemed parochial. Hence, the spectacle of Chinese agents working for the president's reelection in 1996. "If you open a wild bazaar, as we did, you have to expect the occasional pick-pocket," is how Jeffrey Garten explained the China fund-raising scandal.[53]

The wild bazaar was most disturbing in the administration's policies regarding the proliferation of weapons technology to rogue and other untrustworthy regimes.

"Enormous pressure to fudge"

The administration allowed trade to triumph over any serious effort to block an ongoing weapons proliferation revolution. So the power bestowed by missiles and weapons of mass destruction steadily accrued to enemies of the United States, even as corporate bottom lines and political contributions to Clinton swelled.

The administration had a few anti-proliferation successes. It persuaded Ukraine to give up its nuclear weapons after the breakup of the Soviet Union, and it supported the Nunn-Lugar program to help the former Soviet Union secure and reduce its number of weapons of mass destruction.[54] The trouble came when the cause of non-proliferation clashed with the bottom line, in which case the dollar prevailed.

"He wanted to get corporate money," says Gary Milhollin, director of the Wisconsin Project on Nuclear Arms Control and a relentless scourge of policies that spread high technology to dangerous regimes, "and he didn't have much to sell except for export controls. He couldn't trade the environment. He couldn't trade labor. He was looking for something he could trade away without alienating a large portion of his political support. And so what did he find? He found export controls. It was a great disservice to our country. It was on the same moral level as pardoning Marc Rich."[55]

In the 1992 campaign, Clinton issued a plan drafted by Silicon Valley executives saying export "controls are often overly restrictive and bureaucratic, creating a mountain of red tape and costing the U.S. tens of billions of dollars in exports." In September 1993, he wrote a letter to Edward McCracken, CEO of Silicon Graphics, assuring him that reform of the Coordinating Committee for Multi-lateral Export Controls (CoCom) was on the way.[56]

CoCom had minimized the export of strategic technology from the West to the Soviet bloc. Its reform, at the hands of the Clinton administration, meant its wholesale elimination in March 1994.[57] Corporate profits rather than national security would be the most important consideration in American export control policy. In the process the United States was abandoning an important tool to influence the behavior of other countries. Export controls had helped squeeze Argentina and Brazil out of their nuclear ambitions.[58] CoCom's successor was the so-called Wassenaar Arrangement, a much looser regime that allowed countries to decide on their own what technology was safely exportable.[59]

Russia was brought into the Wassenaar Arrangement and the similarly loose Missile Technology Control Regime (MCTR) partly so that American business could sell it more technology. Russia made pledges to be more responsible in its exports, but a typical arms control dynamic took hold in which the administration hesitated to enforce such pledges, as keeping Russia in the agreements became an end in itself. So, ever more blandishments were offered in exchange for Russia's latest promises to abide by earlier promises, in an ongoing cycle of hope triumphing over experience.[60]

Russia inaugurated its entry into the MCTR with missile technology transfers to India that violated the agreement, but the administration gave Moscow a pass on technical grounds of timing. The administration shrugged off a Russian export of missile guidance sets to Iraq in 1995. It balked at Russian plans to build a nuclear reactor for Iran, winning some concessions before Moscow compounded the offense by providing missile assistance to Iran.[61]

The futility of it all prompted Congress to act, passing sanctions on Russia in June 1998 to the chagrin of the administration. "I found the whole episode dispiriting, even distasteful," sniffs Clinton's Russia guru Strobe Talbot.[62] Clinton himself referred to the imperative that had been driving the administration's obfuscation. "What happens if you have automatic sanctions legislation is it puts enormous pressure on whoever is in the executive branch to fudge an evaluation of the facts of what is going on."[63] Clinton vetoed the bill, but acted tough by imposing sanctions on Russian firms that did no business with the United States.[64]

The administration followed much the same trajectory with China. It signed Beijing up to all manner of nonproliferation agreements, opening the spigots for American exports to China. Henry Sokolski writes in his book *Best of Intentions*, "[F]rom 1994 through 1997, U.S. officials approved over a billion dollars in guaranteed U.S. government loans to U.S. firms exporting nuclear-related goods and services to Chinese entities (e.g., Chinese National Nuclear Corporation) known to be assisting Iranian and Pakistani nuclear weapons efforts."[65]

The administration responded to Chinese violations—involving nuclear and missile deals with both Pakistan and Iran—by accepting promises that were soon broken again and resorting to any other dodge to keep from sanctioning China and inconveniencing the American firms doing business with it.[66] Consider the case of the M-11 missiles.

China sold these short-range ballistic missiles and their production technology to Pakistan beginning around 1991. The missiles can be armed with nuclear warheads. The United States had intermittently sanctioned China for the transfers, but the Clinton administration waived the sanctions in October 1994. In exchange, the administration received Chinese promises to end the exports, which, of course, were broken.[67] (In 1992, when Bush had waived similar sanctions, vice presidential candidate Al Gore had called him "an incurable patsy for those dictators he sets out to coddle.")[68] Confronted with photographs of M-11 canisters on the ground in Pakistan, the State Department explained them away.[69] Confronted with certain confirmation of the exports by American intelligence, State simply ignored American sanctions laws.[70]

The winking at Chinese malfeasance stopped only when it endangered American profits. Clinton threatened China with $2 billion worth of tariffs in 1996 to get it to stop pirating American intellectual property.[71] Chinese pirating of American CDs and movies was taken more seriously by the Clinton administration than Chinese missile technology. Disney's interests became the nation's.

C. Michael Armstrong, the chairman of the satellite maker Hughes Electronics and a Clinton supporter, lobbied hard against the M-11 sanctions that were in place until 1994. A White House memo in 1993 worried: "Armstrong is now fairly directly threatening to wage a more public campaign against the administration's sanctions." The sanctions were lifted, and Armstrong was added to the administration's Export Council in 1995 to continue his pressure against export controls from a quasi-official perch.[72]

He could only be delighted when Clinton decided to hand licensing for commercial satellite launches to the export-friendly Commerce Department in 1996, and otherwise eased the way for satellite makers to do business with China.[73] Bernard Schwartz, the chairman of another satellite maker, Loral Space & Communications, felt the same way. He was the biggest contributor to Clinton's campaign in 1996, and the biggest contributor to the Democrats in the 1998 midterm elections, giving $1.1 million to the Democratic Party between 1992 and 1998.[74]

Business considerations also drove the administration's decontrols on the export of supercomputers, which are extremely important in producing ballistic missiles and weapons of mass destruction. In 1996, the administration began drastically increasing the power of computers that could be exported to China and Russia without a government-approved license, and Chinese and Russian military entities reaped a computing windfall.[75]

Silicon Valley loved it. In the run-up to the 2000 election cycle, it favored the Democrats over the Republicans and was the fourth largest industry contributor to the Democratic National Committee.[76]

By 1998, proliferation around the world had reached a tipping point. Henry Sokolski writes that Iran had tested a new ballistic missile "with Russian, Chinese, and North Korean assistance. India tested nuclear weapons and long-range rockets with Russian help. Pakistan replied with nuclear tests of its own and deployed rockets developed with Chinese and North Korean help."[77] The administration bitterly complained about the Pakistani and Indian tests, but it had been unwilling to do anything to keep Pakistan from getting Chinese assistance.[78]

Proliferation represented a frank challenge to Western power.[79] China and Russia were the suppliers, with Pakistan, Iran, Iraq, and North Korea—all outlaw states to one degree or another—the primary recipients. China and Russia figured that the more weapons they put in the hands of regimes hostile to the United States, the greater the chance of constraining American power. And the Clinton administration was happy to sell them both the means to do so.

"One of the sacred texts of arms control"

The Clinton administration was aware of the danger of proliferation. In November 1994, President Clinton called weapons proliferation "an unusual and extraordinary threat," and declared "a national emergency to deal with that threat."[80] In 1997, Madeleine Albright called proliferation "the most overriding security interest of our time."[81] It's just that, as usual, the administration would not back up its talk.

The administration was ill equipped to deal with proliferation, given its political and economic commitment to exporting American technology, its temperamental distaste for unpleasantness with states such as Russia and China, and its overriding faith in the parchment gods of arms control.

The intellectual thread of the 1928 Kellogg-Briand pact, prohibiting the recourse to war to settle international disputes, traced all the way into the Clinton administration. The enduring idea was that international law, enshrined in treaties, could outlaw weapons and associated nasty behavior. In practice, the "arms control process" relies mostly on benign nations imposing limits on themselves in order to create "norms" meant to influence the behavior of other, less benign states.

This explains the Clinton impetus to enmesh the United States in as many arms control treaties as possible, from the Chemical Weapons

Convention to the Comprehensive Test Ban treaty, in a tapestry of self-limitation.[82] The administration confused arms control with national security. It was the ABM treaty that was the most politically contentious of the treaties, and best demonstrated the absurdities of arms control doctrine, even as the Clinton team poured into the treaty the full measure of its devotion.

In an April 1994 speech, Clinton Arms Control and Disarmament Agency director John Holum said, "I turn now to a growing menace [proliferation] that has led some people mistakenly to surmise that we are lessening our commitment to one of the sacred texts of arms control—the anti-ballistic missile (or ABM) treaty.... As a broad proposition, I think that arms control generally has more to offer our national security today than do more weapons systems. We look first to arms control and second—where it has failed or simply come on the scene too late—to defenses."[83]

Madeleine Albright repeatedly said similar things in the final years of the administration, calling the treaty "the basis of most of our strategic thinking."[84]

The theory behind the ABM treaty was the doctrine of "mutually assured destruction," MAD. It rested on the idea that stability was guaranteed and a nuclear first strike would be discouraged if each side in the Cold War had enough missiles to achieve an assured level of destruction against the other side, even after absorbing a first strike. Missile defenses would threaten this equilibrium. For instance, if the United States were able to defend against a Soviet retaliatory attack, it would prompt the Soviets to build more missiles, making the world a more dangerous place.

So went the theory. But the Soviets never bought it. Even after the "stabilizing" ABM treaty was signed in 1972, the Soviets kept right on building offensive missiles.[85] If the theory behind the ABM treaty had always been bogus, it was also outdated with the demise of the Soviet Union and the rise of new rogue-state missile threats.[86] But the administration worshiped the treaty anyway.

In 1993, it immediately slashed funding for missile defense roughly in half.[87] The administration only warmed to missile defense when political pressure from the Dole campaign forced it to. Clinton adopted a plan to possibly deploy a limited defensive system by 2003.[88] When the 2003 timeline slipped, Clinton adopted, under congressional pressure, another plan to possibly deploy a limited system by 2005—scuttled in its turn.[89]

Denying any rogue-state missile threat was essential to the administration's anti-missile defense case, and it did it routinely.[90] Then, a congressionally mandated, bipartisan commission headed by Donald Rumsfeld was charged with determining the nature of the missile threat.[91] The commission's July 1998 report concluded that within five years states such as North Korea or Iran could—with minimal warning, or maybe none—develop missiles capable of reaching the United States.[92]

After the release of the report, chairman of the Joint Chiefs General Hugh Shelton greeted it skeptically. "The commission points out that through unconventional, high-risk development programs and foreign assistance, rogue nations could acquire an ICBM capability in a short time, and that the intelligence community may not detect it. We view this as an unlikely development." One week later, North Korea shocked American intelligence and the world by launching a three-stage Taepo Dong-1 missile with an intercontinental range.[93]

The Rumsfeld report, coupled with the North Korea launch, gave a double boost to supporters of legislation to make it American policy to deploy a missile-defense system "as soon as is technologically possible." Clinton threatened to veto the bill, but when it passed the Senate 97–3 in March 1999 he had no choice but to sign it.[94]

This elevated even further the issue of the ABM treaty in the administration's indulgent relationship with the Russians. The administration's Russian policy was founded both on the belief that the success of Boris Yeltsin offered Russia its only way forward, and on the warm personal sympathy between Clinton and Yeltsin.

Strobe Talbott tried to explain the connection between the two in his memoir, *The Russian Hand*: "The key, as I saw it, might be that Yeltsin combined prodigious determination and fortitude with grotesque indiscipline and a kind of genius for self-abasement. He was both a very big man and a very bad boy, a natural leader and an incurable screw-up. All this Clinton recognized, found easy to forgive, and wanted others to join him in forgiving."[95]

There were limits to how much the United States could influence the domestic affairs of Russia, but the administration's policy was unduly weighted toward aiding Yeltsin's success at any cost, even if it meant watching his cronies steal with abandon. A kind of klepto-state grew up in Russia. As a general matter, more pressure on Yeltsin from Clinton and less bonding over personal dysfunctions would have been appropriate.[96]

The administration, however, did sometimes push the Russians: on Bosnia and Kosovo, and most importantly on NATO. NATO's expansion eastward stabilized Europe, providing an anchor of democratic reform. But the administration pursued expansion only after much worry whether it would be too hard for the Russians to accept. Moscow huffed and puffed, but swallowed the inevitable, as usual. Says a former top Clinton diplomat, "They're pretty quick to reach the right conclusions when we're determined."[97]

What the administration wasn't determined to push for was an end to the ABM treaty. Offending the Russians was bad enough. Offending them in the interest of freeing the United States from the constraints of a thirty-year-old arms control agreement was nearly unthinkable.[98]

The Russians never budged in negotiations over the future of the treaty, because they sensed the administration didn't truly care about changing it. Madeleine Albright said of a December 1998 administration meeting that endorsed exploring missile defense, "I remember that meeting very well, because I looked around the table, and here was the cast of characters who had all been the ones saying that Star Wars was crazy."[99] It showed. At one point, former Clinton defense officials William Perry and John Deutch publicly attacked the administration's missile defense plans—at the urging of senior presidential advisors.[100]

The Russians must have been amused. When Yeltsin's successor Vladimir Putin called Clinton two days after one missile defense test failure, he poked fun at Clinton's ambivalence, saying, "I don't know whether to congratulate you or commiserate with you."[101]

Clinton gave a speech in September 2000 deferring, yet again, plans to build a system. But the speech made an important political and intellectual concession. "Because the emerging missile threat is real," Clinton said, "we have an obligation to pursue a missile defense system that could enhance our security." Ultimately, Clinton and his advisors recognized the changed international environment and knew that ignoring it could create a grave vulnerability for the country—but they loved an outdated arms control treaty too much to do anything about it.[102]

"One of the best things the administration has done"

Arms control was closely related to another Clinton administration obsession—the peace deal. Both feature the same faith that conflicts can be talked out, the same legalism, the same imperative of downplaying the ill intentions of unscrupulous parties.

There is obviously a place for negotiated settlements. The administration successfully forged one in the Bosnian war. But that was largely because one of the parties, the Serbs, had been beaten on the ground, and bombed by the United States. The Dayton accord sealed their defeat. Peace deals become dangerous and immoral when they are an excuse for not defeating or confronting an enemy—or at least recognizing his nature.

The attraction of peace deals, even the most tenuous of them, was obvious for the administration. Peace deals made problems get off the front page. They made for bragging points, and the possibility of Nobel Prizes. They played to the administration's conciliatory international temperament, reflecting Clinton's optimism, fondness for talk, and hope always to win all sides to one point of view. And peace deals had one last advantage: if they were flawed, the odds were they would blow up after Clinton was safely out of office.

The cost of the peace deal as usually practiced by the Clinton administration was fuzzing the difference between the forces of civilization and barbarism, and granting thugs support and power. These were the weaknesses of Clinton's most celebrated peace deals in Northern Ireland[103] and (although the agreements were only interim) in the Israeli-Palestinian conflict. They are also starkly demonstrated in two other Clinton administration peace deals, one minor, the other strategically vital, one representing no threat to American security, the other constituting a danger to this day: Sierra Leone and North Korea.

Sierra Leone had a hellish deal foist upon it. Foday Sankoh led a group of rebels called the Revolutionary United Front (RUF) in Sierra Leone that fought through means of rape, amputation, and unspeakable brutality. They were evil personified. The rebels briefly seized the government in 1997, making the capital of Freetown a pit of horror, but were expelled by Nigerian-led peacekeepers.[104]

The rebels bounced back, waging war from the brush, and the question for the Clinton administration was whether to make the financial effort to aid the flagging Nigerians in crushing them once and for all, or simply admit that it didn't care that much about the fate of Sierra Leone. As Ryan Lizza wrote in a stinging piece in the *New Republic*, "The Clintonites, typically, did neither. Against all the evidence that Sierra Leone could be saved from the RUF only through war, the Clinton administration set out to make peace."[105]

With the extensive involvement of its special envoy Jesse Jackson and its ambassador to Sierra Leone, the Clinton administration largely wrote a deal between the government and the rebels that was finalized in Lomé, Togo, in July 1991. The advantage of the Lomé agreement was that it was something the administration could call a peace deal. Otherwise, it was a catastrophe.[106]

Sankoh was a savage, who should have been executed for crimes against his people. The administration not only helped save him from that fate by lobbying the government to release him after he had been captured, but it made him vice president, handed him control of the country's diamond mines, and gave his forces an amnesty for their atrocities.[107] It was a twisted parody of peace-process moral equivalence.

Once released, Sankoh reorganized his army. The rebels ignored the agreement's requirements that they disarm and stop their illegal diamond trade, and they restarted their campaign of mayhem. Importantly, the agreement had replaced the Nigerian peacekeepers with UN peacekeepers, who weren't as well equipped to protect themselves and therefore were ripe targets. The rebels proceeded to take them hostage and steal their arms. The Lomé agreement exploded. The administration tried to send Jesse Jackson to mediate again, but the government would have none of it. It was only force that saved the situation, as British troops protected the capital from the rebel assault.[108]

Ryan Lizza points out the transparent dishonesty of the administration over the deal. In September 1999, assistant secretary of state for African Affairs Susan Rice said, "The U.S. role in Sierra Leone . . . has been instrumental." That line abruptly changed after the agreement collapsed. A State Department official said in June 2000, "We were not part of that agreement."[109]

Clinton managed to preserve his preening moralism about Africa, saying in February 2000, "We can no longer choose not to know. We can only choose not to act, or to act. In this world, we can be indifferent, or we can make a difference. America must choose, when it comes to Africa, to make a difference."[110] In Sierra Leone, the administration made a difference that only Foday Sankoh could appreciate.

North Korea was a much more important country. But just as in Sierra Leone, the administration arrived at a deal so bankrupt that it was difficult to know whether it would be worse if it failed or succeeded. The stakes in the North Korean crisis of 1993–1994 were high, with the looming possibility of a second Korean War. Caution was appropriate. The administration, however, lurched all the way toward self-abasement.

It allowed itself to get intimidated into a 1994 deal, the Agreed Framework, that was ideal for Pyongyang. The United States poured ever more aid into the country in the forlorn hope that it would moderate the regime's behavior, and when evidence began to accumulate that North Korea was cheating on the deal, the administration ignored it and paid more blackmail. Appeasement of Pyongyang had started as a reflex under pressure and became an ingrained habit.

The administration resolutely stuck to its talking point that the Agreed Framework had been a work of diplomatic genius. In February 1997, as worrisome intelligence about renewed North Korean nuclear activity continued to build, Madeleine Albright said, "The Framework Agreement is one of the best things the administration has done because it stopped a nuclear weapons program in North Korea."[111]

There had been murmurings of a nuclear crisis in the early 1990s, although North Korea reached an agreement at the beginning of 1992 with the International Atomic Energy Agency for inspections. It didn't take long for the IAEA to discover that the North Koreans were hiding something. In March 1993, North Korea announced its nifty solution to the growing mess—it was withdrawing, effective in June, from the Nuclear Non-proliferation Treaty (NPT) that committed non-nuclear powers to staying that way.[112]

This confronted the new Clinton administration with an enormous crisis, obviously not of its own making. North Korea probably already had enough reprocessed plutonium for one or two atomic bombs. Worse, the reactor at Yongbyon would soon reach the end of its fuel cycle, providing a load of fuel rods that if reprocessed would yield plutonium for another half dozen bombs. If North Korea kicked the reactor into full-throttle production, it could provide plutonium for a dozen new bombs a year.[113]

A full-scale nuclear breakout was possible. It would threaten South Korea and American troops there, and change the strategic balance of the region and possibly beyond, since Pyongyang had a practice of selling its weapons far and wide.

The position of the IAEA was clear—North Korea must submit to inspections to determine how much plutonium it had already diverted, and inspections of the reactor and its defueling. The position of the Clinton administration would become equally clear—ditch the IAEA. The Clinton administration wanted to finesse the NPT to allow North Korea to remain in the treaty despite being in violation of it.[114]

The administration embraced North Korea's call for direct talks, thus granting North Korea its wish of muscling South Korea out of the negotiations.[115] The administration held sanctions out as its only available stick, but was extremely reluctant to impose them because North Korea said sanctions would be tantamount to an "act of war."[116] Thus, the administration allowed itself to be spooked out of one of its key points of leverage, and the crisis headed toward a sweetheart deal for North Korea.

On November 7, 1993, Clinton declared, "North Korea cannot be allowed to develop a nuclear bomb."[117] Within a few months, administration officials were saying that Clinton had "misspoken." "Our policy right along," Clinton secretary of defense William Perry explained at the time, "has been oriented to try to keep North Korea from getting a significant nuclear weapons capability."[118] Emphasis on *significant*. Translation: North Korea would be allowed to keep any nukes it had built.

The administration began to have harsh words for the IAEA, because in an exact reversal of the situation that would materialize in the Iraq crisis in 2002, Hans Blix was much tougher and more demanding than the American government. One Clinton official denounced Blix as a "fanatic," while Clinton official Robert Gallucci sneered at the IAEA's "medieval or perhaps Talmudic" operations.[119]

Jimmy Carter, who could out-appease even Bill Clinton, would be the administration's savior. During the Bush administration and earlier in the Clinton presidency, he had sought repeatedly to visit Pyongyang, but had always been turned down. In June 1994, he was on an unofficial but administration-approved mission to Pyongyang, playing the role he would often reprise in the 1990s of rogue-state consigliore. He lost no time in undermining the American position. "In my opinion, the pursuit of sanctions is counterproductive in this particular and unique society," he said. "The declaration of sanctions would be considered as an insult to their country."[120]

As he left North Korea, Carter teared up thinking about what he had accomplished,[121] which was essentially a further offer to negotiate from the North. The administration was ready to grasp at almost anything, and was frightened even by the possibility of having to reinforce American troops in South Korea. "This offer from Kim Il Sung was ambiguous and could very well lead into a cul-de-sac," Perry writes. "Still, it was a hopeful development, since it averted for the time being the potential provocation of the buildup we had proposed."[122]

From this negotiation issued the Agreed Framework of October 21, 1994. North Korea promised to freeze, and eventually dismantle, its nuclear program at Yongbyon, remain part of the NPT, and allow some IAEA inspections, although a full accounting of its weapons program was put off into the future. In exchange, the United States would—in conjunction with South Korea and Japan—build light-water reactors for the North that were supposedly (but not really)[123] less prone to exploitation for weapons purposes than the graphite reactors the North was abandoning. It would deliver five hundred tons of heavy fuel oil a year to replace the energy supposedly lost by North Korea's closing of its reactors.[124]

The deal was a boon to the North. It had leveraged a position that the United States had declared unacceptable at the outset of the crisis—developing nuclear weapons—into a diplomatic and economic triumph. It was springtime for Pyongyang.

It is against U.S. law to sell nuclear reactors to countries in violation of the NPT, so the Clinton administration planned to subcontract the reactor work to allies. Why North Korea needed reactors at all was a mystery, since the same energy needs could be provided by gas-, oil- or coal-fired power plants, which are much simpler to build and maintain.[125]

But the time it would take to construct the nuclear reactors was part of the point. It made for a drawn-out process during which North Korea didn't have to fully perform, in terms of yielding to inspectors or dismantling its nuclear assets, while soaking up economic and energy aid. The regime could be confident that, in the end, it would get nuclear material either from the plutonium stash under IAEA guard that it was refusing to give up, from a secret program still continuing, or eventually from the reactors that would be built for it by the West.

In the meantime, North Korea could test missiles by firing them over Japan, proliferate missile technology around the world, and continuously threaten war, while becoming the largest recipient of American succor in Asia. Food aid was piled on top of the energy aid promised in the Agreed Framework in response to a famine.[126] For the administration, the food aid served an important ulterior purpose: creating the illusion of progress with the North. "Officially a humanitarian gesture, American food aid has become a bribe for North Korea to attend meetings that create the impression U.S. diplomacy is working," wrote former diplomat Robert A. Manning in 1998.[127]

The CIA had thought North Korea would cheat on the agreement all along. "Based on North Korea's past behavior," it wrote in 1995, "the [intelligence] community agrees it would dismantle its known program, [only] if it had covertly developed another source of fissile material."[128]

North Korea was in an ideal position to pick and choose what it would comply with and when, and go back to the United States for yet more concessions after further misbehavior. The Clinton administration, on the other hand, felt compelled to minimize North Korean violations in order to protect the image of the Agreed Framework.

The United States came to believe in 1997 that North Korea had built an underground nuclear facility in Kumchang-ri. The administration still dishonestly maintained that all was well with the Agreed Framework. On July 8, 1998, Albright told Congress, the Agreed Framework had "frozen North Korea's dangerous nuclear weapons program." When intelligence about Kumchang-ri became public in August 1998, Albright told frustrated senators at a hearing that she hadn't known about the information until later in July. The head of the Defense Intelligence Agency, present at the hearing, had to interrupt her: "Madame Secretary, that is incorrect." She had been told many months earlier.[129]

It was clear by the late 1990s to honest observers that North Korea still had a nuclear weapons program, while it was spreading missile technology far and wide and battening itself on American support.[130] The strategic assumptions of the Agreed Framework had been proven false. It was supposed to moderate North Korean behavior, or if not, at least play for time while the regime moved ever closer to collapse. Neither happened, since the framework both rewarded irresponsible behavior and propped up the regime with aid.

The administration was nonetheless eager to try to create an Agreed Framework II, this time focused on missiles. As a State Department official said, "Hopefully, some day soon, we will get those talks back on track and be able to have as much success in the missile area as we had in the nuclear area."[131]

In October 2000, Madeleine Albright visited North Korea to pave the way for a possible last-minute Clinton trip there to cut a missile deal. She called Pyongyang an "impressive and beautiful city,"[132] pronounced Kim Jong Il "jovial and forthcoming and interested and knowledgeable,"[133] and professed to be taken with the "Kim Jong Il-ia," a flower bred in honor of the dictator.[134] She watched and applauded along with Kim at a stadium demonstration that included praise for North Korea's nuclear and missile programs.[135] (Earlier in the year, she had rhetorically given dictators around the world similarly warm treatment when she announced that the State Department would no longer use the term "rogue states," but instead "states of concern.")[136]

North Korea floated the idea of U.S. payments of $1 billion a year for at least three years[137] and free launches of its satellites,[138] in exchange for promising to give up its missile program. Clinton ultimately decided not to go to North Korea in December 2000 because he had run out of time, and a sequel to the Agreed Framework was dropped.[139]

The Agreed Framework itself ended when the North Koreans admitted to an ongoing uranium enrichment program in October 2002, which had been in operation since 1997 or 1998. The program was part of a barter deal in which Pakistan provided nuclear help to North Korea in return for North Korean missiles.[140]

The Clinton administration's fundamental mistake was failing to realize that the nature of the North Korean regime was the problem. The goal should have been to topple the government, rather than propping it up on the basis of empty promises. Any deal should have been much stricter—demanding that North Korea give up its weapons programs and missile proliferation entirely. And it should have included demands that North Korea implement political and economic reforms. This would have required a much stronger stomach for confrontation on the part of the administration, and a much grander effort to muster China and Japan in pressuring the North Koreans. It was much easier to sign a weak deal, and dishonestly sell it as a solution.

When it came undone, it was someone else's problem. In that sense, the Agreed Framework worked marvelously, and qualifies, as Madeleine Albright insisted, as a Clinton administration accomplishment.

THE WARS:

Cowardice-at-Arms

MADELEINE ALBRIGHT HAD A MESSAGE for anti-war protesters disrupting a town hall meeting convened at Ohio State University in February 1998: they had it all wrong. There wasn't going to be any "war" to protest. "We're talking about using military force, but we are not talking about a war," the secretary of state said of the administration's Iraq policy. "I think that it is an important distinction."[1]

When it came to military action, Clinton always blew an uncertain trumpet. His specialty was "in-between" wars of the sort to which Albright was referring. Clinton rejected the traditional American way of warfare, characterized by, in the words of defense expert Eliot A. Cohen, "a compulsion to seize the first available opportunity to close with and destroy the enemy."[2] That was too harsh, too brutal, and required entirely too much clarity of purpose and moral self-confidence.

Instead, Clinton's wars involved military force applied in carefully measured pinches and dashes, ideally against inanimate objects instead of enemy soldiers, with weapons that kept American troops entirely safe, in missions that were marginal, confused, negotiable, or all three.

The interventions of the 1990s had little to do with the national interest, and operated independently of national support. They didn't require national crusades, rallying popular outrage and patriotic sentiment. Instead, they were elite affairs. Selling them to the public was almost an afterthought. Clinton didn't give a speech entirely devoted to Kosovo until he announced the beginning of the bombing campaign.[3] Clinton's wars were launched on executive authority alone,[4] and waged explicitly to avoid producing casualties that might engage the public's interest. Eight times more American soldiers committed suicide in the 1990s than were killed in combat.[5]

The nature of Clinton interventions made for a reversal. Liberals became the hawks. The end of the Cold War bleached American power of what many progressives had found so objectionable about it. It was no longer wielded primarily against left-wing enemies of the United States, in defense of the national interest. Now, the national interest had receded from the rationale behind American interventions, and force was being applied against vaguely right-wing enemies, whether they were the military junta in Haiti or the hateful Serbs in the Balkans. American power began to look more humanitarian and "progressive."

Yet the Clinton administration was still caught in the shadow of Vietnam, and of every other American humiliation. It was dogged by visions of failures past, whether it was the Bay of Pigs, Desert One, or, one of its own productions, Somalia. Dick Morris writes, "I found that every time I discussed Bosnia with the president, we ran into this word 'can't' over and over again. 'What do you mean *can't?*' I said at one meeting. 'You're the commander in chief; where does *can't* come from?'"[6] "Can't" was the overhang of Vietnam, the nagging sense that even in a new era, American power was wrong and bound to fail.

Clinton's attitude toward warfare reflected not just his beliefs, but his personal history and character. "He was terrified by blood," says Dick Morris, "because of his own lack of a service record."[7] He assumed that the American public shared his paralyzing aversion to casualties. Clinton was temperamentally incapable of communing with the warrior strain in the American character, the Americans whose sense of honor would be offended when American troops were killed and would want our enemies to pay.

Clinton's sentimentality helped produce both idealistic statements of purpose soaring toward the grandiose, and a hesitance—because of potential military and civilian casualties—to bring to bear the military power necessary to reach his goals. Force was not just the last resort, but the almost-never resort, to be called back once launched, precisely calibrated even if ordered, and never confused with the antiquated notion of "war."

"They were children in his eyes"

The most consistent opposition to Clinton's interventions came from the military itself. It had been touched by some of the can't-do spirit of the post-Vietnam era, and—more important—had little faith that Clinton could see through difficult interventions. Clinton, in turn, lacked the moral authority to bring the military to heel, and to exercise vigorous civilian leadership over it.[8] At the beginning, he didn't know how to salute, and by the end, he had enmeshed himself in a sex-and-lies scandal that further weakened his already shaky credibility with the military. "The truth was," says former Marine commandant General Charles Krulak, "that he got himself in trouble in a way that conflicted with the core ethics and values system of the military."[9]

"The Clinton administration," says a former top-level Clinton Pentagon official, "got off on the wrong foot in terms of Clinton's own background, which he was uncomfortable with, but that was his own issue. Look at the number of senators who were draft dodgers. But for some reason, Clinton never seemed quite comfortable. And then you add gays in the military and you could make a case that he never recovered. The president personally didn't get over it. I don't think he ever established a level of comfort with the military at the senior levels."[10]

He certainly didn't with Colin Powell. As chairman of the Joint Chiefs of Staff, Powell was a national hero serving a commander in chief who very much wasn't. Clinton could only envy Powell's status, and futilely hope that his ability to bond with black people would somehow win him over.[11] If the president didn't measure up to Powell, neither did anyone else on his team. National security advisor Tony Lake was a conscience-stricken moralizer, often in ill health,[12] serving a president he had trouble getting to focus on world affairs. Defense secretary Les Aspin was a liberal, technocratic former congressman, famous for his indiscipline and rumpled style, trying to preside over the Pentagon.[13]

"Powell overwhelmed most of the new administration," says former Clinton diplomat Richard Holbrooke. "They were children in his eyes, and he was an awesome world figure in theirs."[14]

The problem with Powell was that he had over-learned the lessons of the Vietnam War. His standard for American military intervention was that the United States must have the ability to bring an overwhelming force to bear in circumstances so ideal that they don't often present themselves in the real world. The first Persian Gulf War—with the the United States confronting a woefully inferior Iraqi force in the open terrain of the desert—met Powell's criteria, though he opposed American intervention at the time.[15] So of course he opposed intervening in the civil war in Bosnia, adding a powerful voice to the administration's initial, agonized reluctance to beat back the Serbs.

The irony was that Powell wanted a larger military that would do less, while the Clinton team wanted a smaller military that would do much more, as it engaged in humanitarian interventions the world over.

The military roughly declined by half in the 1990s, with the Army getting sliced from eighteen divisions to ten and the Air Force from thirty-six fighter wings to twenty (a total of fifteen wings were used just in the first Gulf War).[16] Whenever the Clinton administration bragged about reducing the deficit or the federal workforce, it was effectively talking about how it had cut the military. Former Clinton officials Alan Blinder and Janet Yellen write of the 1997 balanced budget negotiations, "discretionary spending had already declined roughly 11 percent in real terms between 1992 and 1997. Further progress would be difficult because the entire cut had, to that point, come from the defense budget."[17] This, not the 1993 budget deal, was Clinton's big contribution to deficit reduction—taken directly out of the hide of America's military.

The number of military interventions increased even as resources dwindled. There had been, by one count, sixteen military interventions during the Cold War. That had jumped to roughly forty-eight after the Cold War's end.[18] The military was forced to rely on increasingly hollowed-out units.[19] It also had to do without significant modernization, as it lived off defense systems acquired in the 1970s and 1980s.[20] Spending to acquire new weapons went from more than $100 billion in 1987 to $44 billion in 1998.[21] By the end of the decade, the Congressional Budget Office was reporting that the military was underfunded by $50 billion a year.[22]

It is hard to generalize about what Clinton asked this reduced force to do. He used the military both too much and not enough. He was a promiscuous user of feckless force, most comfortable when interventions involved—in the jargon of the day—"operations other than war" and very little risk.

Somalia was a dubious, if limited intervention inherited by Clinton that he made an exercise in wildly unrealistic nation building. The invasion of Haiti replaced a right-wing dictator with a left-wing dictator popular with the Congressional Black Caucus. Both of these interventions were misconceived. On the other hand, a dollop of American force in Rwanda might have stopped the slaughter of hundreds of thousands,[23] but the administration refused to engage there and actively worked to keep the United Nations from doing so.

Both Balkan interventions, Bosnia and Kosovo, were warranted, and should have been pursued from the beginning with more vigor and less bull-session agonizing. But they were relatively peripheral to American interests. They should have received less attention than fighting truly important enemies of the United States, such as Saddam Hussein, whose Iraq was a strategic linchpin in the Middle East, and Osama bin Laden, who was waging an open war against America.

But the very fact that the Balkans were less important strategically gave intervening there an added significance for the Clinton administration. The Balkan wars were a use of force cleansed by their very purity of purpose. The United States military had been honed into something higher than a mere instrument of American security. As Army chief of staff General Dennis Reimer said in a 1996 speech, capturing the Clinton aspiration, the U.S. Army was "the rapid reaction force for the global village."[24]

"An unprecedented enterprise"

The first stop in the global village was Somalia. In December 1992, the Bush administration received a United Nations mandate to send American troops to Somalia. Their mission was to secure the distribution of food aid for the starving, war-wracked country.[25] President-elect Clinton was enthusiastic. "I have felt for a long time that we should do more in Somalia. The thing I think is so heartening is that the United States is now taking the initiative.... I think it is high time. I'm encouraged, and I applaud the initiative of President Bush and his administration."[26]

The United States sent thirty thousand troops, in an intervention that was conceived as brief and limited.[27] Bush vowed not to get involved in trying to "dictate political outcomes."[28] The military freed up the flow of humanitarian aid,[29] and as author Frederick Fleitz writes, "was tolerated by the Somali warlords, since it did not threaten the political balance in the country, was a heavily armed and well-organized force, and was deployed for a fixed amount of time."[30]

When Clinton took office, rather than winding down, the mission wound up. In March, the Clinton administration drafted and pushed through the United Nations a resolution establishing a new, wide-ranging mandate. Somalia would be a test case for then–UN ambassador Madeleine Albright's "assertive multilateralism." So the United

States, through the UN, got assertive: factions would be disarmed, and the country made anew. The resolution called for the "reestablishment of national and regional institutions and civil administration in the entire country," the "economic rehabilitation of Somalia," and "conditions under which Somali civil society may have a role, at every level, in the process of political reconciliation."[31]

This wasn't "mission creep," the cliché for gradually widening objectives in a military operation. It was "mission leap."[32] Albright hailed the dawning of a new era. "With this resolution we will embark on an unprecedented enterprise aimed at nothing less than the restoration of an entire country." Warren Christopher spread the good news in a cable to his ambassadors: "For the first time there will be a sturdy American role to help the United Nations rebuild a viable nation-state." Les Aspin shouted from the Pentagon rooftop, "We are staying there now to help those people rebuild their nation."[33]

Even as the operation got more ambitious, its twenty thousand troops, drawn from the armies of two dozen nations, became more lightly armed in keeping with the traditional configuration of UN peacekeepers.[34] On May 4, 1993, the United States officially turned the command over to the UN, although five thousand American soldiers remained.[35] The new mission antagonized the warlords, since it explicitly threatened the basis of their power—the ongoing civil war. The forces of warlord Mohammed Farrah Aideed attacked and killed more than twenty Pakistani peacekeepers on June 5.[36] The next day Albright helped shepherd a resolution through the Security Council calling for the arrest of "those responsible" for the attack.[37]

Albright spelled out in the *New York Times* the full measure of the administration's ambition in an August op-ed piece. "The earlier, American-led intervention ordered by President George Bush was limited to humanitarian relief. But the currently applicable Security Council resolutions call explicitly for the disarming of Somali factions because humanitarian and political goals cannot be assured unless a secure environment is created." She vowed to "lift the country and its people from the category of a failed state into that of an emerging democracy."[38] Albright said that Aideed's soldiers should be "disarmed" and—in a perfect expression of the spirit of Clinton nation-building— "retrained and re-employed."[39] The administration wanted to run a jobs program for Mogadishu.

American teams began conducting raids aimed at Aideed. After one inconclusive raid, Clinton boasted, "We have crippled the forces . . . of warlord Aideed. The military back of Aideed has been broken."[40]

Jonathan Howe—the retired admiral the administration had hand-picked to run the UN operation in Somalia—[41]soon asked for Rangers and the Delta Force to be sent. The administration hesitated, then relented after four Americans in a Humvee were killed by a remote-controlled mine on August 8. Senior administration officials didn't meet to consider the request, although they telephoned one another and Lake had an NSC staffer inform Clinton at Martha's Vineyard. "The president didn't weigh in," a Clinton aide told Elizabeth Drew.[42]

Just as the Rangers were arriving, the administration began to consider a shift to a new approach emphasizing a political settlement. Aideed, like every tyrant and killer around the globe in a confrontation against the United States, contacted Jimmy Carter, who urged Clinton to emphasize more diplomacy. Clinton liked the idea, and the State Department began planning for possible peace talks.[43] Later, Clinton complained that he thought that the anti-Aideed raids had ended with this nascent reorientation, but he made no decision to stop them.[44]

"The Pentagon's understanding of the policy," Clinton defense secretary Les Aspin would explain later, "was to move to more diplomatic efforts but snatch Aideed on the side, if you can."[45] The policy, in other words, was half devoted to seeking a diplomatic accord with Aideed,[46] and half devoted to attempting to capture or kill him. Meanwhile, in September, American officers in the field requested more firepower—artillery pieces, Bradley armored vehicles, M-1 tanks, assault helicopters, and AC-130 Specter gunships.[47]

Secretary of defense Aspin turned down the request because granting the military's demand for such weaponry would send the wrong "message."[48] In other words, American troops should try to capture

Aideed, but not use any weapons judged too threatening. On October 3, in the last in a series of raids that were so similar that Aideed had caught on, two Black Hawk helicopters were shot down, precipitating a vicious and deadly daylong firefight. At midnight, the UN mission's quick reaction force, consisting entirely of American troops, finally arrived at the fight—but for lack of American armor, they arrived in Malaysian personnel carriers and accompanied by Pakistani tanks.[49]

Aideed's attack killed eighteen Americans, wounded seventy-eight, and captured one. Clinton reacted with fury—at what had been done to him.

"This is stupid," he said days after the raid. "How could they be going after Aideed when we're working on the political end?"[50] David Halberstam reports, "There had been, he decided, a shift in policy without his informed approval. That was the key phrase, *his informed approval*, and in his mind effectively let him off the hook. Why hadn't anyone told him about the downside of the policy?"[51] In a meeting with families of those killed, Clinton expressed surprise and wonderment that American troops had still been chasing Aideed.[52] He affected a scandalized detachment from his administration's own policy.

After the Black Hawk Down incident, Clinton managed a red-faced burst of bravado, telling Tony Lake, "I believe in killing people who try to hurt you, and I can't believe we're being pushed around by these two-bit pricks." Soon enough he worried to George Stephanopoulos that he'd given in to the "two-bit pricks" too fast. "I hope I didn't panic and announce the pullout too soon."[53] The political consultants had wanted the troops out before the New Year.[54] Clinton resisted quite such a headlong rush, setting a departure date of March 31, 1994.[55] And initially he sent massive reinforcements to Mogadishu.

"There is a myth here that Mogadishu happens and then immediately we pull the troops out," says Lake. "The fact is that we had a very strong, difficult negotiation with the Congress about how quickly we had to leave. I argued that if you did this, you're going to put a bull's-eye on every American soldier abroad. So we negotiated a buildup where we actually increased our forces, and then did an orderly withdrawal by the next spring. But I think we should have stayed another year."[56]

The reinforcements were sent to Mogadishu only as an empty show of resolve. Immediately after the Black Hawk Down attack, Clinton dispatched former ambassador to Somalia Robert Oakley to Mogadishu to tell Aideed that he was off the hook; the United States would no longer seek his capture. Just days after Aideed's forces had killed eighteen Americans, Oakley delivered the message. Aideed's clan, perhaps taken aback by the American pusillanimity, didn't believe it. Oakley replied, "You'll see for yourself over time that it's true."[57]

Aideed could look forward, shortly after his attack, to becoming part of negotiations for peace.[58] A few days after October 3, there was a White House meeting to plot Somalia strategy.

"It was mostly a discussion back and forth between George Stephanopoulos and [press aide] Dee Dee Myers on how we were going to get sufficient press attention to sending Oakley over to form a coalition government," recalls a former administration official. "When the CIA guys said that all their information is that any coalition government would inevitably fail, there was just silence. And after a while, George and Dee Dee started up talking about positive press. The substance was just a brief interruption in a p.r. meeting."[59]

The public relations effort had its fits and starts. At first, Clinton said the American soldiers had "lost their lives in a very successful mission against brutality and anarchy," and vowed, "you may be sure that we will do whatever's necessary...to complete our mission." About a week later he was saying, even though his administration had authored the UN resolution making nation building the goal, "It is not our job to rebuild Somalia's society." In a letter to Congress, the White House promptly began rewriting history: "The U.S. military mission is not now nor was it ever one of 'nation building.'"[60]

But it was impossible to spin away the disaster. It became clear that Aspin, who had turned down the request for armor, had to go.[61] General Thomas Montgomery, the overall American commander in

Somalia, said the additional firepower might have saved American lives.[62] "There is excellent reason to believe," Donald Kagan and Frederick W. Kagan write in *While America Sleeps*, "that if the helicopters delivering the troops had been accompanied by additional air forces with greater firepower, such as the requested AC-130 gunships or Apache helicopters, the fire from the Somalis could have been suppressed and the disaster averted. If the force sent to extract the soldiers after the mission had been made up of the armored Bradley vehicles and M-1 tanks, their firepower could have been brought to bear for the same purpose."[63]

Somalia was a classic mismatch of rhetoric and reality. Either America is (insanely) committed to rebuilding Somalia, or it's not. Either America is committed to waging a war against Aideed, or it's not. The Clinton administration wanted to straddle, so it could have all the high-mindedness at none of the cost. It ran at the first opportunity, letting a killer of American troops walk free. Tony Lake's "bull's-eye" had indeed been firmly fixed on the back of every American soldier abroad.

The fecklessness in Somalia created the predicate for yet more fecklessness to come. The administration's relations with the military were further poisoned. The military dreads having the rug pulled out from it by easily spooked politicians. "Somalia iced the cake for the military establishment," says former Clinton speechwriter Paul Glastris. "Once that happened, and they said to themselves, 'He did it to us, they did it to us again,' there was never any trust again between the two sides."[64]

As for the administration, it was rattled to the core. "The importance of Somalia was immense," says Dick Holbrooke. "It traumatized the administration, and came very near to taking us down. Had it come closer to the presidential election, it might have. It paralyzed decision making and led directly to Rwanda."[65]

"Acts of genocide may have occurred"

In Rwanda, the administration had helped craft the Arusha agreement in August 1993, an ambitious plan to reintegrate Rwandan society.

The country was riven between the governing Hutus (about 85 percent of Rwandans, who since 1990, had carried out sporadic mass murders of Tutsis) and Tutsis (the other 15 percent, who until 1961 had dominated Rwanda through their cooperation with the country's colonial masters). A UN peacekeeping force was set to police the agreement. The debate over the exact composition and mandate of the force, however, came just as Somalia was going sour.[66]

The Security Council vote took place on October 5, 1993, two days after the Black Hawk Down firefight. Suddenly, saving Rwanda didn't look so important anymore. UN officials on the ground, aware of the potential for horrible violence, wanted up to eight thousand troops. The Western countries wanted no more than three thousand. The Clinton administration—whose multilateralism was becoming considerably less assertive by the day—wanted one hundred. The UN settled on 2,548 troops, who would be confined to the capital of Kigali.[67]

A plane with Rwandan president Juvenal Habyarimana, a Hutu, aboard was shot down on April 4, 1994. His death was a trigger for Hutu extremists who wanted to scuttle the Arusha agreement and kill all the Tutsis. The Hutus almost immediately began their rampage. Over the course of one hundred days, eight hundred thousand people were murdered, mostly Tutsis but also moderate Hutu supporters of the Arusha agreement.[68]

The whiff of mass murder had been in the air by January 1994. A Hutu informant told the UN peacekeepers on the ground that the Interahamwe, the president's private army, was being transformed into a "killing machine." General Romeo Dallaire, the UN commander on the ground, cabled back to headquarters that he planned to seize a weapons cache at the headquarters of President Habyarimana's political party revealed by the informant. The cable became part of a long-running dispute between Dallaire, who wanted to confront the radical Hutus, and UN headquarters, which wanted him to abide by his limited mandate to remain a neutral party merely monitoring implementation of Arusha. Dallaire's minders scotched his plan to seize the weapons. "We wish to stress . . . that the overriding consideration is the need to avoid entering into a course of action that might lead to the use of force and unanticipated consequences. Regards."[69]

The informant had also warned that the extremists wanted to kill a few Belgian peacekeepers on the Somalia model to send the peacekeepers fleeing. When he wanted to seize the arms cache, Dallaire had argued, "You've got to let me do this. If we don't stop these weapons, someday those weapons will be used against us."[70]

On April 7, ten Belgian soldiers were cornered by Hutus and ordered to give up their weapons. When they radioed their superiors for instructions, they were told to do their non-confrontational duty and give up their weapons. The Hutus tortured and chopped them to pieces, dumping a collection of body parts at the Kigali hospital.[71] Dallaire went to view their corpses at the hospital and initially thought there were eleven bodies instead of ten—it was impossible to tell.[72] The savagery was calculated to make the UN wet its multilateral pants. It did.

By April 10, the fourth day of the killing, Romeo Dallaire began to get an inkling of the evil afoot. He pleaded for his troop strength to be doubled to five thousand and for a broader mandate to choke off the catastrophe. He got nowhere. Reports of mass murder began to appear in the Western press, but the Clinton administration was in the process of formulating stringent post-Mogadishu rules for peacekeeping, including that American interests had to be at stake and an exit strategy apparent.[73]

Sensible enough—but the administration insisted that the rules apply not just to the United States, but to every UN peacekeeping mission as well. The theory was that if the United States didn't want to deploy peacekeepers to a hot spot, no one should send peacekeepers, since America would end up bailing out any operation that got in trouble.[74] So, perversely, the administration's multilateralists got in the business of assertively obstructing anyone doing anything about the slaughter in Rwanda.

The administration cut a deal with the Belgians. The Belgians wanted their troops—the best Dallaire had—out, and asked the

United States to provide diplomatic cover by pushing for an end to the mission altogether. The Clinton administration obliged without hesitation. Secretary of state Warren Christopher instructed Clinton's United Nations ambassador Madeleine Albright that "the international community must give highest priority to full, orderly withdrawal of all [UN peacekeeping] personnel as soon as possible." In late April, with the genocide raging at full fury, the UN voted to take Dallaire's force down to 270 troops. Albright said the "small, skeletal" force left would "show the will of the international community"— which it did, although not in the way she meant.[75]

An administration that prided itself on its multilateral regard for the utility of the United Nations, on its idealism, and on its concern for Africa was running away from the scene of an African genocide; not just denying a role for American troops, but working to withdraw all UN troops. This was cowardice and dishonor by proxy.

Almost as soon as Dallaire's force had been whittled away to nearly nothing, the UN felt compelled to take up the matter again because the stink of the corpses, and its shame, had become too powerful. By the end of April, two hundred thousand Tutsis had been killed.[76] Dallaire again pushed for five thousand troops to secure the capital and to create safe havens for Tutsis throughout the country. The Clinton team was opposed and countered with a proposal for safe havens along Rwanda's borders (good luck getting to them).[77]

The Clinton administration stalled a few weeks,[78] and even threatened a veto at the UN.[79] Only on May 17 did the administration relent and vote for a stronger UN presence on the ground.[80] Some 850 Ghanians were supposed to be the leading edge of the new deployment. The administration promised to provide the fifty armored personnel carriers essential to the mission, but refused to donate them to the Ghanians—too expensive—and dragged the UN through a long bureaucratic process of buying them.[81] During the delay, the administration countered charges of inaction by heralding its support for cleaning corpses from Lake Victoria.[82] The personnel carriers didn't arrive in Uganda until the end of June, and not in

Rwanda until August. By then a Tutsi rebel army had conquered the country, and the genocide was over.[83]

At least by then the administration was calling what had happened a genocide. It had gone to agonizing lengths to avoid using the word during the crisis.[84] As late as June 10, the State Department was still refusing to use the word for legalistic reasons.[85]

Asked whether she had guidance to avoid saying "genocide," a State Department spokeswoman said, "I have guidance which, which, to which I—which I tried to use as best I can. I'm not—I have—there are formulations that we are using that we are trying to be consistent in our use of. I don't have an absolute categorical prescription against something, but I have the definitions. I have a phraseology which has been carefully examined and arrived at."[86] The preferred formulation was "acts of genocide may have occurred."[87]

The administration was in denial all around. Clinton diplomats were most worried about the state of the "peace process" in Rwanda. Even when the killing had begun in earnest, Clinton officials held out hope for the process. American ambassador to Rwanda David Rawson told Samantha Power, author of *A Problem from Hell*, "We were naive policy optimists, I suppose. The fact that negotiations can't work is almost not one of the options open to people who care about peace. We were looking for the hopeful signs, not the dark signs. In fact, we were looking away from the dark signs."[88]

The administration was hardly alone in not wanting to intervene in Rwanda. Throughout the 1990s, it often took Republicans to push Clinton into taking foreign policy risks. In this case, Republicans were leaning hard the other way.[89]

To have become part of an effort to staunch the slaughter would have required leadership—imaginative, morally committed, politically bold leadership. It was inconceivable that the Clinton administration would exercise it, and indeed it did the opposite. The administration didn't just not send American troops, didn't just work to scuttle any UN mission, it refused to pay for armored personnel carriers and wouldn't even jam Hutu radio broadcasts of lists of people slated to be killed (a State Department office recommended against it because it would violate free speech).[90] Forced to choose between its ideals and its fears, its fears prevailed with no contest.

What the administration could offer the Rwandans, finally, was apologies and moral posturing—they were easy, after all.[91] Clinton regaled Rwandans with contrition during a March 1998 visit, when he proclaimed that Rwanda's genocide should matter to all the world because "each bloodletting hastens the next, and as the value of human life is degraded and violence becomes tolerated, the unimaginable becomes more conceivable."[92] Clinton no doubt believed that sentiment—so long as it never compelled him to do something politically difficult.

The administration next turned in a characteristic performance in its Haitian policy. Clinton followed his usual pattern of flip-flopping on campaign rhetoric (he said he wouldn't send Haitian refugees back to Haiti, then did);[93] projecting an image of weakness (letting Haitian thugs chase away the USS *Harlan County* with some port-side fist waving);[94] vacillating on deadlines and ultimatums (he huffed and he puffed, but found it very difficult actually to get tough with the powerless Haitian junta he wanted to depose);[95] and ultimately relying on a Jimmy Carter-brokered deal—backed by an invasion force[96]—to return the exiled radical thug Jean-Bertrand Aristide to power,[97] thus sinking Haiti into a left-wing dictatorship in exchange for its right-wing one.[98]

But this was a mere sideshow compared to Clinton's limp performance in the Bosnian war.

"The position of leader of the free world is vacant"

Yugoslavia had exploded in early 1991, with its republics splitting off from what was becoming a rump Yugoslavia dominated by Serbia. Elements of the regular Yugoslav army invaded the splinter republic of Croatia in August 1991 and cooperated with local Serb militia in a brutal ethnic war. It killed thousands and created hundreds of thousands of refugees, as the Serbs waged a campaign of "ethnic cleansing" against the Croats. By the summer of 1992 Bosnia was consumed in a brutal ethnic war too.[99]

The Bush administration reacted to it all with determined passivity. It left handling the unspooling disaster to the Europeans, who were eager to demonstrate their new post–Cold War mettle. Unfortunately, their mettle arrived in Croatia in the form of unarmed volunteer monitors wearing funny white uniforms. The bloodletting ran its course.[100]

Clinton blasted Bush's detachment during the 1992 campaign. He warned, "We may have to use military force. I would begin with airpower against the Serbs to try to restore the basic conditions of humanity."[101] He sounded even tougher immediately after the election, echoing Bush's language about Saddam's invasion of Kuwait. "The legitimacy of ethnic cleansing will not stand."[102] The chest-pounding rhetoric conflicted with the administration's real priority, which was to try to forget about the world while passing the Family and Medical Leave Act.[103]

The proposed solution on the table when Clinton took office was a peace plan devised by UN negotiator Cyrus Vance and EU representative David Owen. It would have divided Bosnia into ten cantons along ethnic lines, under an attenuated central government in Sarajevo. The administration objected to the plan not just on the practical grounds of it being difficult to enforce, but on principle: it unacceptably rewarded aggression and recognized ethnic separation on the ground.[104] And so it did. Owen called it "a peace from hell."[105] But what was the alternative? There were roughly three choices in Bosnia: defeat the Serbs by force, accept an imperfect plan to end the killing, or shut up and wash America's hands of the matter.

The administration's high-minded distaste for the Vance-Owen plan served the cause of indecision, inaction, and slaughter. "Bush had never promised the U.S. cavalry might be on the way," journalist Mark Danner has written. "Clinton had promised strong action—had vowed America would help—and when confronted with the need to supply it, he had offered words; those words did more than disappoint—they instilled hope which the Bosnians paid for with blood."[106] Owen had it right when he warned the Bosnians in December 1992, "Don't, don't, don't live under this dream that the West is going to come in and sort this problem out. Don't dream dreams."[107]

The administration's rejection of Vance-Owen had its roots in a dream of its own. The hardheaded case for American intervention was that Serbia's Communist president Slobodan Milosevic should be stopped from tearing up the conventions of the new, post–Cold War Europe, its peace and freedom guaranteed by NATO. The softheaded Clinton administration case was that mere peace was not enough: toleration must triumph over ethnic hatred and separation. Vance-Owen was considered insufficiently progressive and multicultural. Typically, such high-mindedness in principle was combined with fear-induced waffling in practice.

After months of drawn-out, inconclusive meetings,[108] Clinton in May settled on a policy of "lift and strike." The United States would lift the arms embargo that had kept the Bosnians under-armed, and hit the Serbs with air strikes if they continued their aggression.[109] Secretary of state Warren Christopher was sent to Europe to sell the policy, but gently—very, very gently. As former Clinton NSC staffer Ivo Daalder puts it, in an understatement, "Christopher's nuanced, lawyerly presentation constituted a highly unusual way for a U.S. secretary of state to make a major policy presentation."[110]

The Europeans, realizing that the administration wasn't serious enough to force the issue, predictably balked at the proposal. UN peacekeepers, including British and French troops, had been inserted into Bosnia. They essentially served as hostages against lifting the arms embargo or airstrikes. According to UN thinking, both proposed actions were considered likely to intensify the conflict, endanger the peacekeepers, and inflame the Serbs.[111] So the Europeans stiffed Christopher, the prelude to nearly three years of futility.

Opposition to the Clinton "lift and strike" policy quickly grew in the Oval Office itself. While Christopher was still in Europe, Clinton changed his mind after dipping into Robert Kaplan's book *Balkan Ghosts*, which emphasized the region's bloody history. Clinton called Colin Powell and Les Aspin into the Oval Office to discuss the book. Aspen quickly concluded, "Holy shit! He's going south on 'lift and strike.'" Clinton was also—as he often was, according to Elizabeth Drew—buffeted by an op-ed piece. In this case, it was an article in the *Wall Street Journal* by Arthur Schlesinger pointing out the potential domestic political cost of a Balkan engagement.[112]

After another long round of indecision and reversals,[113] the administration settled on a policy of threatening air strikes to push the Serbs back from Sarajevo and induce progress at the negotiating table. But the French and British insisted on prior UN approval for any strikes, which was a perfect formula for inaction. In the end, nothing much happened. By late September, the peace talks had collapsed, but the administration shrugged it off.[114] Bosnia had become a cynic's delight. By December 1993, the UN commander in Bosnia, British general Michael Rose, said he didn't even bother to read UN resolutions on Bosnia anymore.[115]

In 1994 and 1995, a long series of confrontations with the Serbs ensued, in which the Serbs would commit a provocation and NATO would respond with wrist-slap air strikes.[116] In May 1995, Bosnian Serbs began helping themselves to weapons that they had previously handed over to the UN to be held in "exclusion zones," and stepped up the shelling of Sarajevo and other so-called "safe areas." NATO and the UN huffed, and they puffed, and they responded with a few pinpricks. The Serbs responded by killing civilians all over the country, and taking four hundred UN peacekeepers hostage, chaining some of them to military equipment to serve as "human shields." The suspicion is that, to get them back, the UN promised no further air attacks.[117]

Worse was yet to come. In July, Serb bully-criminal General Ratko Mladic overran the UN safe area of Srebrenica, took the Dutch peacekeepers hostage, and proceeded to separate the women from the men, so the women could be deported and many of the men murdered. The Serbs summarily executed more than seven thousand

Muslim men and boys. The UN had turned down five requests from Dutch peacekeepers for NATO air strikes when Mladic was on the march.[118]

Clinton shouted at Sandy Berger, accentuating the first person in the growing debacle, "I'm getting creamed."[119] He had a limitless capacity to interpret any event, even faraway slaughters, through the prism of his own ego.[120]

Bosnia represented a stark failure of multilateralism. A pure multilateralism can never be "assertive," as Madeleine Albright would have it, but is almost always passive and weak. When no country is willing to take the lead, and to force the issue by threatening unilateral action, inertia rules.[121]

As for the UN, the world's ur-multilateral institution, it considered any peace, even a phony peace that consisted of idly watching Muslims get slaughtered, better than choosing sides. Disillusioned liberal journalist David Rieff writes, "no matter what the Serbs did to the UN, the UN wanted to negotiate with the Serbs."[122] As a UN commander put it in the fall 1994, "[The UN's] mission is to maintain the peace. I don't have enemies, I have partners."[123]

While the UN proved a moral nullity, impetus for a new Bosnia policy came from the Republican Congress. In the summer of 1995, the Senate voted 60–29 and the House 298–128 to lift the arms embargo in Bosnia, pushing the policy that Clinton had tried, then given up, urging on the Europeans.[124] On August 11, Clinton vetoed the bill, on grounds that the embargo should only be lifted in a multilateral fashion, lest Bosnia become solely an American problem.[125]

The congressional votes were pivotal, demonstrating that there was a domestic political price to be paid for his Balkan weakness. Clinton had suffered a major rebuke on an important foreign policy question, and his veto was in danger of being overridden. Worse, his likely presidential opponent, Bob Dole, was the leading critic of his policy, denouncing it as "multilateral make-believe."[126]

At the same time, he was caught in a vise that would make not deploying American troops in Bosnia almost impossible. He had committed to assisting in a NATO withdrawal of UN peacekeepers should that become necessary. The Pentagon had drawn up plans for an operation to deploy twenty thousand troops and helicopters in an extraction. The plans had already been discussed by the NATO council. If the council gave the order to assist the UN's withdrawal, the plan would go into effect, unless Clinton betrayed his own commitment and pulled the plug on it.[127]

He was stuck. The president didn't fully realize the consequences of what he apparently considered a loose promise until June 14, 1995, when assistant secretary of state Richard Holbrooke and Warren Christopher spelled it out to him.[128] Now the question was whether American troops would be deployed as a punctuation mark on a failure, or as part of a solution, and whether they would be deployed sooner, or later—potentially, as a worried Clinton put it, "dropped in during the middle of the [1996 presidential] campaign."[129]

The administration had also lost the excuse of European obstruction, since French president Jacques Chirac had been pushing for months for a stronger American engagement, declaring that "the position of leader of the free world is vacant." Clinton was now weaker and more fearful about a military engagement than the French. According to author David Halberstam, "Clinton was more than a little jealous of the French president."[130]

The administration finally created a plan in August 1995 to divide Bosnia between the ethnic groups and make an all-out push for a diplomatic settlement. If that failed, the administration was prepared to use force.[131] Richard Holbrooke, who had called Bosnia the West's "greatest collective failure since the 1930s," was charged with hammering out the negotiations.[132] He was brilliant, arrogant, and tough as hell. Two factors would make his work easier: a successful Croat offensive, and a major NATO bombing campaign.

The Croats launched their offensive in the summer of 1995. It swept the Serbs before it, and it wasn't pretty. Almost two hundred thousand Serbs were driven from eastern Croatia.[133] At one point, Holbrooke explained to other Clinton officials that his negotiating team had encouraged the Croats to keep going, and that the offensive was properly understood as part of the peace process. "The map negotiations are taking place on the battlefield right now."[134] The Croats understood a truth that the administration had resisted for more than two years: that force is the only answer to determined aggression.

The Clinton administration finally acted on that insight itself after a Serb shell killed thirty-seven people at a Sarajevo marketplace on August 28. Holbrooke demanded "bombs for peace,"[135] beginning a roughly three-week long bombing campaign.[136] The entire campaign amounted to about a day's worth of bombing in Desert Storm, but it was massive by the standards of the Bosnian conflict.[137]

The new policy worked. "We made a real breakthrough," says Holbrooke, "persuading NATO and the UN to bomb the Bosnian Serbs very heavily. That bombing, plus other events, turned things around. This wasn't empty rhetoric anymore; this was diplomacy backed up by precision bombing."[138]

By bombing's end, Holbrooke had the outlines of a deal for a formally united Bosnia that would be divided 51 percent Muslim/Croat, 49 percent Serb, in an arrangement policed by NATO, including American troops. The agreement was fully hashed out and formalized during negotiations at Dayton, Ohio. The administration could have taken a roughly similar deal almost three years earlier, but had dithered until accepting a kind of Vance-Owen lite.[139]

Clinton deployed twenty thousand American troops to implement the agreement, even though 70 percent of Americans opposed sending them.[140] His profile in Balkan courage, however, is mitigated by the fact that he implausibly promised that the troops would be there only a year.[141] And he had come to this pass at all only because he had come to believe that the domestic political price of inaction was too high. His trajectory tracked with that of Dick Morris. Morris had initially opposed intervening in the Balkans. As the domestic political dynamic changed, he became a hawk, declaring, "I want [Clinton] to bomb the s— out of the Serbians to look strong."[142]

Anyone who had followed Clinton's Bosnian meanderings had seen the very opposite of strength.

"NATO is not waging war"

Clinton's next Balkan war came four years later in Kosovo. It was a province of Serbia that had become 90 percent Albanian, but had vital symbolic importance to the Serbs. Serb leader Slobodan Milosevic revoked Kosovo's autonomous status in 1989, and the province had been simmering ever since. A Serb crackdown in Kosovo would risk a refugee crisis that would potentially destabilize the region. Which is why the first Bush administration, on its way out the door, issued its "Christmas Warning," threatening the use of force in the event of Serb aggression in the province.[143]

This warning, and ones like it made later by the Clinton administration, would become part of an attenuated and circular—but ultimately inescapable—justification for war: war had been threatened, therefore it must be waged to maintain American credibility.

The Clinton administration thought a short and splendid war in the Balkans would revitalize NATO and convince the alliance that it could, and should, act "out of area."[144] Kosovo, however, was hardly vital to America's national interest.[145] British prime minister Tony Blair said that the war was waged "in defense of our values, rather than our interests."[146] Sidney Blumenthal writes that the war was necessary to bolster social democratic parties in Europe and the cause of European integration.[147] So, Kosovo was a war of the Third Way, conceived by its supporters as a way to boost a center-left politics committed to multicultural societies and the withering of the nation-state.

The practical catalyst for the war was the Kosovo Liberation Army (KLA), a militant Albanian group that the United States deemed "terrorist." The KLA began carrying out attacks in 1996–1997 on Serbian police and their families, and against Albanians allegedly collaborating with the Serbs.[148] The KLA wanted to provoke the Serbs into a brutal response that would drag NATO into the war. The Serbs duly obliged.[149]

After a long series of threats and negotiations, Milosevic was told to accept a deal dictated to him at a conference with the Kosovars at Rambouillet, France, or get bombed.[150] He decided to get bombed.

Thus NATO began the first war in its history, a campaign that stumbled to success despite its strategic confusion and moral pose.[151]

Days before the Rambouillet talks broke down, Milosevic had launched Operation Horseshoe, a campaign to sweep the Albanians out of the province.[152] On March 24, 1999, the day the bombing campaign started, Bill Clinton said from the Oval Office that NATO's goal was "to protect thousands of innocent people in Kosovo from a mounting military offensive."[153] Two days later, in contrast, General Wesley Clark explained, "It was always understood from the outset that there was no way we were going to stop these paramilitary forces who were going in there and murdering civilians in these villages."[154]

Despite Clinton's dewy-eyed rhetoric, protecting American personnel was much more important to the administration than protecting Kosovar Albanians. Clinton ruled out ground troops at the very beginning.[155] That was because the Kosovo intervention was intended to be an exercise in Vietnam-style signal sending. Chairman of the Joint Chiefs of Staff General Hugh Shelton said the United States was waging an air campaign "that will send a message."[156] Kosovo was really an armed negotiation. Hence, NATO Secretary General Javier Solana's seemingly odd statement at the outset of the Kosovo campaign: "Let me be clear: NATO is not waging war against Yugoslavia."[157]

At a joint press conference with Solana in the opening hours of the campaign, Clark promised to "ultimately destroy [Yugoslav] forces and their facilities and support."[158] Afterwards, Clark writes, "Solana was quiet as we moved back toward his office. 'What do you think?' I asked, hoping to compare notes and draw him out a little. 'The word "destroy,"' he said. 'I am worried; that is all the press will focus on tomorrow.'"[159]

The theory of the war, embraced by Clinton, was that Milosevic would fold quickly under bombing.[160] But Kosovo, an actual province of Serbia, was more important to Milosevic than Bosnia or Croatia had been. He held firm after the initial forty-eight-hour bombing "demonstration"[161] and NATO didn't have enough firepower in place to hit him in earnest. As a German general put it, "We faced an opponent who accepted war, whereas the NATO nations had accepted [just] an operation."[162] A key part of Wes Clark's alternate plan—ground troops—had been ruled out by the president.

So a listless air campaign was all NATO had, conducted at a safe distance so allied pilots wouldn't be in danger. It was signally ineffective in stopping the Serb-cleansing campaign, which proceeded apace. By early April, some 540,000 Kosovars had been expelled from the province.[163]

Maintaining the air campaign at no cost in lives or political turbulence so it could be continued indefinitely became one of NATO's chief aims. It was one of the most precisely calibrated, thoroughly politically vetted campaigns in history. Clark explains, "In the U.S. channel, we would need a complete analysis of each individual target—location, military impact, possible personnel casualties, possible collateral damages, risks if the weapon missed the target, and so forth. This analysis then had to be repeated for different types of weapons, in search of the specific type of weapon and warhead size that would destroy the target and have the least adverse impact elsewhere. And this had to be done to my satisfaction, then sent to Washington where it underwent additional levels of legal and military review and finally ended up on President Clinton's desk for his approval."[164]

The administration had missed the true lesson of the Bosnian war, won by a Croatian ground offensive devoted to killing Serb soldiers. If the war in Kosovo was to be won it meant destroying—there's that word—the enemy with the help of ground troops, or a robust air assault on Belgrade to eliminate the supports of Milosevic's power. Clark pressed for ground troops, earning him the enmity of political leaders in Washington and most of the rest of the military command that didn't want to risk casualties. It wasn't, in this case, "the coalition" that was driving the caution. Tony Blair was gung-ho for ground troops.[165]

But for Clinton, even Apache helicopters, which could closely engage Serb forces, were too risky. Clark relentlessly pushed for them, and Clinton, on April 4, reluctantly agreed to send them. They would never be used. The closest Clinton came to taking any risk in combat was when he deployed one of his most familiar weapons—the flip-flop. He eventually let it be known that he was thinking about ground troops again. To this end, he went so far as to meet with the Joint Chiefs of Staff for the first time of the war.[166]

The real action was in the bombing campaign. As in Bosnia, timidity became a spur to greater aggressiveness, since vigorously bombing Belgrade was a way of avoiding a resort to more unpalatable measures. "One of the reasons we were successful in getting the go-ahead to go downtown was because it was an alternative to ground troops," Clark testified later.[167]

In late April, the bombing campaign shifted into a heightened, strategic phase. It targeted power lines and transformers, bridges, oil refineries, communications systems, cigarette factories (did Hillary approve this target?), fertilizer plants, and TV broadcast houses in Serbia proper in an attempt to make Serb civilians feel the pain.[168] Beginning in mid-May, 85 percent of Serbs were without electric power.[169]

When it became clear that on top of the intensified bombing, the Russians weren't going to stand by Milosevic—thanks partly to skillful Clinton administration diplomacy—the Serb leader capitulated. Clinton had won a victory, if a sour one. He had outlasted and beaten Milosevic, who would be headed out of office and eventually to a war crimes tribunal. And he had ended—albeit a million refugees and 300,000 to 500,000 internally displaced persons later—the Serb abuses in Kosovo.[170]

But no one felt much elation at the result. Wes Clark had become hated at the Pentagon. He was blamed for allegedly dragging the military into an adventure that had nearly become a debacle, and was effectively fired weeks after the war ended.[171] When the Serb forces left Kosovo in relatively good shape, it seemed they had suffered much less damage from the NATO air campaign than advertised. The Albanians flowed back into Kosovo, and the KLA promptly cleansed the area of 250,000 Serbs and gypsies.[172]

The war had suffered from two characteristic Clinton administration flaws—ruling out ground troops in a way that signaled a lack of resolve and not hammering Belgrade sooner. The top commander in Kosovo, Lieutenant General Mike Short, said after the war that in an appropriately fierce opening gambit, "Milosevic and his cronies would have woken up the first morning asking what the hell is going on."[173] Instead, they woke up thinking NATO wasn't serious.

A truly aggressive air campaign required an administration willing to wage real war. The Clinton administration's hesitance to do so, as demonstrated throughout the decade, from Africa to the Caribbean to the Balkans, was noted by parties considerably more dangerous to America than the Serbs.

THE MIDDLE EAST:

The Price of Illusion

O NE OF THE MOST ENDURING POSITIVE images of the Clinton years was "The Handshake," the gesture of reconciliation between the former bitter enemies Yitzhak Rabin and Yasser Arafat, supervised on the White House lawn in September 1993 by a gently nudging Clinton: a benign, optimistic, nurturing presence, looking every bit a Nobel Peace Prize candidate. Beyond the optics, the Handshake had nothing to do with Clinton or his administration. The image that day was a lie, in what it said about the process that produced the Oslo agreement and in what it said about its prospects for success.

The administration fell in love with the Handshake as a kind of international public relations gimmick. It desperately sought to capture another one, in a chase that would blind it to the strategic realities of the Middle East, harming America's interests and neglecting the budding war on terror.

By the end of the decade, the Clinton administration had presided over a catastrophic loss of America's standing in the Middle East. It had responded to Arab recalcitrance and provocations by pressuring its ally, Israel, for more and more concessions. It ignored the rise of a radical terror axis. It allowed Saddam Hussein to survive and thrive, in a continual rebuke to American power that emboldened our enemies and convinced them that the United States could be expelled from the region entirely.

As Middle East expert David Wurmser writes, "The 1990s began with unassailable American regional dominance and overwhelming Israeli regional superiority. It ended with America on the eve of regional ejection and Israel in a military and existential crisis."[1] And it all started with the Handshake.

"Is it proper to ask a president for a hug?"

In the early 1990s, the administration was sponsoring talks in Washington between representatives of the Palestinians—but pointedly not Arafat's Palestinian Liberation Organization (PLO)—and Israel. In secret, Israel and the PLO started a separate negotiating track in Oslo. The administration barely knew about the talks.[2]

In this hush-hush venue, the Israelis and the PLO reached an agreement. Israel would withdraw from Jericho and Gaza, and the West Bank would be set aside for Arafat to establish a proto-state, the Palestinian Authority. The toughest so-called "final status" issues—borders, the status of Jerusalem, the "right of return" for Palestinian refugees, and Israeli settlements—were set aside for later.[3]

This deal fell into the Clinton administration's lap, the diplomatic equivalent of an immaculate conception. When the Israelis finally briefed the administration about the accord, Foreign Minister Shimon Peres told Warren Christopher that he was willing to pretend that the whole agreement had been "Made in the U.S.A." Christopher was taken aback. "I immediately declined, saying we could not even consider such a deception."[4] A high-profile White House signing ceremony was another matter. Christopher lobbied Rabin over the phone to attend with Arafat.[5] George Stephanopoulos writes, "We all knew that a successful ceremony on the White House lawn would be a political boon to Clinton, but we were careful not to say so: Taking credit wouldn't only be crass, it would backfire."[6]

The invitation was an extraordinary coup for Arafat. The United States still officially considered him a terrorist, and for good reason, considering that American citizens, including American diplomats, had been among his victims. Arafat had to make a quick stop in the phone booth, to exchange the trappings of an international outlaw for those of a respectable statesman. The administration urged him not to bring his pistol, to which he had an unnatural attachment, to the ceremony. He was wearing it when he departed Tunis for Washington aboard an Iraqi plane, but ditched it before showing up at the White House. He did, however, wear his military uniform. To comply with a ban on Iraqi aircraft in the United States, Arafat had to scrub his plane of its Iraqi markings.[7]

In preparation for the ceremony, Clinton and his team rehearsed the Handshake until they were confident Clinton could nail it. Clinton practiced with Tony Lake how to fend off an attempted hug or kiss from Arafat. Stephanopoulos told him how to smile just right, a dignified closed-mouth smile that Clinton practiced a few times.[8]

The ceremony went off without a hitch, prompting gales of sentimentality. Barbara Walters, after a brief, fawning interview with Clinton, wondered out loud, "Is it proper to ask a president for a hug?"[9] Did she have to ask?

The day had been a spectacular success, except for the minor matter that Arafat didn't denounce terrorism. Israeli analyst Yigal Carmon describes the scene: "Waiting for the magic words to be uttered any moment, Ehud Ya'ari, the Israel Television commentator who covered the proceedings, used every break in Arafat's speech to announce, 'Now he will denounce terrorism.... Now he will say it.... Now he simply has to say it....' Only after the last paragraph did Ya'ari give up. 'He is not saying it,' he reported, crushed."[10]

That lacuna was, of course, more telling than Rabin's eloquence that day, or all the expressions of high hopes. It was a refusal that emanated from Arafat's core. His ideology combined pan-Arab nationalism with a quasi-Leninist vision of perpetual struggle. The boosters of the peace process simply ignored Arafat's ideological commitment, a failure to take ideas and words seriously. The assumption was that he couldn't quite mean what he was saying in Arabic to his own population, both because it seemed so outrageously backward—especially from the secular, rationalist framework of the Clinton administration—and because believing in its sincerity would fatally undermine the premises of the peace process.

Arafat's ideology would, the administration hoped, be washed away by the power of the peace talks and the glorious vistas opened up by economic development. How could Arafat possibly resist the personal chemistry and "the momentum" generated by the negotiations, constantly reinforced by the charm and warmth of Bill Clinton? The mistaken faith in personal schmoozing and economic development was compounded by a misunderstanding of the very process of the peace process. It wasn't an accident that Oslo happened without the administration's involvement. The important and successful Arab-Israeli agreements had always been hammered out bilaterally and discreetly, without high-profile American pressure on Israel.[11]

All of this contributed to a strategic mistake of the most profound proportions. Former Clinton official Martin Indyk described the administration's strategy in an article in *Foreign Affairs* in 2002. "There was a window of opportunity to negotiate a comprehensive peace in the Middle East. If the negotiations were successful, that outcome would have a profound effect on the region.... The United States should therefore focus its energies on peacemaking, while containing the radical opponents of peace (Iraq, Iran, and Libya)."[12]

The administration, in other words, wanted to peace-process its way to the transformation of the Middle East. In this, it essentially bought the Arab view of the region—that nothing was wrong that couldn't be fixed by solving the Palestinian dispute. Then all the other problems in the Arab world would disappear: the lack of economic development, the poor education, the failure to establish the rule of law, the absence of democratic institutions, and, perhaps above all, the hostility to the West.

This was exactly backwards. It was the nature of the Arab regimes that embittered and prolonged the dispute with Israel. The road to a better Middle East required changing the Arab regimes. The administration found this project uncongenial. It meant embarking on an arduous, risky effort. Arab governments, including nominal allies, would have to be confronted rather than appeased. Saddam Hussein would have to be toppled, as a way of asserting American power in the region and dealing a blow to a linchpin of radical Arab politics. And the Jimmy Carter model of winning international acclaim by pressuring one's own allies as hard, if not harder than one's enemies, would have to abandoned.

Rather than all that, the administration preferred . . . to talk.

"Continue and continue and continue"

Through much of the 1990s, Israel was as eager an adherent to the peace process faith as the Clinton administration, if for different reasons.

Israeli prime minister Yitzhak Rabin was taking a calculated risk. The Arab states had lost their military patron with the fall of the Soviet Union, and thus Israel's military superiority had only increased. It now seemed possible to secure Israel's immediate borders with a peace agreement that would reduce its pariah status in the region and improve its relationship with the United States. Israel would then be in a better position to deal with what Rabin recognized as the foremost future threat to his country—missiles and weapons of mass destruction deployed by Iran and Iraq.

Rabin wanted to leverage Arafat's interests to Israel's ends. By cooperating with Israel, Arafat could achieve, and rule, a Palestinian state. But to get it, he would have to crack down on his own political competition: the growing ranks of Islamic fundamentalists.

It was in these terms that Rabin sold the agreement to the Israeli public.[13] As he put it, the PLO would fight the rising radical threat of Hamas and Islamic Jihad, and could do so without a human rights lobby and a Supreme Court such as constrained Israel.[14] The risk, obviously, was that Israelis were making Arafat a quasi–head of state and arming his police force just as his political fortunes had hit bottom.[15] As the energy in the Arab world shifted to religious fundamentalists, Arafat was yesterday's man lucking into today's dictatorship.

Arafat understood the agreement differently than Rabin. He wasn't going to be Israel's cop. For him, Oslo was in keeping with the Palestinians' "phased plan" of 1974, in which the Palestinians decided to pocket any Israeli concessions as a step toward the ultimate goal of the destruction of the Jewish state.[16] In January 1994, Arafat told Gaza activists that the intifada would "continue and continue and continue."[17]

Attacks against Israelis did indeed continue, and Arafat's own Fatah organization was involved in some of them.[18] Arafat embarked on a delicate walk between placating the Americans, who wanted to see him crack down on the radicals, and allying with Hamas and Islamic Jihad in the assault against Israel. He would dodge and obfuscate before his true goal became undeniably clear in 2000.

Rabin, his fellow Nobel Peace Prize winner, didn't live to see the day. On November 4, 1995, an extremist Israeli opponent of Oslo assassinated Rabin, and dovish foreign minister Shimon Peres took power.[19] "It's kind of conventional wisdom that if only Rabin had lived everything would have been different," says top Clinton negotiator Dennis Ross. "I'm very dubious of that. While on the one hand there's no question that Rabin had developed a certain relationship with Arafat, the fact is that Arafat had developed a relationship with Shimon Peres too. It didn't mean that he was still prepared, when the moment of truth came, to act differently."[20]

Peres forged ahead. He agreed to withdraw Israeli troops from five more Palestinian cities. But a Palestinian terror wave ensured that the hard-line Likud candidate Bibi Netanyahu defeated Peres in the May 1996 elections.

Netanyahu, a tough-minded critic of the peace process, signed two more deals.[21] In January 1997 he agreed to give the city of

Hebron to the Palestinians. Then, at a summit at the Wye River Plan-
tation in October 1998, he agreed to further Israeli withdrawals.[22]
Despite this, the Clinton administration considered Netanyahu the
problem in Israeli-Palestinian relations, because he emphasized
"reciprocity." He wanted the Palestinians to follow through on their
commitments to extradite terrorists, stop anti-Israeli incitement, disarm militants, and amend the PLO charter to excise clauses calling
for Israel's destruction.[23]

This offended the Clinton administration, which thought Netanyahu was asking too much of Arafat. The administration's posture was,
"Trust, but don't verify—and don't even expect promises to be kept."

Natan Sharansky writes of a Clinton official's distressed reaction
when he made the case for having Arafat amend the PLO charter, as
originally promised at Oslo. "There was no way, he told me, that Arafat
could fulfill this promise without endangering his own life. I realized
then that if this official believed that 'strengthening Arafat' precluded
the Palestinian leader from making even this minimal effort to promote
peace and reconciliation, we had no hope of convincing the West to
press Arafat to keep any of his commitments. . . . We were placed in a
diplomatic quagmire where pressure would be exerted on us alone
because we were the side that could 'afford to compromise.'"[24]

The administration had plenty of leverage over Netanyahu, because
Clinton—thanks partly to his moving performance at Rabin's funeral—
was viewed by Israelis as an extremely committed friend. The Clinton
team squeezed Netanyahu hard. "I was kind of the lone holdout on it,"
says Dennis Ross. "Not because I supported what he was doing, but
because I still believed you could bring him along, and I didn't believe
we would in fact sustain a confrontation with him. I thought in the end
you wouldn't weaken him, you would create an illusion on the Arab
side that a wedge is being driven between us and the Israelis, which I
think is always a mistake. What drives Arab acceptance of Israel is a
belief that they have no choice."[25]

The administration openly worked to beat Netanyahu and install
Labor Party candidate Ehud Barak in Israel's 1999 elections. When

Barak won on May 17, 1999, Clinton could hardly contain himself, relating that he was "as excited as a young kid with a new toy."[26] Clinton, toy in hand, headed into the Oslo endgame.

"Let's quit!"

The push for a final deal at Camp David, disastrously, came only a few months after Israel had retreated from southern Lebanon, abandoning a southern security buffer it had held for eighteen years. Israel had fought a low-intensity war in Lebanon against Hezbollah guerrillas supported by Syria and Iran. Unable to negotiate a deal for withdrawal with Damascus, Barak just picked up and left.[27] The withdrawal, hastily made on May 23, took on the feel of an ignominious rout. Iranian Foreign Minister Kamal Kharazi traveled to Lebanon to celebrate Hezbollah's victory, and drew a general lesson from the pullout: "This is the way to liberate occupied Arab lands." The crowds in Gaza shouted, "Lebanon today—Palestine tomorrow!"[28]

It was a severe blow to Israel's military credibility. Palestinian militants could be forgiven for thinking that perhaps Israel could simply leave the West Bank and Gaza as well. Not only did Israel fail to achieve peace on its northern border, but the Arabs urged further attacks against Israel because its withdrawal was supposedly incomplete. To the Arab world, Israel's destruction again seemed tantalizingly possible.[29]

Barak nonetheless wanted another summit, this one at Camp David in July 2000, an all-out attempt to resolve all major outstanding issues.[30] It was a high-stakes forum for the negotiator-in-chief. "Clinton as a negotiator in this kind of setting really was extraordinary in many respects," says Dennis Ross. "He married his seemingly limitless capacity for empathy with his understanding and command of detail." He continues, "Where he was less strong was in some respects he wanted it too much. And when you're dealing with these kinds of parties, if you want it so much, then they don't have to. One had to deal with Arafat in a way not just that you built his confidence, which was where Clinton was extraordinary, one also had to deal with him in a way that made it clear you were prepared to walk away at any moment."[31]

In other words, the negotiations married Clinton's technical proficiency and gift for detail—Sidney Blumenthal boasts that Clinton wanted to know how the garbage would be collected in Jerusalem[32]—with his yearning to get another Handshake on the White House lawn, a legacy. In the end, he convinced the Palestinians only that they could demand anything, and perhaps help bring about a larger strategic defeat for the United States in the region.

At the summit's midpoint, Clinton offered Arafat a proposal. The Palestinians would get 92 percent of the West Bank and all of Gaza. They would receive some territory from inside Israel's pre-1967 borders to compensate for the 8 percent of the West Bank retained by Israel. Most of the Israeli settlements would be dismantled. The Palestinian capital would be in East Jerusalem, and the Palestinians would have "custodianship" over the Temple Mount. Palestinian refugees could return to the West Bank, but not Israel.[33] Barak was willing to negotiate from Clinton's proposal. Arafat ignored it.[34]

On the last day of the summit, Clinton offered a more detailed proposal for arrangements in Jerusalem, but Arafat rejected it. He was not willing to acknowledge any Jewish claim on the Temple Mount, the holiest site in Judaism. He demanded the "right of return" of roughly four million Arab refugees into Israel proper, which would demographically overrun Israel and effectively end its status as a Jewish homeland.[35] It was clear that seven years after signing Oslo, after winning the Nobel Peace Prize, after a dozen-odd visits to the White House,[36] Arafat still considered Israel a Western imperial implantation to be eradicated.[37]

At various points during the summit, Clinton exploded in frustration, bringing a juvenile touch to the otherwise deadly serious proceedings. Clinton stomped out of the room at one point, saying, "Let's quit!" Later, he lectured Arafat. "You have been here fourteen days and said no to everything. These things have consequences; failure will mean the end of the peace process.... Let's let hell break loose and live with the consequences."[38]

Contributing to his anger, no doubt, was that Clinton saw one of his legacies vanishing. No agreement, no Nobel Prize. As he explained to one audience after his presidency, he could have been concentrating on forging another (misbegotten) arms agreement with the North Koreans instead of being stuck with Arafat with nothing to show for it. It turned out that he had bet on appeasing the wrong thug.[39]

Arafat returned to the West Bank from Camp David like a conquering hero—with an emphasis on conquering. He had remained true to his motivating vision of destroying Israel, whether through armed struggle or a massive influx of refugees. Arafat, and the Palestinians, weren't willing to give up their dream, and were right back where they were in 1948—rejecting a proposed state that would coexist with Israel.[40]

The proximate cause of the second intifada—the first began in the late 1980s and ran into the early 1990s—would be Ariel Sharon's visit to the Temple Mount on September 28, 2000. He was making a political point—that Jews would never be denied access to their holiest of holies. The visit was approved by Barak and coordinated with Palestinian Authority security honcho Jibril Rajoub, and Sharon didn't enter the mosque on the site.[41]

The Palestinians whipped up riots that were the beginning of the new intifada, armed with weapons that Israelis had given Palestinian "police" under Oslo.[42] A few weeks later, Arafat said, "Sharon desecrated the al-Aksa mosque and its compound. A new, religious, dimension was added to the Arab-Israeli struggle," with the Israeli government launching a "mass extermination campaign against our people."[43] The Palestinians hoped the conflict would stoke enough international sympathy that an outside force would intervene to constrain the Israelis—on the Kosovo model—or perhaps that a unilateral declaration of a Palestinian state would become possible.[44]

The administration made its ritual calls for Israeli restraint, in keeping with its view that a "cycle of violence" drove the conflict. This cliché posited a moral equivalence between the attacks of terrorists and the legitimate responses of the army of a democratic society. Such "even-handedness" kept the administration from recognizing Arafat for what he was, or from breaking out of a "peace process" that had utterly failed.

Madeleine Albright called Arafat, telling him that yet more nego-tiating concessions would be forthcoming and urging him to stop the violence—to no avail.[45] The administration's Palestinian "peace part-ner" was too busy funding suicide bombers.[46] At an October meeting with Albright in the American ambassador's residence in Paris, Arafat stormed out on the secretary of state, prompting her literally to run after him, ordering the Marine guards to "Shut the gates!"[47] American power was reduced to something out of a Lucy and Desi skit.

With the peace process in tatters, Barak suffered a catastrophic loss of popularity, and resigned in early December, which gave him sixty days to stand for reelection. In desperation, the Clinton admini-stration made an even more generous peace offer to Arafat in Decem-ber. This became the basis for a last-ditch summit in Taba, Egypt, where Israel made more territorial concessions than it had at Camp David. The Palestinians rejected this offer too.[48] Barak lost in a land-slide to Likud's hawkish Ariel Sharon in February 2001.

In response to a massive wave of suicide bombings, Sharon launched a major military offensive in the West Bank, and a war that had been partly submerged and ignored by the leadership of Israel and the United States was fully in the open. And Israel was finally hitting back in earnest.

"They will feel more secure"

The Clinton administration was willing to go to extraordinary lengths to prop up the Arab status quo in the service of the peace process. It begged Arab states to support Arafat.[49] It contemplated pumping international aid to Hafez el-Assad's dictatorial regime in Syria if it reached an agreement with Israel.[50] The peace process froze the United States into accepting what should have been an intolerable

Arab status quo, and prompted it to subordinate to it much more important security issues, whether it was dealing with the weapons programs of Iraq and Iran, or the worldwide Islamic extremist network funded and supported by Saudi Arabia.

To think that Arab governments would sincerely seek peace misread not only the depths of their enmity toward Israel, but their cold self-interest. Tony Lake said at the time that peace would make it possible for Arab governments to "concentrate on the economic well-being of their people; they will feel more secure in meeting their citizens' demands for greater political participation and accountability."[51]

This begs the question: Why would they want to do that? For a corrupt and unpopular government, such political accountability would mean going out of business.[52]

Two of the biggest terror waves in this period, in the spring of 1996 and the fall of 2001, came after the Israelis had made far-reaching concessions. It wasn't frustration with the peace process that prompted the attacks, but the process itself. The attacks were a way for radical Arabs to undermine the push for peace, and weaken the position of the United States and its ally in the cause of eventually expelling the U.S. from the region entirely.

One alternative to the "peace process" was to bolster Arab moderates like Jordan's King Hussein. Hussein, who made his own peace with Israel in October 1994, knew Arafat well enough to expect that the Oslo Accords would fail.[53] A descendent of the Prophet sitting on a Hashemite throne, King Hussein represented the old pre-revolutionary Arab elite. Hussein's enemies were America's enemies. He had deep quarrels with the pan-Arab radicals of the PLO, with whom he had fought a war in the 1970s. The fascist Baathists in Syria were a periodic threat to invade Jordan. And though he hadn't supported the United States in the first Gulf War, the Baathists in Iraq were an enemy as well, having taken power in the wake of a 1958 coup in which a Hashemite king was assassinated.[54]

A sensible policy would have worked to solidify an Israel-Jordan-Turkey axis of decency in the Middle East. Instead, through the peace process, the United States and Israel propped up Jordan's competitors, the PLO and Syria.[55]

The assumptions of the peace process were self-flagellating. David Wurmser writes, "Mistakenly, officials in Washington and Jerusalem identified their own behavior as the sources of anti-Israeli and anti-American violence, instead of recognizing that violence is a manifestation of the despotic nature of their attackers. Both accepted the assertion of the most radical Arab and Muslim tyrants that they had committed so gross an injustice as to engender generations-long rage in Arab and Muslim peoples."[56]

The administration showered particular attention on Hafez el-Assad of Syria. Warren Christopher met with him twenty times in Damascus in four years, becoming, literally, a pain in the neck. "From meeting to meeting," Christopher writes, "there were virtually no deviations in [our] routine, and no surprises, pleasant or otherwise. The structure of our encounters was so fixed and familiar that when, after two years of these meetings, Assad decided I should sit in his customary chair and he in mine, he explained through his translator that he'd been having neck pains and his doctor thought they might be caused by his having to turn in the same direction every time he addressed me."[57]

Assad recognized that a constant palaver with the West gave him diplomatic cover to pursue his strategy of terror to enhance Syria's position in Lebanon and the region generally.[58]

Rabin, Netanyahu, and Barak all tried approaches to Syria, but Assad always balked. Syria had no interest in signing a deal that would contribute to a region-wide peace, since that would inevitably create pressures for it to end its occupation of Lebanon and an opportunity for liberalizing influences to take hold in the region, thus undermining tyrannies like its own.[59] When Assad refused to denounce terrorism at a joint appearance with Clinton in October 1994, a shocked Christopher was at a loss. "The only explanation I could muster was that Assad was immobilized by his ingrained mistrust of Israel."[60] The more obvious explanation was that Assad was pursuing his naked self-interest.

The Clinton team was always surprised when international actors weren't as amenable to good sense as they hoped or expected. When alleged Iranian "moderate" Muhammad Khatami joined radical Palestinian groups in attacking the Wye River Agreement, Clinton official Martin Indyk was, of course, shocked and mystified. He said of the Palestinian groups, "They're yesterday's men, who speak only the language of violence and terrorism and rejection. Why President Khatami would want to associate himself with these people is, I have to say, beyond me."[61]

For the forces of the Arab status quo, Israel was a barometer of American resolve. The combination of America leaning on Israel to appease Arabs and the Israeli concessions created an impression of weakness. The Arabs began to think that they could beat the United States, and why not? Iraq was already doing it.

"Small, self-contained, ultimately inconclusive"

Clinton took the collapsing Iraq policy of George H.W. Bush and shepherded it to utter ruination, adding his own measure of duplicity and calculated fecklessness. By the end of the decade, Saddam had achieved his most important goals and was on the path to working his way out of the postwar constraints on him entirely.

After the first Persian Gulf War, the Bush administration hoped that a military coup might stabilize the country, and allowed Saddam to smash uprisings against him, especially in the Kurdish north and Shi'ite south.[62] Saddam survived, and fought to keep his weapons as well. UN resolution 687 demanded that Iraq end its chemical, biological, nuclear, and ballistic missile programs, under the supervision of international inspectors, the UN Special Commission (UNSCOM). Saddam's strategy from the beginning was to string out the process for as long as possible.[63]

In response to Saddam's obstruction in January 1993, Bush hit eight Iraqi air defense sites, and launched a purely symbolic cruise missile strike on a building once associated with Saddam's nuclear program. Bush had considered a more extensive raid, but backed off, as an official put it, in order to "make a political point. The point is that this was so fast, efficient, low-key and limited that we can do it again one day from now or two or three. Clinton can do it without much stress."[64] In other words, the strikes were so minimal and ineffectual that even Bill Clinton could manage them. President Clinton had his starter's kit for failing in Iraq.

During the campaign, Clinton had, as usual, sounded tougher than Bush. He criticized the administration for having "failed to learn from its appeasement of Saddam Hussein," and hit Bush for leaving "the Kurds and the Shi'ites twisting."[65] The tone changed as soon as Clinton was in position to do something more than just jabber.

During the transition, Clinton had an interview with Thomas Friedman of the *New York Times*, in which he said of Saddam, "I'm a Baptist; I believe in deathbed conversions. If he wants a different relationship with the United States and with the United Nations, all he has to do is change his behavior." His statement played as dangling the possibility of normalizing relations. In the ensuing mini-firestorm in the media, Clinton insisted, "Nobody asked me about normalization of relations." But Friedman had indeed asked. Stephanopoulos, in his familiar cleanup role, had to wring from President-elect Clinton a statement saying that he "inadvertently forgot that he had been asked that specific question about normalization and he regrets denying that it was asked."[66]

Iraq doves held sway in the administration. The foreign policy triumvirate of Tony Lake, Warren Christopher, and Strobe Talbott didn't want to bother with forging a more aggressive Iraq policy, not when there was global economic growth to pursue and peace was about, with some gentle nudges, to break out all over.[67] The insipid Bush approach, dressed up in the doctrine of "dual containment" of Iraq and Iran,[68] suited the administration just fine. It got its first opportunity to exercise this doctrine when evidence emerged that Iraq had attempted to assassinate former President Bush during a visit to Kuwait in April 1993.

The administration was unwilling to act on the CIA's information alone, and in a portentous sign for the coming, overly legalistic war on terror, insisted on calling on the Justice Department to confirm Saddam's involvement. "I soon came to regret," Tony Lake wrote later, "that the Justice Department was given more than a technical role in deciding the issue. While we needed their expert help, they brought to their recommendation a standard of proof that would later hold up in an American court."[69]

After getting the Justice Department's sign-off, the Clinton administration hit the headquarters of Iraqi intelligence with twenty-three cruise missiles. It decided to forego air strikes, to avoid risking any American pilots, and launched the strikes at night, so few people were in the building. The action was also pushed back forty hours after Clinton had approved it so it wouldn't fall on Friday, the Muslim holy day.[70]

James Woolsey, Clinton's director of Central Intelligence, explains how he saw it from Langley. "The CIA forensic experts went over and they took a few days, and they came back and they said it's an Iraqi mukhabarat bomb. And instead of making a judgment based on that, the administration sent the FBI. The FBI took somewhat longer, but came to the same conclusion. So after a while they fired a couple dozen cruise missiles into an empty building in the middle of the night, which is a sufficiently weak response to be almost laughable."[71]

Despite all the precautions to keep Americans and Iraqis from harm's way, and to avoid offending anyone, Clinton was said to be "tense and wobbly" about his decision.[72] "Are you *sure* this is the right thing to do?" he kept asking.[73] Clinton remembered for years afterward the name of an Iraqi killed in the attack.[74]

The administration implausibly spun its pinprick as a hammer blow against Saddam's regime. "We did in fact cripple the Iraqi intelligence capacity, which was the intent of the action."[75] George Stephanopoulos's later judgment was more realistic. "His first military attack was a qualified success—small, self-contained, ultimately inconclusive, but still a short-term victory."[76] Very short-term—Clinton set the price for attempting to murder a former American president at the loss of an empty building.

"Without U.S. involvement or support"

Nonetheless, a threat to Saddam began to gather in the north. Opposition groups had met in the northern city of Salaheddin in October 1992 to create a coalition of opposition groups called the Iraqi National Congress (INC). Under the leadership of Ahmad Chalabi, it steadily built its forces and settled on a plan to attack Saddam's army from the north in early 1995, hoping to punch through his weak and demoralized 38th division.[77]

When Clinton officials got word of the plan, they reacted with outrage. They considered it a rogue CIA operation that the United States was in no position to back, because it had too few aircraft in Turkey to be much of a factor in the north.[78] Actively supporting the revolt would, no doubt, have been risky—which alone was enough to rule it out.

The usual antecedents of failure flashed through the minds of administration officials. Former Clinton National Security Council staffer Kenneth Pollack writes in his book *The Threatening Storm*, "Lake and Christopher both saw the operation as a second Bay of Pigs waiting to happen."[79] The CIA agent supervising the operation was ordered, not by director of Central Intelligence John Deutch, as would be the usual practice, but directly by Tony Lake to pull the plug and inform the INC that "If you go ahead, it will be without U.S. involvement or support."[80] Lake says, "It made the Bay of Pigs look like the German invasion of Belgium. I mean, it had no chance."[81]

A force of ten thousand Kurds from the Patriotic Union of Kurdistan (one of the main Kurdish factions in northern Iraq), together with INC fighters, attacked anyway, and routed two brigades from Saddam's 38th division. They were prepared to try to continue south, but the administration, worried about more formidable Revolutionary Guard units rolling north, demanded that the insurrection halt.[82] It did.

By early 1996, it had become clear how Saddam, if he weren't top-pled, would begin to defeat containment. He would accept the pro-posed UN "oil-for-food" program that would allow Iraq to sell $2 billion worth of oil every six months and devote the revenues to food and medicine, and use his oil business and time to unravel the coali-tion against him. Kenneth Pollack explains how the administration's hawks forecast it at the time. "The oil-for-food deal would eventually alleviate Saddam's domestic situation; if the United States did not make a push on regime change, Jordan would inevitably reconcile with Saddam; several [Gulf] states were becoming more worried about Iran than Iraq; and the Kurds had begun fighting among them-selves again."[83]

In light of the inevitable strategic deterioration, administration hawks wanted a serious push for regime change before it was too late. But Christopher and other doves were unmoved. They argued that their Iraq policy was succeeding. It was easy and left the administra-tion free to focus on peacekeeping in the Balkans and pushing the Middle East peace process.[84]

"Our missiles sent the following message"

The doves were willing only to continue working for a coup.[85] So, the administration's attention shifted from insurrectionists in Iraq to the Baathist exile community in Jordan. These were shady characters eas-ily infiltrated and manipulated by Saddam. The administration's hope was to have them stage a coup by the time of the 1996 elections, so the Saddam problem would be solved relatively painlessly and with very little political risk.[86]

Saddam batted the whole thing away. The coup turned into a deadly fiasco. In July 1996, the plotters were rolled up and executed by the regime, perhaps in the hundreds. An Iraqi agent used captured CIA communications equipment to inform the CIA station chief in Jordan of the failure and suggest that he and the rest of the Americans run back home.[87]

In the north, things went south. The administration had charged the INC with refereeing among the Kurdish factions there, but as the administration shifted its focus to a coup attempt it dropped the financial support to the INC that would have buttressed its position. Without a dominant, unifying INC, the northern factions fell prey to fratricide.[88]

The Patriotic Union of Kurdistan (PUK) had turned to the Iranians by late 1995 for support in their feud with the Kurdish Democratic Party (KDP). Pressed by the PUK and the Iranians, the KDP felt compelled to look to Saddam for protection. Saddam was set up for a nice win. With the support of KDP forces, five Iraqi divisions moved against Arbil, the headquarters of both the PUK and the INC. They took the town, and executed hundreds of INC personnel. Six hundred other members of the INC had to be evacuated to Guam.[89]

In retaliation, and to keep Saddam from overrunning the north further, the administration responded—in the south. It expanded the southern no-fly zone, and—unable to win support from the Saudis and the Turks to launch air strikes from bases on their territory—relied on forty-four cruise missiles to hit southern targets.[90] "Our missiles sent the following message to Saddam Hussein," Clinton said. "When you abuse your own people or threaten your neighbors, you must pay a price."[91] A small price.

"The facts and the truth are not the same thing"

The administration began to call its policy in the north "deconflictualization"[92]—an awkward and inexplicable neologism for an awkward and inexplicable policy. *Washington Post* columnist Jim Hoagland warned of a failing Iraq policy born of "the administration's growing inability to tell the world—and itself—the truth."[93]

As predicted, Saddam had steadily regained the initiative. The boost in prestige from his success in the north allowed him to accept the UN's oil-for-food program without loss of face. That, in turn, gave him oil contracts with which to split the international coalition against him. The administration wasn't prepared to parry Saddam's advances, as Clinton national security advisor Sandy Berger began to assert his dominance in foreign policy. "Sandy Berger had a problem—he saw both sides of the Iraq issue," Kenneth Pollack writes. "Moreover, Berger served a president who disliked the whole issue of Iraq and by his second term wanted to have as little to do with it as possible. Bill Clinton was certainly not looking to make Iraq the centerpiece of his foreign policy. And when the president found himself in domestic political turmoil as a result of the Monica Lewinsky affair, avoiding foreign policy crises became an even higher priority."[94]

1998 would be Saddam's breakout year. He repeatedly pushed his confrontation with the UN inspectors into crises, which the administration did its best to evade and ignore. The Iraqis weren't stupid. They had seen what happened to regimes that defied the United States and United Nations—they got bribes. UNSCOM head Rolf Ekeus quoted the Iraqi foreign minister complaining: "What does North Korea get for its refusal? They get a $4 billion light-water reactor, get a couple billion dollars in addition, plus unlimited oil deliveries. What do we get? We get nothing."[95]

When Saddam was obstructing inspectors in 1997, the administration said his obligations under the inspections regime were non-negotiable. Then, in February 1998, Kofi Annan negotiated an agreement for Iraq's continued (though much reduced) compliance with the inspections.[96] In exchange for Iraq's latest round of assurances, there would be restrictions on searches of Saddam's palaces and a UN guarantee that it would "respect the legitimate concerns of Iraq relating to national security, sovereignty and dignity."[97]

The UN had also, in the midst of all this, doubled the amount of oil Iraq could sell under the oil-for-food program.[98] At the conclusion of the negotiations over the non-negotiable demands, President Clinton reasserted their non-negotiability. "I believe if [Iraq] does not keep its word this time, everyone would understand that then the United States and hopefully all of our allies would have the unilateral right to respond." He talked of the "severest consequences" if Saddam didn't comply.[99]

The administration spent the next few months dodging the import of those words. On June 10, 1998, a U.S. Army lab at the Aberdeen Proving Ground confirmed from pieces of Scud warheads that they had been loaded with VX gas,[100] which the Iraqi regime had, at various times, denied having, producing in large amounts, or loading onto Scuds.[101] The administration sat on the results.

On June 16, Madeleine Albright told a Senate committee, "To date, inspections under this agreement have gone smoothly." On June 24, President Clinton confirmed to Congress that Saddam was living up to his obligations. When the Aberdeen findings were reported in the *Washington Post* on June 22, State Department spokesman James Rubin said only that they represented "apparent" Iraqi defiance.[102]

The administration went further than denying the results of inspections—all the way to interfering with the inspections themselves. It continued a pattern set in North Korea and Rwanda of the administration undermining international bodies when it feared having to deal with the consequences of their work.

In keeping with its deepest instincts, the administration made itself not just unilaterally risk-averse, but multilaterally risk-averse.

Saddam threatened to end inspections on August 3, 1998, prompting the administration to pull back on the inspections to avoid a confrontation. The *Washington Post* reported on the administration's obstruction on August 14.[103] Albright denied that there had been any. An Albright aide explained, in the spirit of Clinton, that, "the facts and the truth are not the same thing."[104] The *Post* eventually reported that the restraint of the inspectors had been going on since the fall of 1997, in defiance of all the administration's tough-on-Saddam rhetoric and its own stated policy of insisting on unfettered inspections.[105]

In the fall of 1998, Saddam said he would end his cooperation with UNSCOM completely. This, at least, was too much for the administration, which tried unsuccessfully to get an increasingly divided UN

Security Council—Saddam had split off France and Russia onto his side—to declare Saddam in "material breach." The administration decided to launch a military strike anyway. On November 14, planes were ordered into the air to hit Iraq. But CNN reported a new offer of cooperation from Iraqi official Tariq Aziz as the planes were en route. Clinton called them back.[106] It was never too late to decide not to do something that he decided to do in an act of near-decisiveness.

The Aziz offer turned out, predictably, to put unacceptable conditions on the inspectors' return.[107] In the wake of this fiasco, administration hawks argued for an extensive air campaign aimed at ousting Saddam. But the ghosts of failures past still loomed. According to Pollack, "other administration officials objected to an open-ended air campaign that, they argued, would be exactly like the mess the United States had created in Vietnam (and that it would soon nearly re-create in Kosovo)."[108]

When Saddam immediately broke his latest promise of cooperation in December, the administration responded with Operation Desert Fox. Beginning the day before the House was scheduled to start its impeachment debate, the four-day affair consisted of 650 aircraft sorties and 415 cruise missile strikes from the sea and air. The attacks worried Saddam enough that he ordered an internal crackdown that briefly reinvigorated the opposition to his regime.[109] But if Rome wasn't built in a day, Baghdad wasn't going to fall in four, nor did the administration have any intention of toppling the regime. Desert Fox was another exercise in punitive message-sending.

The attack was supposed to "degrade"—the euphemism to describe the goal of any military operation that doesn't have a clear goal—Saddam's weapons of mass destruction capabilities.[110] After his presidency, Clinton said of the attack and of Saddam's weapons of mass destruction, "We might have gotten it all; we might have gotten half of it; we might have gotten none of it."[111] None was much more likely. Kenneth Pollack writes, "The fact was that only eleven of the ninety-seven targets attacked were WMD facilities because the administration generally did not know where Iraq was concealing its WMD programs."[112]

The raids stopped, ostensibly to demonstrate ethno-religious sensitivity at the beginning of Ramadan, but really because they were pointless. They had to end sometime, and sooner better than later.[113]

"The echo of Kosovo"

The struggle with Saddam was essentially over. He had ended the inspections, and survived another spaghetti-armed punch from the United States. During the rest of the Clinton administration, Iraq policy would consist of a desultory and pointless air war in the no-fly zones, with the United States loosing two thousand bombs and missiles.[114] The Air Force began to fill the 2,000-pound bombs with concrete because that was cheaper than explosives.[115]

At the finale of the Desert Fox bombing, Clinton said the policy of the United States government was to end Saddam's regime, although he would do nothing to make it happen. In October 1998, Congress had passed the Iraq Liberation Act—unanimously in the Senate—[116] authorizing nearly $100 million to be spent toward Saddam's overthrow.[117] The administration, however, effectively defied the law, refusing to send the money to Saddam's opponents.[118]

The administration was self-deterred from any vigorous action. "The more we discussed the issue with our various superiors," Pollack writes, "the more I heard the echo of Kosovo in their voices: they (and the president) were not looking to back into a war with Saddam the way they had backed into one with Milosevic." In addition, Clinton's attention was elsewhere. "The president wants to finish his term," an official told Pollock, "by making peace between the Arabs and the Israelis, he doesn't want to start a war between us and the Iraqis."[119]

Madeleine Albright, blinkered by the peace process, blamed Israel's recalcitrance for the deterioration of the anti-Iraq alliance in 1998.[120] It was really the other way around—Saddam's strategic defeat of the administration diminished America's influence in the region and made peace less likely.

In 1995, King Hussein had declared against Saddam, reasserting a vision of an Iraq governed again by the traditional Arab elite along decentralized, pluralist lines. This vision made Jordan the potential pivot for reform, along pro-American lines, among the Arab governments of the Middle East.[121]

But the unraveling of the Clinton administration's Iraq policy provided openings for the region's worst governments, and chastened King Hussein. The abandonment of the Iraqi north was a boon to Syria and Iran, both of which asserted their influence there.[122] When Saddam successfully attacked the north in 1996, it was a sign that he would remain in power. King Hussein, sensing which way the wind was blowing, backed off his opposition to Saddam, and worked to heal his breach with the Iraqi dictator.[123]

Syria loosened the economic noose around Saddam by reopening the Syria-Iraq pipeline that had been closed for twenty years, and Jordan and Turkey began to get into the smuggling act as well.[124] There was a rush to embrace Saddam even among supposed American allies. Iraq hadn't been invited to the last Arab summit in June 1996, but was welcomed at the October 2000 summit. The international coalition against Iraq was a shambles, eroding the postwar restrictions on Saddam. The inspectors were gone, international flights to Iraq—banned after the Gulf War—began again, and Iraq was earning $2 billion a year in illegal oil sales.[125]

All of this meant an ill wind would blow through the administration's beloved peace process. A radical axis of Iraq, Syria, and the PLO, not to mention Iran and other terrorist sponsors, united in its hatred of America and its embrace of terrorism, began to define the geopolitics of the Middle East.

Saddam sent supplies and money to the Palestinians, including $10,000 for the families of suicide bombers.[126] So did the Saudis, nominal allies of the United States.[127] In October 2000, after cutting a deal for military cooperation with Syria, Saddam even sent troops marching westward to threaten Israel and create the prospect of a region-wide war.[128] Iran would soon be sending heavy weapons to the

Palestinian Authority.[129] Yasser Arafat, the man on whom Bill Clinton had pinned his entire Middle Eastern agenda and much of his foreign policy, was allied with every nefarious force in the region.

The Clinton administration's grievous errors in the Middle East had many sources, perhaps the foremost of which was that Clinton, a man who always needed to be loved, didn't understand that most Middle Eastern regimes would always hate the United States. The only variable was whether they would hate us but also fear us. Whatever else can be said about the repressive governments of the Middle East—about their cruelty, their close-mindedness, and their folly—none of them were so stupendously foolish as to think they had to fear Bill Clinton.

TERRORISM:

Losing the War

SOMALIA SET THE TONE. Few realized it at the time, but the battle of Mogadishu was one of the opening shots in the United States's war with terrorism. Clinton's retreat at the first significant shedding of American blood broadcast to the world a lack of staying power. Osama bin Laden paid keen attention to America's fecklessness in the 1990s. Indeed, he took credit for being present at the creation.

From his base in the Sudan in 1993, bin Laden saw the American intervention to save starving Somalis as a Crusader occupation. Al Qaeda operatives returned to their former battleground against the Soviets in Afghanistan to retrieve Milan and Stinger missiles, and bin Laden hired a Sudan Airways cargo plane for a Somali arms lift. His aides, including top lieutenant Mohammed Atef, traveled to Somalia to provide training.[1] It was al Qaeda's operational advice to wait until an American helicopter had passed overhead and shoot rocket-propelled grenades at its tail rotor, the tactic that proved so successful for Aideed's forces.[2]

The hasty American surrender recalled the Soviet defeat in Afghanistan, reinforcing the dangerously inflated self-image of the Islamists. They had defeated one superpower from the Hindu Kush mountains, and had dealt a rattling blow to another from the slums of Mogadishu. If eighteen dead could shake America, well then, what could be accomplished by killing thousands?

"It cleared from Muslim minds the myth of superpowers," bin Laden said in his interview with ABC News journalist John Miller in May 1998. "After leaving Afghanistan, the Muslim fighters headed for Somalia and prepared for a long battle, thinking that the Americans were like the Russians. The youth were surprised at the low morale of the American soldiers and realized more than before that the American soldier was a paper tiger and after a few blows ran in defeat."[3]

"We didn't retaliate after Black Hawk Down," says a former top Clinton foreign policy official. "We sent [Robert] Oakley [former American ambassador to Somalia] in to negotiate the release [of a captured American] and then let it go. I had no idea that this became mythology in the Islamist world. We didn't know we were at war with those guys at the time."[4] In other words, it just happened to be the administration's bad luck that it cut and ran against a terrorist conspiracy instead of merely cutting and running against a nasty African warlord.

The 1990s served as an ongoing confirmation of bin Laden's view of America. He waged a steady campaign of murder against Americans, and could hardly get the attention of the Clinton administration until the end of the decade. Even then he encountered a country willing, within bounds, to tolerate terrorist operatives on its own shores and the murder of its nationals, even the crippling of its great warships.

After September 11, 2001, a debate broke out over whether the United States had suffered intelligence and law enforcement "failures" in the run-up to the attacks. To some extent, it had suffered both. But mainly, the predicate for the terrorist mass murder on that day had been set by a massive "policy failure" in the 1990s.[5] The Clinton administration knew of the terror threat—had been told about it in great specificity by American intelligence—but, typically, avoided tough-minded action. The administration did not seriously tighten airport security laws or toughen United States visa requirements. It did not militarily punish countries that provided sanctuary to terrorists or launch sustained attacks on suspected training camps. It did not work to topple Saddam Hussein's regime, so American troops would no longer be stationed in Saudi Arabia as an unintended provocation to Islamists. It did not try seriously to kill bin Laden, or aggressively freeze terrorist assets, or loosen the rules that hampered the FBI and the CIA.

When the catastrophic attack came soon after it had left office, the response of the administration's defenders was typical: it had all been the fault of Louis Freeh at the FBI, or George Tenet at the CIA, or someone—anyone—else. As for Bill Clinton, well, he couldn't be held responsible—he had only been president of the United States for the previous eight years.

Osama bin Laden had in his mind an image of thoroughgoing American softness, a country unable to resist even weak enemies like the street thugs of Somalia or to retaliate forcibly when attacked. In Bill Clinton, he had his ideal foil. Clinton was a weepy, undisciplined, talkative, indecisive, sexually incontinent embodiment of America's alleged weakness and corruption. The Islamists couldn't have created a better symbol of everything they thought was wrong with America, and of why they thought it could be defeated.

In the end, it was Clinton's cowardice that kept him from vigorously fighting the terror war—his fear of risk, his fear of killing people in military attacks, his fear of offending other countries. His ego made him yearn after a great foreign policy crisis to give him a legacy; his moral shallowness kept him from dealing with one when it arrived.

"Bring them to justice"

The first World Trade Center bombing in 1993 should have changed everything in American policy, shattering the conventional wisdom about terrorism. Instead, it was shrugged off. President Clinton, whose empathy for victims of disasters large and small is famous, didn't show up once at the World Trade Center after the bombing,[6] which killed six and caused $510 million worth of damage.[7] He warned people against "overreacting," and said he sympathized with the victims who had suffered "because somebody did something very stupid."[8]

It was considered impossible until that day that Islamic terrorists would undertake operations in the U.S.[9] The attack should have led to tighter enforcement of immigration laws, because their laxity had allowed the perpetrators into the United States. It should have led to the lifting of the "attorney general's guidelines" restricting the activities of the FBI, because reluctance to monitor mosques and religious figures played to the terrorists' advantage. It should have led to a sustained effort to unravel the plot's international connections, because the attack was linked to new forces of terrorism overseas.

Fundamentally, it should have changed how the United States government understood terrorism: terrorism was no longer merely a law enforcement issue; it was war. In the 1990s, Islamic terrorism underwent a revolution. The goal was total—the destruction of wicked America—and the means were indiscriminate violence.[10]

The first World Trade Center bombing was clearly of a different order than previous terrorist attacks. The bombing's ringleader, Ramzi Yousef, told FBI agents after he was captured that he had hoped to collapse one tower into another, causing 250,000 deaths. He picked that figure as his goal because it was the number of people killed at Hiroshima and Nagasaki. On the heels of this attempted mass murder, authorities uncovered another plan to unleash a wave of destruction across New York City—the so-called "bridges and tunnels" plot.[11]

Nevertheless, for the rest of the decade, the Clinton administration treated terrorists as criminals to be arrested and prosecuted rather than as part of a terror network overseas to be eradicated. After guilty verdicts were returned against four of the Trade Center conspirators, an FBI official commented, "The message of this verdict is twofold. That terrorism has invaded the shores of the United States of America, and that [if you're involved in it] you will be caught, prosecuted, and may go to jail."[12] Clinton would repeat a version of that phrase—usually as "bring them to justice"—after nearly every terrorist attack.[13]

He meant it not in the sense of sending terrorists to their eternal reward, but in the literal sense of trying and imprisoning them. This response not only accorded with Clinton's temperamental distaste for the use of military force, but with the way he viewed international relations in the late twentieth-century world. Terrorism was the product of the decline of the nation-state and traditional geopolitics. It was therefore more naturally categorized as crime rather than war.

Historian Mark Riebling writes, "This doctrine was refined by former Carter defense secretary Harold Brown, whom Clinton chose to head the Commission on the Roles and Capabilities of the United States Intelligence Community. Brown redefined international terrorism—traditionally considered a form of political warfare—as a form of 'global crime.' Terrorism joined narcotics transshipment and trafficking in weapons of mass destruction in that category; Clinton nearly always mentioned all three *together*, typically in the same sentence, as if they were the heads of one private-sector hydra, an unsponsored monster that was merely the incidental byproduct of globalization."[14]

The inadequacy of this law enforcement paradigm became more and more obvious throughout the decade, even as it remained Clinton's mainstay against terror.

"The cost of the 'peace dividend'"

This was a catastrophic mistake. The law enforcement focus meant that the lead agency in the war on terror effectively became the FBI, a task for which it was inherently unfit.

As a domestic law enforcement agency, the FBI had to operate in keeping with rules of evidence and high standards of proof that apply in the American courtroom, both of which are inappropriate to waging a terror war. It had essentially no ability to produce intelligence analysis, because its job had always been solving crimes after the fact. "We didn't have any analytical people," says Jim Kallstrom, the former FBI assistant director in New York.[15]

There were numerous prohibitions on the FBI's ability to share information with, and receive it from, the intelligence community. On the one hand, it was often forbidden from acting on information obtained by the CIA because that would raise civil liberties concerns. On the other hand, grand jury rules kept it from sharing crucial information in terrorist cases with the CIA and other agencies.[16] "It was actually illegal, until the passing of the 2001 USA Patriot Act," says Clinton's first director of Central Intelligence, Jim Woolsey, "for the FBI to give material that was obtained pursuant to a grand jury subpoena to the CIA, or indeed, anybody but the prosecutors."[17]

At best, the FBI could hope to detain for prosecution low-level operatives in any given case, while the terrorist masterminds remained untouched in foreign sanctuaries beyond the reach of American law enforcement. Rousting them from those sanctuaries, the essential task, was a job for the American military. "Ultimately, the mistake was the response," says former deputy attorney general Eric Holder. "We put it in the hands of the FBI and the Justice Department, when it should have been in the hands of the Defense Department, because bin Laden was more than the equivalent of a Muslim mob guy."[18]

In short, as Jim Kallstrom puts it, "It was preposterous to think that the FBI could fight global terrorism."[19]

The administration's position on the FBI wasn't even internally consistent. If the FBI was the most important national bulwark against terrorism, why did the attorney general diminish its surveillance powers? Why wasn't the president meeting with Louis Freeh every day to press him on how the bureau was waging the terror war? Clinton didn't even talk to Freeh for a four-year period.[20] If Freeh was as incompetent and unremittingly hostile to the White House as Clinton spinners maintain, why wasn't he replaced?

In keeping with its role of combating global terror, the FBI opened more and more legal attaché offices overseas in the 1990s, intruding on what was traditionally the territory of its bureaucratic rival, the CIA. The agency had long-running difficulties of its own.

In the 1970s, liberals had decided that covert action was essentially incompatible with a free society. The Church Committee (led by liberal Democratic senator Frank Church of Idaho) blasted away at CIA scandals real and imagined. The committee's work prompted retirements en masse from the Directorate of Operations, a body blow to the agency's covert work.[21] The Clinton administration, for its part, adopted a "Church-plus" agenda on intelligence.

Clinton just wasn't that interested in intelligence. It held no short-term political benefits and involved nasty overseas work that should have been made obsolete in the post–Cold War world. He seemed to select his first director of Central Intelligence, Jim Woolsey, almost as an afterthought. "I had no real institutional problems or complaints," Woolsey says, looking back on his brief tenure, "except that a) I didn't have the resources I thought I needed, b) I virtually never got to see the president except in large meetings."[22]

In the thirty months after Woolsey's departure in early 1995, the CIA would be, off and on, without a director confirmed by the Senate for a period that totaled a year.[23] Clinton's pick to replace Woolsey was John Deutch, who openly belittled the agency and its work.[24] He left in December 1996 after engaging in security violations—keeping classified files on his unsecured computer at home—that might have meant prosecution for a junior officer.[25] But not before he further debilitated the agency.

In 1995, New Jersey senator Robert Torricelli—since retired on corruption charges—blasted the agency for hiring as an informant a Guatemalan perhaps involved in a murder. Congress created new restrictions on what kind of informants the CIA could hire, and any new hires had to be approved by a series of special committees—sort of intelligence co-op boards.[26] Hundreds of overseas informants were dropped, and agents were often deterred from securing new ones. Deutch hailed the new Torricelli-inspired recruitment process as more fully consistent with "American interests and American values."[27]

What that effectively meant was that the restrictions that had been placed on the FBI in the domestic sphere were being exported overseas to the CIA's work as well. CIA general counsel Jeffrey H. Smith explained that the CIA would "draw on the experience of the Federal Bureau of Investigation in dealing with informants." The Justice Department's Office of Intelligence Policy Review, which had done so much to hamstring the FBI, began to review the CIA's handiwork as well. The agency was turning into another overly constrained arm of law enforcement.[28]

The administration refocused the CIA on humanitarian interventions, economic security, the environment, and a host of issues associated with global crime—the war on drugs, money laundering, and computer hacking.[29] Terrorism was buried in a blizzard of other boutique, post-historical priorities. "A very fundamental problem was when John Deutch took over the CIA and decided that paramilitary operations against terrorists were a thing of the past and what the CIA had to concentrate on was economic matters," says retired General Wayne Downing, who commanded the U.S. Special Forces from 1993–1996 and was involved in high-level reviews of American counterterrorism policy thereafter.[30] As the director of the National Security Agency told the joint congressional inquiry into September 11, "The war against terrorism was our number one priority. We had about five number one priorities."[31]

The blossoming of new intelligence priorities came at a time when the CIA's resources were being hacked away. "The cost of the 'peace dividend,'" George Tenet later explained, "was that during the 1990s our intelligence community funding declined in real terms—reducing our buying power by tens of billions of dollars over the decade. We lost nearly one in four of our positions."[32]

Mark Riebling describes the baleful dynamic of the Clinton antiterror policy. "The CIA was being asked to penetrate terror cells, but had been denied the means of penetration. The FBI was being asked to analyze the terror threat, but lacked the means to analyze. Each side distrusted the other, yet both were expected to work together. The system had achieved a kind of negative perfection."[33]

The theme of the decade was the Clinton administration making the FBI's and the CIA's work harder, then not even acting on their work when it had the opportunity.

"The subject of abuse from various Western nations"

The problem was that Clinton didn't even mean it when he said the administration would expend every effort to bring terrorists to justice—the sensitivities of Arab allies and the imperative to avoid inconvenient information took precedence. This was dismayingly clear after the Khobar Towers attack in Saudi Arabia in June 1996.

The radical forces that had been building in the Middle East converged on Saudi Arabia in the mid-1990s. The Saudi regime was paralyzed with an ill king on the throne, just as it was finally having to confront modernity, and declining oil prices were increasing the economic stresses. The situation was ripe for exploitation by the Syrians, Iranians, and radical elements of the Saudi government itself, all of which wanted the United States out of Saudi Arabia and the Persian Gulf. Iran had warmed up to its traditional rivals in the Gulf in the 1990s, and urged that, in the words of spiritual leader Ali Khamenei, the Gulf countries "force the aliens to dispense with this intervention."[34]

Al Qaeda rose out of this radical stew. A number of regimes in the region, Syria, Egypt, and Saudi Arabia, had crushed their internal Islamist oppositions over the years. But they recognized that it would be impossible to eliminate the Islamists entirely. They had to reach a kind of accommodation. So they worked to redirect the radical Islamists against Israel and the United States.

Hence the rising tide of incitement throughout the decade against the United States and Israel by even nominally Western-friendly governments such as Egypt. The goal was expelling America from the region, an objective shared by bin Laden. Arab governments thought that America's liberalizing influence threatened their survival. Bin Laden thought that chasing the United States from the region would further his goal of toppling the regimes. This created a short-term confluence of interests, and each side made itself benign to the other. Bin Laden took no direct action against the Saudi government and the Saudi royal family, in turn, financed a global network of Islamic extremism that provided the sea in which al Qaeda swam.[35] Bin Laden and the House of Saud were best of enemies.

For all these reasons, Saudi Arabia was central to the emerging terror threat. At a terrible price, the 1996 Khobar bombing in Saudi Arabia provided the United States with an opportunity to understand and confront the new terrorist conspiracy. But the Clinton administration hid its eyes and flinched from any serious action.

Bin Laden's models for evicting the Americans were Somalia and the Marine barracks bombing in 1983, in which Iranian-sponsored Hezbollah killed 241 American servicemen in Lebanon and prompted President Reagan to abandon an ill-considered peacekeeping mission there.[36] In November 1995, a bomb exploded in central Riyadh at an office of the Saudi National Guard, which had long cooperated with the American military. It killed five Americans and two Indians.[37] In June 1996, a massive bomb exploded at an American base supporting the southern no-fly zone in Iraq. It ripped into the eight-story Khobar Towers complex, killing nineteen American servicemen.[38]

For the Clinton team, desperate times called for the usual measures—a poll. Dick Morris noted in a memo a few days after the bombing:

"SAUDI BOMBING—recovered from Friday and looking great
Approve Clinton handling 73–20
Big gain from 63–20 on Friday
Security was adequate 52–40
It's not Clinton's fault 76–18"[39]

A fraught three-way tug-of-war began over the investigation into the bombing among the Saudis, who didn't want the United States to get at the truth in the case; the FBI, which was determined to ascertain the facts and suspicious of the motives of the White House; and the White House, which loathed its FBI director and was lukewarm about pursuing the case.

The pattern of Saudi non-cooperation had been set after the Riyadh bombing, when the Saudis denied FBI agents access to four suspects, and swiftly beheaded them for finality.[40] In the Khobar case, the shroud of Saudi non-cooperation further clouded a complicated picture that made no sense according to the conventional wisdom that Shi'ite and Sunni terror groups—representing different variants of Islam—could never cooperate.

A Shi'ite extremist group, Saudi Hezbollah, backed by high-ranking officials in the Iranian government, appeared primarily responsible.[41] But bin Laden, who had earlier reached out to Hezbollah,[42] also may have had a hand in the attack, although there is no hard evidence of his involvement.[43] He called both the Saudi bombings "praiseworthy acts of terrorism."[44] And certainly the bombing had sympathizers among the kingdom's radical Wahhabi clerics.

The Saudis may have refused cooperation not just because—as is often argued—they feared that the United States would lash out and bomb Iran in retaliation,[45] but because they wanted to obscure the role of prominent Saudis in the emerging terrorist network.

If the Saudis feared American military retaliation against Iran, they clearly didn't know with whom they were dealing. While the investigation into the murder of nineteen Americans in an Iranian-backed operation was ongoing, the Clinton administration began a campaign to woo Tehran. It is difficult to warm relations with a regime at the same time as pursuing its connections to terror. So by 1998 the administration appeared prepared to forgive and forget Khobar Towers.

"American officials," writes Madeleine Albright biographer Thomas W. Lippman, "stopped saying in public that they suspected Iran of responsibility for the terrorist bombing of the U.S. Air Force residential compound in Saudi Arabia." The administration softened the State Department warning about travel to Iran, waived sanctions against foreign oil firms doing business there, and removed it from the list of major exporters of illegal drugs.[46]

Iran was determinedly, and predictably, unmoved,[47] because anti-Americanism was close to the core of the regime.[48] The administration then deployed its big gun: a soupy, let's-all-get-along near-apology to the Iranians from the president of the United States, which had been a longtime demand of the Tehran terror regime. President Clinton's statement in April 1999, while the FBI was still trying to unravel the Iranian terror plot, ranks among the most shameful things he ever said in office.

"It may be that the Iranian people have been taught to hate or distrust the United States or the West on the grounds that we are infidels and outside the faith," Clinton said. "And, therefore, it is easy for us to be angry and respond in kind. I think it is important to recognize, however, that Iran, because of its enormous geopolitical importance over time, has been the subject of quite a lot of abuse from various Western nations. And I think sometimes it's quite important to tell people, look, you have a right to be angry at something my country or my culture or others that are generally allied with us today did to you fifty or sixty or one hundred or 150 years ago. But that is different from saying I am outside the faith and you are God's chosen."[49]

The outreach to Iran was exactly at variance with Clinton's rhetoric immediately after the Khobar attack. "The cowards who committed this murderous act," Clinton said upon learning of the bombing, "must not go unpunished. Let me say again: We will pursue this. America takes care of our own."[50] Clinton made his semi-apology to Iran before officially requesting its cooperation in the Khobar case, which he did later in 1999 and never backed up with international pressure.[51]

Freeh, and those around him, began to suspect that the administration didn't care that much about finding the perpetrators because if connections with Iran were established it would be forced to take, or at least consider, action against Iran. This meant that getting to the bottom of the case would present what the administration hated most: a difficulty, a risk.

"It was hard," says Dale Watson, who was executive assistant director of the FBI for counterterrorism and counterintelligence. "It was hard because of the question: What would you do if there was a state sponsor behind this?"[52] Instead of lapsing into its default mode of attempting to placate a country like Iran, the administration would have been forced at least to talk tough, and perhaps think about doing something about it. "It was an attitude of look the other way," says Downing, who led a Pentagon review of the bombing in 1996.[53]

"Director Freeh was the only one in Washington," says Mike Rolince, former chief of the international terrorism division of the FBI, "pushing for direct access to suspects, pushing for records, pushing for identities of the people, wanting this investigation to succeed. We got a lot of lip service from people who said that they were behind us, but we knew for a fact that when certain Saudi officials came into town and it was the right time to push them for things the Bureau wanted, we know from other people that the issue wasn't even raised. It was crystal clear to some of us that they were hoping that this whole thing would just go away."[54]

In a meeting that was supposed to be devoted to pressuring the Saudis on Khobar, Clinton got weepy when Crown Prince Abdullah expressed support for him in the Lewinsky affair and didn't push the Saudi hard.[55] Prince Bandar, the Saudi ambassador to the United States, told Freeh that the White House wanted to avoid confrontation with Iran at all costs, even if it meant ignoring the Khobar Towers attack.[56] For its part, the White House thought Freeh was out of control and trying to create American foreign policy.[57] "We weren't out of control," says Dale Watson, "we were working extremely hard to collect information and evidence that we could use possibly to charge and prosecute people with."[58]

That's what the administration professed to be interested in as well. But this was a more complicated case, where the law enforcement approach to terrorism might not help avoid the alternative of waging war.

"What the administration did was latch onto law enforcement as a way of showing that they were doing something," says Jim Woolsey.

"And if you prosecute successfully a small fry, you can claim victory. If you show yourself to be looking for foreign state involvement in something, it's sort of like a pass in football—several things can happen and most of them are bad. You may turn up foreign state involvement, in which case, you've got to do something about it, and that might mean body bags coming back on the evening news. Or you don't do anything about it and you look weak. Or you don't find it, and people say, well, 'You were looking for it and didn't find it, so you're incompetent.' Politically the safest thing to do in a lot of circumstances is to circumscribe your efforts."[59]

In the Khobar case, the law enforcement approach itself risked creating pressure for a military strike. The White House was therefore angered when Freeh—the head of its lead agency in the fight against terror, whose job it was to pursue the facts—pursued the facts.

When Freeh told national security advisor Sandy Berger that there was evidence to indict several suspects, Berger asked, "Who else knows this?" He then proceeded to question the evidence. A reporter for the *New Yorker* who later interviewed Freeh about the case writes that the FBI director thought "Berger...was not a national security advisor; he was a public-relations hack, interested in how something would play in the press. After more than two years, Freeh had concluded that the administration did not really want to resolve the Khobar bombing."[60]

The price of not getting to the bottom of the matter—although the Saudis opened up somewhat in response to Freeh's proddings and allowed the questioning of suspects[61]—wasn't just shrugging off the murder of nineteen Americans. It was failing to understand fully the changing nature of the terror threat. "Khobar provided the keys that unlocked the new terror world," says one terror expert. "Everything you needed to know about the new terror network, the cooperation between all the different sects and factions, the rise of Wahhabi radicalism in Saudi Arabia, the changing dynamic of the Middle East—it all was present in that case."[62]

The administration wanted to look the other way, partly out of deference to the Saudis. This was an outdated reflex. In the 1990s, the Saudis' radical evangelism ran starkly counter to American interests, and even harmed the Clinton administration's dearest project, the "peace process," by funding Palestinian militants.[63] Clinton apparently just couldn't contemplate confrontation with an Arab government, especially one billed as an ally. It would blow away one of the foundations of the peace process—"evenhandedness." So, Saudi recalcitrance was accepted with relative equanimity. "Mr. Clinton never criticized the kingdom publicly or, in my presence, privately," writes Dick Morris.[64]

By 1996, the administration knew that Saudi-supported charities were aiding terrorists. The *Wall Street Journal* has reported, based on a CIA report from the time, that "the Central Intelligence Agency in 1996 provided the State Department and other agencies with detailed reporting on the charity-terror link." The 1996 CIA document said "available information indicates that approximately one-third of these Islamic NGOs support terrorist groups or employ individuals who are suspected of having terrorist connections." The CIA identified Saudi-funded groups as a particular problem, reporting that the Saudi-supported International Islamic Relief Organization had connections to bin Laden and "helps fund six militant training camps in Afghanistan, according to a clandestine source."[65]

These terror-financing groups continued their operations throughout the 1990s, serenely undisturbed by the Clinton administration.[66] The joint congressional inquiry into the September 11, 2001, attacks reported, "According to a U.S. government official, it was clear from about 1996 that the Saudi government would not cooperate with the United States on matters relating to Osama bin Laden."[67]

An attack against American servicemen abroad was not merely a crime. It was an act of war.[68] The Khobar bombing should have prompted severe consequences for both Saudi Arabia, for its financial support for the growing terror network, and Iran, for its direct involvement in the attack. But the Clinton administration couldn't bring itself to change the basis of its relationship with Saudi Arabia, or to punish Iran, which actually got softer treatment after Khobar. Clinton wasn't in the business of subjecting Middle Eastern states to further "abuse from various Western nations."

"Not yet been indicted"

The law enforcement paradigm contributed to one of the great missed opportunities of the decade.

In the spring of 1996, Sudan offered to cough up bin Laden. Sudan was chastened by the recent American decision to withdraw its embassy staff because of the Islamic regime's terror-friendly policies. During his last night in the country, ambassador Tim Carney found Sudan's foreign minister, Ali Othman Taha, suddenly willing to discuss the problem of terrorism. A fitful dialogue began, with a Sudanese official eventually offering to send bin Laden to Saudi Arabia.[69]

The Saudis, eager always to take the coward's way out, refused the idea of accepting bin Laden, given the support he had in the kingdom and the exalted status of his family.[70] The Clinton administration didn't push the issue.[71] "We clearly didn't lean on the Saudis," says a former administration official involved in the negotiations.[72] The administration shouldn't have been willing to take "no" for an answer. But, amazingly, some officials considered the peace process more important. "In the Saudi-American relationship," the *Washington Post* reported in October 2001, "policymakers diverged on how much priority to give to counterterrorism over other interests such as support for the ailing Israeli-Palestinian talks."[73]

Sudan might have offered bin Laden to the administration directly,[74] although the incident is shrouded in mystery and some former Clinton officials deny it.[75] "I can't find a record of them offering him to us," says Tony Lake. "I'm not saying that they didn't do it. I am saying that none of my colleagues have any memory of it, and nobody can find a paper trail."[76]

For whatever reason, the administration at the time asked the FBI and the office of the U.S. attorney for the southern district of New York, Mary Jo White, if an indictment could be made against bin Laden. They said no.[77] Sandy Berger later told the *Washington Post*, "The FBI did not believe we had enough evidence to indict bin Laden at that time, and therefore opposed bringing him to the United States."[78]

This is mind-boggling, given that the CIA had already set up a "virtual station" devoted to bin Laden in January 1996,[79] and according to Tenet, "as early as 1993, [CIA] units watching him began to propose action to reduce his organization's capabilities."[80] Clinton approved a CIA finding in early 1996 that bin Laden was a threat to national security.[81] State Department documents at the time declared him "one of the most significant financial sponsors of Islamic extremist activities in the world today."[82] The southern district of New York indicted him a year or so later.[83]

In their defense of Clinton's counterterror policy, *The Age of Sacred Terror*, two former Clinton NSC staffers, Daniel Benjamin and Steven Simon, explain why the administration didn't want custody of an unindicted bin Laden—in terms that highlight its excessively legalistic approach. "[S]ince he had not yet been indicted, the Justice Department had no grounds to hold him. In the unlikely case that bin Laden was put on a plane to New York, on arrival at Kennedy airport he would have been free to catch a connecting flight to Orlando and visit Disney World, or take the next plane out to Islamabad. The United States had no interest in that happening."[84]

Disney World?

The INS couldn't have held bin Laden on some immigration charge, assuming his papers would not have been entirely in order? He could not have been held as a material witness in connection with the terrorist attacks he was suspected of sponsoring? He could not have been detained on any grounds whatsoever? The cliché is that a grand jury will indict a ham sandwich—but not a ham sandwich funding a terror war against the United States?

The episode betrayed an utter lack of imagination and aggressiveness. If the Sudanese didn't offer to hand over bin Laden to the United States, why didn't the administration ask them to? Thus did the clearest opportunity to prevent September 11 at its root slip away.

The Clinton team was justifiably suspicious of the Sudanese government. But for all of its nastiness, Khartoum had recently betrayed another high-profile terrorist, handing over Carlos the Jackal to the French.[85] The Sudanese ended up expelling bin Laden, which they presumably wouldn't have done if their offers had been in bad faith.

Sudan sent the terror leader to Afghanistan in May 1996,[86] where he would be separated from his Sudanese business apparatus, but otherwise free to operate (he may have drawn on his financial assets in Sudan anyway).[87] Some American officials wanted to consider shooting down bin Laden's plane on his way out of Sudan. But if the administration couldn't even indict him, it wasn't going to think seriously about killing him. According to the *Washington Post*, "it was inconceivable that Clinton would sign the 'lethal finding' necessary under the circumstances."[88]

Getting bin Laden into Afghanistan was a victory by the short-term standards of the administration. Steven Simon told the *Washington Post* in October 2001, "I really cared about one thing, and that was getting him out of Sudan. One can understand why the Saudis didn't want him—he was a hot potato—and, frankly, I would have been shocked at the time if the Saudis took him. My calculation was, 'It's going to take him a while to reconstitute, and that screws him up and buys time.'"[89]

It was a pyrrhic victory. Almost immediately upon his arrival in Afghanistan, bin Laden declared war on the United States.[90] The Taliban provided security guards for him and welcomed his creation of terrorist training camps. Bin Laden, in turn, poured money and personnel into the Taliban. As George Tenet has explained, "While we often talk of two trends in terrorism—state-supported and independent—in bin Laden's case with the Taliban we had something completely new: a *terrorist* sponsoring a *state*." He had the sanctuary to become, in Tenet's words, "a sophisticated adversary—as good as any that CIA has ever operated against."[91]

In helping shuttle bin Laden to Afghanistan, the Clinton team had bought nothing except time and the chance that he would become the problem of some other administration.

"We went after his infrastructure"

From his safe harbor, bin Laden launched al Qaeda's next assault on August 7, 1998. The terror group simultaneously bombed the American embassies in Nairobi, Kenya, (killing 213 and wounding 4,500) and Dar-es-Salaam, Tanzania, (killing eleven). Twelve Americans were murdered in the attacks.[92] There had been warning signs. The American ambassador to Kenya, Prudence Bushnell, repeatedly asked Washington for more security at the embassy, including in a letter directly to Madeleine Albright. She was ignored.[93]

In December 1997, Clinton complained to the *New York Times* about how history seemed determined to rob him of a great crisis from which he could gain a great legacy. "The first thing I had to start with was, you know, we don't have a war," he said. "We don't have a depression, we don't have the Cold War."[94] Well, here was his crisis. A terrorist network had nearly leveled two American embassies simultaneously. He responded with a whimper.

The administration hit back in a classic tit-for-tat manner. Bin Laden hit two targets, so Clinton was going to hit two targets. And he decided to go where he had the most practice—infrastructure. The first target was a cluster of bin Laden training camps near the eastern Afghan town of Khost.[95]

Clinton said of bin Laden two days after September 11, "The best shot we had at him was when I bombed his training camps in 1998. We just missed him by a matter of hours, maybe even less than an hour."[96] Sidney Blumenthal in his book repeats the hour figure.[97] It is a joke.

Anthony Zinni, who at the time was commander of the American forces in the region, has pooh-poohed the idea that the United States came so close. He told journalist Byron York, "There was a possibility [bin Laden] could have been there. My intelligence people did not put a lot of faith in that. . . . As I was given this mission to do, I did not see that anyone had any degree of assurance or reliability that that was going to happen." He continued, "In weighing that out, without great intelligence, it's a million-to-one shot."[98]

Mohamed Odeh, one of the Nairobi plotters, told the FBI that the day before the embassy bombings the word was that "All [bin Laden's] people have been evacuated [because] we're expecting retaliation from the U.S. Navy."[99] Meaning, presumably, a submarine-launched cruise missile strike. Bin Laden knew his adversary well.

In his speech to the nation explaining the retaliatory strike, Clinton said, "Our forces targeted one of the most active terrorist bases in the world. It contained key elements of bin Laden's network and infrastructure."[100] So bin Laden could kill Americans—but only at the price of having his infrastructure degraded. General Hugh Shelton, chairman of the Joint Chiefs of Staff, explained, "We were not going directly after Osama bin Laden. It was an attack on his network of terrorist groups, as I think you can see from the targets. We will continue to go after that if we feel like it's appropriate and if the threats to Americans or American interests continue."[101]

The Clinton administration would never "feel like" it was appropriate again, despite Clinton's pay-any-price, bear-any-burden rhetoric. "Our efforts against terrorism cannot and will not end with this strike. We should have realistic expectations about what a single action can achieve, and we must be prepared for a long battle."[102]

As for the infrastructure at the camp, it consisted of stone, timber, and mud.[103] "What you told bin Laden," says Mike Rolince, former chief of the international terrorism division of the FBI, "is that he could go and level two embassies, and in response we're going to knock down a few huts. If you're bin Laden, that sounds like a real legitimate cost of doing business."[104]

"We used kid gloves after the embassy bombings," says retired General Wayne Downing, who commanded the U.S. Special Forces from 1993–1996. "It was all bull—. Cruise missiles—that's the coward's way out."[105] If the United States was going to hit one terror camp, why not all of them?

"I think the question you have to ask yourself," says Rolince, "is, why didn't we finish the job? We didn't go back. We never went back to the camps and dismantled the neighborhood where these people were allowed to train, test chemicals, recruit, plan operations. On a regular basis, we saw intelligence that documented what they were, where they were, how big they were, how many people were going through there, and the administration lacked the political will to go in there and do something about it. September 11 happened for a number of different reasons—one of which is, we gave the enemy, who numbered in the thousands, a free arena to get ready for the attack."[106]

The other target is infamous: the el-Shifa pharmaceutical plant in Sudan. The Clinton administration thought it was involved in the manufacture of chemical weapons, based on the presence of the chemical EMPTA in the soil. On closer examination, the case against the plant was tenuous. There was one target of undeniable legitimacy, in Khost. But the administration wanted to hit targets at two locations, since al Qaeda had done the same.

It would supposedly "send a signal" that the United States could hit targets simultaneously around the world as well—hence the over-the-top code name for the operation, "Infinite Reach."[107] That was the administration's substitute for a sustained campaign, and to achieve it, "they reached down to any target they could get," says Downing.[108]

A top Clinton foreign policy official confirms as much. "I participated directly in the discussions and at the time two or three other targets were proposed in addition to el-Shifa. None of them had any basis for proceeding, but the chemical plant had this evidence of a presence of EMPTA, which is the precursor of VX and it appeared in soil samples, which the agency felt with reasonable confidence came from close enough to the plant. So we thought, 'Okay, there was enough of a chance there.' And Sandy [Berger's] reason, which I accepted at the time and still accept, was that it could turn out that if this place made VX, and terrorists in Europe, the United States, or the Middle East killed a large number of people as a result, then if we had an opportunity to do what we did and didn't, we would have been subject to the same degree of criticism as we were when we did do it. I think we were lucky, because fortunately only one person was killed in the attack. But I argued very strongly against the other targets."[109]

The criticism of the strike at the time was that it was an attempt by Clinton to distract attention from the Lewinsky scandal. Republicans raised this possibility, as did left-wing demonstrators. "No blood for blow jobs," read one protest sign.[110] Top FBI officials had the same suspicion, and some of them referred to the cruise missiles used in the attacks as "Monica's missiles."[111] But there was a terrorist outrage to respond to, and Clinton should have done more rather than less.

Clinton, as usual, provided justification for the paranoia of his critics. He made a stagy return from his frosty vacation with Hillary on Martha's Vineyard to oversee the military action from Washington. As Peter Baker writes in *The Breach*, "Clinton had no genuine national security reason to leave the island, as the White House had set up all the communications equipment he would need to monitor activities and talk with foreign leaders."[112]

Was the target correct? The administration had on its side the soil sample containing the EMPTA. The chemical has no commercial use, and the CIA thought it could only be part of a process to create VX. But administration officials had to back off their initial claim that no medicines were produced at the plant.[113] Independent researchers couldn't duplicate the incriminating soil sample, and foreigners had regularly been taken on tours of the site, seemingly making it an unlikely venue for the production of weapons of mass destruction.[114]

"I don't think it passes the laugh test, quite frankly," says an FBI official.[115] The judgment of the Monterey Institute's Center for Nonproliferation Studies seems reasonable: "It remains *possible* that at some point in time, a small quantity of a VX precursor chemical was produced or stored in Shifa or transported through or near it. However, the balance of available evidence suggests that the facility probably had no role whatsoever in CW [chemical weapons] development."[116]

So, the target was probably wrong, but that kind of mistake could be forgiven in a war. Only the administration wasn't about to fight one. Clinton barely undertook even the minimal, tit-for-tat el-Shifa strike. About a week afterwards, Clinton explained while still at Martha's Vineyard, "I was here on this island up till 2:30 in the morning, trying to make absolutely sure that at that chemical plant there was no night shift. I believed I had to take the action I did, but I didn't want some person who was a nobody to me—but who may have had a family to feed and a life to live and probably had no earthly idea what else was going on there—to die needlessly."[117]

In the context of Clinton's existential worrying, the criticism of the el-Shifa strike was devastating. Before he made the decision, when it was pointed out to Clinton that he would be attacked for "wagging the dog," the president made brave noises to his aides. "If I have to take more criticism for this, I will."[118] But he wasn't really willing to take the criticism, not for undertaking military action for which he had little stomach in the first place.

Benjamin and Simon write, "The press accounts were so uniformly negative that Clinton himself came to wonder whether the strike was justified. He eventually asked the NSC for a review of all the intelligence on which the decision to strike was based. Those who worked on the memo, which took months of effort, concluded that the call was right."[119] Clinton would, nonetheless, never make such a call again.

The flaccid response to the embassy bombings was part of a general meltdown in the West's image and position in the Middle East in 1998, the year of the rogue. Saddam was outmaneuvering Clinton. The administration was squeezing Israel to make more concessions in the peace process. Israel was suffering a continuing deterioration in its war with Hezbollah in southern Lebanon, from which it would soon withdraw. The president made his near-apology to the Iranians. And the administration showed it would make only the mildest response to direct attacks on its interests overseas.

The world in which the September 11, 2001, attacks were possible had been born.

"Nothing moved"

There is no doubt that the administration knew about the dangerousness of al Qaeda.

"We urgently understood the U.B.L. threat," says a former Clinton official, referring to Usama (or Osama) bin Laden. "There have been former Clinton people on background, saying 'Jeez, we didn't know the threat was that bad.' And my answer is, 'Bull—, we didn't.' The people who were involved in that knew that this was a really big deal. Should we have taken more chances? That's a legitimate question. But it's not legitimate for anyone who worked in the Clinton administration and tackled some of these issues to pass this off and say, 'We didn't know it was that bad.' We did."[120]

Some Clinton defenders want credit for the president's words, for the fact that Clinton occasionally talked about the terror threat—in a version of the characteristic Clinton mistake of considering rhetoric as important as reality. In a 1995 United Nations address, Clinton warned of the growing threat of terrorism.[121] By May 1998, he was saying that the United States must confront terrorism "with the same rigor and determination we applied to the toughest security challenges of this century."[122]

The reason the administration knew about the danger of al Qaeda is simple—it was told. George Tenet has testified to Congress that the CIA was aware of bin Laden's threat by 1993. According to Tenet, the CIA warned as early as 1998 that al Qaeda had already conducted successful tests to elude security at a major American airport and that it had developed plans to hijack a plane on the east coast of the United States.[123] The problem wasn't that the Clinton administration didn't know about al Qaeda or didn't talk about it, but that it didn't undertake concerted action.

There was sporadic movement. In June 1995, Clinton signed PDD-39, streamlining the government's response to a possible terror attack and centralizing authority in the White House, empowering the aggressive NSC staffer Richard Clarke. By 1996, the administration began steadily increasing counterterrorism spending.[124]

There were even tangible successes. The administration hit the accelerator on so-called renditions, in which a foreign country hands over a terror suspect without the publicity of formal extradition. A high-profile victory was the foiling of the millennium plots to bomb the Los Angeles airport and the Radisson Hotel and other targets in Amman, Jordan, which led to the disruption of terror cells in roughly a dozen countries.[125] The administration, however, constantly bumped up against limits imposed by its own unwillingness to consider the fight against terrorism a full-fledged war and its aversion to offending Arab and Muslim governments.

"In the pre–September 11 world, there was always something holding us back," says a former high-ranking Clinton defense official. "If you're trying to control weapons of mass destruction, anthrax strains, for example. If you were just saying common sense things like, 'Isn't it a bad idea that you can FedEx some of this stuff?' Back then you were interfering with academic freedom."[126]

Former NSC staffers Benjamin and Simon offer an example of the imperative of "never offending." A counterterrorism official at the State department wanted to send a cable instructing ambassadors in countries with terrorist problems to alert their host governments to the connections between many Islamic NGOs and terrorists. State's regional bureaus would have none of it. The language was too strong. According to Benjamin and Simon, "Compromises were offered, and the counterterrorism officials in State and the White House fought hard to get the cable sent. But after weeks of battle, the regional bureaus won. The cable was spiked."[127]

The position of Clinton's staunchest defenders on terrorism, like Benjamin and Simon—whose book reflects national security advisor

Sandy Berger's version of events—is that the administration was aware that the United States could face a catastrophic terrorist attack, it just couldn't manage to get its own bureaucracy to act.

Benjamin and Simon offer another example—State Department resistance to pressure from the NSC to do more to protect its embassies overseas. "Eventually, when the backlog of other issues simply grew too large, the NSC relented. Odd as it may seem, a presidential phone call to convince the State Department to protect its own people was something no one could seriously contemplate."[128] Well, why not? It was routine for Clinton, with his prodigious appetite for policy detail, to get involved in minutiae.[129]

In Benjamin and Simon's telling, it was only in budgetary matters that the White House could influence the State Department: "Getting the State Department to give in on a money issue—an area in which the White House had real leverage—was one thing. Persuading it to push terrorism far up its priority list was another."[130]

This is a damning statement of presidential impotence. Bureaucracies are indeed balky and lethargic, which is why it is so important that the president of the United States focus them on what is truly vital—namely, preventing the potential murder of thousands of Americans. This is the most basic test of leadership, and Clinton failed it. If the United States government was distracted from fighting terrorism by other priorities, it is because the Clinton administration gave it so many other priorities: nation building in the Balkans, peace negotiations in the Middle East, protecting the global environment.

A series of government reports in the late 1990s recommended obvious ways to begin addressing the terror threat. In 2000, the Hart-Rudman Commission on National Security in the Twenty-first Century, chaired by former senators Gary Hart and Warren Rudman, and the National Commission on Terrorism, chaired by ambassador Paul Bremer, both recommended a series of commonsense steps. As John Miller summarizes them: "that Afghanistan be designated a sponsor of terrorism, that private sources of funding for terrorists be frozen, that there be a crackdown on student visas, that the CIA and FBI find better ways of sharing information, and that the so-called 'agent scrub' that had discouraged the CIA from recruiting unsavory characters as 'assets' be rescinded."[131]

Each of these steps might have presented its own difficulties, but by the account of even his defenders, Clinton couldn't be bothered to pick up the phone to push any of them.

"Unfinished military business"

The next al Qaeda assault came with the October 2000 attack on the USS *Cole*. A bomb nearly sank the ship and killed seventeen sailors.[132]

Clinton responded to the attack with a non sequitur reflecting his obsession with the peace process. "If [the terrorists'] intention was to deter us from our mission of promoting peace and security in the Middle East, they will fail utterly."[133] The *Washington Post* reported at the time, "While the apparent suicide bombing of the USS *Cole* may have been the more dramatic episode for the American public, the escalation between Israelis and Palestinians took the edge in preoccupying senior administration officials yesterday. This was regarded as the more fluid of the two problems, and it presented the broader threat to Clinton's foreign policy aims."[134]

The investigation quickly slipped into the Khobar pattern, with the sensitivities of the host country, in this case Yemen, trumping all else. Barbara Bodine, the American ambassador to Yemen, didn't want the Yemenis offended by the presence of too many unseemly FBI agents, so she insisted that the contingent be kept to thirty or so. Famed FBI deputy director John O'Neill (he was killed on September 11, 2001, at the World Trade Center, where he had just become head of security) showed up with 150 agents, determined to track every possible lead as quickly as possible.[135]

Initially, Yemeni authorities kept American investigators from even visiting the *Cole*, and they were kept from questioning suspects directly. O'Neill wanted the FBI agents, given the dangerous security environment, armed with compact submachine guns. Bodine, who eventually would ban O'Neill from the country, thought that would be entirely too provocative. In response to constant security threats, in late October most of the FBI agents were sent home, and the remnant left behind was housed offshore on an assault helicopter carrier.[136]

An American warship had been nearly sunk, the investigation into it short-circuited by a recalcitrant government, and now the American investigative team would be scared off by more terrorist threats. It presented a devastating image of American weakness.

The *Cole* attack, meanwhile, went unanswered. Benjamin and Simon write, in defense of the decision not to retaliate in any form whatsoever, "Clearly, jihadists were behind the bombing, including probably al Qaeda, but no claim of responsibility arrived from any known group and there was no intelligence tying the attack to the leadership in Afghanistan. To launch a military strike against targets in Afghanistan on the basis of nothing more than a strong intuition would have gone well beyond any U.S. military precedent."[137]

This is dishonest excuse-making. "I don't think there was much question to most people who looked at the *Cole* that this was al Qaeda," says a former Clinton defense official. "I was comfortable that it was al Qaeda. There was no doubt about it—the level of expertise, everything, pointed to al Qaeda. It may have been a case of people looking for a higher standard of proof. Maybe that's the weasel way out—if it's just too difficult."[138]

John Miller reports, "In fact, some investigators contend that within forty-eight hours of the bombing, the link to bin Laden was firm enough to justify a military response, if that had been the White House's preferred course of action."[139]

Benjamin and Simon plead not only that there was not enough evidence, but that there was not enough time. "The clock was running out on the Clinton administration, and the United States was in the midst of its closest presidential race in a century. Any military action would have constrained the next president's room for maneuver and committed him to a policy he had not chosen."[140] But Clinton wasn't opposed to constraining the president's room for maneuver in other areas. His "save Social Security first" proposal in his 1998 State of the Union address was meant to make it harder for the next president to cut taxes.

Clinton didn't respond to the *Cole* bombing partly because he felt so chastened by the criticism of the el-Shifa attack in Sudan, criticism he had boldly pledged not to be chastened by. "One of the reasons why after the *Cole* there was less done may be in part because of the huge reaction to the Sudan bombings that took place," says a former top Clinton foreign policy official. "Now, after the *Cole*, what more could have been done? We probably could have pushed the Yemenis very, very hard."[141]

Clinton was in a war,[142] and simply wasn't up for it.

"Didn't have the guts"

Los Angeles-class submarines were deployed in "the basket" off Pakistan, where cruise missiles could be launched to hit Afghanistan, for the last two years or so of the Clinton administration. The National Security Council was close to striking three times. But the administration understandably wanted to avoid making a mistake, and once barely averted launching an attack against a hunting party of rich Emiratis.[143]

"A few times we almost launched an attack and found out later that the intelligence was wrong," says a former Clinton official. "I was involved in a situation when we almost launched a cruise missile strike against a hunting party. We almost blew up the royal family of the United Arab Emirates because they were out there pheasant hunting. When you come that close, and you're sitting at that principals meeting, and you have that adrenaline rush, you say, 'F—, we almost smoked these guys.' It's funny now, but it wasn't funny then."[144]

The cruise missile option had limits because it took hours—as much as ten hours of advance warning about bin Laden's whereabouts was necessary—[145] from the time a strike was authorized to when the missile would reach its target. As for other options, Richard Clarke told the *New Yorker* that Clinton authorized the CIA to kill bin Laden after the African embassy bombings.[146] But the CIA had been steadily emasculated over the years, so killing people was no longer one of its strengths. A former intelligence official told the congressional joint inquiry that the CIA's capabilities in this area had "atrophied" prior to September 11, 2001.[147]

The CIA had long been, and was still, operating in a political environment unfriendly to the dark arts of covert action. An intelligence official told the joint inquiry that there was "lots of desire at the working level," but "reluctance at the political level." As long as the Clinton administration wasn't going to work to topple the Taliban, bin Laden had a safe haven protecting him from most CIA action. A former intelligence official told the joint inquiry that the "international political context of this period" presented "an operational environment with major impediments that CIA constantly fought to overcome."[148] Then, there were all the rules in place to constrain the CIA.

According to the joint inquiry, "The CIA could not violate the Constitution, U.S. law, or human rights, including bin Laden's, during these [anti-bin Laden] operations."[149] Bob Woodward recounts the legalistic wrangling over in what circumstances a group of thirty recruited agents in Afghanistan known as "the Seniors" could shoot at bin Laden: "During one period, the leader of the Afghan Seniors had met several times with the CIA station chief from Islamabad, Pakistan, who controlled and paid them. The Senior leader maintained that they had shot at bin Laden's convoy on two occasions in self-defense, which was permissible, but he wanted to go after the convoy in a concerted way, proposing an ambush—shoot everything up, kill everyone, and then run. The CIA station chief kept saying, 'No, you can't, you can't do that.' It would violate U.S. law."[150]

After the embassy bombings, Clinton demanded to be presented options for a military operation on the ground.[151] General Hugh Shelton, chairman of the Joint Chiefs, came up with a proto-plan involving tens of thousands of troops, and emphasized the difficulties involved.[152] It was a typical military plan to scare off civilians from considering a military option.

The administration, of course, scared easily. As John Miller writes, "[N]either Clinton, nor Shelton for that matter, felt the public would tolerate the loss of American lives likely to be incurred in that kind of an operation. Nor did Clinton feel he could sell an Afghan invasion to America's European allies, much less to the moderate Arab states whose cooperation, if only for logistical reasons, was vital."[153]

For its part, the military simply didn't think Clinton was up to it. A former official has explained, "Shelton, like Powell, had eyed up Clinton and decided he didn't have the guts to fight a war. And if you make that conclusion, you're not going to put forward anything in a gray area because you're afraid he's going to wimp out."[154] The military also feared another Desert One, the failed attempt to rescue the Americans held hostage in Iran during the Carter administration. "The military was reluctant," says a former defense official. "It's much easier to take a shot at him with one cruise missile, off one platform, than it is to put one hundred Delta guys on the ground. There's much less chance of something going wrong."[155]

There were potential proxy forces in the region. Uzbekistan was willing. But the CIA had been criticized too many times for cooperating with repressive regimes, and so wanted to take a pass. The Northern Alliance was already confronting the Taliban militarily, and was ripe for American support in the form of increased aid or even direct military operations. But no one, according to Benjamin and Simon, "wanted to place the United States on what might be a slippery slope to a full-scale war in Asia. Serious as the threat of bin Laden was, there was a mismatch between provocation and this suggested response. No one could imagine presenting the American people with a war over a threat they knew so little about and did not view as critical."[156]

The administration didn't give the American people enough credit. It thought the public must be as gutless and risk-averse as it was. It wasn't. Consultant and pollster Dick Morris understood this. He repeatedly pushed Clinton to take on the terror threat, dictating long sections of draft speeches. "We face no Hitler, no Stalin, but we do have enemies, enemies who share their contempt for human life and human dignity, and the rule of law. Our generation's enemies are the terrorists."[157]

The polling definitely backed Morris up. Mark Penn and Doug Schoen reported in an October 1995 memo, "1. Standing up for America. Every time our actions and words are interpreted as standing up for America, our support grows. This has been true in the trade dispute with Japan, our actions on Oklahoma City, and the First Lady in China. This is not a value we say we are doing, it is one that comes through a series of strong, definite actions that have us standing up to threats in the world from a very U.S. point of view."[158]

This is one of the few cases where Clinton didn't follow the polling. A war on terror would have been popular and difficult, while so many other things he did were popular and easy. Besides, there was no groundswell for invading Afghanistan that would have forced Clinton into it. Clinton never had a sense that terrorism would threaten his presidency, or that he would have to confront a congressional revolt over it, the way he did, say, over his weak and faltering Bosnia policy in 1995. Indeed, admitting that we were at war would have been "off message," losing half of the Democrats' crucial 2000 campaign plank of "peace and prosperity."

Then, there was the international audience that Clinton considered so crucial. What would the Europeans say? Benjamin and Simon write, "There was another problem: in 1998–1999, the United States conducted a war in Kosovo and a sustained [four-day] bombing campaign in Iraq called Operation Desert Fox. Several policy makers, especially from the State Department, where the foreign criticism of American actions was perceived most acutely, argued that the United States was increasingly seen as the world's mad bomber."[159] The administration, in other words, was scared by its own shadow, and let the limits of its actions be set by the kind of critics who considered the United States a dangerous and irrational international actor.

So, war was out, and even harsh diplomatic measures were thought to go too far. The administration didn't have much leverage with the Taliban,[160] but continued conversations with Taliban officials in the forlorn hope that the verbal pressure would encourage Taliban "moderates."[161] The administration thought the Taliban could be reasoned with. "They were convinced," says FBI terrorism specialist Mike Rolince, "that the FBI would travel to Afghanistan and brief the Taliban on the strength of our case on the embassy bombings. And we told them in no uncertain terms, 'We don't make it our practice to go over and brief people who are harboring fugitives.'"[162]

The administration wouldn't even go so far as to designate Afghanistan a state sponsor of terrorism.[163] "The omission reflects," according to a report in the *Washington Post* after September 11, "a period that found the State Department more focused on U.S. oil interests and women's rights than on the growing terrorist threat, according to experts and current and former officials."[164] The potential of such a terrorist designation was considered a fearsome stick the administration could wield to coax the Taliban into better behavior. And if the Taliban didn't change, that wasn't so awful either. "This is hard to say and I haven't found a way to say it that doesn't sound crass," Madeleine Albright told the *Post*. "But it is the truth that those [attacks before September 11] were happening overseas and while there were Americans who died, there were not thousands and it did not happen on U.S. soil."[165]

The potential point of leverage on Afghanistan was clearly the sometime American ally Pakistan. Islamabad practically created the Taliban, and forged a close working relationship with al Qaeda. The Pakistanis sent students from their radical madrassas to terror training camps in Afghanistan and then into Indian-controlled Kashmir to wage war over the fate of that disputed province.[166] Throughout the 1990s, Pakistan was actively working against American interests, aiding and abetting Islamic extremism and terrorism, and doing it with impunity.

State Department official Mike Sheehan suggested that the administration give the Pakistanis an ultimatum: cooperate in helping the United States bag bin Laden and shut down the terror camps, or the United States would cut off crucial International Monetary Fund support to Islamabad.[167] Sheehan's plan was considered a non-starter—too risky and confrontational—by the Clinton team.

Talking to the Pakistanis about their nukes—which they had tested in 1998—was considered more important by the arms control–conscious Clinton administration.[168] The administration also operated on the Pangloss-like assumption that it was the best of all possible worlds in the Middle East and Central Asia, and any aggressive move by the United States would only risk making things worse by creating anti-American hostility and toppling nominally friendly governments.

"We were just going nuts about the need to put more of a squeeze on the Pakistanis," says a former Clinton official of hawkish views, who was outnumbered. "And then you got pushed back by the whole counter-proliferation crowd, which was valid, and then the India-Pakistan people were always pushing back with stuff. Mike Sheehan was big on draining the swamp in Afghanistan, and every one of those things ran into resistance from the area guys [at the State Department]."

He continues, "I think when we launched those cruise missiles in 1998 we killed more Pakistani intel officers who were training Kashmiri guerillas than we killed any al Qaeda people. Those training camps used to be an international catch-basin of bad people. And the Pakistani intelligence service was involved in all of that."[169]

A war plan to eliminate al Qaeda would have to wait for a new president. September 11, 2001, of course, changed the realm of the possible in counterterrorism. But a military plan was wending its way to President Bush even before the attacks. The plan was designed to eradicate al Qaeda by supporting the anti-Taliban Northern Alliance and potentially using American air strikes and special operations assaults in Afghanistan.[170] After eight months in office, the Bush administration hadn't yet focused enough on terrorism. The plan proceeded through the policy-review process slowly, and terrorism was relatively low on Attorney General Ashcroft's list of priorities.[171] Even so, in its incipient anti-al Qaeda war plan, the Bush administration seemed already more willing to take risks and apply force against the terrorists than its predecessor.

The September 11 attacks threw the Clinton administration's national security policies into harsh relief. It is impossible to prevent every terrorist attack. That shouldn't be the standard for judging an administration's record. The standard should be whether every reasonable tool at the government's disposal was leveraged to make the terrorists' work more difficult. By that standard, Clinton flunks. He knew about the threat. Yet, he tolerated a terrorist sanctuary in Afghanistan,[172] tolerated Saudi and Pakistani support for terrorism, put the FBI and the CIA in the position of always playing defense, and made the protection of American lives from terrorist attacks no better than a secondary priority of the administration.

The September 11 attacks finally gave Clinton the kind of legacy he had yearned for: one that couldn't be ignored, one that was great in its implications. His could no longer be considered an inconsequential presidency. In leaving the country vulnerable to such an attack after eight years in office, Clinton had achieved the perverse distinction of a monstrous, world-shaking failure.

AFTERWORD

THE MORNING AFTER

THE TERRORIST ATROCITY OF SEPTEMBER 11 was still far away during Bill Clinton's final weeks in office, which were a messy, and appropriate, postlude to his eight years as president.

By November 2000, he had secured what would be his most enduring political legacy, not the election of Vice President Gore as president as he had hoped, but the election of his wife as senator from New York.

Hillary displayed none of Bill's fleshy relish for endless handshaking and hugging along a rope line. If he was all id on the campaign trail, she was all superego. But she picked up his pollster, Mark Penn, and his taste for popular micro-initiatives. After all the Yale Law School dreams of changing the world and all the high-minded Renaissance weekend panel discussions, the most enduring strand of Clintonism turned out to be the focus group.[1]

It worked. Hillary won big, gaining a foothold from which she will almost certainly run for president.[2] This, then, is the foremost Clinton political legacy: They will be back, if not in the Oval Office, then seeking it. It's not called the permanent campaign for nothing.

In the meantime, for Bill, giving up power was hard to do. Although Clinton supposedly didn't want to constrain the next administration

335

ı military strikes in Afghanistan after the bombing of the USS *Cole,*
late as December 2000 he was still weighing whether to go to
Рyongyang to try to strike another arms control deal with the North
Koreans.

A lame-duck president, down to his final weeks or days, doesn't
have many levers of power. Clinton exercised what he could in a
presidential cram session. He issued a raft of executive orders, establishing new environmental rules and creating new national "monuments" to bring notable natural landmarks under federal protection.
About a week before George W. Bush's inauguration, he created
three new national monuments and added nine more just three days
before he was to leave office.³ Presidential pardons and commutations also flew from his pen. As he put it when he was just hours
away from leaving office, "Everybody in America either wants somebody pardoned or a national monument."⁴ And Clinton was determined to accommodate as many of them as his dwindling time in
office allowed.

Clinton granted a stunning 140 pardons and thirty-six commutations of sentences on his last day in office,⁵ a climax to what had
already been a busy Christmas season of clemency. Clinton was worried about his pardon legacy, and afraid he wouldn't seem compassionate enough compared to his predecessors unless he juiced up his
record with as many last-minute acts of clemency as possible.

Just as he had duplicated in his first two years as president the
mistakes of his first two-year term as Arkansas governor, in his final
days as president he repeated the scandal of his final days as governor. Nothing changed because his character never changed—in this
case his eagerness to please and his hunger to exercise his power to
the very last possible moment.

On his way out the door of the Arkansas governor's mansion in January 1981, he commuted the sentences of seventeen prisoners, a
dozen of them murderers or rapists who had been sentenced to life in
prison. According to Gail Sheehy, Hillary had been appalled by the
idea, fearing the future electoral consequences. "Bill, you're out of your

mind! You can't do this, you just can't do this." When he was criticized for the commutations during the next Democratic primary, Clinton dishonestly declared, "I never released a single first-degree murderer from prison. I did not do that." As Sheehy writes, "No, Clinton did not *release* the murderers; he allowed for parole consideration by commuting their sentences."[6]

As president, his frenzied, last-minute acts of forgiveness included clemency for thirty people who hadn't bothered to file the standard petition with the Justice Department, and another fourteen whose petitions had been previously denied. He swept up into his net of clemency all manner of bottom-dwellers, including many who flunked the basic tests for a pardon (having served their sentence and demonstrated good character thereafter) or a commutation (being sentenced unfairly or cooperating with the government).[7] The most notorious pardon was of financier Marc Rich, who had fled the country under indictment for tax fraud and spent the next seventeen years as one of the country's ten most-wanted fugitives.[8]

His estranged wife, Denise Rich, lobbied Clinton on his behalf and pumped $1.5 million into Democratic causes, a chunk of it into the Clinton library.[9] Beth Dozoretz, a major Democratic fund-raiser and a friend of Denise Rich, also pushed for the Rich pardon.[10] When Congress investigated the pardon, both women pled the Fifth Amendment and refused to testify.[11] Denise Rich and Beth Dozoretz were part of a menagerie that quickly grew up around Clinton's screwball clemency process. It featured a bevy of slimy operators eager to buy or sell pardons and commutations. Most of them, as it happened, were Clinton relations.

In an ethical administration, First Relatives surely would have known after eight years that official favors were not for sale. Not surprisingly, no one related to Clinton had gotten such a message. A lawyer for one pardon petitioner said of First Brother Roger Clinton, "Roger related that Bill Clinton had instructed him that since this was his last term in office, Roger should find a way to make a living and use his relationship with the president to his advantage."[12] He did.

Roger, who received payments from foreign governments through-out Clinton's presidency, took $50,000 from the Gambino crime fam-ily and lobbied for the release of drug dealer and mobster Tony Gambino from prison. He benefited from a swindle to sell a pardon to a felon named Garland Lincecum, and may have pushed for as many as thirteen other acts of clemency. First Brother-in-Law Hugh Rod-ham received more than $200,000 to lobby, successfully, for a com-mutation for unrepentant drug dealer Carlos Vignali, and $230,000 for a pardon for a swindler named Glenn Braswell who was under crimi-nal investigation at the time he received it.[13] First Brother-in-Law Tony Rodham received $244,769 from Edgar and Vonna Jo Gregory and lob-bied for their pardon for bank fraud, which was opposed by the Justice Department, but granted by President Clinton.[14]

The veneer of respectability that Clinton's aides had struggled to maintain for eight years was gone. All the grossness was out in the open, because no one was left to protect Clinton from himself. One former Clinton official said that at the end "no one around him [was] strong enough to say no. . . . He was surrounded by enablers. There was no one there to stop him from making mistakes like this."[15]

The pardon scandal raised a collective cry of "good riddance," made all the louder by Clinton's last-minute deal with the indepen-dent counsel's office, in which he agreed to a five-year suspension of his law license and a $25,000 fine for his false statements in the Paula Jones case, which he had always maintained weren't false. David Hal-berstam writes that Clinton "departed the White House as inglori-ously as any president in recent years, save only Richard Nixon."[16] The post-presidency on which he so awkwardly embarked has so far been—appropriately enough—all talk.

In his last year in office, Clinton said of his prospective life after the White House, "I'm going to try to maintain a high level of activity in the areas that I'm particularly interested in. I spent a lot of my life working on reconciliation of people across racial, religious, and other lines. I'm very interested in using the power of technology . . . to help poor countries and poor areas overcome what would ordinarily take years in economic development and education. I'm very interested in continuing my work to try to convince Americans and the rest of the world that we can beat global warming without shutting down the economy.... I'm very interested in promoting the concept of public service among young people.... Those are four things I'll do."[17]

To this point, in the fall of 2003, he has mostly devoted himself to swelling his bank account with $100,000 speaking gigs and partying with glitterati. He is much likelier to show up in the dining room of Nobu than in a soup kitchen. He signed a $10 million book deal, and considered a lucrative contract for a talk show—perhaps, finally, finding his true level. Clinton maintains that he has too many legal bills to do anything other than rake in cash, making the vacuity of his early post-presidency—like so much else—purportedly all Ken Starr's fault.

What he does out of office will help further define his legacy. Former president Richard Nixon rehabilitated his image through the intellectual spadework of writing serious foreign policy books, highlighting one of his strengths in office: his sophisticated grasp of geopolitics and diplomacy. Former president Jimmy Carter rehabilitated his image through the legwork of (sometimes misbegotten) public service, reminding people of one of his personal strengths: an earnest Christian do-goodism.

Out of office, Clinton is likely only to remind us of what was so appalling about his presidency—indiscipline, self-centeredness, and dishonesty.

Consider one small area of his post-presidency: his golf game. He is a great lover of golf, and will no doubt lag behind only presidential duffer Jerry Ford in sheer time spent on the links. Clinton is a good golfer, but cheats on his scores by taking do-over shots, called "mulligans." He brings all his dishonesty, self-pity, and blame-shifting right onto the golf course with him.

New York Times reporter Don Van Natta, Jr. played a post-presidency round with Clinton for his book on presidents and golf, *First Off the Tee*. Van Natta describes Clinton, in a difficult spot, twice hitting shots off a tree after asking his caddy for advice. "Clinton's face reddens, and he bites his bottom lip. Now I see that he is seething. He shoots an unmistakable look of fury at the caddy who I don't think notices. 'I'm pissed off—I shouldn't have done that,' he says to no one in particular. 'Twice in a row I listened and I got screwed! Twice!' Then, he mutters to himself, 'First they told me to aim left...'"[18]

And so it goes. In between the parties and the golf, Clinton's energy will be devoted to talking about his legacy. It is his fate never to rest in his self-aggrandizement and self-justification. He will roam the earth forevermore, claiming credit for imaginary accomplishments and blaming failures on nasty opponents or impersonal forces beyond his control. September 11 has made his work much harder, casting his presidency in a radically different light. It's his Black Tuesday, which shifted perceptions of Calvin Coolidge from successful steward of prosperity to complacent placeholder before the Crash.[19]

Clinton's foreign policy legacy has been a series of ticking bombs. He left a terrorist sanctuary in Afghanistan—it was too hard to do something about it militarily or diplomatically. He left a broken arms agreement with North Korea—it was too hard to admit it had failed. He left a terrorist in control of the Palestinian territories, waging war on Israel—it was too hard to give up on the "peace process." He left a failed Iraq policy, as Saddam gained strength and UN inspectors were barred from the country—it was too hard give it attention over other, more congenial international priorities.

When President Bush had to confront all these problems, many former Clinton aides—who had helped forge the Clinton policy of temporizing that left the problems to Bush in the first place—took to the op-ed pages and airwaves to explain how Clinton would handle them so much more deftly. But, for Bush, papering them over and leaving them to someone else wasn't an option. His doctrine of preemption was the very opposite of the Clinton approach, not just in its willingness to embrace unilateral means and take risks, but in its ends: eliminating threats before they become unavoidable.

America has a knack for getting the leaders appropriate for any given moment. Without Clinton's excesses, there would have been no President George W. Bush, Clinton's opposite in almost every respect. Clinton is chronically late; Bush a stickler for promptness. Clinton tolerated casual wear (or even less) in the Oval Office; Bush insists on coat and tie. Clinton is verbose and slippery; Bush terse and blunt. The most important difference is that Bush represents a different aspect of America, a part of the country that is less touchy-feely, is more insistent on personal accountability, and—importantly—is more at home with the military. It is The Other America.

Bush took office at time when America faced a terrorist network that could only be properly handled by its utter destruction and when the world desperately needed Western, especially American, assertion. His willingness to kill our enemies and to pursue the nation's interests, even when opposed by the "international community," made for a decidedly un-Clintonian posture toward the world. Bush would never launch, and then call back, a military operation, and never agonize at 3 a.m. over whether a military strike might hurt people. He has the moral courage to take risks and, if necessary, to spend American blood in the service of a national goal.

Some argue that the course of the post–September 11 war on terror was inevitable, at least up to the time of the invasion in Iraq. But there is little that is inevitable, and certainly not the conduct of wars. The uncompromising nature of the war on terror reflected Bush's personal qualities (toughness, decisiveness, stubbornness, and moral clarity) that Clinton notably lacked.

If Bush were as self-pitying as Clinton, he would spend every day cursing his predecessor. Besides the foreign crises, he inherited an economy slowing down toward a recession. Corporate America was on a cheating binge that was about to be exposed. The budget surplus was overstated because of inflated revenues from the Internet bubble and federal spending that was much too low on domestic security and the military. All of this coupled with a recession probably meant a return to red ink, even if Bush hadn't cut taxes. So, some of the best

Democratic talking points against Bush—joblessness, corporate crime, the deficit—were inheritances from the Clinton years. Those years required a long morning-after cleanup operation.

Even as late as January 2001, of course, it was hard to imagine what was to come. Clinton got little rest in his final days, raging against the moment when it would all end, and not in the glory he had imagined, but in a whimper of personal disgrace and missed opportunities. When it came time to attend the inauguration of George W. Bush, he literally couldn't keep his eyes open.[20] With his handpicked successor beaten, with the economy slowing down, with corporate scandals building and about to explode, with North Korea working on a new nuclear program, with the September 11 terrorists already in the country, Clinton found on the podium that day a perfect gesture to cap his eight years in office.

He fell asleep.

ACKNOWLEDGMENTS

I WOULD SAY "IT TOOK A VILLAGE" to complete this book, but that would give everyone involved a slightly nauseous feeling. I am nonetheless indebted to many people. William F. Buckley Jr., who has given me the wonderful opportunity to edit his magazine, urged me to write this book, and was supportive throughout. He is a world-class writer, thinker, and mentor. Ed Capano and Dusty Rhodes, the publisher and president of *National Review*, respectively, were patient and solicitous during a long process. Kate O'Beirne, the wisest woman in Washington, was an indispensable source of ideas, advice, and good humor. Matthew Continetti, my research assistant, is a promising young journalist whose intelligence, easygoing way, and book-schlepping abilities were much appreciated. My friend Bill Prillaman, a sharp wit and passionate Yankees fan, gladly reviewed portions of the manuscript and was invariably encouraging and incisive in his comments. David Rivkin, my nominee for the next secretary of state, read several chapters and was an excellent sounding board. Larry Kudlow and John O'Sullivan gave me valuable counsel.

My gratitude to all those who read parts of the manuscript: Alex Alexiev, Paul Michael Wihbey, Chris Frenze, Kevin Hassett, Richard Nadler, Elaine Donnelly, Grace Marie Turner, Mitch Kugler, Cliff May, Alan Reynolds, Keith Payne, and David Pryce-Jones. The responsibility for any errors is obviously mine. Dorothy McCartney provided important research help. Elizabeth Fitton, Jane Jolis, Julie Crane, Duncan Currie and Carlos Ramos-Mrosovsky were always willing to assist with odds and ends. Thanks to friends who were tirelessly encouraging even when my state of "almost finished" stretched on and on: Ric Andersen, Dave Teeuwen, Deroy Murdock, Peter Feld, Alex Preate, Andrew Stuttafford, Jonah Goldberg, Paul Dilion, and Matthew Scully. Jennifer Wotochek's patience and impatience were both helpful in their own ways. She is bright, beautiful, and kind. I couldn't have finished without her. The people at Regnery—Tom Phillips, Harry Crocker, Jeff Carneal, Paula Decker, et al.—were a pleasure to work with. My colleagues Rick Brookhiser, Jay Nordlinger, Ramesh Ponnuru, Kathryn Lopez, and Mike Potemra kept the magazine on an even keel. A special thanks to "Big Daddy," and to Borden.

NOTES

1. THE CONTENT OF HIS CHARACTER

1. Quoted in "International Perspectives," *Newsweek*, December 11, 2000.

2. Sidney Blumenthal, *The Clinton Wars* (New York: Farrar, Straus and Giroux, 2003), 272.

3. Todd S. Purdum, "Clinton Haunted By Impact of His Choices," *New York Times*, August 23, 1998.

4. David Gergen, *Eyewitness to Power* (New York: Simon & Schuster, 2000), 317.

5. Gail Sheehy, *Hillary's Choice* (New York: Ballantine Books, 1999), 142.

6. Bob Woodward, *The Choice* (New York: Simon & Schuster, 1996), 14.

7. Dick Morris, *Behind the Oval Office* (New York: Random House, 1997), 11.

8. George Stephanopoulos, *All Too Human* (New York: Little, Brown and Company, 1999), 5.

9. Todd S. Purdum, "Striking Strength, Glaring Failures," *New York Times*, December 24, 2000.

10. David Maraniss, *First in His Class* (New York: Touchstone, 1996), 352.

11. Interview with Mickey Kantor

12. Stephanopoulos 71

13. Maraniss 172

14. Maraniss 179–180

15. Maraniss 180. Before Clinton headed back across the Atlantic, he had stayed up all night writing a letter to his draft board explaining his lack of genuine interest in ROTC and asking to be drafted instead. He carried it around a few weeks, but never put it in the mail, never quite able to commit himself to this act of principle.

16. Maraniss 198

17. Ibid.

18. William J. Bennett, *The Death of Outrage* (New York: The Free Press, 1998), 44.

19. In February 1992, *Wall Street Journal* reporter Jeff Birnbaum talked to Col. Holmes. Clinton had always referred draft questions to Holmes, who either said he didn't remember the details or had treated Clinton like everyone else. But Holmes had had a change of heart, telling Birnbaum that he felt manipulated by Clinton. Then, Clinton's letter to Holmes after he knew he was in the clear and wouldn't be entering ROTC surfaced. During his first campaign, a congressional race in 1974, Clinton had asked Holmes to return the letter so he could destroy it. But one of Holmes's aides, unbeknownst to Clinton, had made a copy. Clinton thought he was in the clear. David Maraniss recounts a conversation Clinton had in early 1991 with an Arkansas supporter named Ed Howard, who had been a drill instructor in the ROTC program. He told Clinton that he had been badgered by a reporter curious about Clinton's draft history. "'Oh, don't worry about that,' said Clinton. 'I've put that one to bed.' 'Okay,' said Howard. There was a pause, and then Clinton asked, 'What did you tell 'em?' 'Nothing,' said Howard. 'Good,' Clinton said." (Maraniss 324-325, 458)

20. Stephanopoulos 74

21. Maraniss 200-203

22. Stephanopoulos 75

23. Hillary Rodham Clinton, *Living History* (New York: Simon & Schuster, 2003), 240.

24. Maraniss 125

25. Jacob Weisberg, "Clincest," *The New Republic*, April 24, 1993.

26. Ibid.

27. Ibid.

28. Sheehy 11

29. Clinton 297

30. Peter Baker, *The Breach* (New York: Scribner, 2000), 73.

31. Clinton 246

32. Stephanopoulos 325

33. There isn't a record of Clinton explicitly calling Starr evil. But Stephanopoulos writes that Clinton "sure did hate Ken Starr" (Stephanopoulos 379). Clinton called Starr's prosecutors "sick f—" out to get him from the beginning [Bob Woodward, *Shadow* (New York: Touchstone, 1999), 338, 435, and 444].

34. Morris 268

35. So far Clinton has had to look closer to home for his hero treatment. His hagiography has been written by Sidney Blumenthal, the former White House staffer whose oleaginous Clinton worship had long ago discredited him in journalistic circles.

36. David Brooks, "Hollywood Beats Harvard," *The Weekly Standard*, October 5, 1998.

37. Sheehy 213 and 92

38. Sheehy 213

39. Sheehy 96

40. Maraniss 38–41

41. Elizabeth Drew, *On the Edge* (New York: Touchstone, 1994), 95.

42. Sheehy 142

43. Maraniss 422

44. Sheehy 186

45. Joe Klein, *The Natural* (New York: Doubleday, 2002), 25.

46. Sheehy 181

47. James B. Stewart, *Blood Sport* (New York: Simon & Schuster, 1996), 121.

48. Sheehy 100–101

49. Interview with Dick Morris

50. Diane Sawyer and Sam Donaldson, "All Too Human," *ABC 20/20*, ABC News. First aired March 10, 1999.

51. Klein 25–26

52. Stephanopoulos 77. As Stephanopoulos writes, "When a tiny, frail woman named Mary Annie Davis confessed tearfully that she had to choose each month between buying food or medicine, [Clinton] knelt down, took her hand, and comforted her with a hug. Even the hardest-bitten reporters in the room were wiping tears from their eyes."

53. Klein 43

54. Drew 218

55. Drew 210

56. Strobe Talbott, *The Russia Hand* (New York: Random House, 2002), 184.

57. Evan Thomas et al., *Back From the Dead* (New York: The Atlantic Monthly Press, 1997), 5.

58. Clifford Orwin, "Moist Eyes—From Rousseau to Clinton," *The Public Interest*, June 22, 1997.

59. Thomas et al. 233–234.

60. Drew 232

61. Martin Walker, *The President We Deserve* (New York: Crown, 1996), 136.

62. Woodward, *The Choice*, 19

63. Baker 76

64. Anthony Lake, *6 Nightmares* (New York: Little, Brown and Company, 2000), 18–19.

65. Bob Woodward, *The Agenda* (New York: Pocket Books, 1994), 86.

66. Stephanopoulos 372

67. Walker 110

68. Interview with Richard Holbrooke

69. Interview with Don Baer

70. Interview with Howard Paster

71. Morris 308

72. See Dan Barry, "At the Scene of Random Devastation, a Most Orderly Mission," *New York Times*, September 24, 2001.

2. HIS PRESIDENCY: SHRINKING THE OFFICE

1. William Galston and Elaine Kamarck, "The Politics of Evasion: Democrats and the Presidency," *Progressive Policy Institute*, September 1989.

2. Interview with Bill Galston

3. Eliot A. Cohen, *Supreme Command* (New York: The Free Press, 2002), 224.

4. Joe Klein, *The Natural* (New York: Doubleday, 2002), 20.

5. Michael Barone and Grant Ujifusa, *The Almanac of American Politics*, 1994 ed. (Washington, D.C.: National Journal, 1993), xxv. In 1992, Bush forgot why he wanted to be president. He had broken a foundational promise by raising taxes, and had no domestic agenda. It was almost an abdication. Into the vacuum leapt Ross Perot, who tapped a nascent populism by stirring public anger about the budget deficit. The limpness of George Bush's candidacy and the vitality of Perot's created the conditions in which the incumbent president could lose to an Arkansas governor with obvious personal weaknesses. Clinton ran for the nomination in a year when no other Democratic candidate seemed viable. The big shots had been scared off by Bush's post–Gulf War popularity. He bumped along in third place until July 16, when Perot dropped out and implicitly gave his nod to the Democrats (Richard L. Berke, "Perot Says He Quit in July to Thwart G.O.P. 'Dirty Tricks,'" *New York Times*, October 26, 1992.) Perot said that he decided to drop out of the race after he "uncovered" a plot by President Bush to sabotage his daughter's wedding. In his July statement of withdrawal, Perot said that the Democratic Party had been "revitalized." Clinton immediately jumped from 25 percent to a nearly unassailable 56 percent in the polls (Gwen Ifill, "With No Break, Clinton Initiates Campaign Tour," *New York Times*, July 18, 1992). None of this detracts from Clinton's Olympic-quality excellence as a candidate: he understood the issues; kept the Democratic Party united; was articulate and passionate; connected with crowds; and had boundless energy. "I heard him speak in New Orleans in March 1990," says former policy aide Bruce Reed, a centrist. "You could hear a pin drop in the room. People were just spellbound—a Reagan-like ability to tell stories, with some new and real ideas behind it" (Interview with Bruce Reed). Clinton had long dabbled with what would become known as New Democrat politics in Arkansas. He combined that centrism with an ability to hold the Democratic Party base. "Everyone else was in the business of showing up to tell the DNC how goofy it was that we were totally led around by our interest groups," says former spokesman Mike McCurry. "Clinton found an attractive way to talk to mainstream, middle-of-the-road voters in a way that was not offensive to blacks, minorities, union households—the liberal wing of the party" (Interview with Mike McCurry).

6. Martin Walker, *The President We Deserve* (New York: Crown Publishers, Inc., 1996), 164.

7. David Maraniss, *First in His Class* (New York: Simon & Schuster, 1995), 362. Chapter 20 deals with Clinton's disastrous first term as Arkansas governor.

8. George Stephanopoulos, *All Too Human* (New York: Little, Brown and Company, 1999), 132–133.

9. John L. Helgerson, *CIA Briefings of Presidential Candidates, 1952–1992* (Washington, D.C.: Center for the Study of Intelligence, 1996), 40.

10. Clinton delegated significant parts of his authority to the First Lady and the vice president, an unprecedented act of power-sharing that weakened his presidency. David Gergen calls it a "three-headed system for decision-making" that was "a rolling disaster as far as I can tell. It caused untold delays, confusions, and divided loyalties." [David Gergen, *Eyewitness to Power* (New York: Simon & Schuster, 2000), 293]

11. Michael Waldman, *POTUS Speaks* (New York: Simon & Schuster, 2000), 44.

12. "He had a B-team White House staff," says one former Clinton aide (Interview with former administration official). One reason for that was Clinton's insecurity. The way some politicians surround themselves with "yes men," he surrounded himself with "maybe men" who bobbed and weaved along with his indecision. It wasn't until later that Clinton would begin to feel comfortable with figures of more stature. According to Mike McCurry, "Guys like Rubin or Lloyd Bentsen initially intimidated the White House staff, so the White House staff did not like a lot of these extra-heavy people. Over time, Clinton began to gravitate to those people, began to feel more like those were his peers" (Interview with Mike McCurry).

13. Interview with Howard Paster

14. Interview with former senior administration official

15. Interview with Bruce Reed. According to Don Baer, "There were many more people coming out of the experience of the Democratic wilderness years, out of the Mondale campaign, the Dukakis campaign, the congressional Democrats during the 1980s. They attached themselves to Clinton, but didn't necessarily agree with a lot of what Bill Clinton really had come to do as a New Democrat." (Interview with Don Baer)

16. Interview with Howard Paster

17. Stephanopoulos 125–126

18. Elizabeth Drew, *On the Edge* (New York: Touchstone, 1993), 42.

19. Ibid., 48

20. Bob Woodward, *The Agenda* (New York: Pocket Books, 1994), 18. Clinton had never been enthusiastic about the tax cut. He tended to blame it every time something went wrong. When the draft story sank his poll numbers in New Hampshire, Clinton insisted to aides, "the g— f— middle-class tax cut is killing me." (Woodward, *The Agenda*, 21) After the election, focus groups and polling showed that people didn't expect him to keep his promise. So he felt liberated, indeed, not to keep it (Woodward, *The Agenda*, 70, 100).

21. Haynes Johnson and David S. Broder, *The System* (New York: Little, Brown and Company, 1997), 139. At the behest of the country's mayors, the bill funded a dog's breakfast of pork projects: fish atlases, beach parking lots, a cemetery in Puerto Rico, sewage projects, and student drawings of "significant structures" for safekeeping at the Library of Congress (Drew, *On the Edge*, 115; Walker 188). When Republicans balked, Clinton accused them of opposing a program that would create 500,000 new jobs. At the annual White House Easter egg roll, he pointed to the kids and charged that Republicans opposing the stimulus wanted to deny them vaccines (Drew, *On the Edge*, 119). A Senate GOP filibuster killed even the slimmed-down $15 billion version of the bill (Johnson and Broder 139).

22. Sidney Blumenthal, *The Clinton Wars* (New York: Farrar, Straus and Giroux, 2003), 3. He adds, "in Washington almost everything old felt threatened by everything new; the possible imperiled the settled" (Blumenthal 45).

23. Eugene Steuerle, "Tax Policy from 1990 to 2001," in *American Economic Policy in the 1990s,* ed. Jeffrey Frankel and Peter Orszag (Cambridge, MA: MIT Press, 2002), 144–145. With regard to his 1993 budget, Clinton defenders argue that he had somehow been done dirty by the fact that all Republicans opposed his tax increase. But Republicans had just seen a tax increase destroy a Republican presidency. It made sense that they wanted to re-establish their anti-tax credentials.

24. Interview with Bill Galston

25. Johnson and Broder 483–485

26. Michael Barone and Grant Ujifusa, with Richard E. Cohen, *The Almanac of American Politics,* 1996 ed. (Washington, D.C.: National Journal, 1995), xxiv, xxvi.

27. Barone and Ujifusa, with Cohen xxvi

28. Evan Thomas, et al., *Back From the Dead* (New York: The Atlantic Monthly Press, 1997), 220.

29. Gingrich had sensed the Democratic hold on the House gradually loosening. "The Watergate babies," the class of superbly talented liberals swept into Congress in the mid-1970s, had been dropping off, running for the Senate, retiring, or getting beaten (see, for example, "Why House Investigator is Joining the Exodus," about Watergate Baby Matthew McHugh, *New York Times*, May 10, 1992). The South turned more and more Republican, so it became harder for conservative Democrats to hold seats there. Finally, the Democratic majority in the House had become sclerotic, dependent on the institutional advantages of incumbency and increasingly out of touch with the country. "There were a bunch of guys in Congress who really didn't see the changing winds in the political universe," says Howard Paster. "One of the reasons that 1994 happened was that some of our guys didn't stay contemporary." (Interview with Howard Paster).

30. Despite his polarizing image, Gingrich didn't emphasize typical Republican hot-button issues, such as abortion, prayer in school, etc.

31. Thomas et al. 35

32. Interview with Tony Blankley

33. Elizabeth Drew, *Showdown* (New York: Touchstone, 1996), 35.

34. Interview with John Kasich

35. It nonetheless packed a well-disguised blessing. Clinton was freed from the yoke of the congressional Democrats. "The night of the election I remember we were up in the Solarium looking over results," says Don Baer, "and it was finally clear what had happened and that he had to say something the next day, but no one knew what. As we walked down this ramp that goes from the Solarium to the third floor of the White House, he said, 'This could be liberating.' I think what he meant was he was going to be unshackled from congressional Democrats and the liberal wing of the Democratic Party. Anyone who tells you there was a straight line from that moment on is lying." (Interview with Don Baer).

36. Back when he was trying to get Sen. Bob Kerrey's vote for his budget package, Clinton had raised the possibility of quitting: "Now maybe I ought just to pick it up and go back to Little Rock. Chuck it!" (Woodward, *The Agenda*, 335). He had always tended to blame others when something went wrong. Connecticut senator Chris Dodd remembered visiting Clinton in 1981 after his loss for reelection as governor, and staying until 3 a.m. in hopes that Clinton might admit that he had done something wrong. He never did. [Bob Woodward, *The Choice* (New York: Simon & Schuster, 1996), 54].

37. Drew, *Showdown*, 19

38. Dick Morris, *Behind the Oval Office* (New York: Random House, 1997), 15.

39. Robert L. Bartley, *The Seven Fat Years* (New York: Free Press, 1992), ix.

40. Woodward, *The Choice*, 551

41. Robert Reich, *Locked in the Cabinet* (New York: Vintage Books, 1997), 229.

42. Woodward, *The Choice*, 23

43. Woodward, *The Agenda*, 401. He proposed a $500 a child tax credit, making college tuition tax deductible, and expanding tax-free IRA accounts (Woodward, *The Choice*, 46).

44. Stephanopoulos 395

45. Woodward, *The Choice*, 287

46. Michael Barone and Grant Ujifusa, with Richard E. Cohen, *The Almanac of American Politics*, 1998 ed. (Washington, D.C.: National Journal, 1997), 21.

47. Woodward, *The Choice*, 47

48. Interview with Elaine Kamarck

49. Woodward, *The Choice*, 138

50. Stephanopoulos 336

51. Interview with Robert Reich

52. Clinton told Morris of one advisor he hadn't liked: "It took me months to get him moved out of the White House." (Morris 98)

53. Morris 90. There may have been a method in the madness, but it spoke to a deep dysfunction in Clinton's governance, both in how badly the White House had been run and in the fact that there was no bond of trust between Clinton and even his closest advisors. A former senior official explains, "First, there was way too much attention and focus on the 'sausage making' of the first two years. I think he was trying to tamp that down and just not open another window onto the inner workings. Second, I don't think he, in the case of some of the people, really trusted what they would go out and do and say. I'm not suggesting they knew things that would hurt him, but I think he was very worried about some of them, understanding their strong ties with the press." (Interview with a former senior administration official) Another former senior official says, more darkly, "I think he got used to the idea that people around him may have seen things, or have become aware of vulnerabilities, so he had to be careful not to alienate them." (Interview with a former senior administration official)

54. "Panetta took umbrage with that," says a former senior official, "and he was a proud man. He'd been a member of Congress, a leader there, and thought that this was an insult to his authority. He threw up huge walls and obstacles and there were factions and camps and all kinds of ugliness inside." (Interview with former senior administration official)

55. Stephanopoulos 385

56. Interview with Leon Panetta

57. Interview with Don Baer

58. Thomas et al. 11

59. Morris 65

60. Gail Sheehy, *Hillary's Choice* (New York: Ballantine Books, 1999), 192.

61. Morris 124–126

62. Gergen 331

63. Klein 7

64. Morris 237–238

65. Ibid., 83, 85, 220, 93, 165 and 147

66. Reich 278

67. Morris 10

68. Woodward, *The Choice*, 205

69. Interview with Alice Rivlin

70. Woodward, *The Choice*, 207

71. Ibid.

72. Thomas et al. xi

73. Drew, *Showdown*, 315

74. Interview with Dick Armey

75. Thomas et al. 37

76. Woodward, *The Choice*, 237–238

77. Johnson and Broder 583

78. Reich 295

79. Julie Rovner, "Congress and Health Care Reform 1993–1994," in *Intensive Care: How Congress Shapes Public Policy*, ed. Thomas E. Mann and Norman J. Ornstein (Washington, D.C.: American Enterprise Institute and the Brookings Institution, 1995), 184.

80. David Cutler and Jonathan Gruber, "Health Policy in the Clinton Era: Once Bitten," in *American Economic Policy in the 1990s*, ed. Jeffrey Frankel and Peter Orszag (Cambridge, MA: MIT Press, 2002), 833.

81. Drew, *Showdown*, 316

82. Gingrich constantly made Clinton's life easier. He said the Health Care Financing Administration, which administered Medicare payments, would "wither on the vine because we think people are voluntarily going to leave it—voluntarily." (Woodward, *The Choice*, 312; Drew, *Showdown*, 318). He said "voluntarily" twice within six words, but the "wither on the vine" phrase was ripe for exploitation, and the White House exploited it. (Woodward, *The Choice*, 313). Never mind that the Clinton 1992 campaign manifesto *Putting People First* had promised, "We will scrap the Health Care Financing Administration." [Governor Bill Clinton and Senator Al Gore, *Putting People First* (New York: Times Books, 1992), 21]

83. Drew, *Showdown*, 323

84. Woodward, *The Choice*, 323. The White House immediately released a picture of Clinton chatting with Gingrich on the plane.

85. Interview with Dick Armey

86. Even with Gingrich's mistakes, the White House was still in peril and worried about holding congressional Democrats during the first shutdown in mid-November. Clinton sounded defiant, telling Gingrich in the Oval Office on November 13, "If you want this budget signed, you'll have put someone else in this chair." Immediately after Gingrich left the meeting, Clinton turned to Panetta, sounding worried, and said, "OK, Leon, now you gotta figure out the end game." (Thomas et al. 39–41). The Republicans blinked. They sent Clinton an offer that committed him to a seven-year balanced budget, scored by the more pessimistic assumptions of the Congressional Budget Office instead of the Office of Management and Budget. This had been a major GOP demand. Otherwise, Republicans didn't nail down any of their policy priorities (Morris 186). The Clinton team was delighted. When White House aides received the GOP offer by fax, Clinton high-fived each of them (Stephanoplous 405–406). They eagerly signed on.

87. "We had serious debates about the shutdown," says Mike McCurry. "There's nobody who said that we should do this because the Congressional Republicans are going to get blamed for it. I don't think anybody anticipated that. It was actually done on instinct, but also Clinton felt strongly that we had to put the roadblock down then, because if we didn't draw a line in the sand then, we might never recapture momentum." (Interview with Mike McCurry).

88. Republicans were overmatched in the negotiations. Says one staffer, "We would walk in there totally unprepared. Dole couldn't get a word out of his mouth. Armey didn't know the issues. Kasich was running around. It was up to Newt, and the one thing he didn't know how to do was play poker. Clinton knew all he had to do was sit tight." (Interview with former GOP leadership aide)

89. Republicans had always overestimated their leverage. Before the first shutdown in November 1995, they thought they could make Clinton break by putting their legislative priorities on a bill to raise the U.S. debt ceiling. They dared Clinton to veto it. Gingrich even suggested that Republicans would allow the U.S. to default on its debt (Johnson and Broder 595). Clinton officials played along, hyping the risk of a default if the ceiling weren't raised ("a horrendous example in the global financial markets," warned Rubin), both to make Republicans think it was a crucial point of leverage and to make them appear reckless (Dina Temple-Raston and Mike McKee, "Default Fears Eased, But Not Political Fire; Treasury's Rubin Labeled Partisan," *Houston Chronicle*, November 18, 1995). At the same time, Clinton officials had been planning behind the scenes as early as April 1995 to tap various government funds to cover the gap if the ceiling weren't raised, and knew that there was no possibility of a default ("Planned Gridlock: The Clinton Administration's Plan to Block Debt Limit and Balanced Budget Legislation," Memo of the Joint Economic Committee, October 22, 1996). The government could have survived this way for years (Patrice Hill, "Strategy on Budget Planned Last June; Rubin Anticipated Battle with GOP," *Washington Times*, January 30, 1996), and Clinton's veto of the debt limit extension on Nov. 13 was a non-event. The irony was that much of the rationale of the Clinton 1993 economic plan had been to reassure the bond market. Here, two years later, the administration was deliberately engaging in scare-rhetoric to spook it.

90. Interview with Tony Blankley

91. Barone and Ujifusa, with Cohen, 1998 ed., 23

92. Ibid., 24

93. James MacGregor Burns and Georgia J. Sorenson, *Dead Center* (New York: Scribner, 1999), 275.

94. Interview with Mike McCurry

95. Thomas et al. 16

96. Barone and Ujifusa, with Cohen, 1998 ed., 28

97. Thomas et al. 17 and 38

98. Woodward, *The Agenda*, 23

99. Thomas et al. 243

100. Morris 221–231

101. Thomas et al. 140. Even as he resorted to a piddling agenda, Clinton had begun to exploit fully the ability of the president to shape the political environment in ways that floated above the opposition.

It had taken some time for Clinton to realize that he was president, literally. "Clinton said at one point, 'Wait a minute, I'm not a prime minister, I'm a president,'" recalls Elaine Kamarck (Interview with Elaine Kamarck). One presidential tool was executive orders, although most of Clinton's actions didn't even rise to the level of executive orders, and were instead "memoranda to agencies" (Burns and Sorenson 274). The other was rhetoric. Clinton governed partly by logorrhea. He relished the opportunity that State of the Union addresses gave him to address a national audience, stuffing them to bursting with poll-tested items. And he loved any opportunity to ooze empathy. He spoke at six—six—memorial services for Ron Brown (Waldman 119).

102. Waldman 83

103. Interview with Elaine Kamarck

104. James Bennet, "The Guru of Small Things," *New York Times Magazine*, June 18, 2000.

105. Interview with former aide to Senator Bob Dole

106. Reich 339

107. Thomas et al. 208

108. Barone and Ujifusa, with Cohen, 1998 ed., 21

109. Thomas et al. 197

110. Dick Morris had left the Clinton team after the story of his relationship with a prostitute broke during the Democratic convention, but he had been the most important architect of the victory. "I used to argue with him in a way that revealed both the cynicism and the realism behind his position," says Reich. "I'd say something like, 'Dick, we can't go into the 1996 election without a mandate to do anything. If the president's reelected,

miniscule policy ideas like V-chips and school uniforms are absurdly irrelevant. The federal government doesn't even have any say over these sorts of
things. Without a mandate, there's no *point* in being reelected.' And then
Dick Morris would turn around and say to me, 'Look, the American public
is not in any mood for a mandate. What we've got to tell them is, 'You've
never had it so good' and 'You ain't seen nothin' yet,' and be quite the opposite of ambitious." (Interview with Robert Reich)

111. Interview with Dick Morris

112. Interview with Robert Reich

113. Robert D. Reischauer, "Comments on 'Medicare,'" in *American Economic Policy in the 1990s,* ed. Jeffrey Frankel and Peter Orszag (Cambridge, MA: MIT Press, 2002), 972–973; Joseph P. Newhouse,
"Medicare," in *American Economic Policy in the 1990s,* ed. Jeffrey Frankel
and Peter Orszag (Cambridge, MA: MIT Press, 2002), 928.

114. Klein 159

115. Tony Pugh, "Luxury Mentality Drives Tuition Costs Higher," *Detroit
Free Press,* March 3, 2000. The credits ultimately were more marginalia
from Dick Morris's poll-tested grab bag, leaping to the president's attention
when Morris discovered that 55 percent of the public strongly supported
them, and 25 percent somewhat supported them (Morris 85). When
Robert Rubin initially objected that scholarships would be better targeted,
Morris advanced a clinching argument: "Politically, we need a tax cut to
beat the tax cut we expect Dole to propose." (Morris 224)

Former Clinton economist Joseph E. Stiglitz writes, "We provided tax
credits and deductions for higher education, but most of the middle-class
kids who benefited were already going to college; the credits and deductions did make their parents lives' easier, but it was unlikely to have much
effect on enrollments. The money could have been better spent targeting
the very poor, for whom money is a real obstacle—whose parents do not
pay taxes" [Joseph E. Stiglitz, *The Roaring Nineties* (New York: W. W. Norton & Company, 2003), 17].

116. Klein 159

117. Consider, for instance, North Carolina's experience with its program,
called Health Choice: "From FY 1997 to FY 2000, according to Health
Choice's own reports to the federal government, private health insurance
declined dramatically among children with household incomes less than or
equal to 200 percent of the poverty line (the income cap for Health
Choice), while children with incomes just above the cap actually saw
increased private coverage." ("No. 191—Hasty on Health Choice: New
Data Show Adverse Impact on Self-Sufficiency," John Locke Foundation,

Spotlights, March 21, 2001. URL: http://www.johnlocke.org/spotlights/ 2001032140.html).

118. Rebecca M. Blank and David T. Ellwood, "The Clinton Legacy for America's Poor," in *American Economic Policy in the 1990s,* ed. Jeffrey Frankel and Peter Orszag (Cambridge, MA: MIT Press, 2002), 778. The program's focus on children provided a politically seductive way to extend government health care, part of a salami-slice approach that allowed liberals to recover somewhat from the Hillary-care debacle. Another element in that push was the 1996 Kennedy-Kassebaum "insurance portability" bill to prevent people from losing coverage if they switched or lost a job, or from being denied coverage for pre-existing conditions (Johnson and Broder 650). Many states had already adopted similar rules (Cutler and Gruber, "Health Policy in the Clinton Era," 853). Some studies show it did nothing to increase insurance coverage, while others show it may have decreased it slightly, since the regulations increased the price of premiums (Cutler and Gruber, "Health Policy in the Clinton Era," 855).

119. Burns and Sorenson 97–98

120. Klein 215.

121. Robert W. Hahn and Robert N. Stavins, "National Environmental Policy During the Clinton Years," in *American Economic Policy in the 1990s,* ed. Jeffrey Frankel and Peter Orszag (Cambridge, MA: MIT Press, 2002), 622–623.

122. The same fate is likely to await Bush's "No Child Left Behind Act" which follows the same formula.

123. U.S. Newswire, "Report: It Takes More Than Money To Educate; Study Covers Two Generations of Public School Students, 1976–2000," April 17, 2001.

124. Michael Paterniti, "Bill Clinton: The Exit Interview," *Esquire,* December 2000.

125. Michael Barone and Grant Ufijusa, with Richard E. Cohen and Charles E. Cook, Jr., *The Almanac of American Politics,* 2000 ed. (Washington, D.C.: National Journal, 1999), 26.

126. Former Clinton pollster Stanley Greenberg co-authored a 2000 article explaining, "For two years, the country was forced to come to terms with the president's private sexual behavior and his public defense. Democrats saved Clinton's presidency and even made gains in the 1998 midterm elections, but at a price. The Democrats again were identified with 1960s-style irresponsibility" (Anna Greenberg and Stanley B. Greenberg, "Adding Values," *The American Prospect,* August 28, 2000).

127. Interview with former administration official. His last major domestic move was his "save Social Security first" line in his 1998 State of the Union address. It was a more a sound bite than a policy. Clinton didn't actually propose doing anything with the surplus to support Social Security, just vaguely "reserving" it (Martin Feldstein, "Let's Really Save Social Security," *Wall Street Journal*, February 10, 1998). It was mainly a way to forestall significant tax cuts as the federal budget lurched unexpectedly into surplus, while preserving the opportunity to spend above levels agreed upon in the 1997 budget deal. In that sense, "save Social Security first" was a grand success (Waldman 241).

128. Interview with Bruce Reed

129. Interview with former senior administration official

130. Interview with Elaine Kamarck

131. Interview with Bill Daley

132. Alan Ehrenhalt, "Turn, Turn, Turn," *The New Republic*, January 27, 2003.

133. Katharine Q. Seeyle, "Democrats Fleeing to G.O.P. Remake Political Landscape," *New York Times*, October 7, 1995.

134. Peter Roff, "The Peter Principles: Pulling the Switch," United Press International, December 11, 2002.

135. Karlyn H. Bowman, "Attitudes Toward the Federal Government," *American Enterprise Institute Studies in Public Opinion*, August 7, 2003, 11–13.

136. Klein 208

137. Jacob Weisberg, "The Governor-President," *New York Times Magazine*, January 17, 1999.

138. Morris 40

139. Peggy Noonan, *The Case Against Hillary Clinton* (New York: HarperCollins, 2000), 177.

140. Quoted in Ramesh Ponnuru, "Femme Fatale," *National Review*, December 31, 1998. This runs exactly counter to the theory advanced by Sidney Blumenthal: "The allies of conservative presidents are indifference, passivity, and complacency" (Blumenthal 15).

141. Weisberg, "The Governor-President"

3. THE ECONOMY: THE 1980S, PART II

1. William Kristol and Lawrence F. Kaplan, *The War for Iraq* (San Francisco: Encounter Books, 2003), 59.

2. Anne Saker, "Clinton, Gore Busing It. Bush Goes South," *Chicago Sun-Times*, August 23, 1992.

3. Lexis-Nexis shows that the first use of the term "rust belt" in the *New York Times* occurred in 1984.

4. Robert D. Hershey Jr., "This Just In: Recession Ended 21 Months Ago," *New York Times*, December 23, 1992.

5. After 1994, tax increases were unthinkable, and Clinton proposed various new tax credits while signing a substantial tax cut in 1997; after making them pay a terrible political price, he acceded to the balanced-budget goals of congressional Republicans, shrinking the size of government relative to the economy; he was, most of the time, a booster of free trade; and he signed onto significant deregulatory measures.

6. Douglas W. Elmendorf, Jeffrey B. Liebman, and David W. Wilcox, "Fiscal Policy and Social Security Policy During the 1990s," in *American Economic Policy in the 1990s,* ed. Jeffrey Frankel and Peter Orszag (Cambridge, MA: MIT Press, 2002), 73–74; Michael Waldman, *POTUS Speaks* (New York: Simon & Schuster, 2000), 39; Robert Reich, *Locked in the Cabinet* (New York: Vintage Books, 1997), 4.

7. Quoted in Elmendorf, Liebman, and Wilcox, "Fiscal Policy and Social Security Policy During the 1990s," 71.

8. Bob Woodward, *The Agenda* (New York: Pocket Books, 1994), 91, 135.

9. Elmendorf, Liebman, and Wilcox, "Fiscal Policy and Social Security Policy During the 1990s," 74.

10. Elizabeth Drew, *On the Edge* (New York: Simon and Schuster, 1994), 111.

11. Martin Walker, *The President We Deserve* (New York: Crown Publishers, Inc., 1996), 38.

12. Unfortunately, George W. Bush relied on crudely Keynesian arguments when making the case for his string of tax cuts in 2001–2003.

13. Woodward 68

14. Woodward 32. Clinton had his own doubts about the plan's credibility when he adopted it. Before he finally signed off on it, his aides, according to Woodward, noted his "deep, near-terminal ambivalence" (Woodward 40).

15. Woodward 80–81. These numbers tend to lag economic conditions, so the recovery had begun while they were still worsening.

16. Elmendorf, Liebman, and Wilcox, "Fiscal Policy and Social Security Policy During the 1990s," 74.

17. Reich 106

18. Woodward 181

19. Ibid., 315, 324

20. At a crucial meeting of Clinton aides, according to Woodward, James Carville gave a little speech about how his father used to declare everything in his family "the *best*." The idea was that the Clinton team should do the same, even if the economic plan satisfied no one. Begala told Clinton, in the same spirit, "You're not allowed to criticize it anymore." (Woodward 293 and 304)

21. Reich 66

22. If the investments turn profitable, businessmen and investors are willing to pay higher interest rates to get into the game, and their competition for funds bids up rates.

23. As economist Alan Reynolds has written, "In the 1980s, economists began to examine the facts. What they found, as Robert Barro reported in his 1987 *Macroeconomics* textbook, is that 'this belief [of deficits driving interest rates] does not have evidence to support it.' A 1985 analysis by Paul Evans found that historical periods of high budget deficits in the United States did not coincide with high interest rates. A 1993 survey of academic studies by John Seater concluded, 'They are inconsistent with the traditional view that government debt is positively related to interest rates.'"

Reynolds continues, "[M]ortgage rates soared in around 1974 and 1980, when budget deficits were quite small and inflation was high. The deficit was much larger in 1983–1987, but mortgage rates fell along with inflation. After the economy slipped into recession in 1990–1991, the deficit grew substantially larger through 1993, but mortgage rates declined. The deficit then shrank steadily as the economy recovered, but mortgage rates nonetheless edged up in 1994 and again in 2000, before declining in 2001 as the surplus disappeared. In short, mortgage rates clearly move in response to changes in inflation, but neither mortgage rates nor inflation moves in tandem with the budget." (Alan Reynolds, "Do Budget Deficits Raise Long-Term Interest Rates?" *Cato Institute Tax & Budget Bulletin*, February 2002. URL: http://www.cato.org/pubs/tbb/tbb-0202.html.)

24. They eventually spiked up again, but this had nothing to do with the deficit: "The most common journalistic device to convert investor success into political failure is to fret about the fact that long-term interest rates are up from their record lows. This often involves such quackery as pretending the bond market suddenly noticed budget deficits in August that it failed to see in June." (Alan Reynolds, "Higher Interest Rates Reflect Higher Growth," August 7, 2003. URL: http://www.townhall.com/columnists/alanreynolds/ar20030807.shtml.

25. Woodward 67 and 129

26. All things being equal, it was better for the economy that Clinton abandoned any notion of a LBJ-style spending spree. It is government spending, not deficits, that truly dampens investment and economic growth. Ditching his "investments" meant that Clinton had taken a step to the right. Indeed, Clinton came into office touting huge new governmental spending projects to get the economy on track. He left office arguing that it was imperative to save huge government surpluses to keep the economy on track. This represented a shift from liberal Keynesianism to a version of old-fashioned, cornbelt Republican deficit-phobia.

27. Alan Reynolds writes, "Another variation on the 'deficits cause high interest rates' theory—embraced by Office of Management and Budget director David Stockman under President Reagan and by Treasury secretary Robert Rubin under President Clinton—says that budget deficits expected in the future are what affect interest rates. However, there is no evidence that expected deficits have any different effects than actual deficits. Using a variety of statistical tests, a 1987 study by Paul Evans 'found no evidence that interest rates are related to current, past, and expected future budget deficits.'" (Reynolds "Do Budget Deficits Raise Long-Term Interest Rates?")

28. Reynolds "Do Budget Deficits Raise Long-Term Interest Rates?"

29. See the chart in Alan S. Blinder and Janet L. Yellen, *The Fabulous Decade* (New York: The Century Foundation Press, 2001), 18.

30. Woodward 378, 399

31. Blinder and Yellen 29

32. Woodward 400

33. Ibid., 378

34. See the chart "Interest Rate on 10-Year Treasury Bonds" from the Federal Reserve Bank of New York. URL: http://www.ny.frb.org/pihome/statistics/indicators/interest.pdf. Economic writer James Glassman noted days before the 1994 election, "Interest rates were the measure that Clinton officials, right from the start, urged us to watch as the indicator of its success. The Economic Report of the President, published in February, brags about how 'administration policy actions have had a noticeable effect in reducing interest rates,' then notes that rates on ten-year Treasury securities fell from 6.8 percent on Election Day 1992 to 5.3 percent in mid-1993. Yesterday, ten-year bonds closed at 7.9 percent. No wonder this recovery gets no respect." (James K. Glassman, "5 Reasons Why Clinton Isn't Getting Credit for the Recovery," *Washington Post*, November 2, 1994)

35. Joe Klein, *The Natural* (New York: Doubleday, 2002).

36. Nicholas Thompson, "Graduating With Honors: The Hits and Misses of a Protean President," *Washington Monthly*, December 2000.

37. Sidney Blumenthal, *The Clinton Wars* (New York: Farrar, Straus and Giroux, 2003).

38. "Assessing the Current Expansion," The Joint Economic Committee, United States Congress, February 2000. URL: http://www.house.gov/jec/growth/assess/assess.pdf.

39. Christopher Frenze, "Whither the Budget Deficit—And Economy?" The Joint Economic Committee, United States Congress, July 1996. URL: http://www.house.gov/jec/fiscal/budget/whither3/whither3.htm.

40. Ibid.

41. R.W. Apple, Jr., "Democrats' Unease May Slow Clinton on Economic Plan," *New York Times*, February 21, 1993.

42. Frenze, "Whither the Budget Deficit," July 1996. Former Clinton economic advisor Joseph Stiglitz notes how helpful defense cuts were to the Clinton team: "The end of the Cold War meant that if we only brought down military expenditures to a more reasonable level—from the 6.2 percent of GDP that it reached in the peak of the Reagan era to, say, 3 percent, we would have erased more than half of the deficit" [Joseph E. Stiglitz, *The Roaring Nineties* (New York: W.W. Norton, 2003), 35].

43. Waldman 46

44. Frenze, "Whither the Budget Deficit," July 1996. Some of Clinton's advisors expressed the same worries. In July 1993, Laura Tyson and her deputies at the time—Alan Blinder and Joseph Stiglitz—wrote a memo to Clinton. According to Bob Woodward, "The memo said there was another side to the deficit reduction coin, namely, that the president program might contain too much deficit reduction, particularly in the current and following year. The contractionary impact of cutting spending and raising taxes in a weak economy could have a significant adverse impact." (Woodward 306)

45. Martin Feldstein, "Comments on 'Fiscal Policy and Social Security Policy During the 1990s,'" in *American Economic Policy in the 1990s,* ed. Jeffrey Frankel and Peter Orszag (Cambridge, MA: MIT Press, 2002), 124.

46. Growth figures from Council of Economic Advisers, 2003 "Economic Report of the President," Table B-4, 281. URL: http://w3.access.gpo.gov/usbudget/fy2004/pdf/2003_erp.pdf.

47. In his discussion with Clinton about presidential greatness, Dick Morris talked about this as one of the reasons Reagan ranked among the greats: "...he probably permanently lowered the tax rates in America. He began an era of less government" [Dick Morris, *Behind the Oval Office* (New York: Random House, 1997), 306].

48. N. Gregory Mankiw, "U.S. Monetary Policy During the 1990s," in *American Economic Policy in the 1990s,* ed. Jeffrey Frankel and Peter Orszag (Cambridge, MA: MIT Press, 2002), 22.

49. Berenson 74–79

50. Robert L. Bartley, *The Seven Fat Years* (New York: The Free Press, 1992), 4.

51. Mankiw, "U.S. Monetary Policy During the 1990s," 20; Blinder and Yellen 12

52. This is obviously a broad-brush comparison. Neither Reagan nor Clinton served ten-year terms and I'm not suggesting either of them should get credit or blame for all of their decades.

53. Mankiw, "U.S. Monetary Policy During the 1990s," 26, 31

54. Berenson 83–84

55. Ibid.

56. Woodward 304–306

57. Clinton's failure on trade was political, and a result of his attempted Third Way on the issue. He embraced the arguments of anti-trade groups and imported them into the trade process itself through his advocacy of labor and environmental provisions in trade deals. This made the pure free-trade position a non-starter for Democrats. After the Democrats lost Congress in 1994, their business contributions declined and they were more dependent than ever on labor money. It became impossible for most Democrats to be more free trade than even Bill Clinton. The consequences were dire. Developing countries weren't going to sign onto trade agreements with environmental and labor conditions that could be harmful to their economies. So, the Democratic Party collectively supported free trade only with conditions that would make free-trade agreements difficult or impossible to strike. The Seattle ministerial meeting of the WTO in 1999 illustrated the problem. It was billed as a potential giant step forward for free trade, but Clinton blew it up. Developing countries were fatally spooked when Clinton told the press that "ultimately I would favor a system in which sanctions would come for violating" labor standards [Robert Z. Lawrence, "International Trade Policy in the 1990s," in *American Economic Policy in the 1990s,* ed. Jeffrey Frankel and Peter Orszag (Cambridge, MA: MIT Press, 2002), 290]. So, Clinton left Democrats much worse off on trade than when he had started. "Democratic support for pro globalization policies didn't just erode, it evaporated," says Cato Institute trade analyst Brink Lindsey (Interview with Brink Lindsey).

58. Lawrence, "International Trade Policy in the 1990s," 285–309

59. Council of Economic Advisers, 2003 "Economic Report of the President," Table B-2, 279.

60. Joel Kurtzman, "Dancing Past the Recession," *New York Times*, August 12, 1990.

61. Greenspan got help, especially later in the 1990s, from many conditions outside his control—low oil prices, declining health-care costs, plummeting prices for computer chips, and surging productivity. All of these factors lead Blinder and Yellen to call the period from 1996 to 1998 "the good luck period" (Blinder and Yellen 43).

62. Mankiw, "U.S. Monetary Policy During the 1990s," 21–22

63. Eugene Steuerle, "Tax Policy from 1990 to 2001," in *American Economic Policy in the 1990s*, ed. Jeffrey Frankel and Peter Orszag (Cambridge, MA: MIT Press, 2002), 159.

64. Alan Blinder, "Comments on 'U.S. Monetary Policy During the 1990s,'" in *American Economic Policy in the 1990s*, ed. Jeffrey Frankel and Peter Orszag (Cambridge, MA: MIT Press, 2002), 47.

65. Roger K. Lowe, "Clinton Plan Won't Balance Budget in 9 Years, Kasich Says," *Columbus Dispatch*, August 4, 1995.

66. Woodward 185

67. Elmendorf, Liebman, and Wilcox, "Fiscal Policy and Social Security Policy During the 1990s," 80.

68. Steuerle, "Tax Policy from 1990 to 2001," 145–146

69. Reich xiv

70. William A. Niskanen, "The Clinton Regulatory Legacy," *Regulation*, Summer 2001. Liberals like Joseph Stiglitz think Clinton went too far in his deregulation: "When Clinton entered office, I and many others who came to Washington with him hoped that we would restore balance to the role of government. Jimmy Carter had begun the process of deregulation, in such vital areas as airlines and trucking. But under Ronald Reagan and George Bush, America had pushed deregulation way too far. Our task was to find the appropriate middle course and to adapt the regulations to the changes that were going on in the country. We should not have been talking about deregulation so much as finding the *right* regulatory framework. In some areas, we did that; but in others, we were too swept up by the deregulation, pro-business mantra" (Stiglitz, *The Roaring Nineties*, 16).

71. Pamela Samuelson and Hal R. Varian, "The 'New Economy' and Information Technology Policy," in *American Economic Policy in the 1990s*, ed. Jeffrey Frankel and Peter Orszag (Cambridge, MA: MIT Press, 2002), 385.

72. Jeffrey Frankel and Peter Orszag, eds., *American Economic Policy in the 1990s* (Cambridge, MA: MIT Press, 2002), 2.

73. Council of Economic Advisers, 2003 "Economic Report of the President," Table B-50, 335. (These figures reflect productivity growth in the "nonfarm business sector.") URL: http://w3.access.gpo.gov/usbudget/fy2004/pdf/2003_erp.pdf.

74. Blinder and Yellen 63

75. Berenson 162

76. Feldstein, "Comments on 'Fiscal Policy and Social Security Policy During the 1990s,'" 125

77. Elmendorf, Liebman, and Wilcox, "Fiscal Policy and Social Security Policy During the 1990s," 67

78. Paul Johnson, *A History of the American People* (New York: Harper-Collins, 1997), 922.

79. Blinder and Yellen 75

80. Reich xiv

81. Blinder and Yellen 74

82. Hillary Rodham Clinton, *Living History* (New York: Simon & Schuster, 2003), 252.

83. Blumenthal 57–59

84. Ibid., 266

85. Interview with Mickey Kantor

86. Interview with Bill Daley

87. James B. Stewart, *Blood Sport* (New York: Simon & Schuster, 1996), 232–233.

88. Ibid.

89. Martha Sherrill, "Hillary Clinton's Inner Politics; As the First Lady Grows Comfortable in Her Roles, She Is Looking Beyond Policy to a Moral Agenda," *Washington Post*, May 6, 1993. Hillary was quoting the late Republican campaign operative Lee Atwater.

90. Stewart 233

91. Woodward 122

92. Ibid., 145

93. Berenson 101–106. Such estimates are controversial. There are no official figures on executive pay.

94. Mickey Kaus, *The End of Equality* (New York: Basic Books, 1992), 29.

95. Interview with Robert Reich

96. Woodward 155

97. Elmendorf, Liebman, and Wilcox, "Fiscal Policy and Social Security Policy During the 1990s," 74

98. Joseph Stiglitz, "The Roaring Nineties," *The Atlantic Monthly*, October 2002.

99. Interview with former administration official

100. Steven A. Holmes, *Ron Brown* (New York: John Wiley and Sons, Inc., 2000), 249–250.

101. Celia W. Dugger, "Enron's Fight Over Power Plant Reverberates Beyond India," *New York Times*, March 20, 2001.

102. The 1995 Mexican bailout may have seemed necessary to avoid the risk of a Mexican financial collapse, but the action set the stage for the Asian financial crisis, and its attendant IMF bailouts, as it helped investors forget the risks of the "emerging markets" they were pouring funds into. They might have invested with more care if they had taken a bath in Mexico. By the time of the attempted Russian bailout in 1998, investors were gleefully gaming the system, depending on emergency handouts to save them from their irresponsibility [see Paul Blustein, *The Chastening* (New York: Public Affairs, 2001), 173]. The bailouts were meant to combat "financial contagion," government defaults that might prompt more defaults elsewhere. "Contagion," however, was just another word for a sensible financial retreat from parts of the world where market reforms and new investment opportunities were significantly oversold in the hype over globalization. The bailouts attempted to keep the emerging-markets bubble afloat, at least for a little longer. It is difficult, however, for any administration to resist the temptation to "do something" about a significant economy in trouble—George W. Bush bailed out Brazil in August 2002.

103. Stiglitz, "The Roaring Nineties." In general, proposals to tighten accounting rules and strengthen the Securities and Exchange Commission were opposed by Republicans and Democrats alike. As Alex Berenson writes, "The S.E.C. had no natural constituency in the Democratic Party. It had no pork to dole out, and what did unions, environmentalists, or trial lawyers care about the stock market?" (Berenson 140).

104. Andrew J. Bacevich, *American Empire* (Cambridge, MA: Harvard University Press, 2002), 38.

105. "Pace of New Factory Orders Is Reported as Fastest in 14 Years," *New York Times*, April 2, 2002.

106. "Clinton's Economic Legacy," *Washington Times*, September 30, 2002.

107. Stiglitz, "The Roaring Nineties."

108. Ibid.

4. WELFARE & CRIME: A CONSERVATIVE TRIUMPH

1. Interview with Robert Rector

2. Robert Rector, "President Clinton's Commitment to Welfare Reform: The Disturbing Record So Far," *The Heritage Foundation*, December 17, 1993, 3.

3. Hugh Heclo, "The Politics of Welfare Reform," in *The New World of Welfare*, ed. Rebecca Blank and Ron Haskins (Washington, D.C.: Brookings Institution, 2001), 179.

4. Rector, "President Clinton's Commitment to Welfare Reform," 5

5. Robert Rector, "Yet Another Sham Welfare Reform: Examining the NGA Plan," *The Heritage Foundation*, March 18, 1996, 5.

6. Interview with Robert Rector

7. Interview with Bruce Reed

8. James MacGregor Burns and Georgia J. Sorenson, *Dead Center* (New York: Scribner, 1999), 234.

9. Interview with Bruce Reed

10. Hillary Clinton, *Living History* (New York: Simon & Schuster, 2003), 369.

11. Governor Bill Clinton and Senator Al Gore, *Putting People First* (New York: Times Books, 1992),165.

12. Rector, "President Clinton's Commitment to Welfare Reform,"2, 8

13. Ibid., 9

14. Ibid.

15. Ibid., 7

16. Ibid., 9–11.

17. Robert Rector, "How Clinton's Bill Extends Welfare As We Know It," *The Heritage Foundation*, August 1, 1994), 5–6.

18. Rebecca M. Blank and David T. Ellwood, "The Clinton Legacy for America's Poor," in *American Economic Policy in the 1990s*, ed. Jeffrey Frankel and Peter Orszag (Cambridge, MA: MIT Press, 2002), 760.

19. Ron Haskins, "Comments on 'The Clinton Legacy for America's Poor,'" in *American Economic Policy in the 1990s*, ed. Jeffrey Frankel and Peter Orszag (Cambridge, MA: MIT Press, 2002), 812.

20. Haskins, "Comments on 'The Clinton Legacy,'" 813

21. Interview with Robert Rector. The bill had weak work requirements that were phased in far off in the future, and no provisions on illegitimacy.

22. Interview with former administration official

23. Interview with Robert Rector

24. Interview with Senator James Talent

25. Ibid.

26. Elizabeth Drew, *Showdown* (New York: Touchstone, 1996), 92.

27. Heclo, "The Politics of Welfare Reform," 191

28. Interview with Robert Rector. The Republican bill addressed the perverse financial incentive by ending the entitlement nature of welfare—which tied federal funding to the states to the size of their welfare rolls—and moving to a block grant instead. The entitlement had given states no reason to cut their rolls, since reducing them meant less money from Washington. In this way, Wisconsin Governor Tommy Thompson lost bundles of federal money because of his reform successes.

29. Interview with Robert Rector. Conservatives wanted a national family cap that would deny any additional federal welfare dollars to mothers who had another child while on welfare. They pushed also to deny federal cash benefits to teenage mothers. Both of these provisions were defeated. The proposed provisions at least served to spark a national debate on illegitimacy, something to which Clinton had contributed with a couple of stark statements against out-of-wedlock childbearing from his bully pulpit in 1993 and 1994.

30. Evan Thomas et al., *Back From The Dead* (New York: The Atlantic Monthly Press, 1997), 135. To listen to the left, the bill would be the end of poor people in the United States.

31. Burns and Sorenson 226

32. Robert Rector, "The Good News About Welfare Reform," *The Heritage Foundation*, September 5, 2001, 2. Moynihan added that "those involved will take this disgrace to their graves." (Rector, "The Good News About Welfare Reform," 2)

33. Interview with a former administration official

34. Rector, "The Good News About Welfare Reform," 2

35. Heclo, "The Politics of Welfare Reform," 183–184

36. Interview with Bruce Reed

37. Interview with Senator Talent

38. Ibid.

39. Heclo, "The Politics of Welfare Reform," 193

40. Bob Woodward, *The Choice* (New York: Simon & Schuster, 1996), 352.

41. Dick Morris, *Behind the Oval Office* (New York: Random House, 1997), 300.

42. Ibid.

43. Ibid., 300–301. Clinton couldn't really give up the liberal premises, the idea that obstacles were keeping welfare recipients from working, and that it would be unfair to treat them too toughly. He had a lingering case of the liberal's paternal protectiveness—partly well-intentioned, partly romantic, partly patronizing—for the poor.

44. Clinton 368

45. Morris 298

46. Interview with Senator Talent. "From my perspective," says Rector, who was never shy about criticizing welfare bills he considered inadequate, "there were no substantive differences. They didn't weaken anything." (Interview with Robert Rector)

47. Interview with a former administration official

48. Robert Reich, *Locked in the Cabinet* (New York: Vintage Books, 1997), 320. Ron Haskins has identified five major characteristics of the reform bill, from ending the entitlement to the five-year time limit: "Examination of the legislative history of the 1996 reforms reveals that all five were introduced by Republicans and that Republicans, sometimes with strong opposition from Democrats, defended them and refused to allow any to be dropped from the final bill or even substantially modified. All five were in the two bills vetoed by Clinton (in December 1995 and January 1996); all five were in the bill he signed in August 1996" (Haskins, "Comments on 'The Clinton Legacy,'" 815).

49. "Acts of Principle," *New York Times*, September 13, 1996.

50. Robert Rector, "The Continuing Good News About Welfare Reform," *The Heritage Foundation*, February 6, 2003, 6.

51. Ibid.

52. Blank and Ellwood, "The Clinton Legacy," 749

53. Rector, "The Continuing Good News," 3

54. Ibid.

55. Ron Haskins, "Effects of Welfare Reform on Family Income and Poverty," in *The New World of Welfare*, ed. Rebecca Blank and Ron Haskins (Washington, D.C.: Brookings Institution, 2001), 120–121.

56. Rector, "The Continuing Good News," 7

57. Ibid., 9.

58. Interview with Senator Talent. Rebecca Blank and David Ellwood write, "The whole tone of the reform sent a strong message to state administrators that the mission of welfare offices was no longer to determine eligibility and compute the proper amount of the check, but rather to move people quickly off welfare, and, hopefully, into employment." (Blank and Ellwood, "The Clinton Legacy," 764)

59. Rector, "The Continuing Good News," 7. The rate of out-of-wedlock births dipped among blacks from 70.4 percent in 1994 to 68.8 percent in 1999. The percentage of black children living with married couples rose slightly and the percentage living with single mothers dropped slightly. The cause and significance of the slowdown in illegitimacy are open to argument, but, again, the general message sent by the debate over welfare reform, and the effects of reform itself, probably had an effect. As women were moving off welfare, they would no longer be affected by its perverse anti-marriage incentives. And some of the mothers leaving welfare may have looked to a husband to help replace the lost benefits.

60. Later, Clinton was able to get some of the fixes in the bill that he called for upon its signing. He managed to repeal the retroactive cutting off of SSI and food stamps to legal immigrants who were already in the country when the law was enacted—a provision that particularly enraged critics like Wendell Primus [George J. Borjas, "Welfare Reform and Immigration," in *The New World of Welfare*, ed. Rebecca Blank and Ron Haskins (Washington, D.C.: Brookings Institution, 2001), 373]. Prohibitions on new immigrants receiving most types of welfare until they become citizens stood. They seem to have succeeded in depressing immigrant use of welfare, which declined faster than that of native citizens (Borjas, "Welfare Reform and Immigration," 370).

61. Reich 90

62. Haskins, "Comments on 'The Clinton Legacy,'" 816

63. Joe Klein, *The Natural* (New York: Doubleday, 2002), 156.

64. Douglas J. Besharov with Nazanin Samari, "Child Care after Welfare Reform," in *The New World of Welfare*, ed. Rebecca Blank and Ron Haskins (Washington, D.C.: Brookings Institution, 2001), 462.

65. Ron Haskins, "Effects of Welfare Reform on Family Income and Poverty," in *The New World of Welfare*, ed. Rebecca Blank and Ron Haskins, (Washington, D.C.: Brookings Institution, 2001), 107.

66. Haskins, "Effects of Welfare Reform," 115–116. Clinton also increased spending on Head Start from $2.8 billion to $6.3 billion from 1993 to 2000 (Klein 156). Head Start, however, doesn't deserve its exalted place in the liberal imagination. The program has no academic function, and is essentially a jobs program for the women who work in it.

67. If Clinton and the Democrats had maintained unified control of the government, they probably never would have done anything. Other issues would always seem more important—as health care had—and it would be too painful to overcome the objections of close ideological allies, as his first two years in office demonstrated. He would have had to battle his own cabinet, his own party in Congress, the *New York Times*, and most of his own instincts—without a congressional Republican majority exercising leverage over him.

68. Morris wasn't the only voice urging him to sign. "It was flat-out wrong to suggest that President Clinton signed welfare reform only because he was afraid it would be used against him and he would lose the election in '96 if he didn't do it," says Don Baer. "He always said he was going to reform welfare, and the most persuasive argument that was put to him—and I was there—was Bruce Reed's argument that at the end of the day we promised the American people in 1992 we would do this and this is our last chance to do it." (Interview with Don Baer) But since 1992 Clinton had been urging a different kind of reform. Even when the Republican bill was sent to him a third time, even when his foremost political advisor was begging him to sign it, Clinton wrestled with himself over approving it. Would he have signed if Morris had told him a veto would be a political winner? Or even politically neutral? Of course not. The political advantage tipped him off his straddle.

69. Morris 304

70. Sidney Blumenthal, *The Clinton Wars* (New York: Farrar, Straus and Giroux, 2003), 789.

71. Al Gore said in the vice presidential debate on October 13, 1992: "This started with Harry Truman and it was a bipartisan effort from the very beginning. George Bush taking credit for the Berlin Wall coming down is like the rooster taking credit for the sunrise."

72. Henry Ruth and Kevin R. Reitz, *The Challenge of Crime* (Cambridge, MA: Harvard University Press, 2003), 67.

73. John J. DiIulio, "Keeping Crime on the Run," *Blueprint*, Fall 2000. URL: http://www.ndol.org/blueprint/fall2000/diiulio/html.

74. Charles Murray discusses how long it took to make up for the imprisonment slowdown in the 1960s in his essay in "Does Prison Work?" printed by the Institute of Economic Affairs Health and Welfare Unit, Choice in Welfare No. 38, 1997.

75. William Spelman, "The Limited Importance of Prison Expansion," in *The Crime Drop in America,* ed. Alfred Blumstein and Joel Wallman (Cambridge: Cambridge University Press, 2000), 108.

76. Richard Rosenfeld, "Patterns in Adult Homicide: 1980–1995," in *The Crime Drop in America,* ed. Alfred Blumstein and Joel Wallman (Cambridge: Cambridge University Press, 2000), 143.

77. Murray, "Does Prison Work?"

78. Ruth and Reitz 96

79. Alfred Blumstein, "Disaggregating the Violence Trends," in *The Crime Drop in America,* ed. Alfred Blumstein and Joel Wallman (Cambridge: Cambridge University Press, 2000), 13.

80. Spelman, "The Limited Importance of Prison Expansion," 124. The same way Ronald Reagan had determined to bankrupt the Soviet Union with an enormous defense buildup, America had collectively decided to wear down its crime with a relentless, massive prison buildup. The research vindicates the common-sensical insight that locking criminals away reduces crime. One study shows that every incarceration prevents fifteen crimes annually (DiIulio, "Keeping Crime on the Run"). Criminologist Richard Rosenfeld reports that more than a quarter of the drop in murders can be attributed to the prison boom (Ibid.). Imprisonment had a direct and large effect on property crimes. While incarceration rates steadily increased from the 1970s to 2000, burglary and theft steadily decreased along with them (by 71 and 65 percent respectively) (Ruth and Reitz 101). Writer Eli Lehrer suggests a simple comparison: "Crime rates fell in the United States as punishment increased and rose in Britain as punishment decreased" (Eli Lehrer, "Crime Without Punishment; As American Streets Get Safer, Crime in Europe Soars," *The Weekly Standard,* May 27, 2002).

81. Interview with Eric Holder. Holder is careful to stipulate that Clinton polices had an effect too: "Together with the get-tough approach, there was a focus on the underlying social conditions, a greater awareness of the role of social dysfunction. Clinton got it. No one was talking about black victims. A tough-on-crime approach was totally consistent with my point of view, coupled with a focus on good schools, jobs and the role of men."

82. The Clinton administration fellow-traveled with this attack, and generally bought the critique of the police as racist. Heather Mac Donald writes, "No institution made more destructive use of racial profiling junk science than the Clinton Justice Department. Armed with the shoddy studies, it slapped costly consent decrees on police departments across the country, requiring them to monitor their officers' every interaction with minorities, among other managerial intrusions." [Heather Mac Donald, *Are Cops Racist?* (Chicago: Ivan R. Dee, 2003), 29–30].

83. William Bratton describes the culture of the Police Department as he took over: "The organization didn't want high performance; it wanted to stay out of trouble, to avoid corruption scandals and conflicts in the community. For years, therefore, the key to career success in the NYPD, as in many bureaucratic leviathans, was to shun risk and avoid failure." William J. Bratton and William Andrews, "What We've Learned About Policing," *City Journal,* Spring 1999.

84. Mac Donald 103. The stop-and-frisk policies behind this success drove liberals crazy, because stop-and-frisk allegedly discriminates against minorities. Liberals apparently suspend their hatred of guns when they are being carried by young urban males.

85. Bratton and Andrews, "What We've Learned About Policing"

86. Mac Donald 103

87. John E. Eck and Edward R. Maguire, "Have Changes in Policing Reduced Violent Crime?" in *The Crime Drop in America,* ed. Alfred Blumstein and Joel Wallman (Cambridge: Cambridge University Press, 2000), 233.

88. Andrew Karmen, *New York Murder Mystery* (New York: New York University Press, 2000), 25.

89. Mac Donald 118

90. Karmen 24–25

91. Bruce D. Johnson, Andrew Golub, and Eloise Dunlap, "Drugs and Violence in Inner-City New York," in *The Crime Drop in America,* ed. Alfred Blumstein and Joel Wallman (Cambridge: Cambridge University Press, 2000), 176–80.

92. Ruth and Reitz 256–257

93. Johnson, Golub, and Dunlap, "Drugs and Violence," 185–186

94. Ruth and Reitz 170, 177

95. Laura Parker, "Politics Blocks Wider Use of 'Fingerprinting,'" *USA Today,* October 16, 2002.

96. Ruth and Reitz 175–176. One study found, according to Ruth and Reitz, that "as many as 70 percent of felons' most recently owned firearms had been stolen either by the offender himself or by the source from whom he acquired the weapon."

97. Gary Kleck, *Targeting Guns* (New York: Aldine de Gruyter, 2003), 375.

98. Frank Main, "Brady Gun Law Ineffective?" *Chicago Sun-Times,* August 2, 2000.

99. Clinton 203

100. Kleck 376

101. John R. Lott, Jr., *The Bias Against Guns* (Washington, D.C.: Regnery, 2003), 194.

102. Kleck 364

103. Ted Gest, *Crime and Politics* (Oxford: Oxford University Press, 2001),150. Gest also notes, "two-thirds of federal firearms violators have no prior convictions on their record—the main cause of Brady act denials."

104. The bill also had funding increases for prisons and incentives to states to adopt truth-in-sentencing laws—part of the long-running get-tough trend (Gest 201).

105. Kleck 110–112

106. Ibid., 111, 114

107. "Statement by President Clinton on Violent Crime," April 13, 1997.

108. Michael Paterniti, "Bill Clinton: The Exit Interview," *Esquire*, December 2000.

109. Interview with Howard Paster

110. Gest 170

111. Ibid., 179, 183

112. Ibid., 183–186

113. According to a 1997 Justice Department report, "While the COPS Program language has stressed a community policing approach, there is no evidence that community policing *per se* reduces crime" (David B. Muhlhausen, "More COPS Funding Will Not Mean More Cops and Less Crime," *The Heritage Foundation*, June 14, 2001, 2). Ruth and Reitz write that one study "concluded that the substantial numbers of additional police officers did not 'play an independent or consistent role' in violent crime reduction. Further, violent crime reduction efforts cannot be consistently attributed to various forms of community policing implemented through police-community partnerships and/or police organizational changes." (Ruth and Reitz 135)

114. Michael Barone and Grant Ujifusa, with Richard E. Cohen, *The Almanac of American Politics*, 1998 ed. (Washington, D.C.: National Journal, 1997), 29.

5. "THE CHILDREN": NANNY-IN-CHIEF

1. Bob Woodward, *The Choice* (New York: Simon & Schuster, 1996), 210–211.

2. Jean Bethke Elshtain, "Suffer the Little Children," *The New Republic*, March 4, 1996.

3. Hillary Rodham Clinton, *It Takes a Village* (New York: Touchstone, 1996), 290.

4. Elshtain, "Suffer the Little Children."

5. Barbara Olson, *Hell to Pay* (Washington, D.C.: Regnery, 1999), 100.

6. Alexis de Tocqueville, *Democracy in America*, ed. J.P. Mayer, trans. George Lawrence (New York: Harper Perennial, 1988), 692.

7. Clinton 222–223

8. Elizabeth Drew, *On the Edge* (New York: Simon & Schuster, 1994), 22.

9. Health-care reform was at the very heart of the nanny-state agenda. It meant insinuating government much deeper into American life, in the cause of health, always a central nanny-state concern because its core ambition is to make us safer and more comfortable—at the cost of individual freedom. Paul Starr, an architect of Hillary's health care plan, writes, "Political leaders since Bismarck seeking to strengthen the state or to advance their own or their party's interests have used insurance against the costs of sickness as a means of turning benevolence to power" [Paul Starr, *The Social Transformation of American Medicine* (New York: Basic Books, 1982), 235].

10. David Gergen, *Eyewitness to Power* (New York: Simon & Schuster, 2000), 308.

11. Ibid., 309

12. Interview with Bruce Reed

13. Haynes Johnson and David S. Broder, *The System* (New York: Little, Brown and Company, 1996), 105.

14. Jacob Weisberg, "Dies Ira," *The New Republic*, January 24, 1994. (This is another excellent Jacob Weisberg essay.) As a student, he conceived a change in Brown University curriculum that de-emphasized Western civilization and grading, making the school an academic laughingstock compared to the rest of the Ivy League. He led student radicals in a campaign to revitalize the working-class town of Brockton, Massachusetts, an effort that had to be abandoned as Magaziner's shock troops became unpopular with the very poor people they were seeking to help. His plan in 1982 to overhaul the economy of Rhode Island was rejected by voters. In the late 1980s, he devised a better way for General Electric to make refrigerators that flopped and lost the company hundreds of millions of dollars.

15. Johnson and Broder 15

16. Ibid., 113

17. Drew 192

18. Johnson and Broder 31, 169

19. Ibid. 16, 10. The president's economic advisors—and anyone else with a sense of sobriety—were aghast. Treasury secretary Lloyd Bentsen wrote a thirty-eight-page single-spaced memo expressing his doubts (Johnson and Broder 163). Even the administration's liberals were taken aback at what Hillary and Magaziner had wrought. Says Donna Shalala of a White House that heard many calls for caution from within the administration, "On health care, it was just, the program that was developed was too complex, and there, I would argue that there was consensus there was a problem but no consensus on the solution, and therefore, you really had to go to the Hill with principles and start working your way through to get more coverage. A few minutes into it, we knew that. [But] the commitments had been made. Commitments to the First Lady, and to Ira Magaziner, and to a whole organizational scheme for doing it. It wasn't like the President wasn't told that's [a go-slow approach] what he should do." (Interview with Donna Shalala)

20. Julie Rovner, "Congress and Health Care Reform 1993–1994," in *Intensive Care,* ed. Thomas E. Mann and Norman J. Ornstein (Washington, D.C.: American Enterprise Institute and the Brooking Institution, 1995), 189.

21. Porter J. Goss, "Why Seniors Should Look Closely at Health Reform," *Washington Times,* May 31, 1994.

22. Rovner, "Congress and Health Care Reform," 203. As a candid administration official told the *Washington Post,* "From a policy standpoint, the worst outcome would be that we win on universal coverage but don't get the cost controls right, and wind up bankrupting the country as a result"(Steven Pearlstein, "Health Care Reform Bills Caught in Political Labyrinth," *Washington Post,* July 16, 1994).

23. Johnson and Broder 409

24. Interview with a former administration official

25. Christopher Connell, "Lawmakers Propose Heath Care Bill," *Associated Press,* March 3, 1993. Connell writes that the bill "would be financed primarily by raising the Medicare payroll tax from 1.45 percent to 7.9 percent and raising both corporate and income taxes."

26. Robert Reich writes of his feeling at the time, "The health care plan plays into its opponents' hands. It's unwieldy. I still don't understand it. I've been to dozens of meetings on it, defended it on countless radio and TV programs, debated its merits publicly and privately, but I still don't comprehend the whole." [Robert Reich, *Locked in the Cabinet* (New York: Vintage

Books, 1997), 168]. And Reich does not lack intellectual candlepower. "There were only about three or four people in the administration who actually understood the plan," says a former GOP Energy and Commerce Committee aide. "There were probably about twenty people in town all told who understood it. It was the single most complicated piece of legislation Congress ever considered." (Interview with former GOP aide)

27. Johnson and Broder 382

28. Their increasing market share, in turn, made it possible for them to intimidate doctors and hospitals into joining up with them. By 1994, most doctors and hospitals had agreed to reduce their fees for patients in managed-care plans (Johnson and Broder 381). The slowdown in the premium increases would be temporary [Hillary Rodham Clinton, *Living History* (New York: Simon & Schuster, 2003), 248–249], but reduced the sense of "crisis" just as the administration was trying to hype it.

29. Most of these inefficiencies result from the way the current health-care system keeps a true competitive market from operating.

30. David Cutler and Jonathan Gruber, "Health Policy in the Clinton Era," in *American Economic Policy in the 1990s*, ed. Jeffrey Frankel and Peter Orszag (Cambridge, MA: MIT Press, 2002), 832. As health economist Victor Fuchs writes, "[H]ealth services employment in 1990 was more than two and a half times larger than in 1970. What were the millions of additional physicians, nurses, technicians, and others doing if not producing more inpatient and outpatient services?" These services made people healthier. Fuchs points, for instance, to Medicare records that "showed very rapid rates of growth of age-specific, per capita utilization of angioplasties, coronary artery bypass grafts, hip replacements, and many other major surgical and diagnostic procedures. These were real surgeons providing services to real patients, not price inflation." [Victor R. Fuchs, "Comments on 'Health Policy in the Clinton Era,'" in *American Economic Policy in the 1990s*, ed. Jeffrey Frankel and Peter Orszag (Cambridge, MA: MIT Press, 2002), 878]

31. Johnson and Broder 61–62

32. Reaching "universal coverage" is a utopian goal, since people are not stamped in a socialist cookie-cutter. Not everyone is going to want, need, or get access to the same level of health care. Even in countries with government-run health-care systems, like Sweden, Denmark, Britain, and Canada, there is a wide variation of participation in health care, depending on income, geography, and other factors.

33. Johnson and Broder 90

34. Bob Woodward, *The Agenda* (New York: Pocket Books, 1994), 127.

35. Johnson and Broder 209, 324

36. Ibid., 222

37. Greg Steinmetz, "Clinton Health Care Plan Casualty: The Health Insurance Agent," *Wall Street Journal*, November 17, 1993. He writes, "As a health-insurance agent, Lori Proctor was naturally curious about how the Clinton health-care plan would affect her job. So when she visited the White House last month as part of a group of northern Ohio businesspeople, she put the question about her future directly to Hillary Rodham Clinton. The answer left her shaken. 'I'm assuming anyone as obviously brilliant as you could find something else to market,' the First Lady said."

38. Rovner, "Congress and Health Care Reform," 185

39. Paul Starr, "What Happened to Health Care Reform?" *The American Prospect*, Winter 1995.

40. Ibid.

41. Ibid.

42. Rovner, "Congress and Health Care Reform," 200

43. Ibid., 185

44. Starr, "What Happened to Health Care Reform?"

45. Rovner, "Congress and Health Care Reform," 203

46. Ibid.

47. Interview with Chip Kahn

48. Johnson and Broder 209–210

49. Johnson and Broder 212. There is nothing wrong, of course, with such expenditures. Interest-group spending to influence the political debate is an integral part of a free and open political system.

50. Gergen 305

51. Johnson and Broder 460–464

52. Ibid., 461

53. Clinton, *Living History*, 246

54. Johnson and Broder 461

55. Susan Page, "Clinton at Midterm," *Newsday* (New York), January 22, 1995.

56. "This Week With David Brinkley," ABC News, November 13, 1994.

57. Gail Sheehy, *Hillary's Choice* (New York: Ballantine Books, 1999), 339.

58. Woodward, *The Choice*, 55, 133. In a December confab at Camp David, they also hosted: Anthony Robbins (*Awaken the Giant Within*), Marianne Williamson (*A Return to Love*), and Stephen R. Covey (*The Seven Habits of Highly Effective People*).

59. Sheehy 259

60. Ibid., 256

61. Toni Morrison explained in the October 5, 1998 issue of *The New Yorker*: "Years ago, in the middle of the Whitewater investigation, one heard the first murmurs: white skin notwithstanding, this is our first black president. Blacker than any actual black person who could ever be elected in our children's lifetime. After all, Clinton displays almost every trope of blackness: single-parent household, born poor, working-class, saxophone-playing, McDonald's-and-junk-food-loving boy from Arkansas. And when virtually all the African-American Clinton appointees began, one by one, to disappear, when the President's body, his privacy, his unpoliced sexuality became the focus of persecution, when he was metaphorically seized and body-searched, who could gainsay these black men who knew whereof they spoke?"

62. Sheehy 209

63. James MacGregor Burns and Georgia J. Sorenson, *Dead Center* (New York: Scribner, 1999), 257.

64. Clinton 335

65. Peggy Noonan, *The Case Against Hillary Clinton* (New York: Regan Books, 2000), 149.

66. Warren Christopher, *Chances of a Lifetime* (New York: Scribner, 2001), 164. There's nothing wrong necessarily with taking into account race and gender in forming a government. Politics has always involved that sort of symbolism and logrolling. But the administration took it to absurd lengths.

67. Sidney Blumenthal, *The Clinton Wars* (New York: Farrar, Straus and Giroux, 2003), 261.

68. Drew 24, 100

69. Blumenthal 278

70. From Justice O'Connor's decision: "Accordingly, we hold today that all racial classifications, imposed by whatever Federal, state, or local governmental actor, must be analyzed by a reviewing court under strict scrutiny. In other words, such classifications are constitutional only if they are narrowly tailored measures that further compelling governmental interests." URL: http://caselaw.lp.findlaw.com/scripts/getcase.pl?court=us&vol=515&invol=200.

71. George Stephanopoulos, *All Too Human* (New York: Little, Brown and Company, 1999), 364.

72. Presidential Commission on the Assignment of Women in the Armed Forces, *Report to the President*, November 15, 1992, C-49.

73. Stephanie Guttman, *The Kinder, Gentler Military* (New York: Scribner, 2000), 157–159. Military expert Charles Moskos has said, "The Tailhook convention of '91 was the worst event for the Navy since Pearl Harbor."

74. Gutmann 171, 176–177

75. Kingsley R. Browne, "Women at War: An Evolutionary Perspective," *Buffalo Law Review* (Buffalo, NY: University of Buffalo School of Law, Winter 2001), 58–59.

76. Sheehy 263

77. Gutmann 208

78. David Maraniss, *First in His Class* (New York: Touchstone Books, 1996), 203.

79. Drew 45

80. Gutmann 151

81. John Lancaster, "Nearly All Combat Jobs To Be Open to Women; Front-Line Ground Units Would Be Excluded," *Washington Post*, April 29, 1993.

82. "Why American Servicewomen Are Serving at Greater Risk," Center for Military Readiness Report, April 2003. URL: http://cmrlink.org/CMRNotes/M38V8CCMRRPT16.pdf.

83. "Secretary of Defense Aspin Expects to Open New Opportunities for Women with New Direct Ground Combat Rule," News Release by the Office of the Assistant to the Secretary of Defense (Public Affairs), January 13, 1994. URL: http://www.chinfo.navy.mil/navpalib/people/women/rel0113.txt.

84. Philip Shenon, "Denounced for Remarks on Marines, Army Official Quits," *The New York Times*, November 15, 1997. The Center for Military Readiness and the *Washington Times* reported the Lister comment from an audiotaped October 26, 1997 academic seminar in Baltimore, Maryland.

85. Interview with General Charles C. Krulak

86. Browne 67

87. Ibid., 192

88. Gutmann 247

89. Kingsley Browne writes, "The Army, for example, had integrated basic training in the late 1970s but abandoned it in the early 1980s because men were being held back and women were not able to excel." (Browne, "Women at War," 189)

90. "Report of the Federal Advisory Committee on Gender-Integrated Training and Related Issues to the Secretary of Defense," December 16, 1997, 15. URL: http://www.defenselink.mil/pubs/git/report.html. *Time* magazine noted in 1997, "No one who went through boot camp in the 1950s or '60s would recognize the place today." (Gutmann 55)

91. Browne, "Women at War," 234. This kind of dishonesty had dire consequences. The Navy, for instance, was desperate for feel-good stories about female aviators. When pioneer female combat pilot Lt. Kara Hultgreen crashed her F-14 in October 1994 trying to land on the USS *Lincoln*, the Navy publicly led the nation to believe that the mishap had been primarily caused by an engine malfunction [Linda Bird Francke, *Ground Zero* (New York: Simon & Schuster, 1997), 256]. But evidence steadily came to light revealing that pilot error really was the primary cause. On April 25, 1995, Elaine Donnelly published the comprehensive "CMR Special Report: Double Standards in Naval Aviation" exposing how Hultgreen and another woman pilot had systematically been held to a lower standard. In an April 19, 1998, appearance on CBS "60 Minutes," Admiral Stanley Arthur admitted that the Navy had rushed women to the fleet in order to prove a political point: "This was a way that we could at least demonstrate that the—what was viewed as the reluctance of the Navy to deal properly with women coming out of Tailhook could be put aside; that we were, in fact, not the ogres that we were painted to be." ("60 Minutes," April 19, 1998) A sidelight: The late Lt. Kara Hultgreen had an admirable role in the Tailhook controversy. She was groped at the convention, but refused to say she was assaulted or victimized. As she described it to a TV interviewer, "One person who had a lot to drink that night thought he was being clever, witty, and charming. I made it clear that his advances were unwelcome. I told him, 'I'm an officer and an aviator; touch me again and I'll kill ya.' When he came back, he had obviously only heard the 'touch me again' part and interpreted that as an invitation. So I decked him. He crawled away, and we all commented that he was an idiot." She also told the interviewer, "The vast majority of my peers never have and never will require sexual harassment training. They were taught by their parents to treat people with dignity, good manners, and respect" (Gutmann 160).

92. Francke 249

93. Browne, "Women at War," 171

94. Gutmann 155, 197

95. Elaine Donnelly, "Social Fiction in the Ungendered Military," *Washington Times*, April 7, 1997. Donnelly has been a tireless and important defender of the traditional culture of the military.

96. Dalton Pregnancy Policy, SECNAVINST 1000, ASN (MERA), February 6, 1995, 1. URL: http://neds.nebt.daps.mil/Directives/1000_10.pdf.

97. Browne, "Women at War," 192

98. Quoted in Kate O'Beirne, "An Army of Jessicas," *National Review*, May 19, 2003. Author Stephanie Gutmann writes, "A single mother searching for a safe, friendly, compact community decamps at a military base and finds subsidized day care, health insurance for herself and her dependents, a pension program, a housing allowance, and Family Care Centers to listen to her problems." (Gutmann 131)

99. Browne, "Women at War," 206

100. Gutmann 23

101. Browne, "Women at War," 198. The roaring economy had something to do with this too.

102. O'Beirne, "An Army of Jessicas"

103. The traditionalist Marines, notably, were an exception to the recruitment trend (Browne, "Women at War," 197).

104. Dan Barry, "What Firefighters Do the Rest of the Time," *New York Times*, December 15, 2002.

6. INVESTIGATION: WATERGATE'S REVENGE

1. P.J. O'Rourke, "The Bill Show," *The Atlantic Monthly*, March 2003.

2. Interview with Lanny Davis.

3. Ibid.

4. *Morrison v. Olson*, 487 U.S. 654 (1988). URL: http://laws.findlaw.com/us/487/654.html

5. James B. Stewart, *Blood Sport* (New York: Simon & Schuster, 1996), 265. The investigation dragged on so long partly because Hillary made "factually false" statements under oath minimizing her role in the firings ("Ray: First Lady's Answers False in Travel Office Probe, But No Prosecution," *CNN.com*, October 18, 2000. URL: http://www.cnn.com/2000/ALLPOLITICS/stories/10/18/travel.office/)

6. Benjamin Wittes, *Starr* (New Haven: Yale University Press, 2002), 32.

7. The case that precipitated the suit had all the hallmarks of a typical independent counsel case. It arose from a minor dispute in the early 1980s between Congress, which subpoenaed EPA documents, and the Reagan administration, which refused to hand them over. The matter produced a two-and-a-half-year congressional investigation, which in turn resulted in allegations of untruthful congressional testimony against the assistant attorney general, Theodore Olson (*Morrison v. Olson*, 1988). The matter of Olson's testimony was handed over to an independent counsel, who took two years to clear him (Dale Russakoff, "Theodore Olson is Free At Last," *Washington Post*, March 23, 1989).

8. Wittes 69. It is worth noting that conservatives and *National Review* celebrated this dissent at the time. Liberals only grew to appreciate it with Clinton's troubles, and aren't so taken with the rest of Scalia's jurisprudence, although his independent counsel opinion grew directly out of it.

9. Interview with Bernie Nussbaum

10. Bob Woodward, *Shadow* (New York: Touchstone, 1999), 229.

11. Interview with Bernie Nussbaum

12. *Morrison v. Olson,* 1988

13. Woodward 263

14. Interview with Bernie Nussbaum

15. Hillary Rodham Clinton, *Living History* (New York: Simon & Schuster, 2003), 215.

16. Interview with Bernie Nussbaum

17. David Gergen, *Eyewitness to Power* (New York: Simon & Schuster, 2000), 286–289, 290.

18. Clinton 200

19. Gergen 289–290

20. Michael Isikoff, *Uncovering Clinton* (New York: Three Rivers Press, 1999), 35.

21. Larry J. Sabato and S. Robert Lichter, "When Should the Watchdogs Bark?" (Washington, D.C.: Center for Media and Public Affairs, 1994), 9. Indeed, the *Los Angeles Times, Newsweek,* and NBC News would all at one time or another go to extraordinary lengths to try to avoid publishing or airing responsibly reported stories related to Clinton's sexual excess.

22. Interview with Lanny Davis

23. Stewart 212

24. *Morrison v. Olson,* 1988

25. Michael Kelly, "Total War," *The New Republic,* February 3, 1997.

26. "Another Independent Counsel for the Clinton Cabinet," *Newsday* (New York), May 14, 1998.

27. Interview with Robert "Bear" Bryant

28. Joe Conason and Gene Lyons, *The Hunting of the President* (New York: St. Martin's Press, 2000), 352.

29. Woodward 237–238

30. Tim Weiner, "Republicans on Whitewater Panel Want Investigation Into Whether Witnesses Lied," *New York Times,* June 22, 1996.

31. Interview with former Republican congressional staffer

32. Wittes 30

33. Sidney Blumenthal, *The Clinton Wars* (New York: Farrar, Straus and Giroux, 2003), 100.

34. Interview with Kenneth Starr

35. Wittes 74–73. Hilary writes that "Fiske's team was sending so many subpoenas that we had to have an organized system for searching files and providing responses" (Clinton 222).

36. Wittes 101

37. Ibid.

38. Wittes 104; Byron York, "El Sid, Vicious," *National Review*, June 30, 2003.

39. Interview with Sol Wisenberg

40. "Remarks by President Clinton at a White House Press Conference," *The Associated Press*, June 28, 2000.

41. Byron York, "The McDougal Pardon," *National Review*, February 19, 2001.

42. Wittes 104

43. Ibid., 109

44. Ibid., 224

45. Ibid., 125

46. Wittes 94. Even though Fiske had already issued a report about the suicide of Vince Foster, for instance, Starr took three years to duplicate Fiske's conclusion in much greater detail.

47. Gail Sheehy, *Hillary's Choice* (New York: Ballantine Books, 1999), 206.

48. Susan Schmidt and Michael Weisskopf, *Truth at Any Cost* (New York: HarperCollins, 2000), 15.

49. Wittes 100; Robert W. Ray, "Final Report of the Independent Counsel In Re: Madison Guaranty Savings & Loan Association," January 5, 2001, 122, 129. These records seemed to contradict her account to investigators of some of her Rose work.

50. Ray, "Final Report," i

51. Ibid., 22

52. Ibid., 94

53. Joseph Lelyveld, "In Clinton's Court," *New York Review of Books*, May 29, 2003.

54. It is telling that the Clintons paid so little attention to the Whitewater investment—McDougal was just supposed to make money for them. Hillary Clinton writes that in 1986, "For the first time since we became partners in 1978, I demanded to see the books. I've been asked why I had never done that before and how I could have been so ignorant of McDougal's actions. I've asked myself that too." (Clinton 197)

55. David Maraniss, *First in His Class* (New York: Touchstone Books, 1996), 336.

56. Senator Fred Thompson et al., Report of the Committee on Government Affairs, U.S. Senate, 1997 Special Investigation, Section II, 1.

57. Charles G. La Bella and James DeSarno, "Interim Report for Attorney General Janet Reno and FBI Director Louis J. Freeh," July 16, 1998, found in "Janet Reno's Stewardship of the Justice Department: A Failure to Serve the Ends of Justice," Tenth Report by the Committee on Government Reform, U.S. House of Representatives, December 13, 2000, 302.

58. Dick Morris, *Behind the Oval Office* (New York: Random House, 1997), 151. He added: "You want me to issue executive orders; I can't focus on a thing but the next fund-raiser. Hillary can't, Al can't—we're all getting sick and crazy because of it."

59. Thompson, Section II, 17

60. Thomas B. Edsall and Edward Walsh, "FEC Issues Record Fines in Democrats' Scandals," *Washington Post*, September 21, 2002; La Bella and DeSarno, "Interim Report," 223.

61. La Bella and DeSarno, "Interim Report," 223–224; Elizabeth Drew, *The Corruption of American Politics* (New York: The Overlook Press, 1999), 96.

62. Drew 97

63. Thompson, Section II, 16

64. Lanny J. Davis, *Truth to Tell* (New York: Free Press, 1999), 103.

65. Thompson, Section III, 6

66. Louis J. Freeh, "Memo to Attorney General Janet Reno," November 24, 1997, found in "Janet Reno's Stewardship of the Justice Department: A Failure to Serve the Ends of Justice," Tenth Report by the Committee on Government Reform, U.S. House of Representatives, December 13, 2000, 201–202; Thompson, Preface, i

67. Drew 130

68. Freeh, "Memo to Attorney General Janet Reno," 202

69. Ibid., 202–203. Clinton explained the approach himself at a DNC luncheon at the Hay Adams Hotel on December 7, 1995: "We realized that we could run these ads through the Democratic Party, which meant we could raise money in $20,000 and $50,000 and $100,000 blocks. So we didn't have to do it all in $1,000 and run down what I can spend, which is limited by law so that is what we've done." (Freeh, "Memo to Attorney General Janet Reno," 203) A few months later, he elaborated at another

Hay Adams event: "In the last quarter of last year... we spent about $1 million per week to advertise our point of view to somewhere between 26 and 42 percent of the American electorate.... The lead that I enjoy today in public opinion polls is about one-third due to that advertising.... I cannot overstate to you the impact that these paid ads have had." [Christopher Hitchens, *No One Left to Lie To* (London: Verso, 1999), 57]

70. La Bella and DeSarno, "Interim Report," 307

71. Ibid., 247–251

72. Ibid., 250–254

73. "Janet Reno's Stewardship of the Justice Department: A Failure to Serve the Ends of Justice," Tenth Report by the Committee on Government Reform, U.S. House of Representatives, December 13, 2000, 92–93.

74. Freeh, "Memo to the Attorney General," 211

75. Drew 131

76. Thompson, Section II, 4, 12, and Section XIII, 73

77. Thompson, Section II, 6–13. There were the usual farcical touches of a Clinton scandal. DNC fund-raiser Johnny Chung, who visited the White House roughly fifty times between 1994 and 1996, would sometimes sit outside Hillary's office and just stare at her pictures, in a sign of his oft-professed devotion to her. In early 1996, an operator named Yogesh Gandhi wanted to give the president the Gandhi World Peace Award. This was quite an honor, considering a previous recipient had been Ryoichi Sasakawa who, in the words of the *Los Angeles Times*, was a "billionaire former war crimes suspect who made his fortune promoting motorboat gambling." (Thompson, Section IX, 1–2 and Section X, 5–7) The White House wouldn't let Gandhi give the president the award, so he contributed $325,000 to the DNC, which then allowed him to quickly hand it off to him at a fund-raiser (Drew 128). (The money was eventually returned.)

78. Thompson, Section II, 2

79. Drew 105

80. Thompson, Section II, 25

81. Edward Timperlake and William C. Triplett II, *Year of the Rat* (Washington, D.C.: Regnery, 1998), 74–75.

82. Thompson, Section II, 25

83. Drew 92–93

84. "Janet Reno's Stewardship of the Justice Department," 95

85. Drew 106

86. Thompson, Section II, 12

87. Ibid., 13

88. Blumenthal 292

89. Hitchens 58

90. Thompson, Section II, 3

91. "Janet Reno's Stewardship of the Justice Department," vii

92. Carolyn Skorneck, "Attorney General Rejects Call for Special Prosecutor," *Associated Press*, November 8, 1996.

93. Interview with Eric Holder

94. "Janet Reno's Stewardship of the Justice Department,"15–17

95. Ibid., 7–8

96. Ibid., 60; Thompson, Section VII

97. H.R. Conf. Rpt. No. 103-511, 103rd Cong., 2nd Sess., quoted in Jack Maskell, "Independent Counsel Provisions: An Overview of the Operation of the Law," *Congressional Research Service*, March 20, 1998, 4.

98. La Bella and DeSarno, "Interim Report," 235, 307

99. Edsall and Walsh, "FEC Issues Record Fines"

100. Interview with Eric Holder

101. Ibid.

7. SEX: GROPE FIRST, SMEAR LATER

1. Michael Isikoff, *Uncovering Clinton* (New York: Three Rivers Press, 1999), 350.

2. Poor Gene Lyons, the Arkansas journalist, trotted out this explanation on national television as the Lewinsky scandal was breaking. "If you take someone like the president, who a lot of women would find attractive if he came to fix their garbage disposal, and you make him the president of the United States, the alpha male of the United States of America, and you sexualize his image with a lot of smears and false accusations so that people think he's Tom Jones or Rod Stewart, then a certain irreducible number of women are going to act batty around him. And I'm not talking about her personally; I'm saying that's a prediction. And so there's every possibility, with what we've seen, that this could be an entirely innocent affair." (Michael Kelly, "Would You Believe He's a Victim?," *Washington Post*, February 18, 1998)

3. Isikoff 352

4. Barbara Olson, *Hell to Pay* (Washington, D.C.: Regnery, 1999), 91.

5. Kenneth Starr, *The Starr Report* (New York: Public Affairs, 1998) 36. Sidney Blumenthal writes of Clinton, "He knew...that this was not like the Kennedy era, when private lives had been kept private." [*The Clinton Wars* (New York: Farrar, Straus and Giroux, 2003), 344]

6. Jeffrey Toobin, *A Vast Conspiracy* (New York: Touchstone, 1999), 167–170.

7. David Tell, "All the President's Backstabbers," *The Weekly Standard*, June 28, 1999.

8. James B. Stewart, *Blood Sport* (New York: Simon & Schuster, 1996), 70.

9. Joe Conason and Gene Lyons, *The Hunting of the President* (New York: St. Martin's Press, 2000), 113.

10. Blumenthal 343

11. Germaine Greer wrote, "Part of the battle will be won if [women] can change their attitude towards sex, and embrace and stimulate the penis instead of taking it." In his history of the 1970s, *How We Got Here*, David Frum notes that, "While fewer than 40 percent of the women born before World War II had ever given or received oral sex, almost 80 percent of those born since the war have at least tried it."[David Frum, *How We Got Here* (New York: Basic Books, 2000), 198]

12. Isikoff 24

13. Toobin 84

14. Ibid., 174. MacKinnon asked—believing the answer was "no"—"whether women have a chance, structurally speaking and as a normal matter, even to consider whether they want to have sex or not."

15. Stuart Taylor, Jr., "Her Case Against Clinton," *The American Lawyer*, November 1996.

16. Toobin 174–175

17. Bob Woodward, *Shadow* (New York: Touchstone, 1999), 362.

18. Toobin 210

19. Woodward 362

20. Blumenthal 574

21. Toobin 149

22. Peter Baker, *The Breach* (New York: Scribner, 2000), 63.

23. Isikoff 31–33

24. Ibid., 47

25. George Stephanopoulos, *All Too Human* (New York: Little, Brown and Company, 1999), 54.

26. Ibid., 55–56

27. Ibid., 56, 58

28. Ibid., 68

29. Ibid., 61

30. "Governor and Mrs. Bill Clinton Discuss Adultery Accusations," *60 Minutes*, CBS News, January 26, 1992. At another point, Steve Kroft asks,

"I'm assuming from your answer that you're categorically denying that you ever had an affair with Gennifer Flowers." Clinton cryptically replies, "I've said that before and so has she." Try parsing that one. In a hilarious touch in the segment, Clinton blamed the Bush recession for his woes: "It was only when money came out, when the tabloid went down there offering people money to say that they had been involved with me that she changed her story. There is a recession on. Times are tough, and—and I think you can expect more and more of these stories as long as they're down there handing out money."

31. Isikoff 336

32. Stephanopoulos 65. During the taping of the segment, Hillary came on so strong, according to Kroft, "We found ourselves rationing her sound bites to keep her from becoming the dominant force in the interview." [Gail Sheehy, *Hillary's Choice* (New York: Ballantine Books, 1999), 2000]

33. Isikoff 56

34. Elizabeth Drew, *On the Edge* (New York: Touchstone, 1994), 387.

35. Isikoff 56

36. Ibid., 55–56, 225. This prompted an official grievance from a woman who had lost out to Flowers, which was upheld by a grievance committee and then squashed by a Clinton political appointee. As for the job, Clinton advised Flowers on the tapes, "If they ever ask if you'd talked to me about it, you can say no."

37. Isikoff 4

38. Stephanopoulos 228

39. James Stewart has a very detailed account of the troopers' story in *Bloodsport*, chapter 12 and 13.

40. Stewart 320. Even in 1995, Clinton was still mindful of the importance of keeping the troopers and their boss happy. He yelled at Dick Morris for telling a journalist that they had worked together on an ad in 1978 attacking Jim Guy Tucker—the current governor of Arkansas. Morris asked, "What the f— do you care?" Clinton replied, "He controls the state police!" (Sheehy 260)

41. Stewart 320–324, 351–352. Young later admitted calling the troopers at Clinton's request, but denied that he had made any threats.

42. Stewart 351, 356, 363. Stewart writes, "[David] Gergen himself knew little about what had gone on in Arkansas, so he checked with Betsey Wright about the troopers' allegations. She shrugged them off as old news, but Gergen was startled when she said that, as far she could tell, the troopers were telling the truth."

43. Taylor, Jr., "Her Case Against Clinton." Taylor writes, "After receiving a phone call from the president in which the Maraniss book was discussed, Wright, who now is executive vice president of the Wexler Group, a Washington lobbying firm, issued a statement through her lawyer denying Maraniss's account of these interviews. Maraniss responded that he had double-checked every detail with Wright, and she had confirmed them all, before publication."

44. Stewart 363. Hillary Clinton's dishonest way of putting it is, "Another trooper who reportedly claimed that Bill had offered him a federal job for his silence later signed an affidavit swearing it never happened." [Hillary Rodham Clinton, *Living History* (New York: Simon & Schuster, 2003), 208]

45. Stewart 364

46. Isikoff 6

47. Michael Hedges, "Sexual Harassment Suit Filed against President; Woman Claims Clinton Made Advances in '91," *Washington Times*, May 7, 1994.

48. Isikoff 95

49. Conason 344–345

50. Interview with Jones legal advisor

51. Taylor, Jr. "Her Case Against Clinton"

52. Jeffrey Rosen, "One Bite at the Apple," *The New Republic*, February 3, 1997.

53. Taylor, Jr. "Her Case Against Clinton"

54. Stewart 389

55. Isikoff 91

56. Toobin 156

57. Taylor, Jr. "Her Case Against Clinton"

58. Isikoff 20

59. Taylor, Jr. "Her Case Against Clinton"

60. Stewart 173

61. Joe Klein, *The Natural* (New York: Doubleday, 2002), 39.

62. Isikoff 22

63. Taylor, Jr. "Her Case Against Clinton"

64. Conason 122

65. Isikoff 16–17 and 40–45

66. Evan Thomas with Michael Isikoff, "Clinton v. Paula Jones," *Newsweek*, January 13, 1997. Stephanopoulos told the press, he writes, "that even if you believed that Clinton was a womanizer, it wasn't credible that he had acted this way with this woman at this time. That's just not his style, I said. Why I thought I knew that is hard for me to figure out now, but it made sense then." (Stephanopoulos 270)

67. Isikoff 87

68. Toobin 152 and Isikoff 185

69. Toobin 127–136

70. Isikoff 216

71. "Grand jury testimony of Monica S. Lewinsky—Day One," August 6, 1998. URL: http://www.chron.com/cgi-bin/auth/story.mpl/content/chronicle/special/clinton/testimony/lewinsky/lew20.html. This was Monica's very savvy, Clintonesque idea, in her own words: "The gist of it is, I thought that first Mrs. Clinton should do something publicly, maybe on a TV show or something, and talk about how difficult the case had been for her and on her daughter and that he would settle it and it would go away. And then the president should unannounced and unexpectedly go into the briefing room, make a brief statement that he—in an effort to put this behind him, you know, against his attorneys' advice, he was going to pay Ms. Jones whatever it was, however much she wanted, and so that this case would be over with."

72. Clinton 440

73. Toobin 48–49

74. Isikoff 119–120 and 328. When during the encounter Willey asked him if he were afraid that there were people around, Clinton said, in a perfectly characteristic touch, "Yeah, I've got a meeting, but I can be late."

75. Isikoff 121–123, 156, and 367–368. Tripp would maintain that Willey was excited, rather than upset, about Clinton's advance (Conason 287).

76. Isikoff 394

77. Blumenthal 438

78. Starr 55. The president initially referred to Monica as "Kiddo," which made her believe that he could not remember her name.

79. Isikoff 162

80. Ibid., 256, 393–394

81. Isikoff 141. Clinton learned of the ruling when he was attending a NATO-Russia summit in Paris. According to Strobe Talbott's account of the summit, Clinton's "mind was elsewhere. He had just learned that the Supreme Court had ruled that the Paula Jones sexual harassment case, dating back to his days as governor of Arkansas, could go forward while he was in office. From the moment he got the news, he seemed to be sleep-walking through the summit." [Strobe Talbot, *The Russia Hand* (New York: Random House, 2002), 247]

82. Woodward 373–374

83. Sheehy 270

84. Starr 49–51

85. Toobin 86

86. Starr 51

87. Ibid., 52–55

88. Isikoff 352

89. Starr 54

90. Ibid., 82

91. Toobin 87

92. Starr 39

93. Ibid., 58

94. Toobin 90

95. He describes her, for instance, as "alone, scared, sobbing" when later confronted by Starr's prosecutors (Blumenthal 354).

96. Isikoff 288

97. Starr 44

98. Byron York devastatingly dissected his testimony in the February 1999 *American Spectator*.

99. Isikoff 288

100. Starr 76

101. Ann Coulter, *High Crimes and Misdemeanors* (Washington, D.C.: Regnery, 1998), 54.

102. Toobin 242

103. Clinton 471

104. Sheehy 16

105. Ramesh Ponnuru, "I Still Don't Believe Her," *National Review Online*, June 4, 2003. URL: http://www.nationalreview.com/ponnuru/ponnuru060403.asp.

106. Toobin 258

107. Ibid., 244

108. Blumenthal 340

109. Clinton 466

110. Blumenthal 342

111. Ibid., 465

112. Clinton 452

113. "Jones v. Clinton," *CNN.com*. URL: http://www.cnn.com/ALLPOLITICS/resources/1998/clinton.jones/.

114. Waller R. Newell, "The Crisis of Manliness," *The Weekly Standard*, August 3, 1998.

115. Maureen Dowd, "Pulp Nonfiction," *New York Times*, September 13, 1998.

116. Posner 36

117. Starr 40–41

118. Christopher Hitchens, *No One Left to Lie To* (London: Verso, 1999), 78.

119. Ramesh Ponnuru, "Sexual Hangup," *National Review*, February 8, 1999. Ponnuru also writes, "It is not too much to say that contemporary liberalism is built programmatically on the sexual revolution. A wide array of government programs is necessary to further it or deal with its detritus, from sex education to child-care services for single mothers. And support for abortion and gay rights, as aspects of sexual freedom, is the emotional core of modern liberalism; it occupies the place that suspicion of corporate power did for an earlier generation of liberals."

120. Francis Fukayama, *The Great Disruption* (New York: Touchstone, 1999), 90.

121. Toobin 317

8. IMPEACHMENT: AN INDELIBLE STAIN

1. Interview with Kenneth Starr

2. Ibid. "Chagrined and disappointed"—a typical outburst by the crazed Ken Starr.

3. Interview with George Conway

4. Interview with Mickey Kantor

5. Michael Isikoff, *Uncovering Clinton* (New York: Three Rivers Press, 1999), 275.

6. Interview with Eric Holder

7. Byron York, "Beyond His Ken," *National Review*, April 22, 2002.

8. Richard A. Posner, *An Affair of State* (Cambridge: Harvard University Press, 1999), 51.

9. David Tell, "Now She Tells Us," *The Weekly Standard*, April 26, 1999.

10. Posner 50–51

11. David Tell, "Impeach the Perjurer," *The Weekly Standard*, September 28, 1998.

12. Peter Baker, *The Breach* (New York: Scribner, 2000), 433.

13. Jeffrey Toobin, *A Vast Conspiracy* (New York: Touchstone, 1999), 214–219.

14. Kenneth Starr, *The Starr Report* (New York: PublicAffairs, 1998), 159.

15. Starr 180–195, 222

16. Tell "Now She Tells Us"

17. Toobin 335

18. Starr 178

19. Posner 46

20. Starr 240–242

21. Posner 43

22. Ibid., 32–33. The alternative explanation is that Lewinsky voluntarily returned the gifts. But among other evidence, phone records confirm that Currie called Lewinsky the afternoon the gifts were returned; Lewinsky did not call Currie. Posner's discussion of this matter is particularly cogent.

23. Michael Waldman, *POTUS Speaks* (New York: Simon & Schuster, 2000), 34.

24. David Tell, "The Real State of the Union," *The Weekly Standard*, February 1, 1999.

25. Posner 41

26. Starr 228

27. Tell, "The Real State of the Union." Some of the other obstruction charges are not as clean-cut. Clinton's effort to find Lewinsky a job, his defenders argue, might have been—and certainly was initially—an attempt to keep a former girlfriend happy and quiet as a general matter, rather than explicitly to have her lie in the Jones case. The Jones case entered into the equation more explicitly as Lewinsky showed up on the witness list and then was served with a subpoena, but it might have been more difficult to prove obstruction in this instance than the others (Posner 40).

28. Consider an example of how nod-and-wink communication can work, drawn, as it happens, from elsewhere in the Clinton White House. White House counsel Lanny Davis would sometimes want to get White House lawyer Lanny Breuer's approval for one of his preemptive leaks without compromising him by telling him exactly what was going on. Davis explains how it worked. "My method was to ask him a series of hypothetical questions, à la Socrates, aimed at assessing the risks and ramifications of a particular deep-background private placement. I trusted his intelligence and political sensitivities to pick up my message." (Davis 201) Clinton, the Socrates of obstruction of justice, trusted Lewinsky and Betty Currie's antennae in exactly the same way.

29. Woodward 408

30. Posner 222

31. In an editorial meeting at *Newsweek* to discuss Michael Isikoff's budding story, one of the editors referred to Clinton's having committed an "impeachable offense." Isikoff was initially taken aback, then realized the potential impact of his story (Isikoff 329). Lanny Davis, when he first heard the allegations, told his wife: "This could be the worst story of the Clinton presidency. It could threaten the Clinton presidency itself." (Davis 22) Senator Daniel Patrick Moynihan said that if Clinton had sex in the Oval Office "it represents a disorder." (David Tell, "I Know of No Oath," *The Weekly Standard*, August 24, 1998)

32. Ramesh Ponnuru, "I Still Don't Believe Her," *National Review Online*, June 4, 2003. URL: http://www.nationalreview.com/ponnuru/ponnuru060403.asp.

33. Interview with Lanny Davis

34. Starr 247

35. Clinton made meritless claims of executive privilege over the testimony of aides about his sex life, and, in an appropriate touch, lied about them. He told reporters while on an Africa trip that he knew nothing about one of the assertions of executive privilege, when seven days earlier White House counsel Charles Ruff had filed a declaration with a court saying he had discussed the matter with him (Starr 248).

36. David Tell, "The Wages of Sid," *The Weekly Standard*, March 9, 1998. This line of attack was embraced by the likes of Garry Wills, a brilliant historian who writes embarrassingly unsophisticated political columns: "Time to impeach? Yes, probably. To impeach Kenneth Starr." [Garry Wills, "Right Time to Impeach Impeachable Starr," *Times Union* (Albany, NY), October 2, 1998]

37. Toobin 204

38. The prosecutors couldn't have stopped Lewinsky from calling him if she really wanted to. Indeed, when she was briefly out of the prosecutors' control back in the shopping mall, she tried to call Betty Currie. And by the end of the night she had a new lawyer, William Ginsburg, who would prove unremittingly hostile to Starr (Toobin 206).

39. They also say Carter might have tried to recall her just-mailed false affidavit in the Jones suit, thus perhaps erasing her perjury and Starr's leverage over her [Sidney Blumenthal, *The Clinton Wars* (New York: Farrar, Straus and Giroux, 2003), 354]. But even if this had been possible, it wouldn't have changed anything because Lewinsky was still guilty of another crime: attempting to suborn Linda Tripp's perjury in the Jones case.

40. Clinton 442

41. Toobin 216

42. Interview with Jackie Bennett

43. Benjamin Wittes, *Starr* (New Haven: Yale University Press, 2002), 13. The case was dropped after two and half years.

44. They were replaced by the lawyers from Texas. Jerome Marcus, one of the "elves," says of the Texas team: "They were fine lawyers, intelligent people, and very good people, who were committed to it more for the kind of reasons that George and I were committed to it, because it was a way of making a point about who this guy was. They're very good guys who in a million years would not have done this if they did not believe her allegations." He adds, "When the Texas lawyers came in, one of them used to say that the Skadden people would tell them, 'Well, you guys are the Branch Davidians.' And he was thrilled that that's what they thought. The Skadden people were terrified of those guys." (Interview with Jerome Marcus)

45. Isikoff, 83–84, 109–110

46. Interview with Jerome Marcus

47. Interview with George Conway

48. Interview with Jerome Marcus

49. Ibid.

50. Interview with George Conway

51. Toobin 115

52. Interview with George Conway

53. Ibid.

54. Ibid. "He had such an immense faith in his own ability to talk his way out of problems," says Marcus. "But a deposition is a very different place. It's hard, and you're not in control, even if you are the president of the United States." (Interview with Jerome Marcus)

55. Full disclosure: Lucianne Goldberg's son, Jonah, is a friend and a colleague.

56. Isikoff 230–231

57. Interview with Jerome Marcus

58. Interview with George Conway

59. This is what Hillary is referring to when she writes, "We later learned that Reno's recommendation was based on incomplete and false information provided to her by the OIC" [office of independent counsel]. (Clinton 442)

60. Interview with Jackie Bennett

61. Ibid.

62. Interview with Eric Holder

63. Interview with Lucianne Goldberg

64. Isikoff 237

65. Interview with Lucianne Goldberg

66. Ibid.

67. Blumenthal 372

68. Interview with Lucianne Goldberg. She adds: "What no one realizes is that those papers with the Monica stories didn't sell. And Ken Chandler, who was editor-in-chief then, he was getting very nudgy about the whole story because it didn't sell."

69. Ibid.

70. Ibid.

71. Interview with Jackie Bennett. Of course, Lucianne Goldberg's goal was never to help the prosecutors, but simply to get the story out. As for Matt Drudge, like any journalist, he wanted to be the first to break a huge story. *Newsweek's* editors could have learned a thing or two from him.

72. Isikoff 209

73. Interview with Sol Wisenberg

74. Ibid.

75. Baker 129. As Baker puts it, "All but five members of the House had voted to investigate Clinton."

76. Posner 182

77. Baker 443

78. David Tell, "A Sorry President," *The Weekly Standard*, September 14, 1998. There was a precedent for impeaching a president for such offenses—Watergate. Liberal Harvard historian Arthur Schlesinger, Jr., wrote in 1973 that Nixon and his henchmen "had engaged in a multitude of indictable activities," "in perjury, in subordination of perjury, in obstruction of justice, in destruction of evidence, in tampering with witnesses, in misprision of felony." These crimes, Schlesinger wrote, should not be "forgiven and forgotten for the sake of the presidency," but "exposed and punished for the sake of the presidency." (David Tell, "A Crooked President," *The Weekly Standard*, November 9, 1998). Of course, the root of Nixon's criminality was high-stakes political skullduggery, while Clinton's was frustrating a sexual harassment suit—albeit largely for political reasons. The resulting crimes, however, were remarkably similar.

79. Posner 55, 86

80. James Madison, Alexander Hamilton, and John Jay, *The Federalist Papers*, ed. Isaac Kramnick (London: Penguin Books, 1987), 380.

81. Posner 114

82. Baker 180–181

83. Ibid., 442

84. Toobin 278, 304

85. Interview with Kenneth Starr. Starr decided not to reach an agreement with Lewinsky unless she, per standard procedure in such cases, agreed to be interviewed by his prosecutors to assess her credibility.

86. Blumenthal 457–458

87. John M. Broder and Don Van Natta, Jr., "Clinton and Starr, a Mutual Admonition Society," *New York Times*, September 20, 1998.

88. Interview with Kenneth Starr

89. Ibid.

90. Interview with former Judiciary Committee staffer

91. Baker 203

92. Blumenthal 575

93. *Associated Press*, February 13, 1999.

94. Interview with Henry Hyde

95. Baker 442

96. Of course, Republicans shouldn't have voted to impeach if censure was their intention: Impeachment is a tool for seeking the removal of the president, not a way to express disapproval of him. Unfortunately, some moderate Republicans did vote for impeachment as a kind of censure (James Bennett and Alison Mitchell, "Four Who Said Yes on Impeaching Call for Censure," *New York Times*, December 22, 1998). The irony of impeachment's ultimate role as a "censure-plus" is that impeachment's most fervent conservative supporters opposed censure on constitutional grounds, as an extra-constitutional sanction on the presidency.

97. Baker 131

98. Bill said, "I think we saved the Constitution of the United States." (Baker 417) Hillary writes that it was "a colossal miscarriage of the Constitution." (Clinton 492)

99. Blumenthal 461

9. DOMESTIC SECURITY: QUEEN OF THE BUNNY PLANET

1. Paul Anderson, *Janet Reno* (New York: John Wiley & Sons, Inc., 1994) 135.

2. James B. Stewart, *Blood Sport* (New York: Simon & Schuster, 1996), 246.

3. Webb Hubbell, *Friends in High Places* (New York: William Morrow and Company, Inc., 1997), 7. "You think I *have* to appoint a woman, don't you, Webb?" Clinton asked his soon-to-be associate attorney general. Hubbell told Clinton he would be killed politically if he appointed a man. "The right person is out there," Hubbell insisted. "We just have to find her."

4. Hubbell 189

5. Interview with Bernie Nussbaum

6. Jeff Leen, "Miami Nice," *The New Republic*, March 21, 1994.

7. Anderson 74

8. Nancy Gibbs, "Truth, Justice, and the Reno Way," *Time*, July 12, 1993.

9. Anderson 260

10. Lincoln Caplan, "Janet Reno's Choice," *New York Times Magazine*, May 15, 1994.

11. Jeffrey Goldberg, "The Mystery of Janet Reno," *New York Times Magazine*, July 6, 1997.

12. Gibbs, "Truth, Justice, and the Reno Way"

13. Interview with Eric Holder

14. Dick Morris, *Behind the Oval Office* (New York: Random House, 1997), 228.

15. David B. Kopel and Paul H. Blackman, *No More Wacos* (Amherst, New York: Prometheus Books, 1997), 79–81.

16. Ibid., 160–163

17. As a PBS Frontline account puts it, "Although several of the surviving Branch Davidians insist that they did not start the fire, a panel of arson investigators concluded that the Davidians were responsible for igniting it, simultaneously, in at least three different areas of the compound. Unless they were deliberately set, the probability of the three fires starting almost simultaneously was highly unlikely, according to fire experts." URL: http://www.pbs.org/wgbh/pages/frontline/waco/topten.html#branch.

18. Kopel and Blackman, 163–164. Koresh had a long history of having sex with minors, but that wasn't an acute crisis justifying the final raid. As the PBS Frontline account explains, "FBI director Sessions, however, said the next day there was 'no contemporary evidence' of child abuse . . . And Reno revised her statement several months later, agreeing there was no evidence of ongoing child abuse by Koresh, who was wounded in the shootout on February 28, at Mt. Carmel, as the Branch Davidians' residence was known."

19. Elizabeth Drew, *On the Edge* (New York: Simon & Schuster, 1994), 132.

20. Interview with former FBI official

21. Bob Woodward, *Shadow* (New York: Simon & Schuster, 1999), 450. Freeh maintained generally warm relations with congressional Republicans who provided him a measure of political cover.

22. Interview with Dale Watson

23. Woodward 450

24. Sidney Blumenthal, *The Clinton Wars* (New York: Farrar, Straus and Giroux, 2003), 286.

25. Interview with Robert "Bear" Bryant

26. Interview with Bernie Nussbaum

27. Interview with former FBI official

28. Interview with Robert "Bear" Bryant

29. Ibid.

30. Ibid.

31. Mark Riebling, *The Wedge* (New York: Simon & Schuster, 2002), 455–456.

32. Henry Ruth and Kevin R. Reitz, *The Challenge of Crime* (Cambridge: Harvard University Press, 2003), 158–159.

33. Interview with Robert "Bear" Bryant

34. Michael Kirkland, "Reno Declares War on Deadbeat Dads," United Press International, December 22, 1994.

35. Interview with Robert "Bear" Bryant

36. Daniel Benjamin and Steven Simon, *The Age of Sacred Terror* (New York: Random House, 2002), 227.

37. Richard Lowry, "A Better Bureau," *National Review*, July 1, 2002.

38. Glenn R. Simpson, "Hesitant Agents: Why the FBI Took Nine Years to Shut Group It Tied to Terror," *Wall Street Journal*, February 27, 2002.

39. Benjamin and Simon 228. Only after September 11 did Congress relent and approve the "roving wiretap."

40. Lowry, "A Better Bureau"

41. Ibid. FISA allowed for this. It said that intelligence should be the "primary"—not the only—purpose of a FISA warrant.

42. Ronald Kessler, *The Bureau* (New York: St. Martin's Press, 2002), 365.

43. Scruggs won Reno over to the tighter interpretation of FISA during the Aldrich Ames spy case. He argued that the FBI had been having improper contacts with prosecutors, that the case was at risk, and that Reno might be called as a witness in the case to justify her FISA certifications. A shaken Reno told Scruggs to "make sure this did not happen again." (Attorney General's Review Team on the Handling of the Los Alamos Laboratory Investigation, "Final Report," May 2000, Declassified Version Released December 11, 2001, 712–713)

44. Kessler 366. OIPR used the threat of rejecting FISA applications as a tool of coercion to keep the FBI from talking to the criminal division, and warned the FBI that it would testify against it in court if it talked to anyone in the criminal division in such cases. A definitive Justice Department review of the Wen Ho Lee investigation, which was botched partly because of the way FISA was handled, concluded in December 2001: "As a result of these limitations, the FBI has come to view contact with the Criminal Division as both unproductive and dangerous: unproductive because of the constraints OIPR has placed on the advice the Criminal Division may provide, and dangerous because of the perception, again fostered by OIPR, that communication with the Criminal Division may jeopardize an anticipated or ongoing FISA."(Attorney General's Review Team on the Handling of the Los Alamos Laboratory Investigation, "Final Report," 13)

45. Attorney General's Review Team On the Handling of the Los Alamos Laboratory Investigation, "Final Report," 710

46. Kessler 439

47. Neil A. Lewis, "Court Overturns Limits on Wiretaps to Combat Terror," *New York Times*, November 19, 2002.

48. Interview with Jim Kallstrom

49. In addition, an FBI informant in San Diego was in contact with Nawaf al-Hazmi and Khalid al-Mihdhar, who were hijackers on Flight 77, which crashed into the Pentagon. But the informant subsequently said he had no idea about their terrorist connections. If there had been better communication between FBI headquarters and the San Diego field office, the two terrorists might have been put under surveillance. The congressional joint inquiry report into September 11 says, "CIA and FBI Headquarters had information tying al-Mihdhar and al-Hazmi to al-Qa'ida as early as January 2000 and later received information that they were in the United States. The San Diego field office received none of this information before September 11. As a result, the informant was not asked to collect information about the hijackers." ("Joint Inquiry into Intelligence Community Activities Before and After the Terrorist Attacks of September 11, 2001," Report of the Senate Select Committee on Intelligence and the House Permanent Select Committee on Intelligence, December 2002, 158–168. URL: http://www.gpoaccess.gov/serialset/creports/911.html.)

50. This was part of the predicate for the law enforcement environment in which the September 11 terrorists committed their atrocity. It is often the case that the true force of the mistakes of an administration aren't felt until it has left office, and so it was with the Clinton administration's politically correct law enforcement.

51. See Rowley's memo to the FBI at URL: www.time.com/time/covers/1101020603/memo.html. She continues, "Numerous high-ranking FBI officials who have made decisions or have taken actions which, in hindsight, turned out to be mistaken or just turned out badly (i.e., Ruby Ridge, Waco, etc.) have seen their careers plummet and end. This has in turn resulted in a climate of fear which has chilled aggressive FBI law enforcement action/decisions."

52. Kessler 439

53. Benjamin and Simon 347

54. Interview with Mike Rolince

55. Don Van Natta, Jr., "Government Will Ease Limits on Domestic Spying by FBI," *New York Times*, May 30, 2002.

56. Walter Pincus, "FBI Wary of Investigating Extremist Muslim Leaders; Agency May Rethink Hesitancy on Religious Figures," *Washington Post*, October 29, 2001. Pincus writes, "Five months before the February 26, 1993, bombing of the World Trade Center and three years after receiving intelligence about his alleged terrorist background, the FBI opened an investigation of Rahman. Approval to do so came only after months of internal haggling and discussions with Justice Department lawyers over the ramifications of focusing on a religious leader. Although the FBI placed Rahman's bodyguard and driver under loose surveillance, Rahman himself was never questioned or put before a grand jury. Nor were his offices bugged, according to a former senior FBI official. Records of Rahman's mosques in Brooklyn and Jersey City were never subpoenaed, and no wiretaps were put on the mosques' phones, the official said."

57. In their apologia for Clinton's terrorism policy called *The Age of Sacred Terror* two former Clinton National Security Council staffers, Daniel Benjamin and Steven Simon, try to blame the FBI for every counterterrorism failing in the 1990s, including the continuation of the attorney general's guidelines. They maintain that an NSC official asked the FBI in August 1998 whether it wanted relief from the guidelines. According to their account, the FBI didn't: "One reason for the inaction, the NSC thought, was that the Bureau, and perhaps the entire Department of Justice, was suffering from a case of political correctness. The Arab-American community had long complained about the FBI's treatment of Muslims; the Bureau's leadership, agents confirmed, was uneasy." (306) Although their account of the politically correct atmosphere is accurate, as we have seen, it came from the top. Benjamin and Simon are engaged in blame-shifting. President Clinton could at any time have ordered Janet Reno to change the attorneys general's guidelines, whatever the FBI allegedly thought. The guidelines were not lifted until May 2002 by Attorney General John Ashcroft.

58. Interview with Dale Watson

59. Simpson, "Hesitant Agents." This is an excellent report, by one of the *Journal's* best reporters.

60. Interview with Jim Kallstrom

61. James Goldsborough, "Out-of-Control Immigration," *Foreign Affairs*, September/October 2000.

62. The website of the Center for Immigration Studies is a treasure trove of immigration statistics. These numbers can be found online at http:// www.cis.org/topics/illegalimmigration.html

63. Jessica Vaughan, "Shortcuts to Immigration: The 'Temporary' Visa Program Is Broken," Center for Immigration Studies Backgrounder, January 2003. URL: http://www.cis.org/articles/2003/back103.html.

64. "Census Releases Immigrant Numbers for Year 2000," Center for Immigration Studies Analysis, June 4, 2002. The center notes, "The 31.1 million immigrants found in the 2000 Census is unparalleled in American history. It is more than triple the 9.6 million in 1970 and more than double the 14.1 million in 1980. The 11.3 million (or 57 percent) increase, from 19.8 million in 1990 to 31.1 million in 2000, is also without precedent in our history, both numerically and proportionately. Even during the great wave of immigration from 1900 to 1910, the foreign-born population grew by only 3.2 million (or 31 percent), from 10.3 million to 13.5 million." URL: http://www.cis.org/articles/2002/censuspr.html.

65. For more on this theme see the brilliant conservative apostate Michael Lind's *The Next American Nation* (New York: The Free Press, 1995). He calls multiculturalism "the de facto orthodoxy of the present American regime."

66. Andrew Bacevich, *American Empire* (Cambridge: Harvard University Press, 2002), 83.

67. Goldsborough "Out-of-Control Immigration"

68. Scot Lehigh, "Is The Door Open Too Wide?" *Boston Globe*, June 23, 1996. Lehigh writes, "The Jordan Commission proposed changes designed to phase down legal immigration from the current level—a yearly average of 773,000 from 1981 to 1990, some 1.1 million from 1991 to 1994—to about 550,000 a year over five to eight years. At the time, President Clinton offered lavish praise of those recommendations. Then, in January, Jordan died, and with her passing, the commission's recommendations lost momentum in the face of heavy opposition from big business. In March, Clinton flip-flopped, sending word to Congress that he no longer supported proposed reductions in legal immigration. As a result, any real chance of limiting legal immigration this year has been lost."

69. Malkin 196–197

70. Ibid., 74–76

71. Nicholas Confessore, "Borderline Insanity," *Washington Monthly*, May 2002.

72. Ibid.

73. Steven A. Camarota, "The Open Door: How Militant Islamic Terrorists Entered and Remained in the United States, 1993–2001," Center for Immigration Studies, May 2002, 39. URL: http://www.cis.org/articles/2002/theopendoor.pdf.

74. Confessore "Borderline Insanity"

75. Morris 123

76. George Stephanopoulos, *All Too Human* (New York: Little, Brown and Company, 1999), 340–341.

77. Dick Morris, "While Clinton Fiddled," *Wall Street Journal*, February 5, 2002.

78. The right made its contribution to the lawlessness, in the form of business interests for whom borders and immigration laws were an obstacle to employing cheap labor and of libertarian ideologues for whom borders and immigration laws were an infringement on absolute freedom. The Bush administration has tightened up immigration laws somewhat, but was considering a new amnesty for illegals before September 11 and supports continuing the current high levels of immigration.

79. As Steven A. Camarota, an analyst for the Center for Immigration Studies, writes, "Allowing those in the country illegally to hold jobs, receive driver's licenses, open bank accounts, and receive green cards, and failing to detain those who violate the law, conveys to terrorists and non-terrorists alike that one can violate U.S. immigration laws with little difficulty." (Camarota, "The Open Door," 36)

80. Interview with Jim Kallstrom

81. The following section of this chapter is drawn from my 2002 story "Profiles in Cowardice," *National Review*, January 28, 2002.

82. Heather Mac Donald, *Are Cops Racist?* (Chicago: Ivan R. Dee, 2003), 164.

83. Lowry, "Profiles in Cowardice." Other countries have had exactly this experience. In a 1986 case, a pregnant woman booked on an El Al flight from Heathrow to Tel Aviv was pulled aside (pregnant women don't usually travel alone). After questioning, it was discovered that, unbeknownst to her, her Jordanian boyfriend had planted a bomb in her carry-on bag that would have killed all 375 people on her flight.

84. The Bush administration has also been too politically correct when it comes to profiling at airports.

10. THE WORLD: McGOVERN WITHOUT THE CONSCIENCE

1. Thomas W. Lippman, *Madeleine Albright and the New American Diplomacy* (Boulder, CO: Westview Press, 2000), 280–281.

2. George Stephanopoulos, *All Too Human* (New York: Little, Brown & Company, 1999), 216.

3. Andrew J. Bacevich, *American Empire* (Cambridge: Harvard University Press, 2002), 36.

4. Bacevich 35

5. Mimi Hall and Charisse Jones, "Clinton: We Were Wrong on Slavery," *USA Today*, March 25, 1998.

6. Christopher Caldwell, "Presidential Apologies Are an 'Inexpensive Virtue,'" *Wall Street Journal*, March 15, 1999. Caldwell notes that Clinton's apologies were often worded in a deliberately weasely way: "Reporters who were traveling with the president in Africa said he deliberately avoided the word 'sorry' on the lawyerly advice that it might leave the U.S. liable to pay reparations under international law."

7. Lippman 183–184

8. Ibid., 283

9. James Kurth has an excellent discussion of the "post-modern" Clinton foreign policy in an essay in Andrew J. Bacevich and Eliot A. Cohen, eds., *War Over Kosovo* (New York: Columbia University Press, 2001).

10. Michael Mandelbaum, "Foreign Policy as Social Work," *Foreign Affairs*, January/February 1996.

11. At the July 2000 meeting of the G-8, for instance, Clinton helped lead the way on the creation of an international school lunch program. "One of the best things we can do to get children in school is to provide them at least one nutritious meal there every day," he said. [Gary T. Dempsey, *Fool's Errands* (Washington, D.C.: Cato Institute, 2001), 158]

12. Lippman 282

13. Ibid., 9

14. Ibid., 59

15. Ibid., 294

16. Ibid., 281

17. *U.S. Department of State Dispatch*. Washington, D.C.: August 1, 1994. Vol. 5, Iss. 31.; 522–523.

18. Lippman 273

19. Mark Riebling, *Wedge* (New York: Touchstone, 1994), 453. Riebling recounts visiting Langley in 1994: "I heard little about spying or counter-spying, defectors or double agents, disinformation or deception. Instead, I heard about the agency's new focus on 'global crime.' Money laundering, alien smuggling, drug running, toxic-waste dumping, computer hacking—these were 'the new threats'"; "Remarks by the President to Staff of the CIA and Intelligence Community," Central Intelligence Agency, McLean, Virginia, July 14, 1995. URL: http://www.fas.org/irp/news/1995/950714cia.htm.

20. *U.S. Department of State Dispatch*, "Fact Sheet: Global Environmental Issues." Washington, D.C.: July 1995.

21. Paul Lewis, "Western Lands, Except U.S., Ban Export of Hazardous Waste," *New York Times*, March 26, 1994.

22. Thomas W. Lippman, "With Wirth in Position, Old Lines Lose Weight," *Washington Post*, June 30, 1994.

23. Margaret Kriz, "The Greening of Free Trade," *National Journal*, November 20, 1999.

24. Sonya Ross, "Clinton Promises Renewed Push for Senate Ratification of Treaty on Deserts," *Associated Press*, March 31, 1998.

25. Department of State, Public Notice 2876, "Revised Notice of Guidelines for Determining Comparability of Foreign Programs for the Protection of Sea Turtles in Shrimp Trawl Fishing Operations."

26. Rick Weiss and Justin Gillis, "U.S. 'Observers' Lobby Against Trade Curbs on Biotechnology; Accord Would be First to Target Genetically Engineered Products," *Washington Post*, February 13, 1999.

27. Marla Cone, "Global Wildlife Summit Under Way; Environment: Officials from 124 Nations Gather in Florida to Draft Policy on Endangered Animal and Plant Species," *Los Angeles Times*, November 7, 1994.

28. *U.S. Department of State Dispatch*, "Fact Sheet"

29. Gary Lee, "Experts Seek Global Treaty On Toxic Ocean Pollutants," *Washington Post*, November 4, 1995.

30. Interview with former senior Clinton administration official. The same dynamic held in the international effort to ban child soldiers. "Everyone took it to mean," says the Pentagon official, "'No nine-year-olds in Rwanda with AK-47s.' That's bad. But the NGOs took it to mean, you can't join the military until you are eighteen. You can't do any recruiting activity. And again, it's our allies. I'm sitting there in a meeting with these guys, I say, 'You know, this is all about little kids in Africa. This is really what we're talking about, and, you're getting me on seventeen-year-olds graduating from high school in the United States wanting to join the Air Force? You're just trying to screw us.' And they would just look at us and say, 'We would never do that,' and they're laughing the whole time."

31. Sidney Blumenthal, *The Clinton Wars* (New York: Farrar, Straus and Giroux, 2003), 635.

32. "I think," Clinton said at a Third Way summit in Italy in 1999, "virtually every European country has done a better job than the United States in providing adequate family leave policies, adequate childcare policies, adequate supports." The summit's communique emphasized the participants' commitment to more domestic spending and regulation in "a new international social compact." (Blumenthal 670, 674)

33. It helped that both areas had domestic political advantages among blacks and Hispanics respectively.

34. Madeleine K. Albright, "Colombia's Struggles, and How We Can Help," *New York Times*, August 10, 1999.

35. See William J. Clinton, "The Year 2000 State of the Union: The Economy, Education, and Healthcare," *Vital Speeches of the Day*, February 15, 2000, 263.

36. In some precincts of the administration, there was also probably lingering romanticism about Marxist guerrillas.

37. Presidential Decision Directive/NSC-73, August 3, 2000.

38. Warren Christopher, *Chances of a Lifetime* (New York: Scribner, 2001), 237–238.

39. Ibid., 242

40. Lippman 310

41. Steven A. Holmes, *Ron Brown* (New York: John Wiley & Sons, Inc., 2000), 263–264.

42. Bacevich 94

43. Holmes 265

44. The liberalization of South Korea and Pinochet's Chile are classic examples of economic growth creating an entrepreneurial class that successfully pushes for political change.

45. According to Samuel Huntington, "In case after case, country after country, the dictates of commercialism have prevailed over other purposes including human rights, democracy, alliance relationships, maintaining the balance of power, technology export controls, and other strategic and political considerations described by one administration official as 'stratocrap and globaloney.'" (Samuel P. Huntington, "The Erosion of American National Interests," *Foreign Affairs*, September/October 1997)

46. Jeffrey E. Garten, "Clinton's Emerging Trade Policy," *Foreign Affairs*, June/July 1993. This was the symbolic import of the administration creating an Economic Security Council to complement the National Security Council. [Bill Gertz, *Betrayal* (Washington, D.C.: Regnery, 1999), 97]

47. Interview with Dick Morris

48. Interview with Tony Lake

49. Jeffrey E. Garten, "Is America Abandoning Multilateral Trade?" *Foreign Affairs*, November/December 1995.

50. Mandelbaum 26–27

51. Lawrence F. Kaplan, "The Selling of American Foreign Policy," *The Weekly Standard*, April 28, 1997.

52. Lippman 217

53. Kaplan, "The Selling of American Foreign Policy"

54. Ashton B. Carter and William J. Perry, *Preventive Defense* (Washington, D.C.: Brookings Institution Press, 1999), 4, 76.

55. Interview with Gary Milhollin

56. "The Proliferation Primer," A Majority Report of the Subcommittee on International Security, Proliferation, and Federal Services, Committee on Governmental Affairs, United States Senate (January 1998), 37. The Bush administration had already loosened up export controls with the end of the Cold War. Clinton went all the way. "One reason I ran for president," Clinton wrote, "was to tailor export controls to the realities of a post-Cold War world." (Gertz 83)

57. The Proliferation Primer," 37

58. Gary Milhollin, "Testimony Before the Senate Armed Services Committee," July 9, 1998.

59. "The Proliferation Primer," 37. The administration adopted the tolerant, open-minded attitude to non-proliferation enshrined in the Nuclear Non-Proliferation Treaty of 1968. The treaty, which was supposed to maintain the exclusivity of the nuclear club, welcomed the spread of nuclear technology for "peaceful" uses. Membership created a strong presumption of pure intentions. Countries like Iraq, Iran, and North Korea would join precisely in order to get "peaceful" nuclear power that they could divert to sinister uses later. The Clinton administration preferred non-proliferation agreements on this non-restrictive model. Countries would be brought into agreements in the hopes that the very act of signing up would somehow reform them.

60. Henry D. Sokolski, *Best of Intentions* (Westport, CT: Praeger, 2001), 74–76.

61. Ibid., 76–78

62. Strobe Talbott, *The Russia Hand* (New York: Random House, 2002), 261. Talbott writes, "For five years, we'd listened to Russian officials point over their shoulders at the Duma and say, 'Do what we want or you'll have to deal with those crazy people!' Now we were doing much the same thing."

63. Gertz 4

64. Sokolski 78

65. Ibid., 79

66. "The Proliferation Primer," 3–14

67. Ibid., 3–4

68. Edward Timperlake and William C. Triplett II, *Year of the Rat* (Washington, D.C.: Regnery, 1998), 170.

69. "The Proliferation Primer," 4

70. Gary Milhollin, "Testimony Before the House Committees on International Relations and National Security," June 17, 1998.

71. Seth Faison, "U.S. and China Agree on Pact to Fight Piracy," *New York Times*, June 18, 1996.

72. Gertz 141, 164

73. Milhollin, "Testimony Before the House Committees on International Relations and National Security," June 17, 1998.

74. Timperlake and Triplett 173–174; Gertz 164. As Gary Milhollin points out, the purpose of the nation's sanctions laws was to keep countries from importing American missile technology while proliferating missile technology to other countries at the same time. The shift to Commerce, coupled with a change in Chinese proliferation strategy, effectively gutted these laws. (Milhollin, "Testimony Before the House Committees on International Relations and National Security," June 17, 1998)

75. This handed important national security determinations over to corporations, and asked them to ignore their bottom lines, when the whole exercise had been created to enhance their bottom lines in the first place. Silicon Graphics sold Russia four supercomputers in the fall of 1996 that the company claimed it thought would go to "environmental and ecological purposes," but instead wound up in a nuclear weapons lab. Russia's minister of atomic energy boasted that the computers were "ten times faster than any previously available in Russia." China's military reaped a similar windfall. The *New York Times* reported in June 1997 that "China has gone on a shopping spree" for supercomputers. The Chinese Academy of Sciences—developer of the DF-5 intercontinental missile—noted that the computers provided "computational power previously unknown," now available to "all the major scientific and technological institutes across

China." The Commerce Department obligingly avoided sanctioning Silicon Graphics and other computer makers for these sales in violation of U.S. export laws (what was left of them.) ("The Proliferation Primer," 39–41; Milhollin,"Testimony Before the House Committee on National Security," November 13, 1997)

76. Gary Milhollin, "Clinton's Super Computer Push," *Asian Wall Street Journal*, September 19, 2000. Milhollin wrote, "Since January 1, 1999, the computer industry has given more than $3.2 million to the Democratic National Committee, Mr. Clinton's party machine, making it the committee's fourth largest industry contributor, according to the independent Center for Responsive Politics. The industry also shelled out money to the Republican National Committee, but not so generously. It was the ninth largest donor with $1.9 million, according to the center."

77. Sokolski 80

78. Milhollin, "Testimony Before the House Committees on International Relations and National Security," June 17, 1998. Milhollin argued, "India, of course, has watched this happen. India watched China help Pakistan make not only missiles but the nuclear warheads to go on them. India also watched the United States invent every excuse possible not to do anything about it. America asked the Indians to show restraint in nuclear testing, but America was unwilling to put restraints on its own satellite companies by sanctioning China. The Indians no doubt concluded that Uncle Sam was against the spread of the bomb unless it might cost him something. It should not surprise us if our non-proliferation policy lacks credibility."

79. Samuel Huntington argues in *The Clash of Civilizations* that weapons proliferation represents the bleaching away of Western power: "Such weapons, first, enable [non-Western] states to establish their dominance over other states in their civilization and region, and, second, provide them with the means to deter intervention in their civilization and region by the United States or other external powers." [Samuel Huntington, *The Clash of Civilizations* (New York: Touchstone, 1996), 186]

80. Senator Thad Cochran, "Stubborn Things: A Decade of Facts About Ballistic Missile Defense," United States Senate, September 2000, 19.

81. "The Proliferation Primer," 70

82. The administration successfully pushed the Chemical Weapons Convention to ratification in the Senate in 1997, but suffered setbacks in the rest of its arms control agenda: It tried to upgrade the Biological Weapons Convention (unsuccessfully), attempted to seal and ratify START II and START III agreements on offensive nuclear weapons with the Russians (unsuccessfully), lobbied for ratification of the Comprehensive Test Ban Treaty (unsuccessfully), and sought to re-negotiate with the Russians, in order to preserve, the Anti-Ballistic Missile Treaty (unsuccessfully). All these agreements were flawed for their own reasons, but all served to constrain the United States. Just to consider the nuclear pacts: the START agreements would reduce existing U.S. offensive weapons, the CTBT would degrade the reliability of the remaining U.S. arsenal and make it impossible to add new weapons, and the ABM Treaty would forbid missile defenses, therefore supposedly further lessening the need for offensive weapons.

83. "Stubborn Things," 16

84. "Stubborn Things," 51

85. Keith Payne, "Action-Reaction Metaphysics and Negligence," *Washington Quarterly*, Autumn 2001. According to Payne, their subsequent buildup was the biggest in history, from 1,547 intercontinental ballistic missile warheads in 1972 to 6,420 in 1985. He quotes Carter defense secretary Harold Brown saying of the Soviets and offensive missiles in 1979, "When we build, they build; when we stop building, they nevertheless continue to build." For an excellent discussion, on which I rely here, of the flaws of arms control orthodoxy with regard to missile defenses see Keith Payne's essay "The Soviet Union and Strategic Defense: The Failure and Future of Arms Control" in the Winter 1986 issue of *Orbis*.

86. As early as 1993, Les Aspin was saying "the new possessors of nuclear weapons may not be deterrable"—but the administration just couldn't bring itself to act on the insight ("Stubborn Things," 13).

87. "Stubborn Things," 9. Referring to the derisive name given to Reagan-era missile defense plans, Les Aspin declared "the end of the Star Wars era." [Bradley Graham, *Hit to Kill* (New York: Public Affairs, 2001), 23]

88. "Stubborn Things," 31. Sen. Joe Lieberman told a Republican colleague that this proposal was entirely political in nature, meant to deny a potential issue to Bob Dole (interview with former Republican Senate staffer).

89. Graham 83–100

90. In 1995, just as pro-missile-defense Republicans were taking over Congress, the National Intelligence Estimate—the collective work of all the nation's intelligence agencies—reported that no rogue nation would "develop or otherwise acquire a ballistic missile in the next fifteen years that could threaten the contiguous forty-eight states and Canada." (Small comfort for residents of Hawaii and Alaska.) This was convenient for the Clinton administration, which could tell Republicans there was consequently no urgent need for a defense. But only two years earlier, the NIE had said that no such projections could be made reliably beyond ten years. Curious. (Graham 32)

91. Early on, the commission was getting stiffed by the CIA; commission members confronted director George Tenet in person about it, and he quickly relented. "If there was a single moment in the late 1990s when events began to turn in favor of those advocating a national missile defense," Bradley Graham writes, "this was it." (Graham 31)

92. Graham 44

93. "Stubborn Things," 47

94. "Stubborn Things," 53. The bill was the inspiration of an aggressive GOP Senate staffer named Mitch Kugler.

95. Talbott 185–186. Another senior Clinton official says of Talbott's book, "Strobe has a very powerful paragraph, which Clinton hated. The paragraph in which he said that Clinton understood Yeltsin because of the similarities between them."

96. "[W]hen President Clinton," Tony Lake writes, "encouraged Boris Yeltsin to pursue a modern reelection strategy in 1996—relying on television, political consultants, and other such tools—we were reinforcing Yeltsin's dependence on the oligarchs, their wallets, and their leverage. This had the dual disadvantage of increasing the kleptos' political influence while undercutting the role of civil society as a link between Moscow elites and the people." [Anthony Lake, 6 *Nightmares* (Boston: Little, Brown & Company, 2000), 193–194]. In an amusing understatement, Sidney Blumenthal writes that as of 1999, "The Clinton-Yeltsin relationship had been warm and productive thus far, though the hoped-for fostering of reform in Russia had not been wholly successful." (Blumenthal 637–638)

97. Interview with former administration official

98. Meanwhile, in late 1999 the administration also was pursuing Senate ratification of another key part of its arms-control agenda, the Comprehensive Test Ban Treaty (CTBT). The CTBT, banning all nuclear tests by its signatories, was straight out of the missal of arms control orthodoxy, with all its attendant flaws. Its premise was a superstition. Once they were made environmentally safe, nuclear tests by the U.S. and other declared nuclear powers posed no danger whatsoever and had no bearing on whether other, less responsible nations would develop or test nuclear weapons. The tests were simply considered unseemly. The CTBT would have had its most direct effect on the already existing nuclear powers. The more honest arms controllers admitted their ultimate motivation: to prevent the U.S. from developing a new weapon, and to force the existing arsenal to wither on the vine. Clinton hyped the treaty as "the longest sought, hardest fought prize in arms control history." (Susan Milligan, "Treaty Troubles Stagger Clinton; Perceived Flaws, Partisanship Fuel GOP Fight Against Atom Pact," *The Boston Globe*, October 7, 1999). "The CTBT was going to be the centerpiece of their legacy in arms control," says a former Republican Senate staffer. "They thought they could sign almost anything, and send it up to the Senate for ratification. They were shocked by the opposition. They never imagined that this would be the first treaty since Versailles flushed down the toilet. They became so desperate that they had Bob Bell, a former Clinton NSC official and a big advocate of arms control, come to the Hill to brief senators just days after the poor guy had had surgery. I still remember him shuffling in, painfully sitting down on the chair, and pouring on the case for this treaty. No one was convinced. We just gained more and more votes every day." (Interview with former Republican staffer). Republicans didn't just deny Democrats the two-thirds majority they needed for ratification, they mustered a majority, fifty-one votes, against the treaty. (Richard Lowry, "Test-Ban Ban," *National Review*, November 8, 1999)

99. Graham 97

100. Graham 233–234. Deutch told Graham, "I didn't think the administration's proposal had been genuine. I don't believe they put it forward because they really wanted to see it developed. I think they put it forward because they wanted to take the issue out of the 2000 election and sort of quiet it down."

101. Graham 305. When Sandy Berger warned Putin that if Bush, or even Gore, were elected it would be worse for the Russians, Putin smiled and commented sarcastically, "You're a dangerous man." (Graham 278) To checkmate the administration, all the Russians had to do was repeat its rhetoric back to it. Russian Foreign Minister Ivanov said of the treaty in a joint press appearance with Madeleine Albright in September 1999, "As Secretary Albright has just mentioned, it represents a core of the strategic stability." ("Stubborn Things," 57)

102. Graham 330. By May of 2000, even Albright was saying, "We believe that there's a threat to the territory of the United States from the DPRK, North Korea, and from Iran." ("Stubborn Things," 67) It took George W. Bush to cut through the clutter. He withdrew from the ABM treaty in June 2002, producing none of the dire diplomatic effects predicted by critics. There was no new arms race with the Russians. Bush had been determined to take the U.S. down to the number of offensive missiles it strictly needed for its defense, regardless of the state of negotiations with the Russians. The reductions on both sides were formalized into a bare-bones agreement only at the urging of Putin. Like Clinton, Bush had recognized the new emerging rogue missile threat to the U.S., but had the strategic sense and will to act on it.

103. The "peace process" in Northern Ireland has been slowly collapsing. As journalist John O'Sullivan writes, "In effect, the underlying contradiction of the Good Friday Agreement is finally destroying it. It was supposed to end terrorism by bringing the terrorists into the democratic process. But the IRA held onto its weapons (despite some minor cosmetic 'decommissioning'), implicitly threatening a return to terror, in case democracy failed to deliver what it demanded....Is it any wonder that, according to the seized [IRA] documents, the code name given by Sinn Fein-IRA to Blair is 'the Naive Idiot?'" (John O'Sullivan, "The War Is Here, Too," *National Review Online*, October 8, 2002).

104. Ryan Lizza, "Where Angels Fear to Tread," *The New Republic*, July 24, 2000. This is a stunningly damning piece.

105. Ibid.

106. Ibid. Jesse Jackson's full title was "Special Envoy for the President and Secretary of State for the Promotion of Democracy in Africa," a bitterly comical designation in light of subsequent events. Jackson was friendly with the bloody warlord from neighboring Liberia, Charles Taylor, who sponsored the RUF and had extensive experience gaming peace deals in his own country—more than a dozen. Jackson agreed with Taylor's line that the Sierra Leone government should reconcile with the rebels. According to Lizza, the State Department thought it could "mainstream" Sankoh with a peace deal.

107. Ibid.

108. Lizza, "Where Angels Fear to Tread"; Frederick H. Fleitz, Jr., *Peacekeeping Fiascoes of the 1990s* (Westport, CT: Praeger, 2002), 166–167.

109. Lizza, "Where Angels Fear to Tread"

110. William Jefferson Clinton, "Remarks Delivered by the Honorable William Jefferson Clinton, President of the United States of America, at the Official Opening Ceremony of the National Summit on Africa," Washington Convention Center, Washington, D.C., February 17, 2000.

111. Gertz 123

112. Donald Kagan and Frederick W. Kagan, *While America Sleeps* (New York: St. Martin's Press, 2000), 345–353.

113. Carter and Perry 126

114. "Initially, the U.S. government supported the IAEA position," writes William Perry, who became secretary of defense in the midst of the crisis. "But beginning in 1993 some in the Pentagon, especially undersecretary

John Deutch, a chemist, and assistant secretary Ashton Carter, a physicist, began to have their doubts." IAEA inspections, according to Perry, "demanded both too little and too much of North Korea." Too little—because the inspections could never be foolproof, and North Korea's nuclear weapons program should be eliminated entirely instead. Too much—because the inspections proposed by the IAEA of Pyongyang's past plutonium diversion served to reinforce "the North Koreans' belief that they were being singled out by the IAEA for discriminatory treatment, while offering little security benefit." (Carter and Perry 127)

115. James R. Lilley, "New Rules in Korea," *Newsweek*, November 9, 1998. South Korea didn't appreciate this. The *New York Times* reported at the time, "After weeks of watching in silent frustration as the United States tries to negotiate a halt to North Korea's nuclear program, President Kim Young Sam of South Korea lashed out at the Clinton Administration today in an interview for what he characterized as a lack of knowledge and an overeagerness to compromise. Mr. Kim said that he supported the administration's efforts and that ties between Seoul and Washington were strong. But Mr. Kim directly attacked Washington's basic stance in the discussions with North Korea as naive and overly flexible. He said that the North Korean government was on the verge of an economic and political crisis that could sweep it from power, and that Washington should therefore stiffen its position in pressing Pyongyang to abandon its suspected nuclear weapons program." (James Sterngold, "South Korea President Lashes Out at U.S.," *New York Times*, October 8, 1994)

116. Carter and Perry 129. "Some viewed these threats as simply bombast and rhetoric," writes Perry, "but I thought it would be irresponsible to shrug off the threats."

117. Kagan and Kagan 355. To which the North Koreans replied, Clinton is "seriously getting on our nerves." [Michael J. Mazarr, *North Korea and the Bomb* (New York: St. Martin's Press, 1995), 134]

118. Mazarr, 150

119. Kagan and Kagan 357–358

120. Mazarr 162–163

121. Ibid.

122. Carter and Perry 131. Perry had drawn up three options, and in June 1994, Clinton and the National Security Council convened to consider them. But, mostly, the administration was hoping the whole thing would go away. "President Clinton was within minutes of selecting and authorizing one of these deployment options when the meeting was interrupted by a phone call," Perry writes. It was Jimmy Carter on the line.

123. The Clinton administration claimed that the light-water reactors it was willing to provide were impossible to use in weapons production. This was false. The reactors could, depending on how they were operated, produce "reactor grade" material that could be incorporated into nuclear weapons (if less than optimal ones), or "weapons grade" material. This is why the U.S. objected to Germany, and then Russia, offering to build light-water reactors in Iran, and why the IAEA regularly inspects light-water reactors [Gary Milhollin and Diana Edensword, "Sizing Up the North Korean Nuclear Deal," *Foresight* (Tokyo), March 1995].

124. Mazarr 173–174

125. Milhollin and Edensword, "Sizing Up the North Korean Nuclear Deal"

126. Robert A. Manning, "Time Bomb," *The New Republic*, November 30, 1998. The regime naturally diverted the aid to its purposes, prompting Doctors without Borders to quit North Korea.

127. Ibid. Manning continues: "Each time North Korean diplomats come to New York or Geneva, the administration claims an accomplishment. The most recent—and egregious—example of this approach came during the September talks in New York, when even the discovery of the North's suspect nuclear sites and its missile launch over Japan failed to deter the administration from offering 300,000 tons of food, the largest U.S. donation to North Korea ever."

128. Gertz 126–127

129. Gertz 109–111 and 123. The administration eventually was allowed to inspect the facility at Kumchang-ri in early 1999, but not before being held up again. The North Koreans initially demanded $300 million in exchange for the inspection. (Philip Sehnon, "Suspected North Korean Atom Site is Empty, U.S. Finds," *New York Times*, May 28, 1999). It settled on receiving several hundred thousand tons of grain from the U.S. The administration denied that it had cut a deal, but a North Korean official explained: "There was sufficient debate on and agreement on the payment of the 'inspection fee.' The United States, though belatedly... decided to adopt politico-economic measures as demanded by the DPRK." The South Korean government confirmed the North Korean account, meaning Pyongyang was more forthcoming in this instance than the Clinton administration. (Nicholas Eberstadt, "U.S. Aid Feeds North Korea's Nuclear Designs," *AEI On the Issues*, April 1999)

130. In response to congressional outrage, the administration tapped former defense secretary William Perry in late 1998 to review its North Korean policy (Philip Sehnon, "North Korean Nuclear Arms Pact

Reported Near Breakdown," *New York Times*, December 6, 1998). He said
in March 1999, "What they're doing is moving forward on their nuclear
weapons." He added, "We believe this is very serious. The long-range missile program itself suggests in parallel the development of a nuclear
weapons program." (Elizabeth Becker, "Clinton Advisor Says North Korea
is Advancing its Nuclear Program," *New York Times*, March 12, 1999)
Nonetheless, after his review, Perry suggested more diplomatic inducements for Pyongyang (George Wehrfritz, "Traveling Behind Enemy Lines,"
Newsweek, October 23, 2000).

131. Gertz 120

132. Park Shin Il, "Why be a Prop for Pyongyang?" *New York Times*,
November 3, 2000.

133. Robert Kagan, "Springtime for Dictators," *Washington Post*, June 25,
2000.

134. Michael Hirsh, "Pyongyang Diary, Day Two," *Newsweek* (web exclu-
sive), October 24, 2000.

135. Michael Hirsh, "Letter from North Korea," *Newsweek* (web exclu-
sive), October 23, 2000.

136. Graham 165

137. "An American in North Korea," *The Economist*, October 28, 2000.

138. Wehrfritz, "Traveling Behind Enemy Lines"

139. Barry Schweid, "Clinton Decides to Pass up Trip to Pyongyang,
Deferring Missile Talks to Bush," *Associated Press*, December 29, 2000.

140. David E. Sanger and James Dao, "A Nuclear North Korea: Intelligence; U.S. Says Pakistan Gave Technology to North Korea," *New York
Times*, October 18, 2002.

11. THE WARS: COWARDICE-AT-ARMS

1. Andrew J. Bacevich, *American Empire* (Cambridge, MA: Harvard University Press, 2002), 48.

2. Eliot A. Cohen, "Kosovo and the New American Way of War," in *War
Over Kosovo,* ed. Andrew J. Bacevich and Eliot A. Cohen (New York:
Columbia University Press, 2001), 41.

3. Ivo H. Daalder and Michael O'Hanlon, *Winning Ugly* (Washington,
D.C.: Brookings Institution Press, 2000), 224.

4. Andrew J. Bacevich, "Neglected Trinity: Kosovo and the Crisis in U.S.
Civil-Military Relations," in *War Over Kosovo,* ed. Andrew J. Bacevich and
Eliot A. Cohen (New York: Columbia University Press, 2001), 181.

5. Bacevich, *American Empire* 276

6. Samantha Power, *A Problem From Hell* (New York: Basic Books, 2002), 437.

7. Interview with Dick Morris. George Stephanopoulos writes that Clinton sent troops to Bosnia "knowing that any casualties could cost him his presidency." [George Stephanopoulos, *All Too Human* (New York: Little, Brown, & Company, 1999), 383] The sacrifice Americans were willing to make for ethnic comity in the Balkans was indeed limited, but *any* casualties?

8. The military was permitted, for instance, to lumber on, developing antiquated weapons systems in keeping with the Pentagon's bureaucratic politics. Bush defense secretary Donald Rumsfeld is an example of the sort of leadership the Clinton administration couldn't bring to bear.

9. Interview with former Marine commandant General Charles Krulak. He says of Clinton early in his administration, "I think when he came in, he probably didn't appreciate the military, and the military responded by not thinking much of him."

10. Interview with former senior administration official

11. David Halberstam, *War in a Time of Peace* (New York: Touchstone, 2002), 299–300.

12. Elizabeth Drew, *On the Edge* (New York: Simon & Schuster, 1994), 141; Jason DeParle, "The Man Inside Bill Clinton's Foreign Policy," *New York Times Magazine*, August 20, 1995.

13. Halberstam 245–246. When Clinton, in a conversation with Powell, floated the idea of choosing Aspin as defense secretary, the president said, "You know, Les is a real smart guy." Powell writes that he responded to Clinton, "'Smart's not everything in running the Pentagon. Les might not bring quite the management style you're looking for.' The president gave me a noncommittal nod. Retirement began to look appealing." [Colin L. Powell with Joseph E. Persico, *My American Journey* (New York: Random House, 1995), 563]

14. Interview with Richard Holbrooke. Says a former Clinton defense official, "Colin Powell was this incredibly powerful chairman. He acted like the secretary of defense and the chairman of the Joint Chiefs rolled into one. He used to do the politics, he used to do the Hill stuff, he used to do all this. He was very powerful under [President George H.W. Bush's defense secretary Dick] Cheney and then was inherited by the Clinton team. He had this thing figured out every which way." (Interview with former senior administration official)

15. R.C. Longworth, "No Guidelines: When Should U.S. Intervene?" *Chicago Tribune*, August 14, 1994.

16. John Hillen, "Kicking the Can Down the Road," *Washington Times*, May 29, 1997.

17. Alan S. Blinder and Janet L. Yellen, *The Fabulous Decade* (New York: The Century Foundation Press, 2001), 74.

18. Bacevich, *American Empire* 142–143

19. Hillen, "Kicking the Can"

20. John Hillen, "Armed and Unready: Why Are We Pouring Money Into a Military Designed to Fight Wars of the Past?" *San Francisco Chronicle*, October 15, 2000.

21. Andy Dworkin, "Defense Firms Set Sights on the World; Firms Exporting Expands Trade, Keeps Jobs; Critics Say U.S. Policy Increases Chance of War," *Dallas Morning News*, October 19, 1997; Leslie Wayne, "The Shrinking Military Complex; After the Cold War, the Pentagon is Just Another Customer," *New York Times*, Feburary 27, 1998.

22. Hillen, "Armed and Unready"

23. In foreign affairs, it is difficult to come up with hard-and-fast principles. Foreign policy requires judgment, and a deft touch above all else, and the administration lacked both. It is difficult to square an intervention in Rwanda with a limited, national interest–based American foreign policy. But given the practical effects on the ground, it is hard to argue that the United States should have done nothing. Sometimes factors other than the strict national interest figure in international affairs. There is a moral element to international leadership, and there is such a thing as national honor—ours was tarnished by the administration's performance during the Rwandan genocide.

24. John Hillen, "Playing Politics With the U.S. Military," *Wall Street Journal Europe*, December 6, 1996.

25. Frederick H. Fleitz, Jr., *Peacekeeping Fiascoes of the 1990s* (Westport, CT: Praeger, 2002), 131.

26. Donald Kagan and Frederick W. Kagan, *While American Sleeps* (New York: St. Martin's Press, 2000), 328.

27. Ibid.

28. Gary T. Dempsey with Roger W. Fontaine, *Fool's Errands* (Washington, D.C.: The Cato Institute, 2001), 30.

29. Kagan and Kagan 329

30. Fleitz 131

31. Dempsey with Fontaine 25, 32

32. Says Tony Lake: "In Somalia, we inherited a bad mission and made it worse. What we inherited didn't have any endpoint. It was simply to feed people. And point one is that it saved a lot of lives, thanks to both administrations. So it's not an unmitigated disaster. What happened then is we started to develop the mission and follow the argument that you can't help people who are permanently mendicants, so you have to help them feed themselves. And this means nation building, etc. And then it became sort of a bureaucratic routine for a while, while we were working on other issues. In truth, we were sloppy in how we adopted that as the mission." (Interview with Tony Lake)

33. Kagan and Kagan 329–331

34. Kagan and Kagan 329; Bacevich, *American Empire* 144; Fleitz 131

35. Kagan and Kagan 330. Clinton marched with returning soldiers across the South Lawn, in a display meant to demonstrate the president's martial vigor and the fact that the U.S. mission was winding down. Clinton said that the homecoming showed that multilateral interventions "need not be open ended or ill defined." (Drew, *On the Edge*, 158)

36. Fleitz 131–133

37. Thomas W. Lippman, *Madeleine Albright and the New American Diplomacy* (Boulder, Colorado: Westview Press, 2000), 109. According to Elizabeth Drew, no one could recall whether the president, busy focusing "like a laser" on the economy, was consulted. (Drew, *On the Edge*, 320)

38. Lippman 110

39. Dempsey with Fontaine 42

40. Dempsey with Fontaine 36

41. Bacevich, *American Empire*, 143

42. Drew, *On the Edge*, 330–322

43. Mark Bowden, *Black Hawk Down* (New York: Penguin Books, 1999), 96.

44. Drew, *On the Edge*, 323

45. Ibid., 324

46. Bowden 96

47. Kagan and Kagan 331

48. Drew 331. The word "message" is mine, not Aspin's. According to Drew, Powell had scaled back the proposal a bit, approved it, and sent it along to Aspin, bringing it up with him twice.

49. Bacevich, *American Empire*, 144–146

50. Drew, *On the Edge*, 325

51. Halberstam 262–263

52. Dempsey with Fontaine 41

53. Stephanopoulos 214–215

54. Drew, *On the Edge*, 329

55. Kagan and Kagan 332

56. Interview with Tony Lake

57. Bowden 311 and 327. Mark Bowden writes of how terrified the warlord's allies were after the Black Hawk Down incident. "If the reports from local spies were correct, some of Aidid's strongest clan allies had fled the city fearing the inevitable American counterattack. The clan's arsenals of RPGs were severely depleted. Others were sending peace feelers, offering to dump Aidid to ward off more bloodshed. But it was clear listening to the discussion that morning in the White House that America had no intention of initiating any further military action in Somalia." (Bowden 311) He also writes, "I was struck by how little bitterness there is among the men who underwent this ordeal. What anger exists relates more to the decision to call off the mission the day after the battle than anything that happened during it." (Bowden 337)

58. Bowden 311

59. Interview with former administration official

60. Dempsey with Fontaine 41, 25

61. The process of his removal featured Clinton's usual agonizing, hours-long meetings stretching past midnight, and last-minute hesitation (Drew, *On the Edge*, 367).

62. Jonathan Stevenson, *Losing Mogadishu* (Annapolis, Maryland: Naval Institute Press, 1995), 105. It is, however, questionable whether the armor, requested in late September, would have arrived in time. The special forces commander in Somalia, General William Garrison, wrote a letter to Clinton immediately after the battle absolving Aspin of blame: "*armored reaction force would have helped but casualty figures may or may not have been different*" (Bowden 337–341). A subsequent study by the Joint Chiefs reached a similar conclusion (Drew, *On the Edge*, 331). But this strains credulity. Aspin himself called his decision an error in retrospect. A Senate committee concluded the same thing (Bowden 335).

63. Kagan and Kagan 331–332. They add, "More important, the protection offered by these armored vehicles would have obviated the need for the defeated and wounded Rangers to *walk* out of the center of Mogadishu through enemy-held areas back to their bases."

64. Interview with Paul Glastris. David Halberstam elaborates on this theme, "The military did not like Clinton's decision at the very start of his administration to allow gays to serve openly in the military, but they liked it even less when, facing considerable opposition, he had backed off almost immediately. Nor, when Somalia turned into a disaster, had they been pleased. What had happened there was like a terrible death in the family for the military, but they had been equally disturbed by the interior White House response. First came the preoccupation with spin, about which they were aware, and second, as the White House people prepared to go before the Congress to explain what had happened, they made it clear to the military people who came over to help brief them that the White House wanted to minimize its own culpability in the decision to upgrade the mission and go for nation building. The Pentagon people believed that decision had been as much Tony Lake's as Jonathan Howe's, but the perception was that the White House wanted to get Lake's fingerprints off it. It was possible that this was wrong, but that was how they saw the administration. To them it showed that what was for them a matter of life and death, of young men dying, could become for the White House all too easily a matter of images. To many military men the president was charming and talented and seductive. But in their view the primary concern at the White House was not necessarily reality, or at least reality as the military men perceived it. Rather it was the *appearance* of reality—spin. What the people at the White House wanted to do, many military men believed, was to keep certain issues off CNN, or if that was not possible, if they finally exploded out in the world of instant media coverage, to deal with what was going on CNN with an acceptable amount of counterspin—to show they were doing something, even if what they were doing was largely inadequate." (Halberstam 417–418)

65. Interview with Richard Holbrooke

66. Fleitz 150–151

67. Ibid.

68. Ibid., 152

69. Michael N. Barnett, *Eyewitness to Genocide* (Ithaca, NY: Cornell University Press, 2002), 78–79, 82–83.

70. Power 344–345

71. Barnett 98–99

72. Power 332

73. Ibid., 342–357. Dallaire was warned by headquarters, "You should make every effort not to compromise your impartiality..." (Power 352)

74. Ibid., 366

75. Ibid., 367–369. Dallaire refused to go all the way down to 270, retaining roughly 500 troops, saving many lives as a result (Fleitz 153).

76. Fleitz 153

77. Power 378

78. Ibid., 379

79. Barnett 141. During this period, amazingly enough, the genocidal government of Rwanda was a member of the Security Council (Barnett 145).

80. Fleitz 156

81. Barnett 141–144

82. Philip Gourevitch, *We Wish to Inform You That Tomorrow We Will Be Killed with Our Families* (New York: Farrar, Straus and Giroux, 1998), 154.

83. Barnett 144

84. Samantha Power reports that at one meeting in late April a NSC official asked, "If we use the word genocide and are seen as doing nothing, what will be the effect on the November election?" (Power 359)

85. The administration feared the word mainly because it might trigger obligations under the Convention on the Prevention and Punishment of the Crime of Genocide, which notionally requires signatories to act to prevent genocide. Never mind the ridiculous conceit that genocide could be outlawed and prevented by treaty—Rwanda was a signatory (Gourevitch 152–153).

86. Halberstam 276–277

87. Gourevitch 152

88. Power 347. David Rieff would complain of the same dynamic during much of the Bosnia crisis, an "inability to believe that what the murderers said to their domestic audiences reflected what they planned to do better than what they said around the conference table." (See the Oslo peace process for yet another illustration.) [David Rieff, *Slaughterhouse* (New York: Simon & Schuster, 1996),183]

89. After the first week or so of the killing, when American nationals were being withdrawn, Bob Dole declared, "I don't think we have any national interest there. The Americans are out, and as far as I'm concerned, in Rwanda, that ought to be the end of it." (Power 352) This is how Tony Lake describes the situation: "I actually went back and looked at my documents on Rwanda, which was instructive, because I could hardly find any. And so this is an error of omission, not commission. First of all, it was a failure. It was a failure by the international community, it was a failure by the U.S. as a leader of the international community. That said, let's not learn the wrong lessons from it or twist what happened. Was there ever a meeting in which we said, 'We have to make a decision as to

whether to intervene militarily or not, and Somalia was a mess and therefore, no?' No. There was never an explicit meeting that I can find in which
we said that we were not going to enter militarily. Why not? Because it was
unthinkable. Our failure and my failure was in not trying to think the
unthinkable. Why was it unthinkable? Because our whole society didn't
think it was an issue. Go back and look. Certainly in the Congress, but
also among the NGOs, the press, other governments, the UN in New York:
except for the UN people in Rwanda, no one was calling for an intervention." (Interview with Tony Lake)

90. Power 372

91. Madeleine Albright said in 1997 that the international community
should have called the atrocities "what they were—genocide." (Gourevitch
350)

92. Gourevitch 350–351. Says Dick Holbrooke: "You'll hear this from
anyone who has spoken to Clinton about his foreign policy legacy. He
knows what a terrible, tragic error was made in Rwanda, and has repeatedly apologized about it, even going to Kigali twice." (Interview with
Richard Holbrooke)

93. Dempsey with Fontaine 56

94. A week after the Black Hawk Down battle, the ship was set to deliver
six hundred American Seabees and Canadian troops to re-train the Haitian
army and police and begin to rebuild the country in keeping with a resolution for the junta to step aside. A couple of dozen thugs dock-side figured
they could shake their fists and make other threatening gestures and chase
away the world's sole superpower (Kagan and Kagan 333–334). Chanting
"Somalia! Somalia!," they were proven right. The administration argued for
a day or so about what to do, as the ship idled in the harbor, then it turned
away. David Halberstam reports, "Much of the interior debate was about
spin and which would look worse—the *Harlan County* waiting out there
day by day as they debated further in the White House, or the *Harlan
County* turning back."(Halberstam 272) According to George
Stephanopoulos, "So soon after Somalia, no one had the stomach for
another fight." (Stephanopoulos 217)

95. Kagan and Kagan 335

96. Clinton and Stephanopoulos both found the resulting pretend military crisis somewhat enjoyable. "Something about watching grim-faced
officers with medals on their chests and spy photos under their arms hus-
tle through hushed corridors," Stephanopoulos writes, "helped me imagine
what it must have been like to be Ted Sorensen during the Cuban missile

crisis." Clinton had a similar feeling, marveling to Stephanopoulos: "The military's impressive, isn't it?" (Stephanopoulos 308–309, 312)

97. Kagan and Kagan 338

98. Fleitz 14–15. The CIA had had reports that the erratic Aristide was a manic depressive. Clinton didn't much care. "You know, you can make too much of normalcy," he explained to Stephanopoulos. "A lot of normal people are assholes." (Stephanopoulos 219)

99. Kagan and Kagan 260–261

100. Ibid., 260. "The refusal of the Bush administration to commit American power early was our greatest mistake of the entire Yugoslav crisis," Warren Zimmerman, the ambassador to Yugoslavia at the time, writes. "It made an unjust outcome inevitable and wasted the opportunity to save over 100,000 lives" [quoted in Richard Holbrooke, *To End a War* (New York: Random House, 1998), 27]

101. Power 274

102. Kagan and Kagan 400

103. The liberal former Colorado senator Tim Wirth, who became a Clinton State Department official, captured the spirit of the early days. "We can't let Bosnia endanger the best liberal hope for a generation." (Rieff 29) Dick Morris warned Clinton that he didn't want to be another Lyndon Johnson, "sacrificing your potential for doing good on the domestic front by a destructive, never-ending foreign involvement." (Power 306) According to Dick Holbrooke, "Clinton was, especially in his first term, being pulled apart by the fundamental conflict that inhabits every White House, the conflict between domestic priorities and international priorities. But he had been elected on the 'economy stupid' line, and his key advisors were fighting against the pressure to deal with foreign issues as a priority." Holbrooke continues: "Because Clinton himself was famously undisciplined, they didn't want to let him near foreign policy, because they knew from experience that once Clinton got into the foreign policy issues he'd find them so interesting he'd blow all the rest of his schedule away." (Interview with Richard Holbrooke)

104. William G. Hyland, *Clinton's World* (Westport, CT: Praeger, 1999), 30–33.

105. Rieff 118

106. Quoted in Kagan and Kagan 404

107. Power 327

108. "It wasn't policymaking," one official told Drew. "It was group therapy—an existential debate over what is the role of America, etc." (Drew, *On the Edge*, 149) His deliberations were occasionally punctuated with self-pity. "What would they have me do?" Clinton demanded at one point, referring to his critics. "What the f— would they have me do?" (Stephanopoulos 216) In April, Clinton said, memorably, "At this point, I would not rule out any option except the option I have never ruled in, which was the question of American ground troops." (Drew, *On the Edge*, 151) He strained to strike his own particular Churchillian note a few days later. "The U.S. should always seek an opportunity to stand up against—at least speak out against—inhumanity." (Kagan and Kagan 405)

109. Power 249; Drew, *On the Edge*, 155

110. Ivo H. Daalder, *Getting to Dayton* (Washington, D.C.: Brookings Institution Press, 2000), 16. "I'm here in a listening mode," Christopher told the British upon his arrival at Whitehall.

111. Hyland 32

112. Drew, *On the Edge*, 157–158. Vice President Al Gore, who frequently tapped out internal memos rebutting op-eds that tempted Clinton to flip-flop, went to work on his Macintosh. But there was no keeping Clinton from caving on his own policy.

113. David Halberstam recounts an exchange between CNN reporter Christiane Amanpour and Clinton in the spring of 1994: "Didn't he think, she added, 'that the constant flip-flops of your administration on the issue of Bosnia set a very dangerous precedent?' Bingo: she had nailed him, live and in color and in front of the entire world. Clinton was not pleased, not expecting this kind of question. He was obviously angry—his face grew hard and his voice icy. 'There have been no constant flip-flops, madam,' he said. But of course there had been, and well into their second year in office, the Clinton people were still searching for a policy." (Halberstam 283)

114. Drew, *On the Edge*, 274–283

115. Fleitz 120. There were more than fifty resolutions in two and a half years (Rieff 164).

116. Congressman Frank McCloskey, a liberal dove radicalized into a hawk by Bosnia, had become a relentless scourge of the administration. At a fund-raising event, he buttonholed Clinton. "Bill, bomb the Serbs. You'll be surprised how good it'll make you feel." Clinton replied, "Frank, I understand what you're saying, but you just don't understand what bastards those Brits are." Clinton found McCloskey again a little later. "By the way Frank, I really like what you're doing. Keep it up!" What he was doing was accusing the administration of weakness and dishonesty in response to a Serb campaign of genocide (Power 326).

117. Holbrooke 63–65

118. Power 391–423

119. Hyland 39

120. David Halberstam reports that after Srebrenica, Clinton "was once more enraged; it was as if these small-time Serb leaders were personally taunting him." (Halberstam 316)

121. Sen. Joseph Biden had it right at the beginning of the war: "As defined by this generation of leaders, collective security means arranging to blame one another for inaction, so that everyone has an excuse." (Power 302)

122. Rieff 177

123. Rieff 167–177. Under pressure from the Serbs at one point, the UN dropped the word "siege," to refer to what the Serbs were doing to Sarajevo, instead opting for "tactically advantageous encirclement."

124. Elizabeth Drew, *Showdown* (New York: Simon & Schuster, 1996), 251–253.

125. "Statement by President Clinton on Veto of Lifting of Bosnian Arms Embargo," August 11, 1995. Clinton said the "vote to unilaterally lift the arms embargo is the wrong step at the wrong time." URL: http://www.ibiblio.org/pub/academic/political-science/whitehouse-papers/1995/Aug/1995-08-11-Veto-of-Lifting-of-Bosnia-Arms-Embargo.

126. Power 424. In response, Clinton tried blame-shifting: "This distribution of responsibility all grew out of a decision made prior to my presidency—which I'm not criticizing, I say again—to try to say, 'OK, here's a problem in Europe. The Europeans ought to take the lead.'" (Power 429–430)

127. Holbrooke 65–67

128. In his book *To End a War,* Holbrooke has Clinton expressing dismay about being committed to helping in the withdrawal. It was after a dinner with French president Jacques Chirac. Holbrooke writes, "The president and First Lady danced alone to the music of a marine band ensemble that had played during the dinner, then walked over to us. It was a beautiful June evening, and the White House exuded all its special magic. I looked at Christopher, concerned that we would lose the moment. The president joined us and broke the ice. 'What about Bosnia?' he asked suddenly. 'I hate to ruin a wonderful evening, Mr. President,' I began, 'but we should clarify something that came up during the day. Under existing NATO plans, the United States is already committed to sending troops to Bosnia if the UN decides to withdraw. I'm afraid that we may not have that much flexibility left.' The president looked at me with surprise. 'What do you mean?' He asked. 'I'll decide the troop issue if and when the time comes.' There was silence for a moment. 'Mr. President,' I said, 'NATO has already approved the withdrawal plan. While you have the power to stop it, it has a high degree of automaticity built into it, especially since we have committed ourselves publicly to assisting NATO troops if the UN decides to withdraw.' The president looked at Christopher. 'Is this true?' he said. 'I suggest that we talk about it tomorrow,' Christopher said. 'We have a problem.' Without another word, the president walked off, holding his wife's hand." (Holbrooke 67–68) Other Clinton aides have questioned Holbrooke's account, perhaps to protect Clinton from the image of cluelessness that it creates. Holbrooke stands by his story. "President Clinton didn't understand that he had committed the U.S. to support any withdrawal from Bosnia of British and French peacekeepers, a potentially dangerous operation. Christopher and I saw this. I have a handwritten note from Clinton praising the book. It was clear from the president's reaction to our discussion that he did not realize the extent to which we were already committed to Op-Plan 40-104." (Interview with Richard Holbrooke) Says another former Clinton foreign policy aide, "It's absolutely true. I remember the conversation about the so-called UN extraction plan that NATO agreed to do. NATO had a pledge that if the UN got in trouble, that the United States and NATO would come to their rescue. And there was a very elaborate extraction plan. Holbrooke took the president aside with Christopher, 'Do you know what we're obliged to do?' I remember them telling me about it the next day. The president claimed to know nothing about it." (Interview with a former Clinton senior official)

129. Power 424

130. Halberstam 305

131. Lake explained the sterner approach taken with the Europeans. "The thrust was that they had better help get the diplomatic track going in earnest or all hell would break loose and the United States was going to do all those crazy things like bomb the Serbs." (Kagan and Kagan 413)

132. Kagan and Kagan 413

133. Daalder 120–123

134. Holbrooke 172

135. Ibid., 132

136. Power 440

137. Bacevich, *American Empire*, 164. During a brief bombing pause, Serb war criminal Radovan Karadzic worked to forestall its resumption by contacting Jimmy Carter, and offering a deal: no more attacks on Sarajevo, if the UN guaranteed the safety of the Bosnian Serb army. Strobe Talbot had to tell Carter that the administration wasn't interested, leaving Carter—a CNN crew waiting outside his office to breaks news of his latest victory for "peace"—crestfallen. An auspicious sign. (Holbrooke 121)

138. Interview with Richard Holbrooke

139. Halberstam 358

140. Holbrooke 219

141. Hyland 42

142. Stephanopoulos 382

143. Kagan and Kagan 415–416

144. James Kurth, "First War of the Global Era: Kosovo and U.S. Grand Strategy," in *War Over Kosovo*, ed. Andrew J. Bacevich and Eliot A. Cohen (New York: Columbia University Press, 2001), 76–77.

145. For a sound discussion of the American interests involved see Eliot A. Cohen, "Kosovo and the New American Way of War," in *War Over Kosovo*, ed. Andrew J. Bacevich and Eliot A. Cohen (New York: Columbia University Press, 2001), 46–47.

146. Sidney Blumenthal, *The Clinton Wars* (New York: Farrar, Straus and Giroux, 2003), 639.

147. Ibid., 633

148. Dempsey with Fontaine 137

149. Halberstam 366–367. In February 1998, Milosevic made a major thrust into Kosovo, but with a campaign of ethnic cleansing just low-intensity enough to stay on the right side of NATO. "A village a day," went the Serb motto, "keeps NATO away." (Kagan and Kagan 418) By late August 1998, 200,000 Kosovar Albanians had been chased from their homes. [Wesley K. Clark, *Waging Modern War* (New York: Public Affairs, 2001),129]

150. Kagan and Kagan 420

151. At a conference in Washington in September 1998, Clinton had an exchange with Wesley Clark, which the general records in his book *Waging Modern War*. "As he came by to shake hands, he touched my shoulder and said, 'You'll be ready to take care of the Kosovars, won't you?' 'Yes sir,' I said. It was his way of showing he knew what was on my mind. And I hoped it was on his mind, too."(Clark 132) This nurturing sentiment was touching, but it wouldn't be of much use to any of the Kosovars soon fleeing Serb troops through the muck.

152. William A. Arkin, "Operation Allied Force," in *War Over Kosovo*, ed. Andrew J. Bacevich and Eliot A. Cohen (New York: Columbia University Press, 2001), 1–2.

153. Bacevich, *American Empire*, 186

154. Ibid. Albright had pressed Clark prior to the bombing on just this point. If the point was to save the Kosovars, how exactly was the United States going to do it? "Despite our best efforts," Clark explained, "the civilians are going to be targeted by the Serbs. It will just be a race, our air

strikes and the damage we cause them against what they can do on the
ground. But in the short term, they can win the race." (Clark 171) In the
long run, NATO would win the war; but in the short run, a lot of Kosovars
would be pushed out of the province.

155. Blumenthal 639

156. Arkin, "Operation Allied Force," 8

157. Cohen, "Kosovo and the New American Way of War," 60

158. Clark 203

159. Ibid., 203–204

160. Blumenthal 639

161. Arkin, "Operation Allied Force," 4

162. Ivo H. Daalder and Michael E. O'Hanlon, *Winning Ugly* (Washington, D.C.: Brookings Institution Press, 2000), 103–105. As Daalder and O'Hanlon write, "NATO did not expect a long war. Worse, it did not even prepare for the possibility. Many alliance leaders deny that assertion to this day, but the evidence is overwhelming. And the blame begins with Washington, ultimately the most important architect of the air campaign strategy."

163. Clark 234

164. Ibid., 201. And not just Clinton's desk: "It was British law that targets struck by any aircraft based in the United Kingdom had to be approved by their lawyers, the French demanded greater insight into the targeting and strikes, and of course there had to be continuing consultation with NATO headquarters and with other countries, too." (Clark 224)

165. Bacevich, *American Empire*, 190

166. Bacevich, *American Empire*, 188–190. Washington and the army piled operational deadweight on the Apaches in a deliberate effort to keep them from ever being used. They were just for show. Bacevich writes, "In response to manufactured security concerns, the Army insisted on beefing up Task Force Hawk, as it came to be called, with a dozen seventy-ton Abrams tanks and forty-two Bradley fighting vehicles. To support the Apaches, the Army added thirty-seven other helicopters—Blackhawks and Chinooks. A larger, heavier force took longer to assemble, longer to deploy, and was more difficult to support. In all, protecting and sustaining a mere twenty-four attack helicopters ended up requiring 6,200 troops and 26,000 tons of equipment, to include 190 containers of ammunition and enough spare parts to support twice the number of aircraft actually deployed. Moving this mammoth task force to its designated staging area in Albania consumed 550 C-17 sorties. The cost to American taxpayers was an eye-popping $480 million."

167. Arkin, "Operation Allied Force," 16

168. Daalder and O'Hanlon 201

169. Bacevich, *American Empire,* 190

170. Alberto R. Coll, "Kosovo and the Moral Burdens of Power," in *War Over Kosovo,* ed. Andrew J. Bacevich and Eliot A. Cohen (New York: Columbia University Press, 2001), 131.

171. Halberstam 478–479

172. Coll, "Kosovo and the Moral Burdens of Power," 139

173. Arkin, "Operation Allied Force," 27

12. THE MIDDLE EAST: THE PRICE OF ILLUSION

1. David Wurmser, "Time to Rethink Middle East Policy," *The Journal of International Security Affairs,* Summer 2001. Wurmser's analysis of the region and its dynamics is brilliant, and guided much of my thinking for this chapter.

2. David Makovsky, *Making Peace With the PLO* (Boulder, Colorado: Westview Press, 1996), 11, 27–29.

3. PBS Frontline, "Shattered Dreams of Peace," Timeline, June 2002. URL: http://www.pbs.org/wgbh/pages/frontline/shows/oslo/etc/cron.html.

4. Warren Christopher, *Chances of a Lifetime* (New York: Scribner, 2001), 200.

5. Yigal Carmon, "The Story Behind the Handshake," in *The Mideast Peace Process,* ed. Neal Kozodoy (San Francisco: Encounter Books, 2002), 20.

6. George Stephanopoulos, *All Too Human* (New York: Little, Brown & Company, 1999), 190.

7. Carmon, "The Story Behind the Handshake," 20–21; Barry Rubin, *The Tragedy of the Middle East* (New York: Cambridge University Press, 2002), 232.

8. Stephanopoulos 192–193

9. Ibid., 195

10. Carmon, "The Story Behind the Handshake," 21

11. Makovsky 119–130. This was true of Israel's disengagement agreements with the Egyptians and Syrians in the mid-1970s and the 1978 Camp David accords. The secrecy of Oslo kept other Arab parties from pressuring Arafat not to cut a deal, and the absence of the United States convinced the Palestinians that they couldn't rely on the Americans to wring concessions out of Israel. A Syrian official, after Oslo, called Arafat "the son of 60,000 whores." (Rubin 201)

12. Quoted in Kenneth M. Pollack, *The Threatening Storm* (New York: Random House, 2002), 66.

13. Rabin told Israelis, "Stop being afraid. There is no danger that these guns will be used against us. The purpose of this ammunition for the Palestinian police is to be used in their vigilant fight against the HAMAS. They won't dream of using it against us, since they know very well that if they use these guns against us once, at that moment the Oslo Accord will be annulled and the IDF will return to all the places that have been given to them. The Oslo accord, despite what the opposition claims, is not irrevocable." [Yossef Bodansky, *The High Cost of Peace* (Roseville, CA: Prima, 2002), 98]

14. Dore Gold, "Where Is the Peace Process Going?" in *The Mideast Peace Process,* ed. Neal Kozodoy (San Francisco: Encounter Books, 2002), 39.

15. Wurmser, "Time to Rethink Middle East Policy"

16. On the day of the Handshake in September 1993—when everyone was weepy in Washington—Jordanian television broadcast an Arafat speech in which he invoked the 1974 policy: "O my beloved ones: do not forget that our Palestine National Council made the decision in 1974. It called for the establishment of national authority on any part of Palestinian soil that is liberated or from which the Israelis withdraw. . . . Brothers, beloved ones: Palestine is only a stone's throw away for a small Palestinian boy or girl. It is the Palestinian state that lives deep in our heart. Its flag will fly over the walls of Jerusalem, the churches of Jerusalem, and the mosques of Jerusalem." [Douglas J. Feith, "Land for No Peace," in *The Mideast Peace Process,* ed. Neal Kozodoy (San Francisco: Encounter Books, 2002), 26–27]

17. Carmon, "The Story Behind the Handshake," 21

18. Feith, "Land for No Peace," 25–26

19. Hillel Halkin, "The Rabin Assassination: A Reckoning," in *The Mideast Peace Process,* ed. Neal Kozodoy (San Francisco: Encounter Books, 2002), 45–46.

20. Interview with Dennis Ross

21. After Palestinian-Israeli violence early in Netanyahu's tenure, Washington immediately had Netanyahu and Arafat into the White House, sending them to the Map Room to eat lunch together, on the theory that all that was ailing the peace process was that Arafat and Netanyahu hadn't spent enough quality time together. "We all, Israeli and Palestinian aides, hovered in a room outside, waiting, while they sat down and ate couscous together," recalls a Netanyahu aide. "It was ridiculous. Couscous. It was all supposed to be about personal chemistry." (Interview with a former Israeli official)

22. PBS Frontline, "Shattered Dreams of Peace"

23. Natan Sharansky, "From Helsinki to Oslo," *The Journal of International Security Affairs*, Summer 2001.

24. Sharansky, "From Helsinki to Oslo"

25. Interview with Dennis Ross

26. Lisa Beyer with Jamil Hamad, Jay Branegan, and Douglas Waller, "Love at First Wonk," *Time*, July 26, 1999.

27. Ben Barber, "After Oslo . . . ," *The Journal of International Security Affairs*, Summer 2001.

28. Bodansky 305

29. Rubin 211–217. As Egypt's foreign minister put it in October 2000, "Egypt and all Arabs [support] the resistance and Hezbollah in their struggle to liberate the remaining occupied territories. Israel is the one that kept some territories and did not release prisoners. Therefore, it is responsible for what is happening."

30. PBS Frontline, "Shattered Dreams of Peace"

31. Interview with Dennis Ross

32. Sidney Blumenthal, *The Clinton Wars* (New York: Farrar, Straus and Giroux, 2003), 778.

33. Benny Morris, "Camp David and After: An Exchange (1. An Interview with Ehud Barak)," *New York Review of Books*, June 13, 2002.

34. PBS Frontline, "Shattered Dreams of Peace"

35. PBS Frontline, "Shattered Dreams of Peace;" Barber, "After Oslo"

36. John Donnelly, "U.S. Distrust of Arafat Seen No Close Secret; Observer: U.S. Stance May End His Role as Peace Partner," *Boston Globe*, April 25, 2002.

37. Later, a revisionist school would grow up around the summit, absolving Arafat of responsibility. Barak maintains that Clinton called him when these arguments first surfaced and said that "the true story of Camp David was that for the first time in the history of the conflict the American president put on the table a proposal . . . very close to the Palestinian demands, and Arafat refused even to accept it as a basis for negotiations, walked out of the room, and deliberately turned to terrorism. That's the real story—all the rest is gossip." (Morris, "Camp David and After")

38. Hussein Agha, and Robert Malley, "Camp David: The Tragedy of Errors," *New York Review of Books*, August 9, 2001.

39. As he put it to a recalcitrant Palestinian negotiator, "Sir, this is not the Security Council, this is not the general assembly. You can give your lectures there, but don't waste my time. *I have a lot at stake here as well."* (emphasis mine) (Bodansky 319)

40. Rubin 195

41. Morris, "Camp David and After: An Exchange"

42. Barber, "After Oslo." There is evidence that the violence was planned in advance. Benny Morris and Ehud Barak write, "Israeli intelligence (and the CIA, according to Barak) has strong evidence that the Palestinian Authority had planned the intifada already in July 2000. For example, in March 2001 the PA's communications minister, Imad Faluji, told residents of the Ein al-Hilwe refugee camp outside Sidon, 'Whoever thinks that the Intifada broke out because of the despised Sharon's visit to the al-Aqsa Mosque is wrong, even if this visit was the straw that broke the back of the Palestinian people. This intifada was planned in advance, ever since President Arafat's return from the Camp David negotiations, where he turned the table upside down on President Clinton' (*Al-Safir,* Lebanon, March 3, 2001)." (Benny Morris and Ehud Barak, "Camp David and After—Continued," *New York Review of Books,* June 27, 2002)

43. Rubin 219–220

44. Barber, "After Oslo"

45. Dennis Ross and Gidi Grinstein, "In response to 'Camp David: The Tragedy of Errors,' (August 9, 2001)," *New York Review of Books,* September 20, 2001.

46. Reuel Marc Gerecht, "Hardly Intelligent; How the CIA Unintentionally Aids Terrorism in the Middle East," *The Weekly Standard,* June 10, 2002.

47. "Arafat Storms Out of Paris Meeting, Albright Chases," Reuters, October 4, 2000. The report said, "Palestinian President Yasser Arafat angrily stormed out of Middle East peace talks in Paris on Wednesday but was persuaded to return by Secretary of State Madeleine Albright running after him, witnesses said. Arafat, who met Albright and Israeli prime minister Ehud Barak for several hours late on Wednesday, rushed out of the U.S. ambassador's residence and jumped into his car shouting 'This is humiliation. I cannot accept it!' Albright, like Arafat clearly audible over a portable telephone on which a Palestinian negotiator was talking to a Reuters correspondent, ran out after him shouting to residence guards, 'Shut the gates! Shut the gates!' Once the gates to the courtyard of the elegant residence in central Paris were closed, Arafat got out of his car and returned to the residence for another meeting with Barak and Albright, the Palestinian negotiator said."

48. Morris, "Camp David and After"

49. Rubin 201

50. Steven Greenhouse, "U.S. Hints at Better Ties if Syria Signs Peace Pact With Israel," *New York Times*, October 25, 1994.

51. Rubin 202

52. As author Barry Rubin writes, "For the existing regimes, having the conflict to deflect attention away from democracy, economic reform, and civil liberties was of the utmost value." (Rubin 194–5)

53. Makovsky 155

54. David Wurmser, *Tyranny's Ally* (Washington, D.C.: The AEI Press, 1999), 82, 95–96.

55. Ibid., 96

56. Wurmser, "Time to Rethink Middle East Policy," 48

57. Christopher 217–218

58. Rubin 156

59. Ibid., 203–207

60. Christopher 223

61. Thomas W. Lippman, *Madeleine Albright and the New American Diplomacy* (Boulder, CO: Westview Press, 2000), 185.

62. Wurmser, *Tyranny's Ally*, 10–11

63. Donald Kagan and Frederick W. Kagan, *While America Sleeps* (New York: St. Martin's Press, 2000), 369–376.

64. Kagan and Kagan 379–380

65. Lawrence F. Kaplan and William Kristol, *The War Over Iraq* (San Francisco: Encounter Books, 2003), 50.

66. Stephanopoulos 157–159

67. Pollack 65

68. Laurie Mylroie, *The War Against America* (Washington, D.C.: The AEI Press, 2001), 123.

69. Anthony Lake, *6 Nightmares* (New York: Little, Brown & Company, 2000), 17.

70. Christopher 235

71. Interview with James Woolsey

72. William G. Hyland, *Clinton's World* (Westport, CT: Praeger, 1999), 172.

73. Evan Thomas, et al., *Back From the Dead* (New York: The Atlantic Monthly Press, 1997), 1.

74. Lake 20

75. Kagan and Kagan 383

76. Stephanopoulos 165

77. Wurmser, *Tyranny's Ally*, 13–14; Pollack 72

78. Pollack 72–73

79. Ibid.

80. Wurmser, *Tyranny's Ally*, 15

81. Interview with Tony Lake. He continues, "And suddenly we get word in Washington that Chalabi has announced that we're supporting this effort. We had betrayed the Kurds twice—in the mid-1970s and in 1991. I was of the view that we should not do it again, by encouraging them in this quixotic effort and then being unable to save them. After a unanimous decision within the government, we agreed we had to tell him we wouldn't support him on this. And to make sure that he got the message clearly, I sent him the message."

82. Pollack 72–73

83. Ibid., 78–79

84. Ibid.

85. Ibid., 79

86. Wurmser, *Tyranny's Ally*, 20–25

87. Ibid., 25

88. Ibid., 26

89. Ibid., 26–27; Pollack 81–84

90. Pollack 83

91. Kaplan and Kristol 51. This surely wasn't what Kurdish leaders had in mind when assistant secretary of state for Near Eastern Affairs Robert Pelletrau had told them prior to Saddam's thrust that the Iraqi dictator had been warned of serious consequences should he move against the North (Wurmser, *Tyranny's Ally*, 27).

92. Wurmser, *Tyranny's Ally*, 29

93. Jim Hoagland, "Saddam Prevailed," *Washington Post*, September 29, 1996. Hoagland writes of how Clinton decided on the missile strikes after Saddam invaded the North. "The most damaging part of Clinton's too-little, too-soon response in Iraq may well be the way in which he reached it. Strategy briefings were conducted on the campaign trail in harried circumstances, usually by telephone or fax. Clinton did not return to Washington for a face-to-face meeting in the White House with his principal cabinet officers to discuss the use of force or the difficult strategic problems of keeping the multinational coalition on Iraq solidly together. A cabinet-level group met without him four times as the crisis escalated. Clinton left the impression of a partially engaged president who checked off the least ambitious, least risky option box on a decision list prepared by Lake."

94. Pollack 83–87

95. Kagan and Kagan 387–388

96. Wurmser, *Tyranny's Ally*, 30

97. Pollack 89–90

98. Mylroie, *The War Against America*, 158

99. Wurmser, *Tyranny's Ally*, 33

100. Ibid., 31

101. Pollack 90

102. Wurmser, *Tyranny's Ally*, 31–32

103. Barton Gellman, "U.S. Sought To Prevent Iraqi Arms Inspections; Surprise Visits Canceled After Albright Argued That Timing Was Wrong," *Washington Post*, August 14, 1998. Gellman writes, "The behind-the-scenes campaign of caution is at odds with the Clinton administration's public position as the strongest proponent of unconditional access for the inspectors to any site in Iraq. . . . Last week, as Albright reportedly sought to rein in [UNSCOM chief Richard] Butler, the administration was retreating from the vows it made six months ago to strike immediately and with significant military force if Iraq failed to honor a Feb. 23 agreement that resolved the last such crisis over inspections. At that time, administration spokesmen described a 'snap back' policy of automatic military retaliation if Iraqi president Saddam Hussein violated his agreement with UN Secretary-General Kofi Annan. Now the administration argues, as White House spokesman P.J. Crowley said yesterday, that Iraq is proposing 'a cat-and-mouse game' and 'we're not going to play.'"

104. Lippman 161–162. Lippman writes how the *Washington Post* story appeared to show that Clinton had decided to "waffle once again on an issue of principle, forcing Albright to back down from what had been an absolutist position. The reality was that the administration had changed its policy toward Iraq; having reached the conclusion that Saddam Hussein would never allow weapons inspectors full access, Clinton and Albright fell back on a policy of isolation, hoping to keep Saddam Hussein bottled up until he is finally toppled from power. They never explained the shift publicly, however, and as far as anyone knew, the United States was still supporting a vigorous inspection program. The *Post*'s story appeared to expose the policy as a sham."

105. Barton Gellman, "U.S. Tried to Halt Several Searches; Intervention Began Last Fall," *Washington Post*, August 27, 1998. Gellman noted in another story, "Last February 17, having given conditional approval for the largest bombing campaign of his presidency, Clinton urged a Pentagon audience in a speech to 'imagine the future': 'What if [Saddam Hussein] fails to comply and we fail to act, or we take some ambiguous third route which gives him yet more opportunities to develop this program of weapons of mass destruction and continue to press for the release of the sanctions and continue to ignore the solemn commitments that he made? Well, he will conclude that the international community has lost its will. He will then conclude that he can go right on and do more to rebuild an arsenal of devastating destruction. And someday, some way, I guarantee you, he'll use that arsenal.' Clinton called off the warplanes when Iraq agreed on February 23 to give arms inspectors unconditional access to any site they chose. But now that Iraq has withdrawn from that agreement, Clinton has chosen the 'ambiguous third route' he warned against." (Barton Gellman, "Shift on Iraq May Signify Trade-Off; Sanctions Reinforced, but at Expense of Arms Inspections," *Washington Post*, August 17, 1998)

106. Pollack 91

107. Mylroie, *The War Against America*, 164

108. Pollack 92

109. Ibid., 92–93

110. Ibid.

111. Interview on CNN's "Larry King Live," July 22, 2003

112. Pollack 93

113. Ibid., 93–94

114. Andrew Bacevich, *American Empire* (Cambridge, MA: Harvard University Press, 2002), 152.

115. Kaplan and Kristol 55

116. Laurie Mylroie, "Senate Unanimously Passes Iraq Liberation Act," *Iraq News*, October 9, 1998. URL: http://www.fas.org/news/iraq/1998/10/981009-in.htm.

117. Pollack 91

118. Kaplan and Kristol 54

119. Pollack 99

120. Wurmser, "Time to Rethink Middle East Policy"

121. Wurmser, *Tyranny's Ally*, 81–101

122. Ibid., 124

123. Pollack 84

124. Ibid., 101

125. Laurie Mylroie, "Iraq: Out of the Box," *The Journal of International Security Affairs*, Summer 2001.

126. Ibid.

127. Scott MacLeod, "No Apologies From This Saudi," *Time*, May 20, 2002. MacLeod writes, "In an interview with TIME last Friday, Saudi

Foreign Minister Prince Saud al-Faisal condemned suicide attacks against civilians but acknowledged that the families of the bombers have benefited from millions in Saudi aid given to the relatives of Palestinians killed since the beginning of the intifadeh. There are 1,800 families receiving aid,' he said. 'How would [bombers' families] feel if all their neighbors were getting food and medicine, and they were singled out and not getting food and medicine?'"

128. Pollack 104

129. Robert Satloff, "The Peace Process at Sea: The Karine-A Affair and the War on Terrorism," *The National Interest*, Spring 2002.

13. TERRORISM: LOSING THE WAR

1. John Miller and Michael Stone, with Chris Mitchell, *The Cell* (New York: Hyperion, 2002), 161–162.

2. Mark Bowden, *Black Hawk Down* (New York: Penguin, 2000), 110.

3. Miller and Stone 188

4. Interview with a former senior administration official

5. As the Joint Congressional Inquiry into September 11 put it, the failures that created the environment for the attacks related to "issues that transcend the Intelligence Community and involve questions of policy." (quoted in Mark Riebling, "Counter-Counterterrorism," *National Review*, November 25, 2002)

6. Dick Morris, *Off with Their Heads* (New York: ReganBooks, 2003), 72.

7. Daniel Benjamin and Steven Simon, *The Age of Sacred Terror* (New York: Random House, 2002), 12.

8. Byron York, "Master of His Game," *National Review*, October 15, 2001.

9. Miller and Stone 100

10. For a discussion of the new terror threat see, "Countering the Changing Threat of International Terrorism," Report of the National Commission on Terrorism, June 2000. URL: http://www.fas.org/irp/threat/commission.html.

11. Benjamin and Simon 7–20

12. Charles J. Shields, *The 1993 World Trade Center Bombing* (Philadelphia: Chelsea House, 2002), 86.

13. After a bombing in Riyadh in November 1995, Clinton promised to "work closely with [the Saudis] in identifying those responsible for this cowardly act and bringing them to justice." After the Khobar bombing, he said, "We are ready to work with [the Saudis] to make sure those responsible are brought to justice." After the African embassy bombings, Clinton said, "we will use all the means at our disposal to bring those responsible to justice, no matter what or how long it takes." [Laurie Mylroie, *The War Against America* (New York: ReganBooks, 2001), 217, 222, 233]

14. Riebling, "Counter-Counterterrorism"

15. Interview with Jim Kallstrom

16. Mark Riebling calls this separation "the wedge." He writes, "Fighting back tears, an agent from the FBI's New York office told Congress how his Washington bosses had ordered him *not* to track suspected terrorist Khalid al-Midhar. Precisely because the CIA had told the FBI that Midhar was an al Qaeda operative, the FBI could do nothing: Data obtained through intelligence channels cannot be used to launch a criminal investigation. Midhar was let be. Thirteen days later, he helped hijack the plane that struck the Pentagon. The agent's testimony, delivered to a shocked audience at a September [2002] hearing of the Joint Intelligence Committee, spotlighted a great flaw in our national security system: the wedge between law enforcement and intelligence." He continues, "Though President Clinton failed in his ambition to 'reinvent government,' he did manage to reinvent national security. His core innovation was to expand the FBI's powers while reducing the CIA's." (Riebling, "Counter-Counterterrorism")

17. Interview with Jim Woolsey

18. Interview with Eric Holder

19. Interview with Jim Kallstrom

20. Elsa Walsh, "Louis Freeh's Last Case," *New Yorker*, May 14, 2001.

21. Miller and Stone 128

22. Interview with Jim Woolsey

23. Benjamin and Simon 240

24. Peter Beinart, "Teach In," *The New Republic*, November 12, 2001. Beinart writes, "Even former DCI Deutch remarked in 1995 that 'compared to uniformed officers, they [CIA agents] certainly are not as competent.'"

25. David A. Vise and Vernon Loeb, "Reno Weighs Recommendation to Prosecute Former CIA Chief," *Washington Post*, August 26, 2000.

26. Miller and Stone 133

27. Mark Riebling, *Wedge* (New York: Touchstone, 2002), 458–459.

28. Ibid.

29. Riebling, *Wedge*, 453; "Remarks by the President to Staff of the CIA and Intelligence Community," Central Intelligence Agency, McLean, Virginia, July 14, 1995. URL: http://www.fas.org/irp/news/1995/950714cia.htm. Clinton said, "Now, instead of a single enemy, we face a host of scattered and dangerous challenges, but they are quite profound and difficult to understand. There are ethnic and regional tensions that threaten to flare into full-scale war in more than thirty nations. Two dozen countries are try-ing to get their hands on nuclear, chemical, and biological weapons. As these terrible tools of destruction spread, so, too, spreads the potential for terrorism and for criminals to acquire them. And drug trafficking, orga-nized crime, and environmental decay threaten the stability of new and emerging democracies, and threaten our well-being here at home. In the struggle against these forces, you, the men and women of our intelligence community, serve on the front lines. By necessity, a lot of your work is hid-den from the headlines. But in recent months alone you warned us when Iraq massed its troops against the Kuwaiti border. You provided vital sup-port to our peacekeeping and humanitarian missions in Haiti and Rwanda. You helped to strike a blow at a Colombian drug cartel. You uncovered bribes that would have cheated American countries out of billions of dol-lars. Your work has saved lives and promoted America's prosperity."

30. Interview with Wayne Downing

31. Quoted in "Threats and Responses; Excerpts from Report on Intelli-gence Actions and the Sept. 11 Attacks," *New York Times*, July 25, 2003.

32. George J. Tenet, "Written Statement for the Record of the Director of Central Intelligence before the Joint Inquiry Committee," October 17, 2002, 17. URL: http://www.cia.gov/cia/public_affairs/speeches/2002/ dci_testimony_10172002.html. It was thought that the CIA could "surge" resources to deal with any emerging threat. By 1998, when it had become devastatingly obvious that al Qaeda was waging war against the United States, the CIA was asked to "surge" resources in support of Operation Southern Watch in Iraq (the ongoing substitute for dealing with Saddam Hussein), to discover more about the India and Pakistan nuclear tests, and to aid the humanitarian war in Kosovo. "In early 1999," says Tenet, "we surged more than eight hundred analysts and redirected collection assets from across the Intelligence Community to support the NATO bombing campaign against the Federal Republic of Yugoslavia."

33. Riebling, *Wedge*, 461

34. Barry Rubin, *The Tragedy of the Middle East* (Cambridge: Cambridge University Press, 2002), 134.

35. The extreme variant of Islam practiced in Saudi Arabia, Wahhabism, is deeply anti-modern, anti-Western, and lends itself to violent fanaticism. Both to increase its influence abroad and co-opt radical clerics inside the kingdom, the Saudi royal family has pumped its massive oil riches since the 1970s into funding Wahhabi activities overseas—into Islamic "chari-ties," religious literature, and mosques. Terror expert Alex Alexiev reckons that it is "the largest worldwide propaganda campaign ever mounted," dwarfing even the propaganda budget of the Soviet Union during the Cold War. The Saudi spending spree changed the inflection of international Islam, giving it a more radical bent. The charities—controlled by the Saudi government even if they were nominally private—often funneled money to extremists and terror groups. Wahhabi-controlled mosques, seeded in most major Western cities, provided the nodes for a worldwide network of Islamic extremism (Alex Alexiev, "The End of an Alliance," *National Review*, October 28, 2002).

36. Reagan's decision to leave after the bombing was disastrous, creating a template for terrorist success against the U.S. In the mid-1990s, bin Laden met with the mastermind of the Marine barracks bombing, Imad Mughniyeh, the head of Hezbollah's security service. An al Qaeda member later explained to U.S. authorities, "Based on the Marine explosion in Beirut . . . and the American pullout from Beirut, they will be the same method, to force the United States out of Saudi Arabia." [Peter L. Bergen, *Holy War, Inc.* (New York: The Free Press, 2001), 85]

37. Benjamin and Simon 241

38. Bergen 88

39. Byron York, "Clinton Has No Clothes," *National Review*, December 17, 2001.

40. Benjamin and Simon 242

41. Louis J. Freeh, "Statement of Louis J. Freeh, Former FBI Director, before the Joint Intelligence Committees," October 8, 2002, 33. He testified, "The direct evidence obtained strongly indicated that the 1996 bombing was sanctioned, funded, and directed by senior officials of the government of Iran. The Ministry of Intelligence and Security (MOIS) and Iranian Revolutionary Guard Corps (IRGC) were shown to be culpable for carrying out the operation. The bombers were trained by Iranians in the Bekka Valley. Unfortunately, the indicted subjects who are not in custody remain fugitives, some of whom are believed to be in Iran."

42. Bergen 85

43. Mylroie 223

44. Rubin 166

45. Benjamin and Simon 225

46. Thomas W. Lippman, *Madeleine Albright and the New American Diplomacy* (Boulder, CO: Westview Press, 2000), 179–182. Lippman writes, "Those who say that no major foreign policy initiative has Albright's name on it may not appreciate the importance of her effort to rebuild relations with Iran." (Lippman 176)

47. Lippman 181–182

48. As the founder of the Islamic republic, Ayatollah Khomeini, put it, "America is the number one enemy of the deprived and oppressed people of the world. There is no crime America will not commit in order to maintain its...domination.... Iran is a country effectively at war with America." (Rubin 135) The administration nonetheless kept trying. In the spring of 1998, it dropped its policy of "dual containment," designed to bottle up both Iraq and Iran. According to Lippman, "[w]ithout saying so, Albright had deftly engineered a retreat from 'dual containment,' a policy that had strong support in Congress." The administration further loosened sanctions against Iran, and noted, hopefully, in the State Department's annual report on terrorism that Iran "apparently conducted fewer anti-dissident assassinations abroad in 1998 than in 1997." (Lippman 182–185)

49. Lippman 184

50. York, "Clinton Has No Clothes." He reiterated the next day, "Let me be very clear: We will not rest in our efforts to find who is responsible for this outrage, to pursue them and to punish them."

51. The National Commission on Terrorism wrote in 2000: "In October 1999, President Clinton officially requested cooperation from Iran in the investigation. Thus far, Iran has not responded. International pressure in the Pan Am 103 case ultimately succeeded in getting some degree of cooperation from Libya. The U.S. government has not sought similar multilateral action to bring pressure on Iran to cooperate in the Khobar Towers bombing investigation." ("Countering the Changing Threat of International Terrorism," 17)

52. Interview with Dale Watson

53. Interview with Wayne Downing

54. Interview with Mike Rolince

55. Walsh, "Louis Freeh's Last Case." Sandy Berger told Walsh that Clinton was tough with the Saudis, but others with knowledge of the meeting disagreed. "Clinton, they said, mentioned Khobar only briefly. 'It was along the lines of 'Would you be kind enough to continue cooperation?'" one source said. Mostly, they remembered the Crown Prince consoling Clinton about his legal troubles. At one point, the Crown Prince, who was wearing a black robe, said to Clinton, 'All those who attack you and are making such a big issue out of this'—the Lewinsky affair—'should be like the lint on my robes. One should just throw them off.' The Crown Prince shook his robe. Clinton, by many accounts, was almost crying. 'He also told Clinton that he would talk to people on the Hill and tell them they should respect the presidency and not wipe the floor with it.' Clinton and the Crown

Prince then had a long conversation about the Middle East and the internal situation in Iran—and the importance of supporting moderate elements there. After Clinton left, according to these sources, the Crown Prince was puzzled. Bandar had warned him to expect some 'very important questions' about Khobar, but Clinton had not raised them. 'What's going on?' the Crown Prince asked Bandar."

56. In fall 1997, the case against one of the Khobar suspects fell apart. According to Walsh "Freeh was frustrated, Bandar told an associate, but in the White House people acted like it was a 'gift from Heaven.' From that moment on, Bandar believed, political pressure from the White House ceased for good. In Bandar's view, Clinton was a romantic who had become excited by the possibility of converting his Iranian adversary. Bandar told Freeh that he had once told White House officials that the Saudis could close the investigation, so that no one would have to retaliate against Iran. 'I bet they were smiling,' Freeh responded." (Walsh, "Louis Freeh's Last Case")

57. Benjamin and Simon 301

58. Interview with Dale Watson

59. Interview with Jim Woolsey

60. Walsh, "Louis Freeh's Last Case"

61. Freeh, "Statement of Louis J. Freeh, Former FBI Director, before the Joint Intelligence Committees," 32.

62. Interview with a terrorism expert

63. Niles Latham, "Even Arafat's Fed up with Saudi Terror Tie," *New York Post*, December 3, 2002. Latham writes, "Saudi Arabia's double dealings with terrorists has become so pervasive that even PLO boss Yasser Arafat has gotten upset over it. The *Post* yesterday obtained a letter from Arafat's diplomatic envoy in Riyadh to the Saudi official in charge of fundraising for the Palestinian uprising. In the letter, the envoy complains that too much of the kingdom's money is going to the Hamas terror group. Written in flowery Arabic and dated Dec. 30, 2000, the PLO envoy Abu Mazen states to Emir Salman Bo Abed al-Aziz, the chairman of the 'Popular Committees for Support of Palestinian Fighters,' that he was asked by Arafat to plea for more Saudi aid to the Palestinian Authority and Arafat's Fatah party. 'The Saudi committee responsible for transferring the contributions to beneficiaries is sending large sums to radical committees and associations, including the Islamic Association which belongs to Hamas and brothers belonging to the Jihad in all areas,' Abu Mazen wrote."

64. Dick Morris, "While Clinton Fiddled," *Wall Street Journal*, February 5, 2002.

65. Glenn Simpson, "U.S. Officials Knew of Ties Between Terror, Charities; Officials Had Information Many Years Before 9/11 Attacks, Report Indicates," *Wall Street Journal*, May 9, 2003.

66. The Bush administration has placed greater pressure on the Saudis, but is still much too tolerant of their duplicity and radical evangelism.

67. "Joint Inquiry into Intelligence Community Activities Before and After the Terrorist Attacks of September 11, 2001," Report of the Senate Select Committee on Intelligence and the House Permanent Select Committee on Intelligence, December 2002, 110. URL: http://www.gpoaccess.gov/serialset/creports/911.html.

68. As Louis Freeh has put it, "Khobar represented a national security threat far beyond the capability or authority of the FBI or Department of Justice to address. Neither the FBI director nor the attorney general could or should decide America's response to such a grave threat. While on the one hand, Khobar demonstrated the capability of the FBI, acting in cooperation with its foreign counterparts overseas, to work successfully under extremely complex conditions to pursue criminal cases; it also demonstrated that an act of war against the United States—whether committed by a terrorist organization or by a foreign state—can receive only a limited response by the FBI making a criminal case against those harbored beyond the reach of law enforcement." (Freeh, "Statement of Louis J. Freeh, Former FBI Director, before the Joint Intelligence Committees," 33)

69. Benjamin and Simon 244–246

70. Ibid.

71. Miller and Stone 151

72. Interview with a former senior administration official

73. Barton Gellman, "U.S. Was Foiled Multiple Times in Efforts to Capture Bin Laden or Have Him Killed; Sudan's Offer to Arrest Militant Fell Through After Saudis Said No," *Washington Post*, October 3, 2001.

74. Miller and Stone 151–152

75. Tenet has testified that the "CIA has no knowledge of such an offer" (Tenet, "Written Statement for the Record of the Director of Central Intelligence before the Joint Inquiry Committee," 4).

76. Interview with Tony Lake

77. Miller and Stone 152

78. Gellman, "U.S. Was Foiled Multiple Times in Efforts to Capture Bin Laden or Have Him Killed"

79. Vernon Loeb, "Where the CIA Wages Its New World War; Counterterrorist Center Makes Many Arrests, Pursues Bin Laden With Aid of FBI,

NSA," *Washington Post*, September 9, 1998. Loeb writes, "The bin Laden 'station' formed in January 1996 was given the freedom to operate as though it were an overseas office, the official said. It was founded after analysts kept coming across bin Laden's tracks as they investigated the World Trade Center bombing, bombings against U.S. servicemen in Saudi Arabia and attacks against tourists in Egypt."

80. Tenet, "Written Statement for the Record of the Director of Central Intelligence before the Joint Inquiry Committee," 3.

81. Miller and Stone 150

82. Gellman, "U.S. Was Foiled Multiple Times in Efforts to Capture Bin Laden or Have Him Killed"

83. Miller and Stone 215

84. Benjamin and Simon 247

85. Gellman, "U.S. Was Foiled Multiple Times in Efforts to Capture Bin Laden or Have Him Killed"

86. Benjamin and Simon 247

87. Gellman, "U.S. Was Foiled Multiple Times in Efforts to Capture Bin Laden or Have Him Killed"

88. Ibid.

89. Ibid.

90. Benjamin and Simon 140

91. Tenet, "Written Statement for the Record of the Director of Central Intelligence before the Joint Inquiry Committee," 5–6

92. York, "Master of His Game"

93. Miller and Stone 205. Meanwhile, back in Washington, Clinton had another important thing to worry about—saving his presidency in his sex-and-lies scandal. Former White House speechwriter Michael Waldman writes of the Friday after the embassy attacks, "That morning, speechwriter Jeff Shesol and Ann Lewis gave Clinton a lyrical radio address honoring the victims of terrorism in Kenya. He recorded it, and then told them he wanted a new speech with hard news. 'This just won't break through. It just doesn't do what I need right now,' he told them." [Michael Waldman, *POTUS Speaks* (New York: Simon & Schuster, 2000), 227]

94. York, "Master of His Game"

95. Bergen 120

96. York, "Master of His Game"

97. Sidney Blumenthal, *The Clinton Wars* (New York: Farrar, Straus and Giroux, 2003), 466. Blumenthal writes, "The missiles missed bin Laden by an hour."

98. York, "Master of His Game"

99. Bergen 121. As Bergen points out, it's highly unlikely that bin Laden would stay at the same camp where he had given a press conference in May and met ABC reporter John Miller in the same month.

100. Bergen 119

101. Bill Gertz, *Breakdown* (Washington, D.C.: Regnery, 2002), 18.

102. From the "Joint Inquiry into Intelligence Community Activities Before and After the Terrorist Attacks of September 11, 2001," quoted in "Threats and Responses; Excerpts from Report on Intelligence Actions," *New York Times*, July 25, 2003.

103. Bergen 122

104. Interview with Mike Rolince

105. Interview with Wayne Downing

106. Interview with Mike Rolince

107. Andrew J. Bacevich, *American Empire* (Cambridge, MA: Harvard University Press, 2002), 153.

108. Interview with Wayne Downing

109. Interview with a former senior administration official

110. Christopher Hitchens, *No One Left To Lie To* (London: Verso, 2000), 87. Hitchens, a brilliant polemicist in any circumstance, is particularly devastating when writing about the Clintons.

111. Interview with a former FBI official

112. Peter Baker, *The Breach* (New York: Scribner, 2000), 50.

113. Benjamin and Simon 259, 355–356

114. Bergen 123–124

115. Interview with an FBI official

116. Bergen 125

117. Hitchens 89

118. Benjamin and Simon 358

119. Ibid., 360

120. Interview with a former senior defense official

121. Miller and Stone 215

122. Ashton B. Carter and William J. Perry, *Preventive Defense* (Washington, D.C.: Brookings Institution Press, 1999), 153. In June 1998, Sandy Berger was calling bin Laden "the most dangerous non-state terrorist in the world,"(Miller and Stone 215) and after the embassy attacks in August, he maintains, "terrorism became my number-one priority." (Riebling 464)

123. Tenet, "Written Statement for the Record of the Director of Central Intelligence before the Joint Inquiry Committee," 3, 10

124. Benjamin and Simon 230–231, 247

125. Ibid., 251–252, 311–312

126. Interview with a former senior defense official

127. Benjamin and Simon 293–294. There was a government-wide tendency to consider other things more important. A bill in early 2000 to crack down on money laundering, important to al Qaeda's operations, was killed in Congress (Benjamin and Simon 314).

128. Benjamin and Simon 292

129. Former defense secretary Bill Perry writes of how important it was to have the president active in efforts to de-nuclearize the Ukraine. "The effort had the constant support and intervention of President Bill Clinton and Vice President Al Gore. The president once even found himself discussing the technical details of the disposition of rocket fuel with the president of Ukraine." (Carter and Perry 76) After Clinton became engaged in Balkan diplomacy in 1995, Dick Holbrooke writes, "Not for the first time, I observed the value of—indeed, the necessity for—direct, personal presidential involvement to overcome bureaucratic stalemates or inertia and give policy direction and strategic purpose." [Richard Holbrooke, *To End a War* (New York: Random House, 1998), 81–82]

130. Benjamin and Simon 293

131. Miller and Stone 334

132. Ibid., 229

133. York, "Clinton Has No Clothes"

134. Ibid.

135. Miller and Stone 230–231

136. Ibid., 232–237

137. Benjamin and Simon 324

138. Interview with a former senior administration official

139. Miller and Stone 235. Miller continues, "Jama al-Badawi, the first suspect picked up by Yemeni authorities, apparently even admitted to having trained in al Qaeda camps in Afghanistan and to having fought in Bosnia with bin Laden forces in 1994."

140. Benjamin and Simon 324

141. Interview with a former senior administration official. An inadvertently amusing passage in Sidney Blumenthal's book boasts, "President Clinton and Vice President Gore carefully avoided using the bombing of the *Cole* as a pretext to attack Bush's unsure command of foreign policy during the campaign." (Blumenthal 751)

142. When Louis Freeh and Dale Watson went to brief senators Richard Shelby and Bob Kerrey after the bombing of the *Cole*, both senators told them that the FBI could track down the facts, but ultimately it was a national security matter, to be treated as an act of war (Freeh, "Statement of Louis J. Freeh, Former FBI Director, before the Joint Intelligence Committees," 33).

143. Benjamin and Simon 280–281

144. Interview with a former senior administration official

145. Bob Woodward, *Bush at War* (New York: Simon & Schuster, 2002), 6.

146. Jane Mayer, "The Search for Osama; Did the Government Let Bin Laden's Trail Go Cold," *New Yorker*, August 4, 2003. Clarke complained that the CIA wasn't aggressive enough in following through. An intelligence official told the *New Yorker* in reply, "That's bull—. Risk-taking depends on political will allowing you to take the risk. It wasn't until after September 11 that people wanted the gloves to come off."

147. "Joint Inquiry into Intelligence Community Activities," 293

148. Ibid., 299, 293

149. Ibid., 292

150. Woodward, *Bush at War*, 6–7

151. Clinton declared at one point during a meeting, "It would be nice to drop a bunch of guys in black uniforms into one of bin Laden's camps in the middle of the night. Wouldn't that scare the s— out of him?" (Miller and Stone 219)

152. Benjamin and Simon 294

153. Miller and Stone 219

154. Benjamin and Simon 319

155. Interview with a former senior administration official

156. Benjamin and Simon 338–339

157. Bob Woodward, *The Choice* (New York: Simon & Schuster, 1996), 203–204. Bob Woodward recounts Morris launching into this particular anti-terror riff, which appalled other Clinton officials. Clinton eventually used some of the language in a speech marking the fiftieth anniversary of the UN charter. Clinton said, "Our generation's enemies are the terrorists and their outlaw nation sponsors . . . the briefcase or the car bomb." Woodward writes, "He went no further, proposed no action, pledged no retaliation, and the remarks went largely unnoticed."

158. Evan Thomas et al., *Back from the Dead* (New York: The Atlantic Monthly Press, 1997), 235.

159. Benjamin and Simon 284

160. Miller and Stone 216

161. Benjamin and Simon 274

162. Interview with Mike Rolince

163. Mary Pat Flaherty, David B. Ottaway and James V. Grimaldi, "How Afghanistan Went Unlisted as Terrorist Sponsor," *Washington Post*, November 5, 2001.

164. Ibid.

165. Ibid. The *Post* story is worth quoting at length. "Each year, the U.S. State Department formally rebukes and imposes penalties on governments that protect and promote terrorists. But since 1996, when the Taliban seized power in Afghanistan, the nation harboring Osama bin Laden has never made the department's list of terrorist-sponsoring countries. The omission reflects more than a decade of vexing relations between the United States and Afghanistan, a period that found the State Department more focused on U.S. oil interests and women's rights than on the growing terrorist threat, according to experts and current and former officials. Even as its cables and reports showed growing anxiety, the department vacillated between engaging and isolating the Taliban. It was not until 1998, when two U.S. embassy bombings were linked to bin Laden, that officials knew they must directly address Afghanistan's protection of the terrorist's organization. U.S. diplomats held out hope that the threat of adding Afghanistan to the terrorism list was 'one card we had to play' in pressing the Taliban to turn over bin Laden, according to a former Clinton administration advisor. The lack of a coherent policy toward Afghanistan was part of a broader miscalculation by the U.S. government, experts now realize. By allowing terrorism fueled by anti-American rage to take root in Afghanistan, officials underestimated the potential for danger."

166. Benjamin and Simon 145–146

167. Ibid., 315

168. Ibid.

169. Interview with a former senior administration official

170. Michael Elliott, et al., "They Had a Plan," *Time*, August 12, 2002.

171. Benjamin and Simon 340

172. So long as the terrorists had a base to operate from with relative impunity, they would always be on the offensive. George Tenet has testified of the post–September 11 terror war, "Nothing did more for our ability to combat terrorism than the president's decision to send us into the terrorist's sanctuary. By going in massively, we were able to change the rules for the terrorists. Now they are the hunted. Now they have to spend most of their time worrying about their survival. Al Qaeda must never again acquire a sanctuary." (Tenet, "Written Statement for the Record of the Director of Central Intelligence before the Joint Inquiry Committee," 17)

AFTERWORD

1. Michael Tomasky, *Hillary's Turn* (New York: The Free Press, 2001), 8. He writes, "She was an extremely—at times, maddeningly—cautious candidate who spent her time talking about things like utility rates and upstate technology corridors."

2. She lacks her husband's natural political touch, but she lacks many of his weaknesses as well. Mickey Kantor says it with such conviction it sounds almost like a warning, *"Never* underestimate the talent of Hillary Clinton." (Interview with Mickey Kantor)

3. Barbara Olson, *The Final Days* (Washington, D.C.: Regnery, 2001), 83.

4. Ibid., 81

5. Ibid., 118–121

6. Ibid., 141

7. "Justice Undone: Clemency Decisions in the Clinton White House," Executive Summary, House Committee on Government Reform (March 14, 2002), 5–7. URL: http://news.findlaw.com/hdocs/docs/clinton/pardonrpt/int031302hcgrcprdrpt.pdf.

8. "Justice Undone," Executive Summary, 1

9. Olson 137

10. "Justice Undone," Executive Summary, 4

11. Ibid.

12. Ibid., 6

13. Under public pressure, he returned some of the Vignali money, but not all. He gave the Braswell money back.

14. "Justice Undone," Executive Summary, 6–17

15. Stephen Braun and Richard A. Serrano, "Clinton Pardons: Ego Fed a Numbers Game; Clemency: A Desire To Add To His Legacy, Coupled With a Flood of Last-Minute Pleas from Every Corner, Overwhelmed the System," *Los Angeles Times*, February 25, 2001.

16. David Halberstam, *War in a Time of Peace* (New York: Touchstone, 2002), 492.

17. Byron York, "Party Guy," *National Review*, March 11, 2002.

18. Don Van Natta, Jr., *First Off the Tee* (New York: PublicAffairs, 2003), 215–217. One of Clinton's methods for cheating was to take multiple shots, pretending that the ones after his first were merely "practice shots," then playing whatever shot happened to be the best; another was to take "gimme putts," simply assuming that he would make a putt without bothering actually to make it. Both methods come into play as Van Natta goes on to describe what happened after Clinton hit the tree twice. "Clinton stands between two golf balls and asks, 'Which one is my first one?' He lines up the closer one to the hole, but the caddy says, 'I think that's your second shot.' 'Which one is my first one?' Clinton asks again. His first one is about ten yards farther from the green than the second shot. 'Aw, s—, I just feel so mad about that one, I don't know what to do,' Clinton says. 'I blew two strokes here. I twisted the goddamn club and hit into the tree.' He hits the chip, but it goes over the green and settles somewhere behind it. He stomps off to the golf cart without finishing the hole. His ball is lying 6; it would take him a minimum of two strokes to get in the hole, for an 8. On his scorecard, Bill Clinton writes a 6—the angriest, ugliest bogey you've ever seen." When Van Natta asks Clinton about his reputation for dishonesty in golf and why Republicans criticized him for it, the former president launches into his explanation for nearly everything. It was unfair, a conspiracy to get him. "Well," Clinton said, "the Republicans did it because it was part of their strategy to deny my legitimacy. They decided they would say that because Perot got nineteen percent of the vote [in 1992] and nobody could get a majority that even though I had won an overwhelming electoral victory that I was not legitimate. They just decided from the day I was elected to just keep attacking me. They had some friends in the press because I was the designated fall guy in '92, and I didn't fall. So they sort of wanted to keep writing those stories."

19. Historian Richard Norton Smith has made this comparison. He told Byron York, "September 11, it can be argued, is Bill Clinton's Black Tuesday." (York, "Party Guy")

20. Melinda Hennberger, "The Speech: In His Address, Bush Lingers on a Promise to Care," *New York Times*, January 21, 2001. She writes, "Over one shoulder, the new president's proud parents were carefully keeping their emotions within the bounds of modesty. Over the other, his predecessor, Bill Clinton, briefly nodded off, jerking awake at one point during an Inaugural Address that included a sharp jab at him."

INDEX